1008279000

The Politics of Budgets

While governments prefer to alter budgets to fit their ideological stances, domestic and international contexts can facilitate or constrain behavior. *The Politics of Budgets* demonstrates when governments do and do not make preferred budgetary changes. It argues for an interconnected view of budgets and explores both the reallocation of expenditures across policy areas and the interplay among budgetary components. While previous scholars have investigated how politics and economics shape a single budgetary category, or collective categories, this methodologically rich study analyzes data for thirty-three countries across thirty-five years to provide a more comprehensive theoretical approach: a "holistic" framework about the competition and contexts around the budgetary process and an examination of how and when these factors affect the budgetary decision-making processes.

Christine S. Lipsmeyer is a professor in the Department of Political Science at Texas A&M University. Her research interests merge many areas of political science, including comparative political economy, public policy, governing institutions, and political behavior.

Andrew Q. Philips is an associate professor in the Department of Political Science, University of Colorado Boulder. His research interests are in political economy and comparative politics, as well as methodological interests in machine learning, time series, panel and compositional data.

Guy D. Whitten is the Cullen–McFadden Professor of Political Science, as well as the Director of the European Union Center at Texas A&M University. His research focuses on comparative political economy, comparative public policy, and political methodology.

The Politics of Budgets

Getting a Piece of the Pie

CHRISTINE S. LIPSMEYER
Texas A&M University

ANDREW Q. PHILIPS
University of Colorado Boulder

GUY D. WHITTEN
Texas A&M University

CAMBRIDGE
UNIVERSITY PRESS

Shaftesbury Road, Cambridge CB2 8EA, United Kingdom

One Liberty Plaza, 20th Floor, New York, NY 10006, USA

477 Williamstown Road, Port Melbourne, VIC 3207, Australia

314–321, 3rd Floor, Plot 3, Splendor Forum, Jasola District Centre, New Delhi – 110025, India

103 Penang Road, #05–06/07, Visioncrest Commercial, Singapore 238467

Cambridge University Press is part of Cambridge University Press & Assessment, a department of the University of Cambridge.

We share the University's mission to contribute to society through the pursuit of education, learning and research at the highest international levels of excellence.

www.cambridge.org
Information on this title: www.cambridge.org/9781107179318

DOI: 10.1017/9781316832073

© Christine S. Lipsmeyer, Andrew Q. Philips, and Guy D. Whitten 2023

This publication is in copyright. Subject to statutory exception and to the provisions of relevant collective licensing agreements, no reproduction of any part may take place without the written permission of Cambridge University Press & Assessment.

First published 2023

A catalogue record for this publication is available from the British Library.

Library of Congress Cataloging-in-Publication Data
NAMES: Lipsmeyer, Christine S., 1970– author. | Philips, Andrew Q., 1990– author. | Whitten, Guy D., 1965– author.
TITLE: The politics of budgets : getting a piece of the pie / Christine S. Lipsmeyer Andrew Q. Philips & Guy D. Whitten.
DESCRIPTION: First Edition. | New York : Cambridge University Press, 2023. | Includes bibliographical references and index.
IDENTIFIERS: LCCN 2022048412 (print) | LCCN 2022048413 (ebook) | ISBN 9781107179318 (Hardback) | ISBN 9781316631287 (Paperback) | ISBN 9781316832073 (epub)
SUBJECTS: LCSH: Public administration. | Budget–Government policy. | Budget–Political aspects.
CLASSIFICATION: LCC JF1351 .L56 2023 (print) | LCC JF1351 (ebook) | DDC 352.4/8–dc23/eng/20221115
LC record available at https://lccn.loc.gov/2022048412
LC ebook record available at https://lccn.loc.gov/2022048413

ISBN 978-1-107-17931-8 Hardback
ISBN 978-1-316-63128-7 Paperback

Cambridge University Press & Assessment has no responsibility for the persistence or accuracy of URLs for external or third-party internet websites referred to in this publication and does not guarantee that any content on such websites is, or will remain, accurate or appropriate.

— To Anna and Meghan

Contents

List of Figures		*page* ix
List of Tables		xiii
Acknowledgments		xv
1	Introduction	1
	1.1 The Complexity of Budgets	4
	1.2 Explaining Budgets	7
	1.3 Political Competition, Context, and Budgets	10
	1.4 A Methodological Contribution to the Study of Budgets	11
	1.5 Political Competition and Budgeting: The Plan of the Book	13
2	A Theory of Budgets	17
	2.1 Studying Political Budgeting	18
	2.2 What Is Missing?	32
	2.3 Our Theoretical Approach: A Contextual Theory of Budgets	40
	2.4 Bringing It All Together	51
	2.5 Appendix	54
3	Political Competition and the Expenditure Pie	59
	3.1 Ideology, Institutional Context, and Spending Tradeoffs	62
	3.2 Politics and Spending Tradeoffs: Research Design and Modeling Strategy	77
	3.3 When Politics Matters for Expenditure Tradeoffs	81
	3.4 Conclusion	88
	3.5 Data Appendix	89
	3.6 Statistical Appendix	92
4	The Effects of Elections, Economics, and International Shocks on the Expenditure Pie	115
	4.1 Electoral Considerations and Spending Tradeoffs	118

	4.2	Domestic Economic Circumstances: How Unemployment and Growth Affect Spending Tradeoffs	123
	4.3	International Circumstances	131
	4.4	Contexts and Expenditure Tradeoffs: Research Design	142
	4.5	When Electoral, Economic, and International Conditions Influence Spending Tradeoffs	143
	4.6	Conclusion: Context, Ideology, and Tradeoffs	153
	4.7	Appendix	156
5	Four Sides of the Budgetary Ledger		158
	5.1	The Big Picture: An Overview of Budgetary Components	160
	5.2	Research Design and Modeling Strategy	165
	5.3	Budgetary Component Results	168
	5.4	Ideological Influences and the Role of Institutional Context	174
	5.5	The Effects of Ideology and Institutions on Budgetary Components	181
	5.6	Conclusion: Four Components of the Larger Budget	185
	5.7	Data Appendix	187
	5.8	Statistical Appendix	189
6	The Effects of Elections, Economics, and External Shocks on the Budgetary Ledger		203
	6.1	Modeling Strategy	205
	6.2	The Effects of Elections	206
	6.3	The Effects of the Domestic Economy	212
	6.4	The Effects of the International Economy	223
	6.5	The Effects of International Conflict	232
	6.6	Conclusion	238
	6.7	Appendix	240
7	Conclusion: The Budgetary Mix		244
	7.1	Theoretical Contributions	245
	7.2	Methodological Contributions	247
	7.3	Chapter Summaries and Findings	249
	7.4	Future Research Questions	252
	7.5	Conclusion	255

References   257

Index   277

Figures

1.1	Screenshots from budgetary games	*page 3*
2.1	Economic affairs spending as a percentage of total expenditures in five nations, 1975–2010.	22
2.2	Measuring total spending (a) and distributions of budgetary change (b).	24
2.3	UK spending categories (a) and budgetary change measures (b)	27
2.4	An illustration of expenditures and revenues (a) and deficits (b) in Finland	31
2.5	Conceptualizing a single budgetary category	34
2.6	Conceptualizing single budgetary categories obscures tradeoffs	36
2.7	Interconnected budgetary components	38
2.8	Interconnected budgetary components in Finland	39
2.9	A compositional theory of expenditures	42
2.10	Politics and external factors affecting broader budgetary components	49
2.11	The larger web of political budgeting	52
2.12	Summary of our theoretical argument	53
3.1	Budgets *do* change, as shown in the United Kingdom	60
3.2	Initial theoretical diagram	71
3.3	Taking into account institutional and electoral pressures on a government's general budgetary priorities	76
3.4	The effects of shifts in ideology on expenditures under a majority government	82

List of Figures

3.5	The effects of shifts from left to right government under majority versus minority government	86
3.6	The effects of shifts from right to left government under majority versus minority government	87
3.7	Stylized example of our simulation approach to predicting compositions	97
4.1	Summary diagram	117
4.2	Highlighting how election considerations affect the budgetary composition	122
4.3	Highlighting how economic factors affect the budgetary composition	124
4.4	Competing expectations about economic performance and policy priorities	125
4.5	How international factors affect expenditure compositions	132
4.6	The effects of elections on expenditures	145
4.7	The effects of ideology on expenditures under an increase to unemployment	147
4.8	The effects of ideology on expenditures under a positive shock to growth	148
4.9	The effects of ideology on expenditures under a positive shock to openness	150
4.10	The effects of ideology on expenditures under a positive shock to hostilities	152
4.11	Further evidence of a lack of a political budget cycle effect	157
5.1	Possible causal relationships between the four budgetary components	165
5.2	The effects of an expenditure change impulse	169
5.3	The effects of a revenue change impulse	170
5.4	The effects of a deficit change impulse	172
5.5	The effects of a budgetary volatility impulse	173
5.6	Updated illustration of how each of the four budgetary components affect one another	174
5.7	The effects of a one standard deviation (within) increase in expenditures on the deficit	183
5.8	The effects of a one standard deviation (within) increase in revenues on the deficit	184
5.9	The effects of a one standard deviation (within) increase in the deficit on revenues	185
5.10	The effects of moving from left to right government	186

List of Figures

5.11	The pVAR is stable	194
5.12	Orthogonalized impulse response function for change in expenditure shock	198
5.13	Orthogonalized impulse response function for revenue change shock	199
5.14	Orthogonalized impulse response function for deficit change shock	200
5.15	Orthogonalized impulse response function for budgetary volatility shock	201
6.1	The effects of elections on the budgetary ledger	212
6.2	The effects of the domestic economy on expenditures	220
6.3	The effects of the domestic economy on revenues	221
6.4	The effects of the domestic economy on deficits	222
6.5	The effects of the domestic economy on budgetary volatility	224
6.6	The effects of openness on the budgetary ledger	230
6.7	The effects of international conflict on the budgetary ledger	236

Tables

2.1	How conceptualizing a single budgetary category obscures tradeoffs	page 35
2.2	Country–year coverage	57
3.1	General spending priorities by government ideology	72
3.2	Panel unit root tests: dependent variables	101
3.3	Panel unit root tests: continuous independent variables	102
3.4	No evidence of residual autocorrelation across our compositional seemingly unrelated regression	104
3.5	Random and fixed effects estimates of ρ suggest it is extremely small	104
3.6	Main compositional results	106
3.7	Compositional seemingly unrelated regression with fixed effects	108
3.8	Random effects compositional results	110
3.9	Pooled seemingly unrelated regression, dropping imputed vars	112
4.1	Expected reactions to an election shock	123
4.2	Expected reactions to an unemployment shock	128
4.3	Expected reactions to a growth shock	130
4.4	Expected reactions to a globalization shock	137
4.5	Expected reactions to a hostilities shock	141
5.1	Percentage of years in deficit spending, 1960–2011 for a sample of OECD countries	163
5.2	Summary of the results from Granger causality tests	174
5.3	Panel unit root tests: budgetary component	190
5.4	Panel VAR results	193

5.5	Granger causality tests	196
6.1	Expenditure single-equation results	240
6.2	Revenues single-equation results	241
6.3	Deficit single-equation results	242
6.4	Budgetary volatility single-equation results	243
6.5	Very weak evidence of residual autocorrelation across our Chapter 6 models	243

Acknowledgments

Although we did not realize it at the time, our work on this book began with a series of conference papers in which we explored the impact of changing profiles of political parties' supporters on their policy positions and governmental actions. Those papers have yet to be converted into publications, and by many standards could be classified as intellectual "dead ends," but they forced us to think about what drives political parties to take particular stances on policy issues and what they do when in government. From a different angle, our discussions about policy priorities, partisan supporters, and government power ultimately became the framework for this book.

Around that same time, we began a more fruitful set of collaborations with Amanda Rutherford (Philips, Rutherford, and Whitten 2015, 2016b; Lipsmeyer et al. 2019) in which we explored the viability of testing theoretical expectations about political budgeting in the United States with "dynamic pie" models, that is, models for a compositional dependent variable observed across time. We quickly realized that while there was potential for testing existing theories about politics and budgets with these models, this approach also opened up extensive possibilities for testing much more realistic theoretical expectations about political tradeoffs in ways that better fit with basic understandings of how the political processes that govern budgets *actually* worked. Thus, what began as a project on political methodology to develop better theory-testing tools quickly evolved into an exercise to craft new theoretical ideas about political budgeting around the world. In fact, the more we delved into the literature the more it became clear that most articles and books only tested one facet of political budgeting – be it social expenditures, defense, or deficits – rather than looking at the larger budgetary picture as a whole. This was the theoretical gap we were seeking to fill.

We pitched a rough idea for a book manuscript to Robert Dreesen at Cambridge University Press and he encouraged us to send him a formal proposal. We owe a special debt to Robert and his team for their patience with us as we worked on this project and ran way past our promised delivery dates.

Throughout our time working on this book, we were incredibly fortunate to be able to present early versions of our ideas to audiences that included many of the authors whose work inspired us to study political budgeting in the first place. Earlier versions of this project were presented to audiences at the following venues: multiple annual meetings of the American Political Science Association, the Centre for Competitive Advantage in a Global Economy (CAGE, The University of Warwick), the 10th Anniversary Conference of the Comparative Agendas Project, the Data Analytics Colloquium (jointly sponsored by the National Chung Hsing University and the University of Texas at Dallas), multiple annual meetings of the European Political Science Association, University of Colorado Boulder, University of Essex, University of Georgia, the Instituto de Estudos Socias e Politicos in Rio de Janeiro, the Latin American Political Methodology Meetings at the Universidad Católica del Uruguay, multiple annual meetings of the Midwestern Political Science Association, University of São Paulo, University of Strathclyde, Texas A&M University, the St. Louis Area Methods Meeting, National University of Singapore, University of Texas, Washington University, and the Wirtschaftsuniversität Wien. Thank you to all of these audiences for their critiques, questions, and suggestions.

As our long list of presentations makes clear, we have benefited tremendously from the professional community. Any attempt to list all of the colleagues who gave us helpful feedback and encouragement on this work will clearly be incomplete and we apologize to those who belong on this list who we may have accidentally overlooked. With that said, in alphabetical order we thank the following individuals: Christopher Adolph, Despina Alexiadou, Andy Baker, Ryan Bakker, Lorena Barberia, Frank Baumgartner, David Bearce, Neal Beck, Allyson Benton, Cristina Bodea, Jake Bowers, Christian Breunig, David Brown, Ricardo Ceneviva, Bill Clark, Harold Clarke, Scott Cook, Brian Crisp, Sir John Curtice, Sebastian Dellepiane, Raymond Duch, Derek Epp, Martial Foucault, Robert Franzese, Matthew Gabel, Julian Garritzmann, Jeff Gill, Zachery

Greene, Fernando Guarnieri, Jude Hays, Tim Hellwig, Tim Hicks, Karl Ho, Stephen Jessee, Bryan Jones, Yoo Sun Jung, Andrea Junqueira, Ali Kagalwala, Gary King, Mike Koch, Chris Koski, Fernando Limongi, John Londregan, Santiago López-Cariboni, Janica Magat, Erik McDaniel, Anthony McGann, Ken Meier, Nathalie Mendez, Sara Mitchell, Jacob Montgomery, Natália Moreira, Peter Mortensen, Eric Neumayer, Santiago Olivella, Sunita Parikh, Thomas Plümper, Philipp Rehm, David Rueda, Amanda Rutherford, Tom Scotto, Laura Seelkopf, Mike Seiferling, Glauco Peres da Silva, Patrick Cunha Silva, Beth Simmons, Flávio Souza, Elizabeth Stein, Sven Steinmo, Randy Stevenson, Margit Tavits, Cameron Thies, Vera Troeger, Clay Webb, Laron Williams, Christopher Wlezien, Samuel Workman, and Samantha Zuhlke. Of this list we would especially like to acknowledge Ali Kagalwala and Janica Magat, who provided excellent research assistance on this project, and Mike Seiferling, who very early on in the project walked us through the availability (as well as lack thereof) of IMF budgetary data.

We also owe a special thank you to the two departments in which we have worked during the writing of this book. All three authors were at Texas A&M University in the Department of Political Science when this project was initially started. Since fall 2017, Philips has been in the Department of Political Science at the University of Colorado Boulder. We thank the members of these departments who kindly sat through presentations and discussions of many iterations of "that book project" and who gave us tremendous feedback.

Last, but certainly not least, we would like to thank our friends and family who put up with us through this process. To all of you who asked, "How's the book going?" we appreciated it. Sometimes, you received a grunt, and other times, you listened patiently to an extended explanation. It meant a lot to us.

We dedicate this book to two very important people: Anna Henri Lipsmeyer Whitten and Meghan Winget.

I

Introduction

It isn't easy to be a Budget Hero...
Michael Skoler, executive director of the Center for Innovation
in Journalism at American Public Media

In 2008, the Wilson Center with American Public Media launched an online game pitched toward both kids and adults called *Budget Hero*. By 2013, the game was in its fifth version and had been played over 1.7 million times.[1] Using the US Congressional Budget Office budget model, the game showed players the results of making a range of budgetary decisions about taxing, spending, the deficit, and debt, while incorporating their stated values and preferences into those decisions. Players could choose from over 70 policies. For instance, they could decide whether or not to tax sugary drinks – some 55 percent were in support of this – or to create a government option for healthcare, a policy which players who identified as Democratic or Green were 450 percent more likely to enact than Republican or Libertarian players.[2] Players also could decide on "spending and cutting across categories like defense, education, Social Security, and more."[3] While *Budget Hero* is no longer available online, a

---

[1] www.wilsoncenter.org/article/the-future-health-care-and-the-independent-vote. Last accessed May 18, 2021.
[2] Sources: www.wilsoncenter.org/article/the-future-health-care-and-the-independent-vote and www.wilsoncenter.org/article/budget-hero-weekly-report. Last accessed May 26, 2021.
[3] Source: www.cnet.com/news/budget-hero-2-0-fun-with-debt-ceilings/. Last accessed May 26, 2021.

successor game, *Fiscal Ship*, allows players to choose from a wide variety of policies, while simultaneously trying to reduce long-term government debt (see Figure 1.1 for examples of both games). An inherent tradeoff occurs since players, "need to find a combination of policies that match [their] values and priorities AND set the budget on a sustainable course" (original emphasis).[4]

While games such as *Budget Hero* and *Fiscal Ship* are just that – *games*, about budgets – the issues players encounter when trading off various parts of the budget reflect real-world budgetary complexities and decisions that policy-makers are forced to make.[5] When confronted with these issues, players quickly learn the difficulties of trying to keep the country on a good course. One *CNET* reporter wrote that *Budget Hero*, "quickly becomes a depressing exercise in futility that might even make you feel sympathy for politicians faced with tough choices."[6] Or, as the executive director of the Center for Innovation in Journalism at American Public Media succinctly put it, "It isn't easy to be a budget hero in the game."[7]

The games described here illustrate the importance of budgets and the complex decisions that lie at the heart of government policy-making. Budgets are the backbone of any government. Yet they involve difficult tradeoffs that may or may not be consistent with a government's ideological vision and, in turn, with the priorities of its supporters. Without the push and pull of spending and revenues, a government cannot defend the nation, provide for its people, or fund public policies. While these *outcomes* of budgets tend to grab the most attention of politicians, the media, and social scientists, in this book we revert the attention back to what makes all of the rest of that possible – budgets.

Deciding how to allocate resources and how to pay for those resources is at the heart of politics. But, in academic circles, the larger competitive picture inherent in these decisions is often overlooked in favor of focusing on smaller arguments. Governments and their oppositions

---

[4] www.brookings.edu/research/the-fiscal-ship-as-a-teaching-tool/. Last accessed June 16, 2021.

[5] Games like *Budget Hero* are not alone; there are many other city/nation-building games with a focus on government, budgets, and policy, e.g., *Democracy 2* (http://positech.co.uk/democracy2/index.html, *Tropico* (www.kalypsomedia.com/us/games/tropico-6/) and Sid Meier's *Civilization* (https://civilization.com/). Last accessed July 2, 2021.

[6] Source: www.cnet.com/news/budget-hero-2-0-fun-with-debt-ceilings/. Last accessed May 26, 2021.

[7] Source: www.americanpublicmedia.org/blog/new-online-game-empowers-anyone-to-be-americas-budget-hero. Last accessed May 26, 2021.

Introduction

(a) Budget Hero

(b) Fiscal Ship

FIGURE I.I. Screenshots from budgetary games
Sources: Budget Hero: The Woodrow Wilson International Center for Scholars' Serious Games Initiative. *Fiscal Ship*: The Woodrow Wilson International Center for Scholars' Serious Games Initiative and The Brookings Institute's Hutchins Center on Fiscal & Monetary Policy, https://fiscalship.org/.

can debate raising corporate tax levels or disagree about decreasing unemployment benefits, while not mentioning how these decisions will affect other revenue streams, policy programs, or deficits. However, as anyone who budgets their own or their family's finances knows, changing part of one budget can require jostling other budgetary pieces. Throughout this book, not only do we acknowledge the interconnectedness of the budgetary components, we also theorize and model them together as parts of complex processes. The political competition involved in making budgetary decisions across policy areas and budgetary tools may be a complicated fiscal web. Add to that the understanding that there are external factors with which governments must contend as well, and the budgetary brainteaser becomes even more apparent. In this book, we set out to unravel the pieces of this budgetary puzzle.

1.1 THE COMPLEXITY OF BUDGETS

Budgets shape many relationships in society. How resources are allocated can keep the peace in families, retain governments in office, appease stockholders, or ward off the pressure of international organizations. Deciding how to spend resources, how to pay for these expenditures, and if – and when – to run a deficit are quite common decisions for many entities, ranging from individuals and firms all the way up to national governments. Surprisingly, research on budgets has tended to focus on specific parts of the budgetary process at the expense of ignoring the intertwined nature of the many facets of budgetary decisions. In other words, previous work has often not accurately reflected the complicated reality of the budgetary process.

While scholars have been interested in the size of government budgets, there has been little attention given to how governments rearrange the pieces of their budgets. In contrast to this scholarly work, much of the "real-world" political discussions of budgetary behavior revolve around the reallocation of spending resources or the interplay between aggregate budgetary components: expenditures, revenues, deficits, and budgetary volatility. These budgetary situations involve questions of resource allocation and tradeoffs among various parts of the budget. Most importantly, these decisions ultimately have economic, political, and social implications.

1.1 The Complexity of Budgets

Spending decisions reflect elements of a zero-sum game, since expenditures involve tradeoffs, where political forces negotiate for pieces of the funding "pie." Advocates for devoting more resources to particular spending categories constantly compete with each other over a limited budget that results in their preferred policy areas becoming larger or smaller relative to other categories. Movement of funds across areas has become an integral part of informed dialogues about budgetary processes. Moreover, these decisions often result in "winners" and "losers" who either benefit from, or are left worse-off by, changes in budgetary allocations. Josh Clark and Chuck Bryant, on the podcast *Stuff You Should Know*, colorfully illustrate this when describing the US budgetary process:

… Congress says, "here's the total amount of money that we're gonna spend this year," and it goes to the appropriations committee in the Senate, and the appropriations committee in the House. And then each of them says "ok, we've got this whole, let's divvy it up into 12 slices" – not necessarily equal slices; I think that'd probably be pretty lazy – but they say, "you know, agriculture and rural development, you're gonna get this much this year, commerce, justice and science, you're going to get this much, like this slice of the pie." And they do that over 12 departments that roughly correspond to the different cabinet posts in the federal government.
That's right, and its up to those subcommittees – those 12 different ones – once they get their little slice of pie, to then decide how to eat that pie – or eat that piece of the pie. (*How Government Shutdowns Work*, September 10, 2019)[8]

Along these lines, there is substantial anecdotal evidence that governments do think compositionally about budgets. In 2010, for example, when Chancellor Angela Merkel announced plans to cut Germany's national deficit, it set off waves of speculation about potential tradeoffs driven by budgetary competition. She chose "investment over redistribution" that resulted in cutting benefits, while largely sparing business subsidies (*The Economist* 2010).[9] In this instance, the winners were businesses, who kept their subsidies; the losers were those receiving redistributive benefits. As another illustration, consider how, when members of the European Union (EU) argued over a proposed increase in the budget, there were calls that this "shadow boxing … deviate[d]

---

[8] https://open.spotify.com/episode/6ber BE1NUu9fiIOQ4gJcke. Last accessed October 12, 2019.
[9] www.economist.com/europe/2010/06/10/slash-and-bounce. Last accessed January 17, 2020.

from the real challenge: agreeing on the composition of the budget" (*The Guardian* 2012).[10] As these examples from the American, German, and EU contexts illustrate, journalistic and political discourses frequently acknowledge and discuss the competition that surrounds budgetary compositions; however, it has mostly flown under the radar for social scientists interested in budgetary questions.

In addition to the competition involved in reallocating spending budgets, the close interconnectedness of the overarching budgetary tools – total government spending, government revenues, budget deficits, and budgetary volatility – also highlights the political decision-making surrounding budgets. Each of these budgetary components is important in its own right and explaining how governments shape them is a key aspect of understanding budgetary processes more completely. However, these components are not independent budgetary parts. For instance, if a government needs to cover an increase in expenditures, does it choose to finance it with increased revenues or instead run a deficit? While the phrase "tax and spend" is often used by politicians, governments, and the media when discussing government finances, social scientists have tended to tackle each part separately. Put another way, although revenues and expenditures do indeed lead interconnected lives, scholars have largely ignored these relationships, instead choosing to emphasize individual explanations of spending, revenues, and deficits.

We argue that the way forward in explaining budgetary behavior is to acknowledge that the budgetary process is complex, to engage with the components that make up the overall budgetary composition in more realistic ways, and – ultimately – to highlight the competition that surrounds budgetary decision-making. For social scientists to understand the competitive nature of budgets, they must first think theoretically about how these dynamics are interlinked and how economic and political factors can shape governments' decisions about these relationships. When governments make budgetary choices, not only is the decision-making process often complicated, but the ramifications of altering budgets have the potential to be quite substantial. Recent shifts in the Australian budget, for instance, illustrate the significance of such budgetary decisions. After taking over the government in 2014, the Liberal/National coalition imposed a budget with, "big spending cuts that fell most heavily

---

[10] www.theguardian.com/commentisfree/2012/oct/31/eu-budget-value-not-size-important. Last accessed October 31, 2015.

on Australians least able to bear them." However, with their political fortunes taking a turn for the worst, the coalition reversed course in May 2015 and instead focused on increasing revenue by "cracking down" on multinational tax avoiders (*The Economist* 2015).[11] This example of shifting from a reliance on spending cuts to increasing revenue shows the importance of understanding both the movement of resources within expenditures (i.e., the policies cut or protected by the government), as well as the broader decision of expenditures versus revenues.

By targeting only part of the budgetary equation, current theories and empirical research lack an understanding of how policy-makers balance their options between expenditures, revenues, and deficits. As Gist (1982, p. 862) explains, "… it would strain credulity to argue that competition and trade-offs do not occur in the context of increasing budgets; the problem is how best to demonstrate them." For instance, by emphasizing only expenditures, this leaves a gap in our understanding of how the push and pull between revenues and deficits may alter our expectations about spending increases or decreases. A similar issue arises when focusing on only revenues; we miss out on the reasons why revenues might be shifting. An emphasis on deficits may offer what appears to be the broadest budgetary picture. But, when looking at deficits alone, researchers are less able to theorize about the behavior on both sides of the budget that can lead to a shortfall or surplus. When deficits increase, is it due to an increase in spending, holding revenues constant, or a decrease in revenues, holding expenditures constant? In addition to spending, revenues, and deficits, we argue for adding a fourth element to this budgetary picture: budgetary volatility. How much absolute shifting of resources is there? Although spending tradeoffs offer us a picture of relative reallocation, an often-overlooked aspect of expenditures is the stability or volatility of budgets and its influence on the other budgetary components. Only when we take all four of these into account can we get a more complete picture of the overall budgetary process, and one that better reflects actual political behavior.

1.2 EXPLAINING BUDGETS

Given how much is at stake when it comes to government budgets, in this book, we place the politics of budgetary compositions and the

---

[11] www.economist.com/asia/2015/05/13/marking-time. Last accessed January 17, 2020.

interconnectedness between budgetary components front and center. In order to accomplish our goal of explaining the competition that surrounds budgets, we need to tackle both the theoretical understanding of government decision-making, as well as the methodological complexity of multiple moving parts within and between budgetary components. Ultimately, then, our aspirations and contributions are twofold.

First, we present a holistic theoretical framework from a novel, more realistic viewpoint that acknowledges all sides of the budgetary process. Our theory explains how political competition affects many facets of budgets and emphasizes when contextual pressures will alter the relationships between politics and budgets. In addition to our primary focus on how politics affects budgets, we also emphasize when other conditions – such as electoral pressures, economic constraints, or international forces – change governments' calculations on budgets away from their priorities. There is much theoretical and empirical research on these contexts (which we discuss in Chapter 2) on which we build our expectations. Therefore, at times, we have competing expectations that result in theoretical "tournaments" to uncover the complex relationships. For the compositional side of our argument, we focus on tradeoffs within expenditures, explaining if and when governments make relative changes across spending categories. This more closely mirrors the behavior (and rhetoric) of political competition. In order to tackle individually the revenue and deficit components of the budget, we highlight the politics that surrounds each one with a focus on both domestic and international economic and political conditions. When we theorize about the interconnectedness of budgets, we study total expenditures alongside budgetary volatility, revenues, and deficits, enabling us to explore the interlinked movements of the budgetary components. A common goal in all of these parts of the book is to explain how politics and contexts shape the tradeoffs either between specific categories or between the various budgetary pieces.

Our second contribution is to combine innovative methodological approaches with a number of graphical strategies that clearly and concisely illustrate the relationships and findings. Although these approaches can be methodologically sophisticated at times, we strive to present our results comprehensibly. We rely on figures and graphs to show the results of these models, while placing numeric tables of the more complicated methodological details in chapter appendices. Although we are using these approaches and techniques to analyze budgets, scholars with similar data structures will find these tools helpful. Together, our contributions are applicable to a broad set of literatures that cross-cut disciplines,

1.2 Explaining Budgets

including political economy, public policy, government behavior, political institutions, and methodology.

We are, by no means, the first to examine budgets. The existing literature on budgetary behavior has often focused on individual components. Examples of this research range from spending on individual public policy areas such as defense (Whitten and Williams 2011; Töngür, Hsu, and Elveren 2015), public order (Wenzelburger 2015), or social welfare (Hicks and Swank 1992; Lipsmeyer 2002; Avelino, Brown, and Hunter 2005; Stasavage 2005; Jensen 2011*b*) to explaining behavior surrounding revenues (Garrett 1995; Garrett and Mitchell 2001; Swank and Steinmo 2002; Sausgruber and Tyran 2005; Plümper, Troeger, and Winner 2009; Dolls, Fuest, and Peichl 2012). Others have focused on fiscal balance, deficits, or, at times, incorporating the difference between total expenditures and revenues (Hahm, Kamlet, and Mowery 1995; Cheibub 2006; Potrafke 2019). While budgetary volatility remains less studied, both economists and political scientists have discovered its usefulness when studying budgets (Tsebelis and Chang 2004; Brender and Drazen 2008). Despite such extensive literatures on aspects of the budget, scholars have spent less time thinking about budgets collectively.

That is not to say that budgetary categories have exclusively been treated in isolation. For instance, research on expenditures has extended to studying various policy areas together. Where researchers have considered spending on multiple policy areas, they typically have used individual models for each policy type and, then, made comparisons across each model (Swank and Steinmo 2002; Soroka and Wlezien 2010; Gerber and Hopkins 2011; Castro and Martins 2018). While these approaches are forms of tradeoffs, they do not fully capture the reality of budgetary compositions.[12] For instance, if we assume that a government prioritizes welfare policy because the percentage of total spending on it increases, then we are implicitly comparing welfare expenditures to spending on all other policies, but it is impossible to determine from which other spending areas the corresponding decreases occurred. In this book, we take that next step and decipher the increases and decreases in expenditures as explicit tradeoffs across policy areas. Although understanding specific budgetary aspects remains an important part of budgetary behavior, realizing how the budgetary components fit together remains a puzzle.

---

[12] Exceptions to this – where tradeoffs are actually modeled as such – include Breunig and Busemeyer (2012), Lipsmeyer, Philips, and Whitten (2017), and Jacques (2021).

In addition to research on disaggregated expenditure categories, much work on budgetary aggregates – budgetary volatility, expenditures, revenues, and deficits – also exhibits a similarly narrow focus. Most research tackles only one aspect of the budgetary picture, rarely acknowledging that the other components are all parts of the same interconnected budgetary process.[13] While we investigate the competitive tradeoffs in expenditures in two chapters of this book (Chapters 3 and 4), we also theorize and explore how political competition can affect the other budgetary components in Chapters 5 and 6. Rather than considering them as individual pieces, we think of them as moving parts in the larger budget with a focus on understanding the variation in how governments use them. Since we focus our theoretical argument on the larger budgetary picture, we are better able to acknowledge the complexity of the decision-making process, incorporate multiple factors into our argument, and produce more realistic causal inferences about political budgeting.

1.3 POLITICAL COMPETITION, CONTEXT, AND BUDGETS

By emphasizing the role of political competition, we tackle the issue of how governments shape budgets by investigating expenditure reallocations, as well as the interconnectedness between spending, revenues, deficits, and volatility. Competition over budgetary changes occurs because of the different policy preferences in the political arena, where victorious political parties and governments are able to alter the composition of budgets to suit their desired outcomes. With representative government comes the assumption that votes and elections matter; therefore, governments should have the ability to shift resources between policy areas to match their ideologies, culminating in different budgetary configurations depending on who is in power. However, we argue that governments' abilities to fulfil their ideological visions may not always come to fruition. Instead, governing institutions, electoral considerations, and economic and international circumstances may help or hinder them as they attempt to shift budgets toward their preferred ideological directions.

Although we begin our story about politics and budgets in a familiar home of political competition – political ideologies of parties and governments – the reality is more complicated. In thinking more realistically

---

[13] See Kato (2003) and Beramendi and Rueda (2007) for exceptions. On expenditures and financing through deficits see Franzese (2002*b*).

about how politics affects budgets, we incorporate the broader contextual environment into our theory of competition and emphasize how economic, political, and international pressures affect governments' abilities to match reallocations to their preferences. Whereas previous researchers typically have included these pressures as control variables – or left them out entirely – in previous theories and/or models of government spending, we focus on how they shape governments' budgetary behavior.[14] By overlooking how contexts can influence governmental behavior, previous research has been unable to explain why ideological differences in governments may have varying effects on budgetary outcomes.[15]

We argue that governments want to change budgets to suit their priorities and supporters, but the surrounding political, economic, and international contexts affect their abilities to institute these preferred policies. While others have acknowledged and explored how various environments can shape government behavior on specific policies, we provide a more comprehensive theoretical approach by considering how, and when, these contexts affect the budgetary decision-making processes. By examining how external shocks simultaneously affect the timing and magnitude of spending reallocations and the tradeoffs between budgetary components, we present a broader theory that acknowledges the political competition surrounding budgets.

1.4 A METHODOLOGICAL CONTRIBUTION TO THE STUDY OF BUDGETS

In crafting a book that mirrors realistic budgetary behavior, we have an advantage over previous research due to several recent developments in statistical methods and the presentation of results. These methodological advances with respect to modeling budgets are the second significant contribution of this book. We highlight that budgets – both subcategories of expenditures such as defense, health, and social expenditures, as well as broader components like revenues and deficits – all reflect tradeoffs. Yet researchers armed with conventional approaches to research design

---

[14] Lipsmeyer (2011) is a rare exception in the extant literature that examines the impact of contextual factors interacting with government ideology.

[15] This interactive argument about government spending mirrors work by scholars who study individual-level preferences and have found that the contexts in which individuals operate influence their policy attitudes (Wlezien 1995; Gingrich and Ansell 2012; Zhu and Lipsmeyer 2015; Compton and Lipsmeyer 2019).

and methodology have found it difficult to incorporate such tradeoffs into their investigations of policies and budgets, something we elaborate on more in Chapter 2. In this research, we draw on models from both the analysis of compositional data and those that allow for endogeneity between systems of equations.

Many variables of interest are compositional in nature, making them subcategories of a larger total. For instance, over the course of a typical day, an individual may spend 8 hours sleeping, 10 hours at work or commuting, and 6 hours engaging in leisure. These subcategories sum to a total of 24 hours and can be expressed as a composition or as parts that convey information about the whole (e.g., 33 percent of one's day is used for sleeping). Likewise, we can think of subcategories of the expenditure budget, such as defense, education, or health spending as compositional data that, when expressed as a percent of total expenditures, sum to 100 percent.[16] Such compositional data cause a host of problems with estimation, which we discuss in detail in Chapter 2. Although methods to transform such dependent variables into a form in which they can be modeled have been available for some time (Aitchison 1986; Katz and King 1999; Tomz, Tucker, and Wittenberg 2002), it is only recently that these models were adapted for budgets (Breunig and Busemeyer 2012; Funk and Philips 2019; Jacques 2021) and budgets in a dynamic context (Philips, Rutherford, and Whitten 2015, 2016a). To be clear, while it is not uncommon to examine multiple budget categories *separately* (c.f., Avelino, Brown, and Hunter 2005; Saez and Sinha 2010; Bove, Efthyvoulou, and Navas 2017), we stress that, by not including all budgetary categories and by not estimating them in a single model, scholars are likely unable to uncover the important relationships between tradeoffs that are occurring across these categories.

Another methodological advance on which we rely is useful when we turn to the aggregate budgetary components – total revenues, expenditures, deficits, and budgetary volatility. As the theory that we develop throughout the book suggests, these pieces are not independent from one another. When expenditures increase, a number of possibilities may follow, including a corresponding increase in revenues, an increase in deficits, an increase in volatility, or some combination of these. Using standard dynamic modeling techniques that typically assume independent variables are at least weakly exogenous, it is difficult to make claims about whether

---

[16] Equivalently, we can think of each category of the budget as a proportion summing to one.

one budgetary aggregate is driving another. We incorporate advances in estimating and presenting the results of panel vector autoregressive models (Holtz-Eakin, Newey, and Rosen 1988; Abrigo and Love 2016) that allow us to relax exogeneity assumptions, test claims about which budgetary category may be driving another, and facilitate simple visual interpretations of the results.

A final methodological contribution in *Competition for Pieces of the Pie* is a heavy emphasis on the visual presentation of results. For expenditure compositions, our starting point is the strategy first developed by Philips, Rutherford, and Whitten (2016a) for modeling compositional variables over time. We use their advice for presenting the results from our statistical models using dynamic simulations – in which we can observe how a change in an independent variable in one period affects the entire composition of the budget over both the short and long run. However, we also expand on their figures by incorporating a relatively recent plot type in order to illustrate our results for expenditure compositions. In later chapters, we model the budgetary components of deficits, revenues, expenditures, and budgetary volatility. Once again, we use variations on recent innovations in exploring the statistical and substantive significance of dynamic regression results to see how political, economic, and international factors affect these budgetary components. These include impulse response functions to visually show the implications from our panel vector autoregressive model findings (Abrigo and Love 2016). Since many of these approaches can be complicated, we relegate more complex discussions of our methodological and visual approaches to chapter appendices for interested readers. We also include tables of regression results in these appendices for those seeking more traditional results.

1.5 POLITICAL COMPETITION AND BUDGETING: THE PLAN OF THE BOOK

The focus of this book remains firmly on the political story of changing budgets, so we combine our interest in the composition of budgets with a desire to understand more about how the various parts of budgets are interlinked. We start by exploring how previous scholars have studied budgets and discuss how our theoretical argument and methodological approaches build on this work, offering a realistic and holistic view of budgetary decision-making. Then, focusing on our empirical analyses, we set up each chapter to build on the findings in the previous chapters.

Following this logic, our theoretical expectations and the empirical models move from measuring and explaining more specific budgetary components to focusing on the broader budgetary process as the chapters progress. Next, we offer further details about what to expect in each chapter.

We build our overarching theoretical argument in Chapter 2 by focusing on how political competition influences the allocation of budgetary resources. Beginning our political story with the role that political parties (and the governments that they form) have in the budgetary process, we emphasize how governments in power craft budgets. While this means that the ideological vision of the parties in government should influence the allocation of resources, we argue that this simplistic view does not take into account the reality of government decision-making. Although governments might prefer certain budgetary tradeoffs that fit their ideological preferences and appease their supporters, the sobering realities of the world around them may affect their abilities to achieve such changes. Therefore, we build our contextual theory by arguing how political, economic, and international conditions may alter governments' expected behavior. For instance, when the economic environment around governments changes, it may cause unexpected – at least from what their ideological priorities would suggest – changes in budgetary behavior. Economic conditions may hamper a government's ability to alter the budget in desired ways. Alternatively, economic shocks may provide flexibility to governments to make changes outside of their normal calculations. In Chapter 2, we also explain our methodological approaches to studying budgetary tradeoffs and interconnectedness. While we explain many of the specific technical details in the individual chapters – and their appendices – we do offer a general discussion about their importance there.

In Chapter 3, we focus on the most often studied part of the budget – expenditures. Here, we emphasize the tradeoffs within government spending by explaining how political competition affects the reallocation of expenditures. We show how the political ideology of the government can shape the tradeoffs that governments make when redistributing spending across policy categories. While the emphasis in research on expenditures has tended to be on when governments increase spending on policy areas, we are also able to uncover the areas where governments take away resources. This other half of the equation can become just as competitive as the increases. Since our main emphasis is on how various contexts affect these ideological relationships, we then move to highlighting how

1.5 Political Competition and Budgeting

political institutions can constrain or facilitate governments' abilities to reallocate. Relying on results from compositional models of time-series cross-sectional data, we show how a government's ideology has different effects on these spending tradeoffs under a majority or minority government, highlighting how institutional power affects governments' budgetary abilities.

Looking at contexts outside of government institutions, in Chapter 4, we consider how various external environments may shape governments' reallocating of expenditures. We focus on how electoral, economic, and international conditions alter the political relationships highlighted in Chapter 3 by creating tournaments of theoretical expectations. Domestically, we focus on the influence of electoral timing and economic conditions when thinking about contexts that push or pull government budgetary behavior. The timing of elections may pressure governments to shift resources to electorally "friendly" policy areas during electoral periods as a means of attracting voters. Additionally, changing economic situations (i.e., growth and unemployment) can affect governments' abilities to make preferred spending tradeoffs. For international forces, we investigate how globalization and international conflict may prevent or push governments to reallocate budgets away from their ideological perspectives.

In Chapter 5, we acknowledge that, in reality, decisions made in one budgetary component may influence the decisions governments make in other areas. Bringing together the various parts of the budget, we explore how expenditures, revenues, deficits, and volatility are interlinked. Through panel vector autoregressive models, we are able to relax assumptions about exogeneity and test our theoretical ideas about how all of the component parts of political budgets influence each other and how political factors may affect these relationships. We end this chapter by using the knowledge gleaned from the VAR models to investigate how government ideology and the political context of majority status influence all four budgetary components.

Building on our understanding of the interconnectedness of budgetary components from Chapter 5, in Chapter 6, we combine those details with our theoretical argument about political competition and contexts. We analyze how domestic economic situations, globalization, and international conflict influence government behavior on all four budgetary pieces (i.e., expenditures, revenues, deficits, and volatility). Similar to Chapter 4, our argument is based on our expectations that context may affect how easily governments are able to push these budgetary components in their preferred ideological direction.

In Chapter 7, we spend time reviewing and highlighting our theoretical and methodological contributions, emphasizing that our goal is to better mirror the difficulties of budgetary decision-making in the real world. But here, we also highlight the connection between budgets, political competition, and representation. We argue that political competition matters for these budgetary and policy decisions and, by extension, that the outcomes of elections matter. Governments with different ideological priorities behave differently when it comes to budgetary decisions, and they react in varying ways to contexts and shocks. Who wins elections and how they represent their supporters have real ramifications for the distribution of resources and for who pays a government's bills.

While this book will help to shape the future of studies about the political budgeting process through both its theoretical and methodological contributions, our theory and methods go beyond budgetary behavior. Government decisions and the pressures surrounding that process transcend budgets. Thinking strategically about when governments will appease supporters with their policy decisions versus those times when environments help or hinder them to go beyond their ideological priorities would benefit all researchers of public policies, governments, representation, and decision-making. Methodologically, both the approaches and the graphic depictions of results can inform other studies of compositional dependent variables, while the use of VAR models and graphs can help social scientists as they strive to consider how complex relationships work.

2

A Theory of Budgets

A budget is more than just a series of numbers on a page; it is an embodiment of our values
　　　Senator Barrack Obama in a 2005 speech to the
　　　　　American Legion

We start from the basic premise that everything in a budget is linked to everything else. Looking within expenditures on policy areas, as well as into the other main component parts of budgets – revenues, deficits, and volatility – it is clear that these pieces are inter-connected. As such, when we set out to explain linkages between politics, contexts, and budgets, it is important to consider how these relationships will play out across different budgetary components. In this chapter, we present a holistic theory of political budgeting and then provide an overview of the research design and methods that we use to test the empirical propositions that follow from it.

Like most social science research, this work builds on previous ideas and approaches to studying budgets and their components, so we begin by considering how the extant literature has tackled the relationship between politics and budgets. This focus allows us to highlight the theoretical interests and research questions that informed earlier work, while discussing research design strategies and empirical methods used to test the resulting hypotheses. By viewing our theoretical argument and research design through the lens of earlier studies, the contributions of our research become more apparent, as do ideas for future avenues for budgetary research. To best illustrate these previous approaches, and to situate our own work, we include examples of the various types of budgetary studies using data we assembled for this book.

We continue this chapter by presenting a broad overview of our general theoretical argument concerning political competition, contextual constraints, and budgetary components. This framework structures the remaining chapters as they focus on explaining specific budgetary components, the interconnectedness of these pieces, and specific political, institutional, and economic drivers of our argument. Note that, while our general theory flows through the various chapters of this book, in each one we present a specific theoretical picture that corresponds with our expectations for a particular component or components of the budget. Each chapter also includes research design details, as well as an appendix with more discussions about our modeling strategies and data issues relevant to that particular chapter. To conclude each chapter, we return to our holistic view of budgets with an eye on take away points future work.

2.1 STUDYING POLITICAL BUDGETING

Discussing research on "political budgeting" involves a wide array of questions and theories. However, there remain two key aspects to which scholars have turned (and have continued to revisit): politics and economics. For instance, when asking why different governments alter budgets in various ways or when theorizing about how rising unemployment affects government decision-making, the intertwined nature of politics and economics continues to structure the discussion of how and when governments shape budgets.

Many of the theories, and much of the research on political budgets, start from the assumption that different types of governments result in different budgets. Governments can vary in a number of ways, such as their ideological type, size (single-party or coalition), or power status (majority or minority). Scholars have theorized about how these types of variations in governments affect budgets and budgetary components.[1] Although they have made significant strides in understanding some of the intricacies of how government characteristics relate to budgetary

---

[1] Potrafke (2017) provides an overview of a large sample of scholarly findings (heavily tilted toward the economics literature), with a table of over 100 articles listed by the type of spending and revenue dependent variable and how left–right partisan ideology affects them. Imbeau, Pétry, and Lamari (2001) document this literature quantitatively through a meta-analysis.

2.1 Studying Political Budgeting

behavior, there still remain questions about the timing of budgetary changes and how different types of governments react to external circumstances.

When considering the timing of budgetary changes, environments, such as political factors, may also play a role. But politics is just one of the contexts that surrounds budgetary decisions. While studies that focus on the politics of budgets tend to downplay the influence of economic factors in order to stress the political stories, the appearance of strong ties between economic conditions and budgetary latitude remains. Previous research has spent many-a-page discussing the possible relationships between unemployment and government spending or growth and deficits, but questions about how the ebb and flow of the economy and, in particular, unemployment and growth influence budgets remain. In this book, we explore both political and economic drivers of budgets and focus on how these changing conditions can affect the behavior of governments when it comes to the timing of budgetary changes and shifts.

In the vast literature on political budgeting, scholars have tackled many important questions about government behavior using a range of theories, and they have tended to use three main types of approaches:

- Studies focusing on single budgetary categories.
- Studies of budgetary changes.
- Studies of aggregate budgetary components.

While each of these types of research has provided a wealth of insights into the relationships between politics, economics, and budgetary behavior, they have largely ignored or greatly simplified the complex tradeoffs and inter-workings of budgetary components that are at the heart of political budgeting. We rely on a framework that uses these "three types" of approaches to studying budgets to help us understand what previous research has uncovered about politics and budgets, while also using it to explore questions and issues that remain.

2.1.1 Studies Focusing on Single Budgetary Categories

Budgetary research that focuses on a single budgetary category is quite common. Using this approach, scholars seek to answer questions about how various factors influence spending on a specific policy or policy area over time and/or across countries. The emphases in these types of studies tend to be on explaining individual budgetary categories, with less interest in the broader budgetary ledger.

A commonality within this approach is an underlying theoretical element of "budgetary incrementalism" (Lindblom 1959; Wildavsky 1964; Danziger 1976; Bunce and Echols 1978; Berry 1990), whereby previous budgetary amounts affect current budgetary levels.[2] Budgetary decisions in the current year are not divorced from previous ones, so acknowledging how budgets from one year to the next are related has both theoretical and research design ramifications. In fact, questions about the factors that influence policy budgets over time drive much of this research. For instance, work on why governments alter spending on defense policy (Whitten and Williams 2011; Bove, Efthyvoulou, and Navas 2017) or welfare spending (Hicks and Swank 1992; Lipsmeyer 2002; Allan and Scruggs 2004; Vergne 2009) emphasizes how politics affect individual parts of the budget over time and across countries.[3]

Under this heading, we also include research that compares multiple individual policies, while still analyzing each one separately. In other words, although researchers ask questions about how factors will influence budgets across a range of policies, they still consider each budgetary category in isolation from the others by estimating separate models. Examples of this approach include Avelino, Brown, and Hunter (2005), who are interested in questions about how politics influences spending in various (but yet) single welfare policy categories across Latin American countries, and Castro and Martins (2018), who theorize about the effects of electoral cycles on disaggregated public spending in separate models for each policy area.[4] Whether the research question focuses on a single budgetary category or on multiple individual budgetary categories, work of this type tends to treat the influence of politics or economics on individual budgets as independent processes.

---

[2] While there are differing viewpoints on how best to conceptualize this theory, as well as how to operationalize it, as summarized by Berry (1990), there are several common approaches. Here, we are interested in the basic premise of incremental changes in the budget from year to year.

[3] While much of this research acknowledges that budgets are theoretically long-run processes, there are exceptions that do not consider these temporal relationships (e.g., Huber and Stephens 2001).

[4] The logic behind this type of study fits a range of budgetary work where the interest lies in understanding a part of the budget independently from the whole. Franzese (2002b), for instance, seeks to explain an aggregated measure that combines multiple categories of spending or revenues. Bove, Efthyvoulou, and Navas (2017), in addition to running separate expenditure category models, also estimate a ratio of two expenditure categories to test the "Guns versus Butter" hypothesis. Bräuninger (2005) also estimates a ratio-type measure.

2.1 Studying Political Budgeting

We can specify a typical model that incorporates the incrementalism of budgets, as well as the political and economic factors, as:

$$\text{Category Spending}_{it} = f(\text{Category Spending}_{it-1} \\ + \text{Politics}_{it} + \text{Economy}_{it} + \text{Controls}_{it}), \quad (2.1)$$

where "Category Spending$_{it}$" is a measure of spending in a particular budgetary category in country "i" during time (usually a year) "t." While Equation (2.1) is clearly a simplification of this body of research, scholars usually theorize that spending on a budgetary category is a function of past spending (Category Spending$_{it-1}$) and some combination of political (Politics$_{it}$) and economic (Economy$_{it}$) factors, as well as controls (Controls$_{it}$) that typically include demographic measures and other factors thought to influence spending in those particular categories.

Since the research questions that drive these studies focus on how the right-hand side political and economic factors affect spending, researchers tend to rely on variation across time and countries (or subnational units within a single country). When estimating these types of models using time series data collected from multiple countries, the category spending measures need to be standardized to make comparisons sensible both across countries and over time. Researchers commonly standardize such categories of the budget (e.g., health or defense expenditures) by expressing them either as a percentage of total budgetary expenditures or as a percentage of GDP. In Figure 2.1, we illustrate this type of dependent variable by plotting spending on one category (e.g., economic affairs) as a percentage of total annual expenditures for five nations – Austria, Denmark, France, Sweden, and the United Kingdom – from 1975 to 2010.[5] As we can see from this figure, there is substantial variation in this measure both between and within nations over this period. There also appears to be relatively high persistence in the percentage of the budget in a given country going toward economic affairs from year-to-year. Despite relatively small amounts of change in the short-run, across the entire period there are substantial movements; there is a clear "dip" in spending on economic affairs in Austria, France, and the United Kingdom from about 1980 to 2000, while for Denmark and Sweden there is overall a steady

---

[5] These data are from the International Monetary Fund's Classification of Outlays by Function of Government (COFOG). The economic affairs budget consists of spending on economic, commercial, and labor affairs, as well as spending on agriculture, forestry, energy, mining, manufacturing, construction, transportation, and communication. More details about these data are available in the Appendix (Section 2.5).

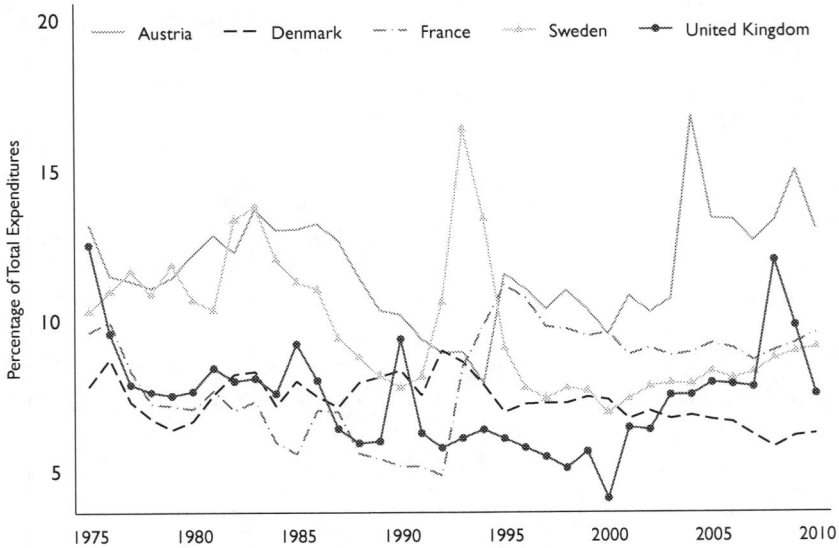

FIGURE 2.1. Economic affairs spending as a percentage of total expenditures in five nations, 1975–2010.
Source: International Monetary Fund's COFOG dataset.

decline with substantial changes in some years. This approach to studying budgets, then, typically asks questions about this variation within countries (or sub-regional units) over time or across countries (and/or over time).

2.1.2 Studies of Budgetary Changes

A second type of research on political budgeting has focused on questions about budgetary changes. While research that highlights budgets on individual policy areas tends to be interested in explaining why spending levels rise or fall, some scholars are drawn to understanding why or when budgets as a whole shift and change. This approach views them – in particular expenditures – through an aggregate lens, where scholars emphasize changes in overall budgets over time.

Similar to research on individual policy budgets, work on budgetary change began by studying the stability or instability of budgets with an emphasis on whether budgets changed incrementally with small shifts (Dahl and Lindblom 1953; Lindblom 1959; Wildavsky 1964). From this start, scholars then focused more on the timing of budgetary changes, as

2.1 Studying Political Budgeting

well as on the magnitude of these alterations. Using examples from two research programs, we can explore this budgetary change approach. First, work on punctuated equilibrium seeks to explain the distribution and shifts in budgets, questioning the expectation of budgetary incrementalism. Second, research on aggregated budgetary change translates spending into overall change measures and asks questions about when and why budgets might change at certain times rather than at others.

Scholars who study budgets from a punctuated equilibrium perspective view budgets at a macro level, directly challenging some elements of incrementalism (Baumgartner and Jones 1991, 2010; Baumgartner et al. 2009).[6] Proponents of punctuated equilibrium theory argue that budgets are characterized by "periods of extreme stability and short bursts of rapid change" (Baumgartner and Jones 1991, p. 1044). In a more statistical sense, they argue that inputs to governments (e.g., election results) will mostly be normally distributed, but outputs from governments (e.g., spending changes) will be leptokurtic, reflecting a tendency for these measures to change little in most time periods and then change greatly in a few time periods. These periods of extreme change, or "punctuations," are far larger than we would expect to see given a normal distribution. Explanations for this have focused on institutional factors that resist new information, termed "institutional friction" (Baumgartner et al. 2009). Slow budgetary incrementalism is common for most years, leading to a build-up of friction that results in earthquake-like periods of extreme budgetary change (Fagan, Jones, and Wlezien 2017). Thus, the punctuated equilibrium perspective substantially differs from budgetary incrementalism by arguing for the existence of extraordinary budgetary changes during certain periods rather than the slower-moving process of incrementalism.

Figure 2.2 illustrates the difference between a spending type of approach and a punctuated equilibrium type of measure for budgeting. First, we show annual measures of total expenditures as a percentage of GDP for Denmark and Spain in Figure 2.2a. Then, we turn these data into annual change measures and display the distributions using histograms in Figure 2.2b. In each of the histogram plots, we also plot a standard normal distribution and report underneath each one the kurtosis measure for the displayed distribution of annual budgetary changes. The value of

---

[6] While applying punctuated equilibrium theory to the budgetary process is relatively recent, it does build on an earlier literature that focused on extreme or atypical budgetary changes across years (see, Kanter 1972; LeLoup and Moreland 1978).

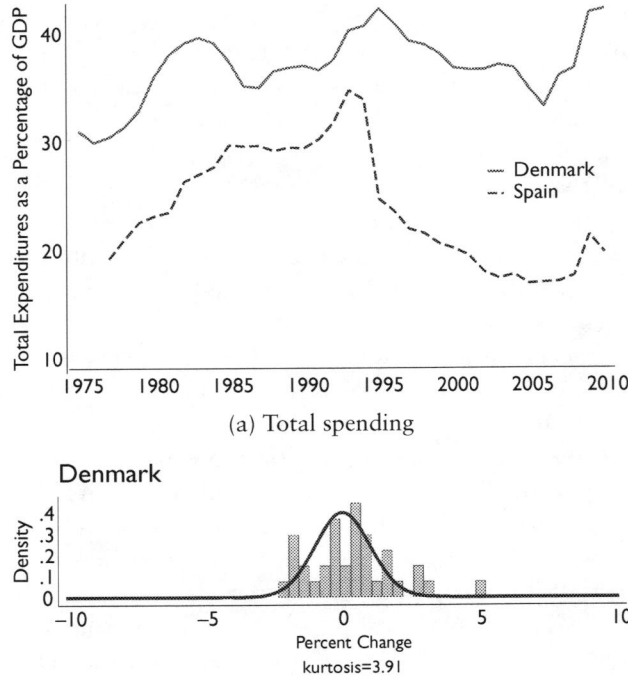

(a) Total spending

(b) Distribution of changes in total spending

FIGURE 2.2. Measuring total spending (a) and distributions of budgetary change (b).

kurtosis for a normal distribution is three, so the theory of punctuated equilibrium predicts that the distribution of changes in total spending will be greater than three due to more extreme increases and/or cuts than we would expect from a normally distributed set of numbers.[7] Both the

---

[7] Kurtosis is a statistical measure (a scaled version of the fourth statistical moment) of the size of the tails for a distribution of numerical values, with larger values indicating a larger number of extreme deviations from the center of a distribution of numbers. A value of three indicates that the distribution has the same kurtosis as the standard normal

2.1 *Studying Political Budgeting*

figures – as well as the numbers under them – tell us that while the values for the distribution of budgetary changes in Denmark are fairly close to those of a normal distribution, the values for Spain are not.[8] This is driven by a substantial number of big changes in total expenditures in the Spanish data, as can be seen in Figure 2.2a. Across the data that we analyze in this book, our results are similar to those of Baumgartner et al. (2009); the kurtosis values for changes in total spending for most of the nations are greater than three, and thus are consistent with the expectations of the theory of punctuated equilibrium.[9]

Rather than focusing on budget size or distribution, our second example of budgetary change asks: When is change more or less likely to occur? Building on questions and theories about when politics and economics will influence the amount of change in budgets, both Brender and Drazen (2013) and Tsebelis and Chang (2004) developed indices in order to understand when there will be more or less budgetary volatility. Unlike the measures used by Baumgartner et al. (2009) that rely on spending totals, these researchers create change measures by aggregating changes in spending across multiple budgetary categories to create indicators of budgetary volatility. With the focus on studying the amount of change over time, Brender and Drazen (2013) create a measure that allows for comparisons across time and countries (or units). Referred to as I_{it}, they calculate it as:

$$I_{it} = \frac{\sum_{i=1}^{J} |e_{jit} - e_{ji,t-n}|}{2}, \quad (2.2)$$

where e_{jit} is the percentage of expenditure for budgetary category j in country i at time t.[10]

---

distribution. Values above three suggest a leptokurtic distribution (i.e., a "peaked" distribution that will produce more outliers than the standard normal distribution), while those below three are said to be platykurtic (i.e., a "flattened" distribution that will produce fewer outliers than the standard normal).

[8] Indeed, Shapiro–Wilk tests for normality suggest that total expenditures (and the change in total expenditures) for Denmark are normally distributed, while the same values for Spain are not.

[9] While the main focus of empirical analyses to test the theory of punctuated equilibrium have been analyses of distributions of changes, Fagan, Jones, and Wlezien (2017) model the determinants of large budgetary shifts.

[10] Such a measure ensures that $0 \le I_{it} \le 100$. Tsebelis and Chang (2004) calculate a similar measure as:

$$BD = \sqrt{(a_{1,t} - a_{1,t-1})^2 + (a_{2,t} - a_{2,t-1})^2 + \cdots + (a_{n,t} - a_{n,t-1})^2}, \quad (2.3)$$

For taxes, Ashworth and Heyndels (2002) use a similar approach when they create a measure of "tax turbulence," the sum of the absolute year-to-year change in a given tax category (payroll, income, etc.). In all of these works on various types of budgetary change (Ashworth and Heyndels 2002; Tsebelis and Chang 2004; Brender and Drazen 2013), the focus is on what political or economic factors affect the amount of movement across time, highlighting institutional and political culprits. Brender and Drazen (2013) conclude that elections and leadership changes lead to greater budgetary volatility, although these changes are mostly in more economically developed countries and require multiple years to come to fruition. Tsebelis and Chang (2004) find that, after controlling for automatic stabilizers in the budget (e.g., changes caused by rising unemployment), budgetary volatility tends to occur more when the veto players in government – key actors whose agreement is needed to enact policy change – hold similar ideologies than when they are ideologically distant. Alternatively, Ashworth and Heyndels (2002) conclude that there is less shifting of taxes during election years; however, the fragmentation of government power does lessen the tax turbulence. In other words, more institutional checks on budgets lead to less change in both spending and taxes over time.

As an illustration of this type of research, we first show, in Figure 2.3a, the proportion of spending across eight categories in the United Kingdom from 1975 to 2010. Then, in Figure 2.3b, we summarize the combination of the absolute value of changes across all of these categorical spending measures using Brender and Drazen's one- and four-year measures of budgetary change. As we can see from this figure, their one-year change measure identifies a smattering of years with particularly large changes across budget categories: in the mid-to-late 1980s, a run of years in the mid-1990s, and 2007. The four-year measure also identifies the mid-1980s and the mid-1990s as periods of relatively high levels of volatility across categories in UK spending, but these values are higher for the latter period because of the run of consecutive years of large one-year changes. Comparing the one- and four-year measures also shows how longer-run changes (i.e., the four-year measure) can dwarf short-run

where BD is the "budget distance" between two budgets for the same country in consecutive years calculated across different categories of expenditures ($a_1, a_2, \ldots a_n$). Although these two measures are calculated and scaled differently, they are highly correlated. Across the data included in our analyses, the correlation coefficient for the Brender and Drazen 1-year measure of change and the Tsebelis and Chang measure is .99.

2.1 Studying Political Budgeting

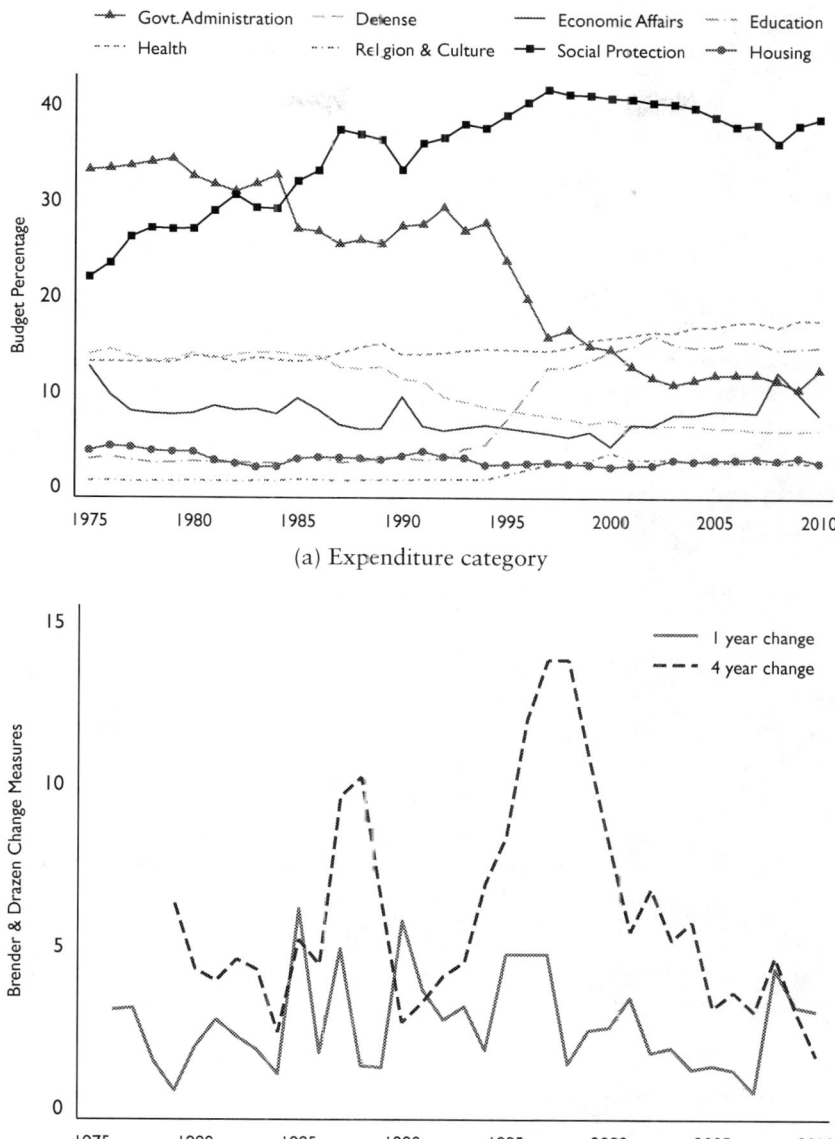

(a) Expenditure category

(b) Brender and Drazen's change measures

FIGURE 2.3. UK spending categories (a) and budgetary change measures (b)

changes (i.e., the one-year measure). From the comparison of the graphs in Figure 2.3, we can see how, when compared to research on individual policy budgets, questions about budgetary change prioritize overall systemic shifts to specific budgetary increases or decreases.

2.1.3 Studies of Aggregate Budgetary Components

The third type of research on political budgeting has emphasized the broader components of the budgetary landscape by focusing on single pieces: usually expenditures, revenues, or surpluses/deficits.[11] Large literatures have investigated how politics and economics may affect these individual components, exploring, for example, how governments shape revenue types or deficit levels, as well as how economic conditions affect total government expenditure patterns.

A fundamental (yet simplified) expectation of political budgeting is that, for any country in a given year, we would see the following budgetary relationship:

$$\text{Deficit} = \text{Expenditure} - \text{Revenue}. \quad (2.4)$$

If expenditures in a given year are greater than the revenues taken in, the government runs a deficit; if revenues exceed expenditures, there is a budgetary surplus.[12] Despite the intuitive algebra of budget balances, reality is typically more complicated than Equation (2.4), because of a variety of accounting conventions in terms of where and when certain types of transactions are reflected in these budgetary aggregates (e.g., Jacobs 2008; De Renzio and Masud 2011; Burger and Hawkesworth 2013). Nonetheless, a substantial amount of the literature on political budgeting has focused on the impact of different political and economic factors on one of these aggregated measures of budgets.[13]

Similar to Equation (2.1), that illustrated research models of single expenditure categories, Equation (2.5) shows a typical way to theorize and model research on a single aggregate budgetary component:

---

[11] Harrinvirta and Mattila (2001) build separate models of three parts of the budget: expenditure, revenue, and fiscal deficits (as a percentage of GDP), but they do not include measures of the other components in each model.

[12] This also could result in budget surpluses. For simplicity, we use the term "deficit" to denote the balance of expenditures and revenues.

[13] Since we are discussing this relationship in the short-term, the focus is on deficits, although researchers have tackled the topic of debt or the accumulation of deficits over time (e.g., Alesina and Passalacqua 2016).

2.1 Studying Political Budgeting

$$\text{Budgetary Component}_{it} = f(\text{Budgetary Component}_{it-1}$$
$$+ \text{Politics}_{it} + \text{Economy}_{it} + \text{Controls}_{it}), \quad (2.5)$$

where Budgetary Component$_{it}$ is a measure of total expenditures, budgetary volatility, total revenues, or the deficit in country "i" at time "t." While research on a single component, such as deficits, shares modeling characteristics with those of single categories, such as defense spending, the former type of studies focus on the aggregate level, not on individual categories within the components.

Research on the three components of Equation (2.4) (plus budgetary volatility) is wide-ranging, with scholars seeking to explain levels and/or changes through a variety of theories and using an assortment of political, economic, and international factors. Standardized versions of these measures – usually expressed as a percentage of GDP – allow researchers to test their theoretical expectations across countries and years. For example, exploring how politics relates to these components is a common theme with work on surpluses or deficits as a percentage of GDP (e.g., Cheibub 2006; Bäck and Lindvall 2015), government expenditures as a percentage of GDP (e.g., Bawn and Rosenbluth 2006; Martin and Vanberg 2013), government revenues as a percentage of GDP (e.g., Huber, Ragin, and Stephens 1993; Harrinvirta and Mattila 2001; Sakamoto 2008), and budgetary change as a percentage of budgetary volatility (Tsebelis and Chang 2004; Brender and Drazen 2013). In these instances, the foci are on how politics – in the form of governments, elections, regimes, or institutions – shape various components of the larger budget (total expenditures, total revenues, or the deficit).

We show an example of the data used in this type of research in Figure 2.4, where we plot government expenditures and revenues for Finland on the left (Figure 2.4a) and the Finnish budgetary deficit on the right (Figure 2.4b).[14] A few interesting aspects stand out. First, not only do expenditures and revenues steadily increase over time – perhaps suggestive of the budgetary incrementalism theory discussed in Section 2.1.1 – but both budgetary instruments track each other closely. Revenues closely matched, and even exceeded expenditures in some years until around

---

[14] Our measure here is the actual deficit; however, in previous literature, researchers commonly used the annual change in debt as a measure of deficit spending (e.g., Roubini and Sachs 1989b; Hahm, Kamlet, and Mowery 1995; De Haan and Sturm 1997; Weisstanner 2017). In addition, we find that some scholars, for example, Cusack (1999) and Seiferling (2019), equate "net lending/borrowing" with deficit/surplus, but this appears to be caused by a data source necessity rather than a theoretical choice.

1990, when expenditures rapidly expanded. Looking to the context, in the 1990s, Finland experienced a massive economic downturn, with GDP declining around 14 percent between 1990 and 1993, and unemployment hovering near 20 percent by 1994 (Honkapohja et al. 1999). Expenditures went from less than 30 percent of Finland's GDP to over 45 percent between 1990 and 1995, highlighting the strain on the budget during Finland's "Great Depression." With the recovery in the late 1990s, there was another switch such that revenues surpassed expenditures, although, as the "Great Recession" began shortly before 2010, expenditures once again overtook revenues. Overall, it is hard to discern whether expenditures are driving revenues, or the other way around (this is something we explore more in Chapter 5); regardless, it is evident that the two are closely interlinked.

Turning to Figure 2.4b, we see that, when deficits are greater than zero, expenditures outpace revenues, and, when deficits fall below zero, revenues out-pace expenditures. This figure would appear to suggest that Finnish deficits exhibited standard business cycle behavior between 1975 and about 1990, although the government ended with a surplus for nearly every year during this period. Starting around 1990 – and then peaking sharply with the Finnish Great Depression – deficits rose to nearly 20 percent. We can see the corresponding differences between expenditures and revenues in Figure 2.4a as a further illustration of these rising deficits; the nearly flat revenue line from about 1990 to just before 1995 could not possibly offset the sharp rise in expenditures, resulting in a massive increase in deficits. One possible explanation for this could be that transfers and unemployment insurance programs expanded during this period, while the government's revenue stream decreased during the downturn (Honkapohja et al. 1999). However, by the mid-to-late 1990s, the government was once again running a surplus that mostly continued until the Great Recession of the late 2000s. All of these patterns in Figure 2.4 suggest a close relationship between deficits, revenues, and expenditures exists, similar to the one posited in Equation (2.4).

2.1.3.1 Summarizing the Three Approaches to Studying Budgets

Considering these three types of research approaches – focusing on the trajectory of a single budgetary category, exploring the distribution and timing of budgetary change, and modeling an aggregate measure of national budgets – we see quite a few commonalities. First, across these three approaches, scholars tend to be interested in how governments,

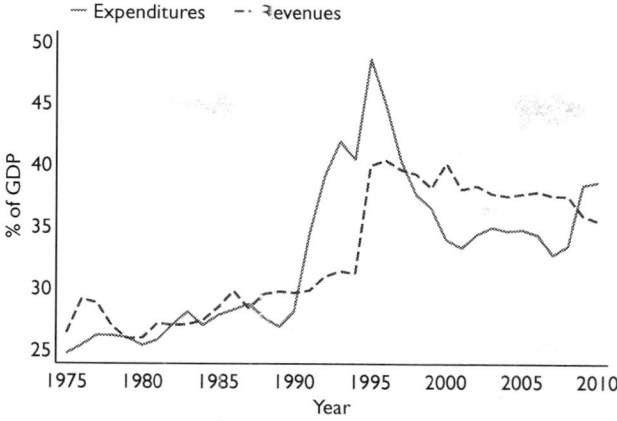
(a) Expenditures and Revenues

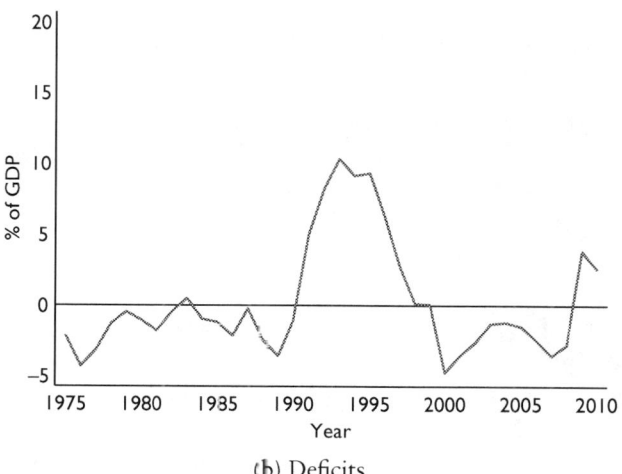
(b) Deficits

FIGURE 2.4. An illustration of expenditures and revenues (a) and deficits (b) in Finland

political institutions, and economic factors relate to budgets. Of course, they vary in their arguments about how politics and economics affect budgets that result in these different approaches, but this starting point remains a common theme. Second, the research question or theoretical argument drives the approach chosen. Questions about welfare policy and constituent groups, for example, tend to lead to one approach, while a puzzle about regime change and budgetary stability follows a different path. This has resulted in detailed research on pieces of the budget at various levels, while also guiding us to our last commonality. While each of these three types of previous approaches to studying budgets offer guidance about complicated relationships, all three remain incomplete. With a focus on a specific aspect of the budget, researchers are able to offer explanations for pieces of the budget, but the larger budgetary picture remains under-explored.

In Section 2.2, we build upon these three types of research by offering an alternative approach to the study of budgets. Acknowledging where previous research has fallen short or been incomplete, we bridge these ways of studying budgets and offer a new way to consider budgetary behavior. Our approach brings the wide field of budgetary studies together by incorporating elements from each of these three established types under a single unified framework.

2.2 WHAT IS MISSING?

While the established literature has uncovered many details about political budgeting at the individual policy, policy volatility, and aggregate levels, we are struck by how compartmentalized much of this research is. For example, researchers of individual policy budgets tend to ignore theories and existing research on aggregate policy change. Similarly, one finds little overlap between work on total spending and research on budgetary deficits or total revenue. Therefore, finding ways to build on and combine the significant resources available in these three types of research approaches offers substantial possibilities for expanding budgetary research.

We begin by considering two major shortcomings in the broad literature on budgets. First, with few exceptions, researchers have ignored the compositional tradeoffs that are occurring within the expenditure categories of budgets. While studying expenditures for more than one policy area is not uncommon, we have found that treating spending in different policy areas as interlinked is quite rare. The second oversight is that scholars have mostly ignored the simultaneous interplay between expenditures, revenues, budgetary volatility, and the deficit components of budgets. As we discussed in Chapter 1, although such tradeoffs and inter-workings are at the core of most detailed descriptive accounts of political budgeting, we argue for focusing a theory of political budgets around these connections to bring them front and center.

2.2 What Is Missing?

2.2.1 Tradeoffs within Expenditures

First, consider how research into political and economic factors on single expenditure categories views budgets. While thinking of budgets as spending on one category or one policy area can provide valuable insights into political budgeting, it is important to recognize the simplifying assumptions inherent in this approach (Philips, Rutherford, and Whitten 2016a). While, theoretically, researchers often focus on more than one policy area, for the most part, each spending area is treated in isolation in their empirical analyses (c.f., Milesi-Ferretti, Perotti, and Rostagno 2002; Castro and Martins 2018). While such approaches are common, they fail to acknowledge how spending on each policy area links together with expenditures in other areas.

A related issue arises with regard to the "omitted" category that researchers inadvertently create when they focus on only a single category. As we illustrate in Figure 2.5, conceptualizations that examine a single expenditure category implicitly aggregate political budgeting behavior into two parts: the proportion of total government expenditures spent on one budgetary area – represented as category "a" – and everything else.[15] In this hypothetical example, the share of the total budget going toward category "a" increases from 14 to 25 percent over the four time periods. This shift for "a" means expenditures on all other categories combined are decreasing as a share of the budget, although it is not clear how that decrease is distributed among the other categories. In other words, the grey areas in Figure 2.5 are "black boxes," where other budgetary changes could also be occurring, but we are unable to decipher them. Moreover, some budgetary categories in these grey areas may be declining faster than others, so gains in "a" may be coming at the expense of some categories in the grey areas more than others. Once again, we are unable to tell if this is true, given the current conceptualization of only a single budget category, as shown in Figure 2.5.

Although researchers may ask questions about how politics and economics influence expenditures on a specific category or policy area, they are typically analyzing that policy area in relation to the remainder of the budget in its totality, whether they intend to or not. For example, if we

---

[15] Models with a dependent variable measured as a particular expenditure category expressed as the percentage of gross domestic product have a slightly different interpretation. Yet a somewhat similar issue occurs, since any observed changes may be caused by an increase or decrease in the expenditure category (holding GDP constant) by a change in GDP itself (holding expenditures constant) or some combination of the two.

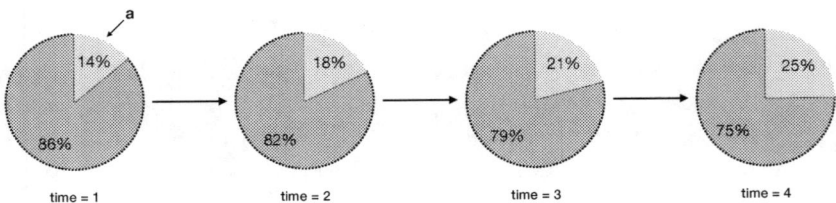

FIGURE 2.5. Conceptualizing a single budgetary category

theorize about why rising unemployment would increase social welfare spending, then we should also acknowledge that this shift in unemployment may affect policy areas in the remaining budget (the "black box" represented by the grey area in Figure 2.5). It is crucial, though frequently overlooked, to remember these tradeoffs when theorizing about political budgeting.

From both the theoretical and methodological viewpoints, it is essential to keep in mind this lumping together of all other categories when interpreting the results from these models. This means that, in a model specified along the lines of Equation (2.1), researchers must interpret the estimated effect of any independent variable that is statistically significant in terms of its impact on the tradeoff between spending on that budgetary category and everything else. An equally important – but seldom-recognized – implication of such conceptualizations is that the failure to find a statistically significant relationship for a particular independent variable does not mean that the independent variable has *no* impact on spending for that budgetary category. Rather, it just indicates that the independent variable has no impact on the tradeoff between spending on that budget category and spending on *everything else*. This grouping of everything else may obscure substantial tradeoffs between the category of interest and the other categories which have been combined.[16]

Another way to illustrate this point appears in Table 2.1 and Figure 2.6. If we imagine that the "black-box" category – shown in Figure 2.5 as

---

[16] In Section 5.2 of the supporting information document for Philips, Rutherford, and Whitten (2016a), the authors provide an illustration of this concern using a model of military spending as a percentage of overall government spending in the federal budget of the United States. Results from this model indicate how many of the independent variables that one would commonly expect to be related to defense spending are not statistically significant. However, when they model tradeoffs across multiple spending categories using the techniques described in Chapter 3, they found these independent variables are statistically significant in ways that comport with theoretical expectations.

2.2 What Is Missing?

TABLE 2.1. *How conceptualizing a single budgetary category obscures tradeoffs*

Time	Category a	Category b	Category c	Category d	Total
1	14	40	36	10	100
2	18	40	31	11	100
3	21	40	27	12	100
4	25	40	21	14	100

the grey sections of the pie – is actually comprised of three budgetary categories "b," "c," and "d," then we might observe something like Table 2.1. Here, spending on category "b" stays at 40 percent throughout the four time periods, while the proportion of spending on category "c" declines from 36 to 21 percent. Spending on category "d" increases over the time period, although this increase from 10 to 14 percent is not as large as the increase for category "a," whose share rises from 14 to 25 percent of the budget. All categories continue to sum to 100 (the total size of the budget). If we had relied on the "black-box" conceptualization of Figure 2.5, we would have been unable to see this interesting variation and simply concluded that categories "b," "c," and "d," when combined, are declining relative to "a."

We also present the data from Table 2.1 in Figure 2.6 to see the issue visually. When we focus on the changes in a single category, such as "a," the only take away point is that, while spending increases for it, the budget for the remaining areas together (b + c + d) is declining. This emphasis masks the fact that while spending in category "c" does indeed decline across the time periods observed, spending in area "d" increases and spending in area "b" stays the same. In other words, the increased share of expenditures going toward "a" is coming solely at the expense of "c," not "b" or "d."[17] By shedding light on how changes in one category affect all other categories simultaneously, this conceptualization of budgets as compositions offers chances to analyze the relative increases and decreases across budgetary categories.

2.2.1.1 Budgetary Volatility As a Mirror of the Budgeting Process

While we have critiqued the existing literature for not broadly acknowledging these tradeoffs in budgets, this blind spot applies less to those

---

[17] Although "a" is taking up a larger share of the budget relative to both "b" and "d."

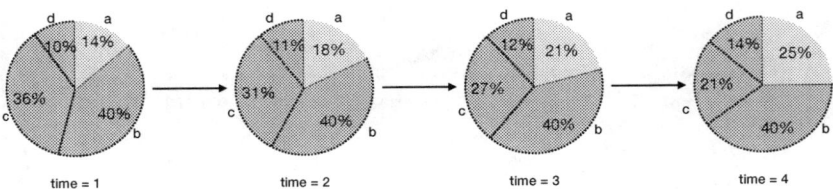

FIGURE 2.6. Conceptualizing single budgetary categories obscures tradeoffs

researchers who focus on measures of budgetary volatility. Recall from our discussion in Section 2.1.2 that this type of research relies on conceptualizing budgets as multiple categories. This essentially shifts the focus from thinking of budgets along the lines presented in Figure 2.5 to those presented in Figure 2.6, where the budget is now more realistically represented as consisting of multiple slices from the same pie. A measure such as that constructed using Equation (2.2) summarizes the total amount of change as a percentage of allocations to categories within the budgetary pie over a particular time period (Brender and Drazen 2013).[18] However, note that this approach of a single budgetary change measure focuses attention on *how much* change is happening inside the pie. It is important to keep in mind that such measures are not appropriate for answering questions about *what type* of changes are happening. In other words, which categories are changing and which are not? And what is the direction (increasing or decreasing) of these changes?

Understanding the amount of volatility across the budgetary categories is a shift toward acknowledging that policy expenditures are connected. While budgetary change measures rely on disaggregated expenditures at the policy category level, both the measures and their conceptualizations differ from work on single and aggregated policy spending. These measures focus on the big picture of overall shifts in budgets over time, but they are grounded in an understanding that lower-level changes in expenditures can provide significant budgetary signals. We see these measures of expenditure volatility as an essential measure of budgetary competition and argue that researchers should include them along with the other components discussed in Section 2.1.3.

---

[18] For instance, the Brender and Drazen (2013) measure of budgetary change was given as $I_{it} = \frac{\sum_{j=1}^{J} |e_{jit} - e_{ji,t-n}|}{2}$. Note, however, that while they analyze various time intervals, here we focus on the interval from $t-1$ to t.

Conceptualizing budgetary expenditures as compositions of more than two parts and as tradeoffs that occur between those parts is consistent with the way most people think about and discuss budgets. For instance, Berry (1990, p. 185) points out how, "budgetary choices for one category of spending may affect choices for another category." Adolph, Breunig, and Koski (2020, p. 26) note that, "even in political systems where policymakers are able to finance expenditure with new debts, every spending decision bears an opportunity cost and thus invites controversy into the budget process. In short, every year legislators and heads of government in the American states and elsewhere must face trade-offs across budget priorities." This more realistic approach to budgetary spending – that recognizes the very real tradeoffs policy-makers are forced to make when allocating budgets – opens up opportunities to theorize and hypothesize about how governments, politics, and economics shape public policy.

2.2.2 Interplay between Budgetary Components

The second shortcoming focuses on the issue of compartmentalization within budgetary research, whereby researchers focus on just a single aspect of the overall budget, such as expenditures, revenues, or deficits. While work on individual budgetary components offers many insights into that part of the budgetary process, understanding the simultaneous interconnectedness of these larger budgetary pieces remains underexplored. Research on how politics and economics affect one part of the budget has mostly ignored the endogenous nature of what is occurring in the other major components of the budgetary process. An external shock (e.g., a change in government or a decline in growth) to any one major budgetary component is likely to influence both that part and the other major components. Even if expenditures, revenues, and deficits do not work perfectly in lockstep – as displayed in Equation 2.4 – few would argue that they are independent of each other.[19]

In Figure 2.7, we illustrate the interconnectedness of the various budgetary components: total expenditures, total revenues, budget deficit, and budgetary volatility. We presented three of these pieces in Equation (2.4), where total expenditures and total revenues result in budget deficits. The fourth component is the budgetary volatility measure, and we include it

---

[19] Methodologically, in order to account for this, we would need to move to a system of equations written as:

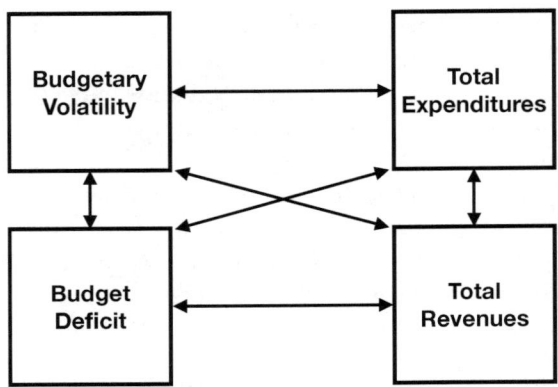

FIGURE 2.7. Interconnected budgetary components

since budgetary change can affect – and in turn be affected by – the other budgetary components.

$$\begin{aligned}
\text{Total Expenditures}_{it} &= f([\text{Present and Past Values of Aggregates}] \\
&\quad + \text{Politics}_{it} + \text{Economy}_{it} + \text{Controls}_{it}) \\
\text{Expenditures Volatility}_{it} &= f([\text{Present and Past Values of Aggregates}] \\
&\quad + \text{Politics}_{it} + \text{Economy}_{it} + \text{Controls}_{it}) \\
\text{Total Revenues}_{it} &= f([\text{Present and Past Values of Aggregates}] \\
&\quad + \text{Politics}_{it} + \text{Economy}_{it} + \text{Controls}_{it}) \\
\text{Total Deficit}_{it} &= f([\text{Present and Past Values of Aggregates}] \\
&\quad + \text{Politics}_{it} + \text{Economy}_{it} + \text{Controls}_{it}),
\end{aligned} \quad (2.6)$$

where [Present and Past Values of Aggregates] in each equation is a combination of the past value of the aggregate on the left side of the equal sign, as well as the past and present values of the other three aggregates. For example, in the first line where the left-hand side variable is Total Expenditures$_{it}$, if we were using only one lag of the other aggregates, then [Present and Past Values of Aggregates] would be equal to

$$\text{Total Expenditures}_{i,t-1} + \text{Expenditures Change}_{it} + \text{Total Revenues}_{it} + \text{Total Deficit}_{it}$$
$$+ \text{Expenditures Change}_{i,t-1} + \text{Total Revenues}_{i,t-1} + \text{Total Deficit}_{i,t-1}. \quad (2.7)$$

Instead of ignoring the obviously endogenous relationships between these four different budgetary aggregates, such an approach embraces and models endogenous relationships. We pursue such a strategy in Chapter 5.

2.2 What Is Missing?

When combined, these four components show a more complete picture of a nation's budget. Turning again to Finland, Figure 2.8 offers an example of this approach using data over the years of our study. Organized to match our schematic in Figure 2.7, the four pieces – expenditure change, total expenditures, total revenues, and deficits – illustrate the same budgetary conditions for Finland but from different angles. Previously, when discussing Figure 2.4, we noted that Finland experienced a depression in the early 1990s, and we can see this reflected in Figure 2.8 by the large spikes in the budgetary volatility measure (the top-left plot). Of course, such a measure does not say *where* such changes are occurring in response to worsening economic conditions in Finland in the 1990s. Other components also shift rapidly around this time. Both expenditures (top-right plot in Figure 2.4) and deficits (bottom-left) rise sharply, suggesting that the government responded to the depression by increasing expenditures (as a share of GDP) and paying for this increase by growing fiscal deficits to nearly 10 percent of GDP at its peak. While revenues (bottom-right plot) were increasing in Finland since the 1980s as a share of GDP, it was not until 1995 that they skyrocketed, which then corresponds with a decline in budget deficits in Finland throughout the rest of the period.

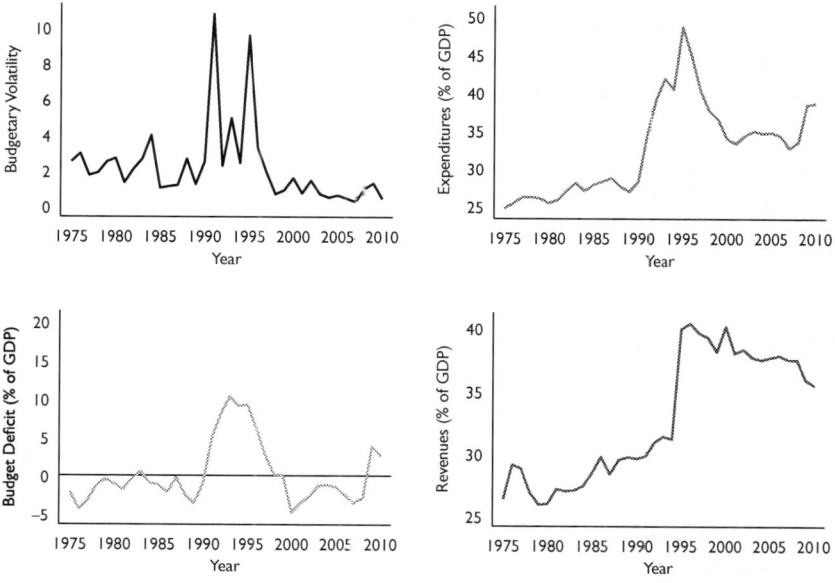

FIGURE 2.8. Interconnected budgetary components in Finland

This example in Figure 2.8 of examining each of the larger budgetary pieces simultaneously, highlights the interconnected nature of these budgetary pieces and illustrates what an investigation into these missing relationships would add to our knowledge about the politics of budgets. This vision of the budgetary components as being interlinked is not unique; many scholars have made assumptions, either explicitly or implicitly, that some components affect others.[20] What we argue has been overlooked in much of the literature is an argument and corresponding analysis about the many relationships in Figure 2.7.

2.3 OUR THEORETICAL APPROACH: A CONTEXTUAL THEORY OF BUDGETS

In *Competition for Pieces of the Pie*, we seek to address these shortcomings in the approaches to studying political budgeting through both theoretical and methodological contributions. Our core theoretical idea is that political competition and external factors combine to shape both expenditure compositions, as well as the larger interlinked components of national government budgets. While we cover multiple aspects of budgets in this book, our argument concerning competition and context drives our theoretical story throughout the various chapters.

In translating our theoretical argument into testable propositions, we first focus on how and when political competition influences tradeoffs in the composition of budgetary expenditures. Ideological differences across governments ground our expectations, but we emphasize the various contexts that surround their decision-making. In fact, we note that these conditioning domestic and international factors often lead to mixed results and competing theoretical expectations that can be found in the extant literature. We thus provide a more comprehensive theoretical picture of budgets by unpacking how and when these environments affect governments' abilities to alter spending priorities. Next, we combine all four larger budgetary pieces – expenditures, expenditure change, revenues, and deficits – in a single model in order to allow each of them to affect one another. This allows us to better understand (and model) which budgetary categories themselves may be causing one another. Last, after developing

---

[20] The overall picture is not unique, although researchers may debate the inclusion of "Budgetary Volatility" as a component in this figure. Yet we contend that all of these budgetary components have not been modeled simultaneously (as in Equation (2.6)), not just to examine how exogenous factors affect these four components, but how they in turn affect one another.

2.3 Our Theoretical Approach: Context and Budgets

an understanding of the mechanisms at play in these interconnected components, we apply our theoretical argument about competition and context to the four components in order to better understand the politics behind budgets.

2.3.1 A Compositional Theory of Budgetary Expenditures

In budgets, tradeoffs occur between spending categories, but previous research has largely overlooked the information available in these compositions. Therefore, we set out to explain these political decisions. Our focus first is on how, within the expenditure pie, a relative increase in one policy area results in a relative decrease in at least one other area. Rather than comparing one policy area to all other policies, thereby leaving us with a pie of only two categories (i.e., as we showed in Figure 2.5), we argue that theories need to consider the broader budgetary composition in order to better understand the tradeoffs involved. By focusing on the relative shifts between multiple policy areas, we can theorize about and empirically test the relationships between the competitive political environment, the broader context, and expenditure reallocations. In doing so, our theory better reflects the complex decisions about the tradeoffs that policymakers make when allocating public spending.

In answering the question of how politics affects expenditures, we highlight the political competition for resources. Figure 2.9 illustrates the first part of our theoretical approach, which we present in Chapters 3 and 4. Our theorizing about budgets begins with the idea that governments of various ideological stripes protect specific policy areas in order to benefit their supporters, while cannibalizing other policy areas. This latter notion is key, since, "how parties target those cuts says just as much about their agenda as which budgets they increase" (Adolph, Breunig, and Koski 2020, p. 29). While parties might emphasize budgetary categories that are particularly important to their constituents, they are just as likely to retrench in budgetary categories that they do not prioritize or in those their opponents on the opposite side of the ideological spectrum *do* prioritize.

As illustrated by the top of Figure 2.9, parties that form governments differ in both their ideologies and their core supporters.[21] These

---

[21] A large literature argues that political parties might target swing voters instead of their core constituents when seeking to win votes in the next election (c.f., Lindbeck and Weibull 1987; Dixit and Londregan 1996; Kwon 2005; Kitschelt and Wilkinson 2007). For our purposes, we refer to "core supporters" as simply the stable base of support that

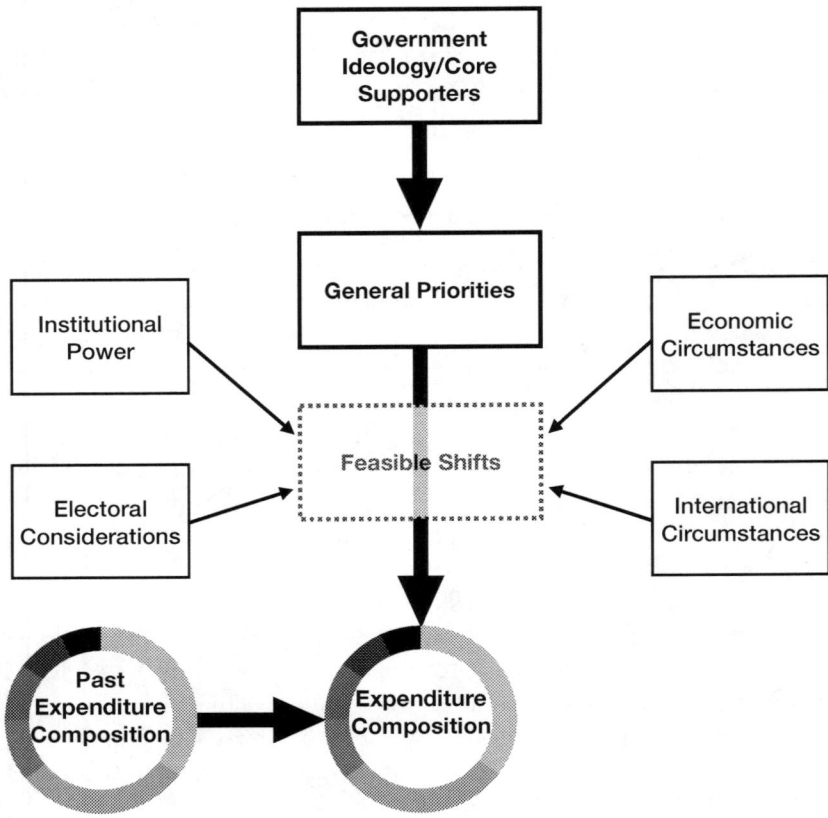

FIGURE 2.9. A compositional theory of expenditures

differences lead to varying general priorities that result in the allocation of budgetary resources.[22] We argue that governments will consciously alter the composition of expenditures, shifting resources across policies to reflect their supporter- and ideologically-driven priorities. However, as depicted in Figure 2.9, we expect that the circumstances and contexts surrounding them will have an impact on their abilities to make relative spending changes.

tends to share the same budgetary allocation desires as the government; this may include swing voters if they share similar views about the budgetary priorities of the government.

[22] There is substantial evidence that political parties follow through on their ideologically defined campaign pledges once in office (Lipsmeyer 2009; Thomson et al. 2017).

2.3 Our Theoretical Approach: Context and Budgets

What could condition the link between ideology and budgets? In our holistic theoretical approach, we focus on the interplay between the general budgetary priorities of governments and four factors that moderate their ability to move the composition of expenditures in order to fulfil these priorities: institutional power, electoral considerations, economic circumstances, and international circumstances. We represent these contexts by the four outer rectangles in Figure 2.9. While governments may allow parts of the expenditure composition to increase or decrease through a lack of action – for instance, by allowing the real value of social insurance benefits to decline with inflation, leading to a relative budgetary decrease – we argue that such non-actions also reflect conscious decisions about budgetary tradeoffs. Thus, changes in the relative size of pieces of the pie, as depicted in Figure 2.9, reflect strategic choices by governments. We discuss each of these contexts in more detail later in this chapter. Last, since budgets are largely incremental, we also incorporate past expenditure compositions into our theoretical model, as shown at the bottom-left of Figure 2.9. Any policy changes performed by governments are likely to be slow-moving and, thus, must be large enough to overcome such budgetary inertia. Therefore, we believe that this incrementalism is just as important in shaping how budgets change, as is the desire of various government types and the four factors that may aid or hinder such changes.

Thinking about how and when political competition shapes expenditures is a key element of our theory. In our examination of the complexity of budgets and the other factors that can affect them (economic, political, and international pressures), we answer three main contextual questions. First, when would we expect politics to matter? Second, although political competition can be a driving force behind compositional alterations, when do the broader contexts and shocks influence the ability of governments to shape budgets to match their own preferences? And third, are governments willing to break from their desired ideological budgeting priorities to respond to external shocks?

As Figure 2.9 highlights, our theory about the broader context of tradeoffs involves multiple types of contexts and pressures, and we emphasize that these "shocks" influence how and when political competition shapes budgets. By focusing on institutional, electoral, economic, and international pressures, we can explore how these environments affect governments' budgetary behavior. This allows us to answer the question: "On budgets, do ideologically distinct governments react differently to similar shocks?"

2.3.1.1 Political Competition and the Institutional Context

One of the factors that may affect whether or not governments institute their preferred budgetary compositions is their institutional power or status. While governments have a desire to distribute budgetary resources to fit their ideological visions, whether they can succeed may depend on whether or not they have the power to accomplish their goals. As shown in Figure 2.9, institutional status alters the ability of governments to enact change. While ideology is a useful heuristic through which political parties and governments define their core beliefs about both the size and scope of government, the institutional environment can alter how well governments are able to translate their ideologies into their preferred budgets.

As previous research on fiscal deficits, as well as on spending on specific policies and revenue areas has demonstrated, institutional arrangements can restrict or enhance a government's ability to implement desired policies (Hallerberg and Marier 2004; Tsebelis and Chang 2004; Bawn and Rosenbluth 2006; Cheibub 2006; Martin and Vanberg 2013, 2020). To study these relationships, scholars have explored the effect of institutions in various ways. How characteristics of governments and corresponding electoral systems influence spending levels has been a key concern when explaining how institutions influence policy (Persson and Tabellini 2004; Kang and Powell 2010). The set-up of coalition governments, the number of members in a coalition, or government members' oversight abilities, for instance, can limit a party's ability to push policy in its preferred ideological direction (Martin and Vanberg 2004, 2011; Lipsmeyer and Pierce 2011; Bäck and Lindvall 2015). In relation to the budgetary balance, previous research has stressed the importance of institutional rules in determining the level of expenditures relative to revenues (Von Hagen and Harden 1995). Higher deficits, for example, are associated with coalition governments (Alesina and Drazen 1989).[23] This body of research on the institutional arrangements of governments has emphasized how these conditions affect whether governments can enact their preferred policies, but it has not considered that institutions may alter how political competition influences the allocation of budgetary resources. In other words, we are interested in how the political competition in different

---

[23] The converse is sometimes true as well; concentrated economic and political power can lead to institutions that distort revenues such as income tax (Ardanaz and Scartascini 2013).

institutional contexts influences governments' abilities to make tradeoffs between relative spending across policy areas.

Highlighting specifically the policy power of majority versus minority governments, scholars have argued that coalitions with enough votes to push legislation through a parliament have the upper hand in following through on their ideological agendas (Lijphart 1984; Strøm 1990b). Much of the literature linking government status and budgets has been focused on whether minority governments spend more and run higher deficits, not on if they can follow-through on their ideological priorities (Roubini and Sachs 1989b; De Haan, Sturm, and Beekhuis 1999; Perotti and Kontopoulos 2002). Potrafke (2019) points out that the empirical results on deficits and government power have been mixed, with some work finding a positive effect of minority governments, while others find no difference between majority and minority governments. Here, our question is not about the direct effect of government power, but whether governments are better able to alter budgets to their liking when they have majority status. The institutional power or context of governments, then, may influence their abilities to allocate budgets in their preferred ways, since holding parliamentary support may facilitate government policymaking. How the institutional context eases or restricts governments' abilities to shift budgetary compositions alters when we would expect to see tradeoffs between and within the budgetary components. Unlike previous theories on the intervening role of institutions, we argue that these factors can influence how governments shape the compositions of budgets, emphasizing that governments consider relative changes to policies rather than piecemeal alterations. Therefore, the institutional context will influence when political competition is likely to shape tradeoffs across expenditures.

2.3.2 Electoral Context

Elections are a key aspect of democratic governance, and there continues to be an expectation that electoral dynamics affect the timing of government behavior. In the realm of budgets, scholars have focused on whether or not governments change expenditures either to shore up their partisan supporters before an election (Cox and McCubbins 1986; Calvo and Murillo 2004; Nichter 2008; Herwartz and Theilen 2017) or to expand their electoral fortunes to new groups of supporters (Dixit and Londregan 1996; Kwon 2005). To explore this relationship between governments, elections, and budgets, researchers have emphasized various parts of the budget with redistributive spending, "visible" policies, and infrastructure/administration being key areas. What these have in common is a focus on policy areas with short-term gains for electorally important groups of voters.

We consider how governments may reallocate resources to benefit themselves before and after an election and present competing arguments that emphasize the ideologically important policy areas of left and right governments. With a nod to our ideological argument, we expect that governments may play to their supporters by shifting relative increases to their preferred policy areas. However, we also take into account the possibility that governments can attract voters through short-term redistributive benefits, because even right governments may receive an electoral benefit from a relative increase to social welfare.

2.3.2.1 *Economic Circumstances*

Similar to institutions and elections, economic upturns and downturns may also enable or constrain governments' abilities to alter budgetary compositions to fit their ideological visions. Although previous research explains how government ideology shapes welfare policies differently depending on economic conditions (Alesina and Roubini 1992; Perotti and Kontopoulos 2002; Lipsmeyer 2011), we argue that this relationship transcends welfare policy, and even expenditures themselves. What governments choose to cut or fund, as well as how they choose to fund it (i.e., through deficits and/or revenues), may depend on their ideologies. However, both positive and negative economic shocks may pressure governments to change not only the composition of expenditures, but also the larger budgetary balance between components, potentially coming at the expense of their ideological preferences and supporters' priorities (Adolph, Breunig, and Koski 2020).

By considering the economy as a context that affects when and how government ideology shapes budgetary allocations, we argue that governments act strategically when faced with different economic conditions. We consider a tournament of expectations of how economic shocks can alter the effect of government ideology on budgetary allocations. For instance, under the constraints imposed by an economic downturn, budgetary allocations may be less about pleasing ideological core supporters and more about appeasing a larger swathe of the public. But another possibility exists – that governments use resources to buffer their support-

2.3 Our Theoretical Approach: Context and Budgets

ers from the hardship which leads to a narrowing of funds to their key policy areas. In contrast, in a positive economic environment, we assert that governments may have the liberty either to enact budgetary changes that emphasize their ideological interests and shore up their supporters or to expand their budgetary goals and resources to policy areas that may attract new electoral supporters. These competing expectations are also relevant to the tradeoffs among budgetary components, with economic pressures influencing government behavior on spending, expenditure volatility, revenues, and deficits.

2.3.2.2 *International Circumstances*

We also argue that international conditions may affect whether or not governments can alter their budgets in their preferred directions. Research on specific policy areas has highlighted arguments concerning the influence of global and international pressures (Hays 2009; Plümper, Troeger, and Winner 2009; Walter 2010). With varying levels of integrated labor markets and difficulties of moving capital, governments face international pressures that affect their abilities to shape public policies (Lipsmeyer and Zhu 2011). Here, we adjudicate an ongoing debate in the literature between a compensating argument, whereby governments attempt to buffer their domestic populations from the hardships created by globalization (Rodrik 1998; Garrett and Mitchell 2001; Swank 2002; Hays 2009) and an efficiency argument, where governments need to retrench in order to counteract the declining revenues from mobile capital (Garrett 2001; Bretschger and Hettich 2002; Devereux, Lockwood, and Redoano 2008; Meinhard and Potrafke 2012). Alternatively, there is the possibility that outside forces such as globalization essentially have no effect on domestic policy-making (Iversen and Cusack 2000; Pierson 2001; Swank and Steinmo 2002).

Ultimately, we are concerned with how left and right governments behave in the face of globalization, not with the direct effects of globalization on budgetary aspects. While some scholars find little evidence of partisan differences in the face of globalizing pressures (Dreher 2006; Potrafke 2009), research on budgetary reallocations and globalization concludes that governments react differently to these shocks, depending on their ideologies (Garrett 1998; Burgoon 2001; Lipsmeyer, Philips, and Whitten 2017). While these previous theories have emphasized specific policy areas (e.g., welfare or economic affairs) and implicitly mentioned tradeoffs between spending areas and/or expenditures and revenues, we tackle the necessary business of looking at the many pieces of the budgetary puzzle.

Outside of economic considerations on the global stage, researchers have also demonstrated that involvement in military conflicts can drive spending priorities (Ostrom 1978; Palmer 1990; Whitten and Williams 2011; Philips, Rutherford, and Whitten 2016a). The general expectation has been that governments of the right will tend to prioritize military spending more than governments of the left. While examining whether ideological differences shape military spending is common (Mintz 1989), analyses of how conflicts – often proxied by combat deaths or militarized interstate disputes – affect expenditures are far less common (Russett 1982; Gupta et al. 2004; Philips, Rutherford, and Whitten 2016a). Even more rare is examining how conflicts interact with ideology to shape budgetary outcomes (Whitten and Williams 2011; Töngür, Hsu, and Elveren 2015). Under conflict conditions, we offer competing theoretical possibilities for how ideology will affect budgets. While conflict may overwhelm ideological differences, leading to left and right governments reinforcing military spending, we argue that ideological preferences may drive which policies they defund. Both left and right governments may reallocate to defense, but they may fund secondary "butter" policy areas that offer economic benefits. We develop expectations about how ideology may be conditioned by conflict involvement to affect not only defense expenditures, but also all other expenditure categories.

2.3.3 The Larger Web of Political Budgeting

The acquisition of revenues, the redistribution of expenditures, and the balancing of budgets are some of the most important, but also complex, activities of government. We contend that our argument about how the political, economic, and international contexts affect whether or not governments can push their ideological budgetary preferences holds for all budgetary components, not just the allocation of expenditure categories. Ideological visions about power and the ideal size of the state can lead governments to espouse differing ideas on revenues, expenditures, deficits, budgetary volatility, and the tradeoffs between these larger budgetary components. Similarly, various contexts can constrain or liberate governments' abilities to follow-through on their ideal positions when it comes to these other budgetary pieces.

Our argument about how political, economic, and international environments can moderate the effect of government ideology helps to explain

2.3 Our Theoretical Approach: Context and Budgets

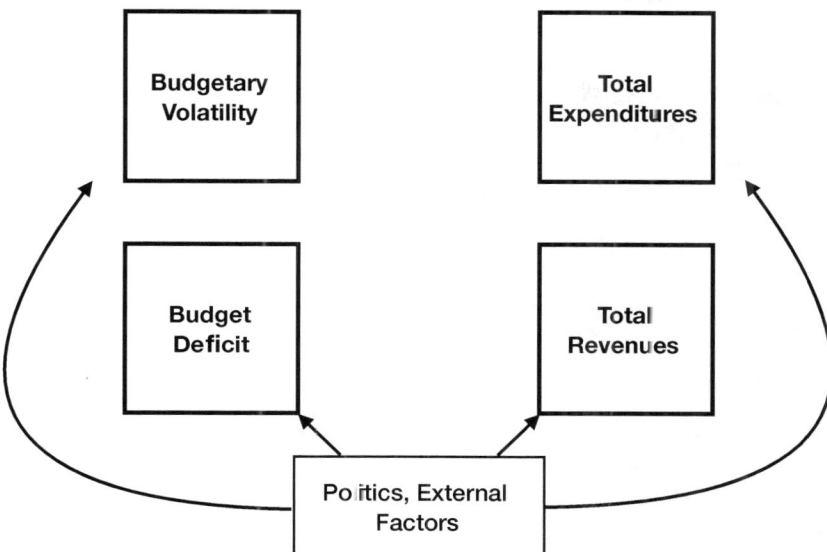

FIGURE 2.10. Politics and external factors affecting broader budgetary components

government budgetary behavior in general. Figure 2.10 illustrates our theoretical thinking about this larger web of political budgeting. Since governments make choices about how they use various fiscal instruments, in this figure we indicate such political manipulation through the use of arrows from the political and external factors to each component of the budget.

Scholars have used ideology as a starting point for explaining levels of revenues, expenditures, and deficits. For instance, they have argued that left governments prefer public over private when it comes to societal responsibilities, and these preferences lead to higher total expenditures, as well as more spending on specific types of policies, such as welfare (Hicks and Swank 1992; Schmidt 1996; Franzese 2002b; Allan and Scruggs 2004; Bawn and Rosenbluth 2006). Parallel arguments appear on the revenue side of the budgetary ledger, where researchers expect left governments to require and raise more revenues than right governments, while also arguing for the use of different tax instruments (Huber, Ragin, and Stephens 1993; Basinger and Hallerberg 2004; Cusack and Beramendi 2006; Plümper, Troeger, and Winner 2009). With deficits, we find similar ideological contentions that left and right governments use these fiscal adjustments in different ways and at varying times (Alesina and Roubini 1992; Boix 2000). Budgetary volatility is the one component without an obvious ideological prior. Because it relies on absolute budgetary change, both left and right governments may be likely to make changes, although the left may increase more, while the right decreases. Therefore, the various contexts may influence left and right governments in different ways on volatility. While these varying arguments for expecting ideological differences across the range of budgetary components continue to help guide us in our political thinking about budgets, questions remain about the generalizability of many of these ideological explanations.

Should we expect ideology to always be the driving factor in governments' budgetary decisions? We argue this is not always realistic: "given the inherent surprises of public life, parties must adjust to what comes at them, often necessitating movements that would not be predicted by partisan ideology alone" (Epp, Lovett, and Baumgartner 2014, p. 866). At times, scholars have turned the expected ideological relationships between governments and budgetary pieces on their heads. For instance, researchers have found evidence that government ideology does not always foretell spending on individual policies, such as education or health (Jensen 2011a,c), and there is evidence that governments of different ideological leanings behave similarly in relation to revenue creation (Swank and Steinmo 2002; Herwartz and Theilen 2017). Similarly, researchers looking at deficits find complicated relationships between spending and revenues that result in ideologically different governments appearing to rely on deficits in common ways (Tavares 2004; Potrafke 2017; Seiferling 2019). In a different vein, work on budgetary volatility focuses more on government or institutional change rather than expecting a right or left government to alter the status quo (Tsebelis and Chang 2004). These mixed expectations and findings indicate how much researchers still do not understand about the relationships between governments, policies, and budgets. Given that left and right governments offer different policy platforms and resource allocations, when are they able to implement these differences? Alternatively, when do budgets indicate similar political behavior by these seemingly disparate governments? Although we begin with government ideology, we anticipate that the reality of competitive budgetary tradeoffs is more complicated than this single dimension.

Through our argument about context, we are better able to understand when governments institute their ideological visions through expenditures, revenues, deficits, and volatility. Realistically, governments make choices constrained or liberated by the surrounding situations. For example, an international military conflict may limit a government's options when it comes to reallocating expenditures. Alternatively, a strong economy may allow governments the freedom to cut revenues or the deficit. While we lean on existing literature's emphasis on individual budgetary components, ultimately, we acknowledge the interconnectedness of these budgetary components and examine them together.

2.4 BRINGING IT ALL TOGETHER

Governments make budgetary tradeoffs that affect conflicting groups and interests (Franzese 2002b). In other words, the competition over budgets has consequences that go beyond ideological arguments, political swagger, and the movement of numbers in a spreadsheet; it also affects society, power, and the lives of citizens. In our argument, we recognize that it can be unrealistic to evaluate change in one part of the budget without considering how it relates to the larger budgetary picture. There are strong reasons to think that all four of the major budgetary aggregates – total expenditures, budgetary volatility, total revenues, and budget deficit – are intertwined or endogenous to each other, but this outlook on budgetary decision-making remains less explored and understood.

We can illustrate this theoretical approach by altering Figure 2.10 to show the interconnectedness of the budgetary components. In Figure 2.11, the additional arrows between the budgetary pieces indicate the two-sided nature of these relationships, where everything is connected. The lower rectangle houses the political competition and contextual environments that shape these connections, indicating how they affect each component and these linked relationships. By focusing on the interplay between all four of these budgetary aggregates, we argue for understanding more of the nuances that occur in budgetary processes. Combining this thinking with that from Figure 2.9 shows how our theoretical framework is holistic, where political competition influences the tradeoffs in the budget by altering the compositions of expenditures and the other major budgetary components. However, an important part of our theory is that the contexts in which governments find themselves will affect their abilities to allocate resources to suit their preferences.

Combining all of the aspects of our theoretical argument, Figure 2.12 illustrates how the different components of the budgetary process fit together in a single theoretical diagram. The top of the diagram

A Theory of Budgets

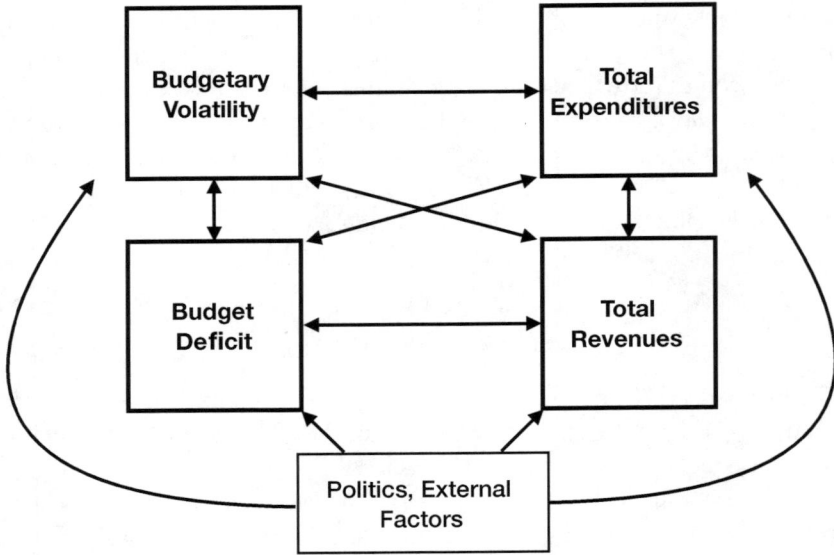

FIGURE 2.11. The larger web of political budgeting

illustrates our discussion about the budgetary process for the composition of expenditures and the four contextual factors that affect the ability of governments to shift budgets in the direction of their general ideological priorities. The middle of the figure shows that not only does the past composition of expenditures largely determine current spending – as might be expected according to the literature on budgetary incrementalism – but also that, by construction, the difference between the past and current expenditure compositions comprises the expenditure volatility measure.[24] The expenditure volatility measure is just one of four budgetary components on which we focus; the others are government deficits, total revenues, and expenditures. Since all four are closely related and may be driving one another, we adopt a relatively conservative theoretical expectation that all components are linked. In turn, we argue that the same types of institutional, economic, and international contextual factors affect the relationships between government ideology and these budgetary pieces.

---

[24] Recall that this measure is constructed by aggregating all budgetary change in expenditure categories into a single statistic (Tsebelis and Chang 2004; Brender and Drazen 2013).

2.4 Bringing It All Together

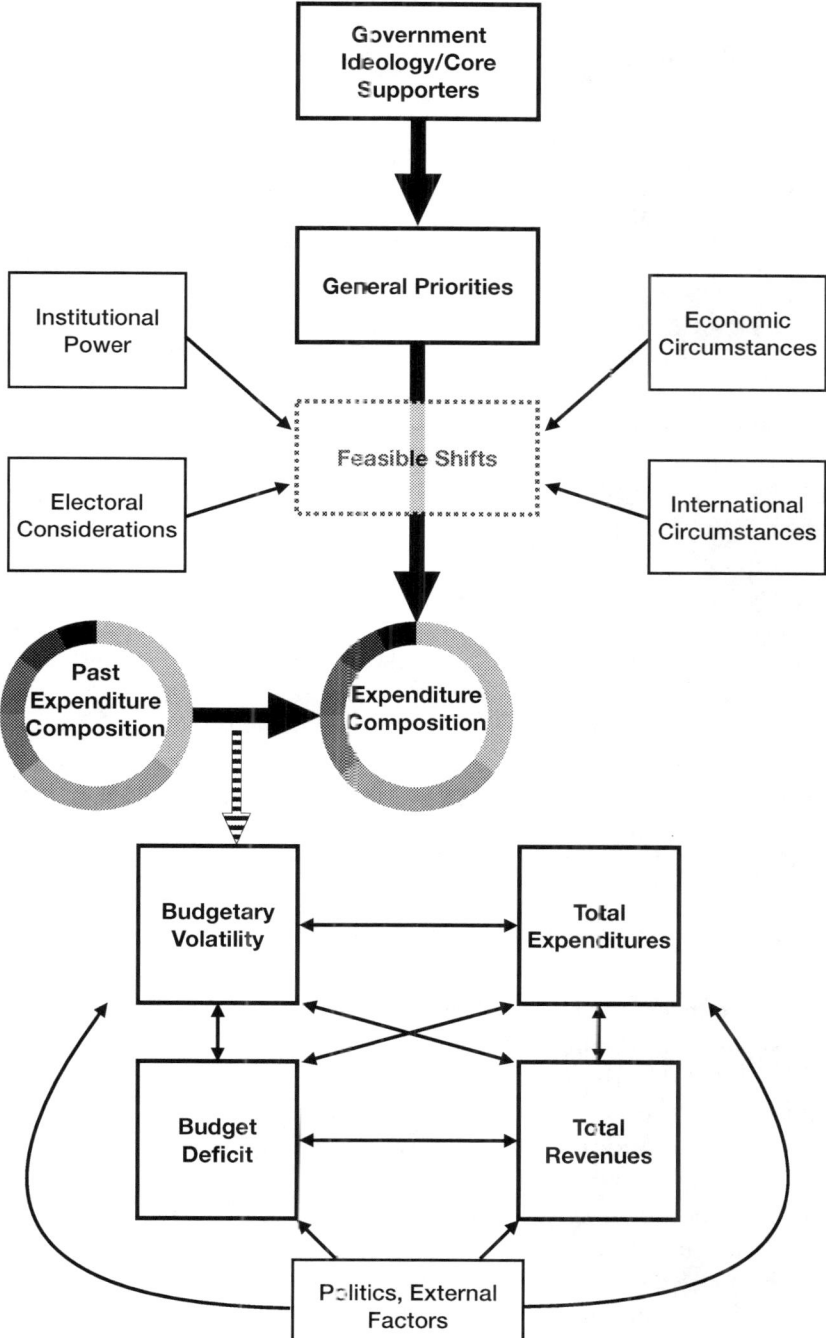

FIGURE 2.12. Summary of our theoretical argument

Figure 2.12 also outlines the progression of the rest of the book. Chapters 3 and 4 address the top half (i.e., modeling expenditure compositions) of the figure. In Chapter 3, we explore how governments' ideologies and general priorities influence tradeoffs in expenditure compositions and we point out how institutional factors might temper their ideologies and affect which relative shifts are feasible. We scrutinize the right side of the top of Figure 2.12 in Chapter 4, in order to see how elections and economic and international factors affect governments' behavior on the budgetary composition.

In Chapters 5 and 6, we turn to the broader budgetary component pieces for the second part of our argument, illustrated in the bottom half of Figure 2.12. Chapter 5 takes a general approach to exploring the entire bottom part of Figure 2.12, emphasizing the interconnectedness and endogeneity of the relationships in order to test which budgetary components may be causing one another. We also investigate how government ideology and political context together affect these components before moving to Chapter 6. There, we use the knowledge gleaned in Chapter 5 about the causal relationships between our interconnected budgetary components to grasp how the same electoral, economic, and international contexts we examined in Chapter 4 might also alter governments' ideological preferences on these four budgetary components. In Chapter 7, we conclude with a discussion about how our findings fit into, and build on research on budgets, representation, government behavior, political economy, as well as methods and visualization. We also offer suggestions on where the future of budgetary research is headed.

2.5 APPENDIX

Throughout the book, a large part of our data come from the International Monetary Fund's Classification of Outlays by Function of Government (COFOG) series. It is the most extensive, detailed dataset on expenditure allocations available for a large number of countries. We use both the historical COFOG dataset (1972–1989) – referred to as the GFSM 1986 – as well as the next most recent dataset, the GFSM 2001. In our country–year coverage, about 28 percent of the data are from the historical dataset.

There are some differences between these two datasets for which we needed to account (Wickens 2002). First, the GFSM 2001 does not have the expenditure category, "not elsewhere classified by major group" (category B14), as the GFSM 1986 does. In the GFSM 2001, this part of the budget is classified as "general public services," so we included it in this category. Second, the GFSM 2001 includes a new category, "environmental protection," while the GFSM 1986 does not categorize these expenditures separately. Instead, part of this category is included in housing, community amenity affairs, and services. Third, the GFSM 2001 classifies outlays on research and development (R&D) as a separate subcategory within each of the main category divisions. In most GFSM 1986/COFOG divisions, expenditures on research and development are not identified separately. This did not pose a problem for our analysis, since we are using the main categories rather than subgroups within those categories.

We focus on eight expenditure categories: education, government administration, defense, economic affairs, housing, health, religion and culture, and social protection. These were the most disaggregated categories available over a long enough time period for a substantial number of countries. While there are 10 total categories in COFOG, we excluded environmental protection for the reasons listed (i.e., it does not exist in the GFSM 1986), and we also excluded spending on public order, since these data were often missing when all other categories were not. We believe this is justified since there appears to be no clear consensus on which categories to include/exclude in the COFOG data. For instance, while Castro and Martins (2018) include all 10 categories, Shelton (2007) excludes the environment category, Sanz (2011) lumps public order into general public services, while incorporating housing with expenditures on the environment, Gemmell, Kneller, and Sanz (2008) exclude public order and the environment, and Brender and Drazen (2013) make no mention of public order or the environment in their analysis of budgetary change.

We detail each expenditure category below (Pitzer 2001):

- **Education** expenditures mainly consist of government spending on education at all levels (e.g., primary, secondary, post-secondary).
- **Government Administration** consists of spending on general government services, such as the executive and legislative branches, financial and fiscal affairs, economic foreign aid, public debt transactions, and general transfers between levels of government. This is called "public services" in the COFOG dataset, but we prefer the term "government administration," since it mostly concerns the day-to-day operations of

government rather than transfers, spending, and services that directly affect the public.
- **Defense** expenditures include all foreign and domestic military expenditures, foreign military aid, and civil defense.
- **Economic Affairs** include government spending on all economic, commercial, and labor affairs, spending on agriculture, forestry, fishing, energy, mining, manufacturing, construction, transportation, and communication.
- **Housing** includes spending on water and lighting, as well as housing and community development.
- **Health** expenditures mainly consist of public health services, including hospitals and outpatient services, as well as spending on medical products and equipment.
- **Religion and Culture** includes public broadcasting and publishing, recreational and sporting expenditures, and cultural, religious, and community services.
- **Social Protection** consists of expenditures on the sick and disabled, old age, survivors, families and children, and unemployment.

Another issue that arises is that different governments use different aggregations of "government" when compiling their expenditures. We use general government expenditures wherever possible, then central government expenditures if general expenditures are missing, and then budgetary central government if both were missing.[25] As Seiferling (2013) points out, this ranking of data sources produces the largest coverage possible. For our country–year coverage, about 85 percent was sourced from either historical or general government data, 11 percent from central government, a little over 1 percent from the budgetary central government, and 2 percent was linearly interpolated. In our analysis of expenditure compositions using the COFOG data (Chapters 3 and 4), data were missing and linearly interpolated for the following country–years: United Kingdom (1995–1996), France (1994), Luxembourg (1996–1997), Norway (1978–1979), Greece (1978–1979), Spain (1986), New Zealand (2003 and 2008), Bulgaria (1995–1997), and Slovenia (1997–1998). We explore the robustness of our results to dropping these imputed observations in Section 3.6, and find that our results remain robust to omitting these observations.

---

[25] Note that this excludes state and local government expenditures.

2.5 Appendix

TABLE 2.2. *Country–year coverage*

Country	Expenditure Years	Revenue Years	Deficit Years
Australia	1975–2010	1975–2010	1975–2010
Austria	1975–2010	1975–2010	1975–2010
Belgium	1996–2010	1996–2010	1996–2010
Bulgaria	1991–2010	1991–2010	1991–2010
Croatia	1996–2010	1996–2010	1996–2010
Cyprus	1977–2010	1977–2010	1977–2010
Czech Republic	1994–2010	1994–2010	1994–2010
Denmark	1975–2010	1975–2010	2975–2010
Estonia	1996–2010	1996–2010	1996–2010
Finland	1975–2010	1975–2010	1975–2010
France	1976–2010	1976–2010	1976–2010
Germany	1975–2010	1975–2010	1975–2010
Greece	1975–2010	1975–2010	1975–2010
Hungary	1992–2010	1992–2010	1992–2010
Iceland	1997–2010	1997–2010	1997–2010
Ireland	1983–2010	1983–2010	1983–2010
Italy	1996–2010	1996–2010	1996–2010
Japan	2005–2010	2005–2010	2005–2010
Latvia	1996–2010	1996–2010	1996–2010
Lithuania	2005–2010	2005–2010	2005–2010
Luxembourg	1975–2003	1975–2003	1975–2003
Malta	1983–2010	1983–2010	1983–2010
Netherlands	1975–2010	1975–2010	1975–2010
New Zealand	1975–2010	1975–2010	1975–2010
Norway	1975–2010	1975–2010	1975–2010
Portugal	1996–2010	1996–2010	1996–2010
Slovak Republic	1997–2010	1997–2010	1997–2010
Slovenia	1996–2010	1996–2010	1996–2010
Spain	1977–2010	1977–2010	1977–2010
Sweden	1975–2010	1975–2010	1975–2010
Switzerland	1981–2010	1981–2010	1981–2010
United Kingdom	1975–2010	1975–2010	1975–2010
United States	1975–2010	1975–2010	1975–2010

Table 2.2 lists all countries and years for expenditure, revenue, and deficit data. For the budgetary aggregates, missing data are the country–years listed. Note that we did not interpolate these missing observations. For deficits: Australia (1995–1998), Greece (1991–1994), Italy (1981–1985 and 1990–1994), Japan (1991–2004), Luxembourg (1998), Malta (1979), New Zealand (1989–2000), Portugal (1977 and 1991–1994), and Switzerland (1985–1990). For revenues: Greece (1991–

1994), Italy (1990–1994), Malta (1979), New Zealand (1989–2000), Portugal (1991–1994), and Switzerland (1985–1989). For expenditures: Greece (1991–1994), Italy (1981–1985), Japan (1991–1993), Malta (1979), New Zealand (1989–2000), Portugal (1977), and Switzerland (1985–1989). The country–years for budgetary volatility are the same as for expenditures.

3

Political Competition and the Expenditure Pie

> *As Prime Minister between 1979 and 1990, I had the opportunity to put these convictions into effect in economic policy. We intended policy in the 1980s to be directed towards fundamentally different goals from those of most of the post-war era.*
>
> Margaret Thatcher

During elections, parties and candidates present competing visions of the future to potential voters. At the heart of these governing alternatives lie policy priorities. Once in power, governments have the ability to allocate resources to their preferred policy and budgetary areas, fulfilling their campaign promises by increasing spending in particular areas, while retrenching in others (Lipsmeyer 2009; Thomson et al. 2017).

This process is far from easy. In budget negotiations at the cabinet and parliamentary level, there are often intense discussions about shifting resources to line up with policy priorities. In New Zealand, for example, the coalition government in 2016 argued that a rising population should be a key concern. In response, it shifted funds to key policy areas affected by the population influx, such as schools, hospitals, housing, and roads (New Zealand Budget 2016 "Health and education the main winners, smokers lose out," *NZ Herald News*).[1] This strong link between party or government priorities and the distribution of budgetary resources across policy areas remains a key feature of representative governance.

---

[1] Source: www.nzherald.co.nz/business/news/article.cfm?c_id=3&objectid=11645338. Last accessed August 29, 2015.

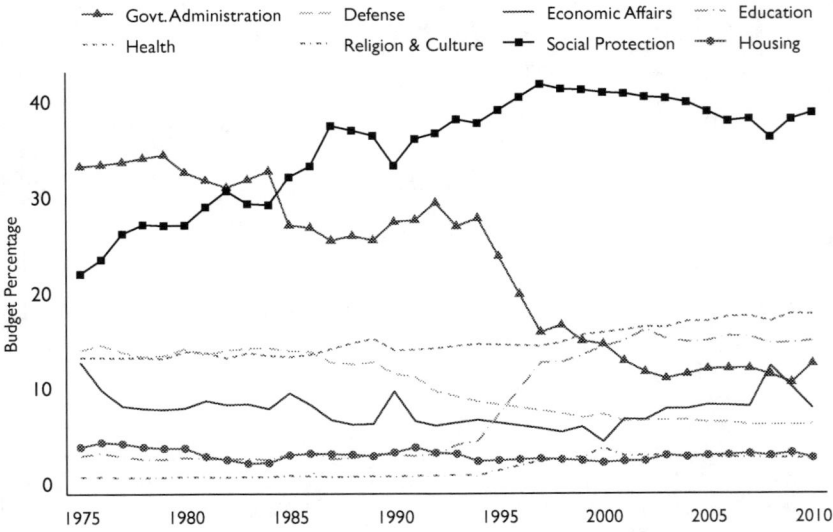

FIGURE 3.1. Budgets *do* change, as shown in the United Kingdom

Since each government has slightly different priorities, spending on policies should move up and down in response to changes in government, although – as we emphasize throughout this book – this is likely to be conditional on additional factors such as institutions (Tsebelis and Chang 2004; Cheibub 2006; Martin and Vanberg 2020).

Of course, despite the fact that budgetary allocations may not always reflect the ideological priorities of governments, budgetary shifts *do* occur. Figure 3.1 – first discussed in Chapter 2 but shown again here – demonstrates this using data from the United Kingdom. Across the five decades covered in the figure, we can see that there were substantial gains in relative spending (i.e., as a percentage of total expenditures) on social protection and education. This contrasts with substantial declines in relative spending on government administration and defense. Recognizing and explaining these types of changing proportions is key to understanding government behavior.

A simple approach to this process would be one where the electoral winners set a course for implementing their policy goals, and, once doing so, the outcome is assured. Then, there should be little difference between desired spending on public policy and actual policy expenditures. For instance, if a government wants to raise spending on education by 10–20 percent, then the budget will reflect this policy desire. If a left government's manifesto proposes an 8 percent cut to defense spending, then once they gain power such a cut will quickly be realized. In reality, such close and timely relationships between government preferences and policy budgets are unlikely. Budgets are not blank slates. Spending commitments tend to be difficult to change quickly, so budgetary decisions tend to be best considered in terms of changes from the status quo.

As discussed in Chapter 2, budgets tend to be slow-moving, and substantial changes are likely to occur only gradually or during certain times (Wildavsky 1964; Baumgartner and Jones 1991; Epp, Lovett, and Baumgartner 2014).[2] Moreover, as an extensive literature on budgetary incrementalism suggests, budgets may deviate only slightly from year to year (Dahl and Lindblom 1953; Lindblom 1959; Natchez and Bupp 1973; Bunce and Echols 1978).[3] Even if budgets do change over the medium- and long-run, other factors – such as the level of development or institutional constraints – may affect the ability of successive governments to shift budgets based on their ideological differences (Imbeau, Pétry, and Lamari 2001; Brender and Drazen 2013; Potrafke 2017).

Governments differ in their abilities to alter budgets, because factors other than their ideological preferences may play a role in whether they succeed in tilting budgets in their preferred directions. Coalition government dynamics and the varying degrees of government power can influence whether governments can shape budgetary allocations to suit their policy agendas. Consider two recent examples in Denmark and Norway. The discussion that surrounded Denmark's 2016 budget focused on the possibilities of early elections and government collapse. This was largely attributed to the difficult negotiations between the minority Liberal Party (Venstre) government and its non-government parliamentary party supporters, the Liberal Alliance and the Danish People's Party (*Irish Examiner*, November 18, 2016). Similarly, in Norway, the minority coalition of the Progress Party and the Conservatives agreed to significant compromises in their 2015 budget in order to appease their two

---

[2] Because of the "stickiness" of budgets, scholars typically employ some form of autoregressive model that takes into account the persistence in budgets over time (Bawn and Rosenbluth 2006; Whitten and Williams 2011). Such persistence also exists in research on budget balances (e.g., Alt and Lassen 2006) and revenues (e.g., Alt and Lowry 2000; Swank and Steinmo 2002; Beramendi and Rueda 2007). Domke, Eichenberg, and Kelleher (1983) make the distinction between long-term and short-term tradeoffs between expenditure categories; our estimation strategy explicitly allows us to examine both of these effects.

[3] For a review of this literature, see Berry (1990).

non-government parliamentary support parties. Both instances highlight how political dynamics – in the form of coalition/government power (or the lack thereof in these instances) – can prevent budgetary allocations from coinciding with partisan visions.

In this chapter, we argue that political competition and institutional factors affect the distribution of budgetary resources. Moreover, this is especially true regarding tradeoffs between policies. As an analysis of the 2003 German budgetary process explains: "these changes would probably affect primarily the distribution of spending between different departments rather than the bottom-line figures" ("Economic policy: 2003 budget foresees expenditure reduction by 0.5%").[4] Such a claim fits with our theoretical argument that focuses on a compositional approach to understanding the politics of these relative tradeoffs among spending categories. When looking for where the political "action" is, we turn to asking questions about the budgetary allocations between multiple policy areas simultaneously, instead of focusing on either total expenditures or the changing size of a single policy category.[5]

In Section 3.1, we pose and answer a series of important questions regarding the ideological and power determinants of expenditure tradeoffs. If governments desire to alter expenditure categories to fit their ideological visions, under what conditions are they best able to do so? From an institutional perspective, are some governments better able to push through their budgetary preferences than others? Ultimately, the question asked throughout this book is: what circumstances help or hinder governments to fulfil their budgetary visions?

3.1 IDEOLOGY, INSTITUTIONAL CONTEXT, AND SPENDING TRADEOFFS

In considering the relationship between politics and budgets, a substantial body of research has debated the influence of government ideology and partisanship on public policy expenditures. The common theoretical tie has been that if a government's ideology shapes its policy priorities, it should follow that governments will allocate budgetary resources according to their broader visions of government responsibility

---

[4] country.eiu.com.srv-proxy2.library.tamu.edu/article.aspx?articleid=555443655#. Last accessed January 17, 2020.
[5] We leave analyses of "total" budgetary aggregates, such as total expenditures, revenues, deficits, or volatility for Chapters 5 and 6.

3.1 Ideology, Institutional Context, and Tradeoffs

(Hibbs 1977; Tufte 1978; Blais, Blake, and Dion 1993; Alesina and Rosenthal 1995; Boix 1998).

This expectation of a link between government policy preferences and their budgetary outlays has a long tradition in academic research. However, the results from empirical tests of this proposition have been mixed (Potrafke 2017). Some research points to ideologically driven budgetary changes for both total spending, as well as specific policy areas (Swank 1988; Hicks, Swank, and Ambuhl 1989; Huber, Ragin, and Stephens 1993; Potrafke 2020). In contrast, others have found few to no differences across different ideologies in terms of government expenditures (Imbeau, Pétry, and Lamari 2001; Potrafke 2012).[6] For instance, in a meta-analysis of the effects of partisanship on government spending, Imbeau, Pétry, and Lamari (2001) find that there is little evidence of a systematic difference in policy between left and right governments after 1973.

What explains these mixed results in existing empirical research? One answer may have to do with how researchers have approached government decision-making. Governments that vary along ideological lines may reallocate their existing budgets in different ways, while not substantially altering the bottom line. In other words, while total expenditures may remain unchanged, the distribution (in terms of relative allocation shares) across budgetary categories will shift. Therefore, focusing on how left and right governments alter the total budget may hide ideological changes at a more disaggregated level.[7] Alternatively, theorizing about spending on a specific policy area may ignore the concern that the possible explanations for why governments change the budget for that policy area may have varying effects and ramifications for the budgets of the other policy areas. When studying one budget area independently, researchers would only ascertain an increase or decrease in that particular category of spending, while overlooking changes that may be occurring in the other budgetary categories. In other words, just because budget category "A" (our category of interest) is changing does not mean that categories "B" and "C" are

---

[6] While we are interested in the general budget, there is a large literature focused specifically on welfare spending that has found mixed results when considering the role of political factors (see, for instance, Blais, Blake, and Dion 1993; Bandau and Ahrens 2020).

[7] Imbeau, Pétry, and Lamari (2001, pp. 24–25) disagree and explain that, "as the substantive stakes of left–right party rivalry shifted away from social welfare and toward the overall size of the public sector, the frequency of success and the effect size of individual tests of partisan impact on the overall size of the state have tended to increase relative to tests of partisan impact on welfare."

remaining constant; they might also be rising or falling relative to "A" or even relative to one another.

That changing governments may not lead to aggregate shifts in budgets but rather movements in the relative shares of the budget is a closer theoretical fit to the reality of political competition and – we argue – an under-appreciated fact in the extant literature.[8] When competing in elections, parties put forth their policy goals, espouse their ideas, and stress their priorities. The picture that they draw is not one-dimensional; they tend to touch on multiple policy areas. Unfortunately, as discussed in Chapter 2, for the most part, current empirical models for explaining the influence of competing government visions on budgetary outcomes are more solitary than governments' behavior in the real world.

While it is not uncommon for researchers to focus on more than one policy area at a time in their theoretical discussions, they nearly always treat the decision to increase or decrease a particular spending area as an independent one in their analyses. For instance, Milesi-Ferretti, Perotti, and Rostagno (2002) analyze the role of electoral rules on the "composition" of budgets (i.e., transfers to households, public goods spending, and total primary expenditures), although each is modeled separately. This treats each expenditure category as if it were set in isolation from every other category, ignoring the implicit tradeoffs that are at the center of policy-making. In another example, Hicks and Swank (1992) find that center and left governments spend more on welfare categories (consisting of social security, health, and some in-kind benefits), but they combine these categories into a single measure. It also remains unclear what changes in other categories (e.g., defense, education) are occurring in response to such shifts in welfare.

Even articles that analyze many categories of the budget do not account for the fact that changes in one budgetary category are likely to affect other categories. For instance, while Castro and Martins (2018) examine a total of 10 expenditure categories, their analysis is unable to explain which categories gain a greater share of the budget in response to a declining share in one of the other categories. As a final example,

---

[8] This is not to say that there is *no* literature that looks at disaggregated budgetary categories, see, for instance, Hicks and Swank (1992); Lipsmeyer (2002); and Brown and Hunter (2004). Our claim is that not only is it necessary to focus on disaggregated policy areas, we also need to look at all areas *simultaneously* in order to see which budget categories are gaining and losing in response to changes in government ideology.

3.1 Ideology, Institutional Context, and Tradeoffs

consider Bräuninger (2005), who analyzes the effect of partisanship on both social security and economic affairs. He uses a measure of the relative share of the budget between these two categories but dismisses the remaining budgetary categories when conceptualizing this as a composition.

To summarize, all of the works discussed in this section use common approaches to studying budgets. Yet, despite the compositional language often used, their inferences are drawn from comparisons of the effects of various political factors on transfers and public goods in separate, isolated models, rather than in a single comprehensive model of how changes in various factors (e.g., political, institutional, or economic) lead to tradeoffs between spending on the relevant parts of the budget.[9] In our approach, budgetary spending on one policy is intertwined with spending on other policy areas. This leads to viewing budget areas as parts of a composition and to seeing decisions as tradeoffs, and this viewpoint translates into different theories and models than previous work on political institutions and budgets. While an increase in the amount spent on a particular policy area may indicate a government's priority for that area, this is not always the case. Without considering the up-tick in spending relative to other budgetary areas, it becomes problematic to assume that a spending increase or decrease in absolute terms is related to the government's budgetary priorities. Therefore, when thinking about the politics of budgeting, we argue for a competitive theory of budgets, one where policy areas compete for funding and where governments make spending choices across all policy areas simultaneously. Viewing budgets as a competitive arena that reflects governments' priorities places the focus squarely on the politics of these government decisions.

---

[9] To some extent, Dreher, Sturm, and Ursprung (2008) have the closest modeling strategy to our approach. In fact, they refer to their model as "compositional" in that they are modeling a system of equations, where the dependent variable in each equation is a percentage of the total budget, and they use seemingly unrelated regressions to estimate these equations. Our approach differs from theirs in two important ways. First, by leaving their dependent variables in percentage formats (what we refer to in Chapter 3 as y_{ijt} values), they are working with dependent variables that are bounded and, thus, subject to all of the problems associated with compositional data. We discuss this issue more in Section 3.6. Second, they do not include either present or past values of other budgetary categories in their models of each budget category. They, thus, are not able to directly model tradeoffs across budget categories.

3.1.1 Institutional Constraints

How would we expect government ideology and the surrounding institutional contexts to shape our competitive theory of budgetary spending? Building on a long line of research that shows an ideological influence on spending decisions, we argue that changes in the ideological makeup of governments should play a critical role for budgetary tradeoffs (Bräuninger 2005; Bove, Efthyvoulou, and Navas 2017; Lipsmeyer, Philips, and Whitten 2017; Potrafke 2017; Castro and Martins 2018). However, variation in how much power a government wields over reallocating budgets may influence when governments actually succeed in implementing their preferred ideological changes.

Once parties achieve their goals of winning a place in government, they have an opportunity to reallocate government budgets to suit their policy preferences. We agree with Bawn and Rosenbluth (2006, p. 256) that, in terms of guiding principles, "all groups prefer more rather than less spending on themselves, and that 'ideological differences' are more about types of spending than amounts." When disentangling government policy preferences, previous research has relied on a number of cleavages, core among them being variation in preferences over government intervention. In discussing government intervention (and correspondingly, government size), redistribution remains a key way to differentiate parties and governments.[10] Left parties and governments tend to embrace redistributive policy areas and to support government intervention in society and the economy more generally. In contrast, right governments advocate for market-driven solutions for redistributive policy areas that reflect their general inclination away from government intervention in the broader social and economic spheres (Boix 1998). These different approaches to intervention and redistribution often lead to expectations based on budget sizes, with left governments supporting larger budgets than the right, since government involvement can lead to bigger government responsibility in society and the economy.

Considering the institutional complexities surrounding governments, the expectation that ideological differences always drive budgetary behavior may not fit with reality. Scholars have highlighted how various political institutions can shape overall spending, as well as spending on specific policy areas. With a focus on systemic institutional

---

[10] Case in point, Whitten and Williams (2011) find that redistributive preferences are meaningful for decisions on military spending.

3.1 Ideology, Institutional Context, and Tradeoffs

variation, some researchers have looked at how governments behave differently on budgets in consensus versus majoritarian democracies, with more dispersed power in consensus-oriented countries leading to larger governments (Lijphart 1999; Tavits 2004). Similarly, Persson and Tabellini (2004) investigate welfare spending variation in presidential and parliamentary democracies, finding that parliamentary systems have higher welfare expenditures. Research that focuses on electoral rules shows how the type of election may be a factor in why proportional representation systems tend to be associated with higher levels of government spending (Persson and Tabellini 1999; Milesi-Ferretti, Perotti, and Rostagno 2002; Kang and Powell 2010). However, as Persson, Roland, and Tabellini (2007) illustrate, these institutions at the pre-government formation stage may not have direct effects on government spending; instead, they influence the creation of different types of governments that lead to varying budgetary levels. Ultimately, then, these types of political institutions help to shape the governments that form, and the variation in these decision-makers affects the differences in total budgetary expenditure levels.

If we shift to looking at the governmental institutions that affect decision-making surrounding budgets, then these differences in power and status may more directly influence governments' budgetary behavior. Scholars have pointed to how increasing the number of parties in a government can lead to higher spending due to the fragmentation of decision-making, as well as the diffuse electoral concerns and supporters of multiple parties (Volkerink and De Haan 2001; Perotti and Kontopoulos 2002; Bawn and Rosenbluth 2006; Persson, Roland, and Tabellini 2007). Many of these arguments rely on a common pool resource problem element, whereby all government parties have incentives to strive for benefits for themselves at the expense of other parties (Hallerberg and Marier 2004). However, the conclusion that more parties lead to higher spending levels is also called into question, since Martin and Vanberg (2013) show that this relationship disappears once the role of financial institutions is taken into account.[11] Crepaz and Moser (2004) also argue that the tie between politics and budgets is less about the number of government actors and more about institutional diffusion and the

---

[11] Similarly, Hallerberg, Strauch, and Von Hagen (2007) argue that centralizing fiscal decisions within the finance ministry limits the ability of governing partners, although their interest is largely on overall budget balance.

necessity of collective decision-making.[12] A common theme in these works concerning institutions and budgets continues to be the ease or difficulty that governments have in altering budgetary levels.

Much of the previous research that connects governments, institutions, and expenditures has targeted total government spending or spending on specific policy areas,[13] and this leads them to theorize about how government ideology or various types of political institutions relate to increases or decreases in those areas. For example, Milesi-Ferretti, Perotti, and Rostagno (2002) conclude that proportional electoral systems can result in larger governments, leading to larger overall total expenditures. Similarly, increasing the number of parties in a coalition may push up overall government spending (Bawn and Rosenbluth 2006). While approaching budgets in this way can offer straightforward – although sometimes conflicting – expectations about politics and expenditures, these same theoretical assumptions may not hold when explaining tradeoffs *within* total spending.[14]

In moving this theoretical discussion to a compositional framework, we consider the budgetary tradeoffs that governments will prefer based on their underlying ideological preferences. A key implication of this approach is that, even when the overall size of the total budget does not move up or down, we should still be able to uncover the political machinations involved with spending reallocations among categories of the budget. Governments may tradeoff expenditures without significantly altering their overall totals, so our institutional story focuses on whether or not governments have the power to shift their budgets to suit their ideological preferences.

Despite all parties attempting to follow through on their ideologically defined campaign pledges (Thomson et al. 2017), some governments will be more likely to succeed than others. The power disparity between majority and minority governments shows how government status can help or hinder a government's ability to shift spending. Unlike a majority government – where the executive and legislative coalitions complement each

---

[12] Crepaz and Moser (2004) create an index that adds electoral rules and corporatism to the number of effective legislative parties.
[13] There is a vein of research on welfare policy that focuses on changes in benefit structures (replacement rates, generosity levels, etc.), and scholars have found that both government ideology (Scruggs 2004) and institutions, in the form of legislative committees, are influential (Martin and Vanberg 2020).
[14] At times, scholars use the term "compositions" when discussing spending on an individual policy or policies (e.g., Persson and Tabellini 2004).

other – the party or parties comprising a minority government require extra legislative votes to pass their preferred legislation (Strøm 1990a; Laver and Shepsle 1996). Often this involves compromises on various elements, such as altering policy expenditures (Lipsmeyer 2011), relying on deficit spending (Falcó-Gimeno and Jurado 2011), or diluting electoral promises (Artés and Bustos 2008). Denmark's negotiations over the 2015 government budget illustrate these power dynamics in a minority government: "The governing coalition will need to negotiate a temporary alliance with other parties in parliament in order to conclude a final budget deal, which will not be easy given an increasingly fractured political consensus and contrasting views on welfare and social policy."[15] At other times, the ability of governments to enact policy change may be hamstrung by coalition partners. For instance, coalition fights over healthcare reform in Germany in 2010 were so intense that a Free Democratic Party (FDP) official called Christian Social Union (CSU) members "wild pigs," while the CSU general secretary referred to those in the FDP as "bush leaguers."[16]

As these examples show, governments differ in how much power they have to shape budgetary allocations. In considering variation across governments, the power of government parties *vis-a-vis* the opposition can also significantly affect their ability to push through their desired budgetary allocations. Research on public policy has argued that, when governments have a majority of seats in the lower house of parliament, they are better able to implement their ideological budgetary preferences through spending changes. Alternatively, minority governments are often forced to make compromises, leaving them with a watered-down version of their ideal budget. Although some researchers have combined government power and party systems when discussing governments' abilities over fiscal outcomes (Roubini and Sachs 1989b), a key factor is that governments backed by a majority of parliamentary support have an easier time realizing their fiscal priorities than minority governments, who must appease non-governmental parties (Edin and Ohlsson 1991; Herwartz and Theilen 2014).[17] Blais, Blake, and Dion (1993) and

---

[15] http://country.eiu.com.srv-proxy1.library.tamu.edu/. Last accessed September 19, 2014.
[16] *The Economist*, "Slash and bounce: Germany's budget deficit." June 10, 2010.
[17] When Roubini and Sachs (1989b, p. 923) evaluate the influence of government power, their measure ranges from a "single-party majority government" (the most powerful) to a "minority parliamentary coalition" (the weakest). However, when Edin and Ohlsson (1991) pull this measure apart, they find that the true relationship is between minority governments and deficits, not with multi-party systems. Lipsmeyer (2011) finds similar

Lipsmeyer (2011) find that majority status significantly affects left governments' abilities to increase both overall spending, as well as welfare spending, respectively. Therefore, when considering budgetary tradeoffs, government power may be key in whether or not they are able to institute ideological reallocations.

In tackling how ideology and institutions fit into our compositional framework, we first theorize about the types of tradeoffs that right governments would prefer versus governments on the left. Then, we consider how the power of a government – in regard to majority status – will affect the composition of budgetary allocations.

3.1.2 Theoretical Expectations

We begin with a fairly simple set of expectations about how governments will reallocate budgets based on their policy preferences and core supporters. We then argue that institutional pressures, in the form of government power, can help or hinder governments by influencing when they are able to make tradeoffs that fit their ideological priorities. While we maintain a narrow focus on institutions in this chapter, in Chapter 4 we develop and test theoretical expectations about how domestic and international circumstances shape governments' abilities to follow through on their general priorities.

In Figure 3.2, we illustrate the basic argument using our theory of competitive budgets. The general priorities of a government are shaped by the combination of the government's ideological position and the concerns of their core supporters, as shown at the top of the figure. This, in turn, directly affects the composition of the budget. Yet, because budgets change in an incremental fashion (c.f., Dahl and Lindblom 1953; Lindblom 1959; Natchez and Bupp 1973; Bunce and Echols 1978), the "Past Expenditure Composition" will also have a major impact on the current year's expenditure composition. Thus, Figure 3.2 illustrates how the general priorities of governments will shape the incremental changes in budgetary compositions over time. Note too that Figure 3.2 is a simplistic view of reality; we have not yet taken into account how the institutional context surrounding governments affects such reallocations in the budgetary composition.[18]

---

relationships with welfare spending when splitting the measure between power and government size.

[18] Nor do we consider domestic and international factors that are the subject of Chapter 4.

3.1 Ideology, Institutional Context, and Tradeoffs

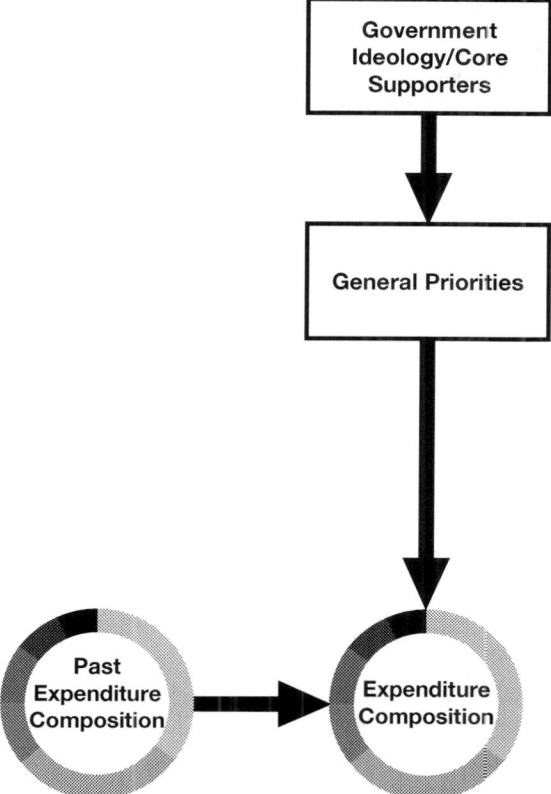

FIGURE 3.2. Initial theoretical diagram

In Table 3.1, we set out our expectations about the spending priorities of the various budgetary policy areas according to governments' ideological leanings (left or right), using the eight expenditure areas discussed in Section 2.5.[19] Given the nature of tradeoffs, we anticipate that governments will tend to emphasize some categories (represented with checkmarks) at the expense of other budgetary categories (those without checkmarks).

Overall, the biggest ideological difference is reflected in the reliance on state responsibility and resources. Left governments focus their attention on policy areas that support redistributive efforts, attempting

---

[19] In Section 3.5, we provide detailed descriptions of specific policies that compose each category.

TABLE 3.1. *General spending priorities by government ideology*

Policy Area	Left Government	Right Government
Defense		✓
Economic Affairs		✓
Education	✓	✓
Government Administration	✓	
Health	✓	✓
Housing	✓	
Religion and Culture		
Social Protection	✓	

Note: A ✓ means that a government prioritizes a policy area over those without a ✓.

to use government resources to buffer society from market forces and lifecycle hardships (e.g., income loss, disability, illness, or injury), while also using the power of government to supply public goods and services. Right governments, in comparison, turn less to the state for assistance and responsibility, instead relying on private and market-driven factors to fill gaps between groups in the labor market and society. This is not to say that right governments' visions see *no* role for government in society. As we will see later in this section, there is reason to believe they have a vested interest in increasing both health and education expenditures. But, given that we are focused on trading off resources (not the size of the budget), right governments are less likely to prefer reallocating expenditures toward redistributive policies. We expect them to favor other areas (i.e., defense, economic affairs, education, and health) and to rely on non-governmental outlets.

To organize our theoretical argument, in Table 3.1, we begin by discussing the specific policy areas most preferred by the left and then the right. We also consider policy areas where the preferences of the left and right governments overlap. Such policy priority overlap may be caused by either a consensus between the left and right on the importance of the particular category or a lack of ideological guidance on that policy area. As emphasized in Figure 3.2, these priorities are in isolation, without any institutional constraints on a particular government's ability to enact policy change.

Starting with the priorities of left governments, in Table 3.1, we expect that they will differ from right governments by generally prioritizing the following areas: government administration, housing, and social

3.1 Ideology, Institutional Context, and Tradeoffs

protection. Relative increases in these three categories should arise from left governments shifting funds away from defense and economic affairs. Government administration is a traditionally left policy area and highlights the idea of a "bigger" government, since it involves expenditures on day-to-day operations of government. Similarly, although housing expenditures can vary – ranging from subsidies to less restrictive housing requirements for low-income families – and, although it is typically one of the smallest spending categories, we expect left governments to spend relatively more than right governments.[20] Finally, another traditionally left budgetary area is social protection, where governments budget resources to alleviate hardship along redistributive lines. Given left governments' emphasis on more involvement in the economy (Boix 1998), we expect relative increases in this area.[21]

Although right governments prefer smaller government, they still have budgetary priorities when reallocating resources. Even with perhaps a smaller overall pie than left governments, we still very much expect right governments to prioritize how that pie is allocated. We expect them to emphasize policies that focus on national security and business growth. This translates into expectations of increased funds for defense and economic affairs, while shifting funds away from government administration, housing, and social protection. Defense is generally seen as a preferred policy area of more conservative governments; thus, we expect right governments to favor increasing the proportion of the budget spent on defense (including both domestic and foreign commitments) at the cost of other areas.[22] Conservative governments also favor allocating relatively more resources to economic affairs than their left counterparts, because of their emphasis on private, market, and business interests. Right governments would rather use resources to help businesses remain or become more competitive than have them rely on state subsidies (and increase the overall size of the government's footprint).

---

[20] Housing also includes expenditures on water, lighting, and community development, which we also expect left governments to be in favor of increasing.

[21] Such expectations, and evidence, about left governments preferring greater social protection are not universal. For instance, Breunig and Busemeyer (2012) find no effect of Social Democratic governments on the proportion of the budget spent on labor market policies. Similarly, Lipsmeyer, Philips, and Whitten (2017) find very few differences *prima facie* and instead conclude that left governments respond much more to labor market shocks by increasing labor market protection; something we explore in Chapter 4.

[22] See Whitten and Williams (2011) for a different spin on this ideological expectation.

3.1.2.1 *When Ideological Expectations Coincide*

Conclusions from previous research about the influence of government ideology on two budgetary areas, education and health, are mixed. This leads our expectations about these categories in Table 3.1 to fall under what we call "general priorities" for both left and right governments. For education, there is some debate about whether or not government ideology shapes its funding and, by extension, preferences for relative funding in this policy area.[23] Some scholars argue that education follows a redistributive model, whereby left governments emphasize universal education, while the right prefers private alternatives, leading to ideological differences in expenditures (Castles 1982; Boix 1998; Iversen and Stephens 2008; Rauh, Kirchner, and Kappe 2011). Others contend the opposite. Rather than left governments championing education spending, it is right governments that have electoral incentives to increase education expenditures, especially spending on tertiary education (Busemeyer 2007; Ansell 2008, 2010).[24] From a budgetary competition viewpoint, left governments may spend *less* on education than right governments, preferring instead to allocate resources toward welfare policies that offer a greater redistributive return (Jensen 2011a). Therefore, when considering governments' ideological relationships with education, we have mixed expectations, since both the left and right may prioritize education.

When considering health, we once again find conflicting expectations. The redistributive model offers a starting point with a right/left ideological continuum where left governments increase public health spending, and governments from the right prefer to decrease expenditures (Herwartz and Theilen 2014; Bellido, Olmos, and Román-Aso 2019). Despite this, other research has found either declining ideological effects on health spending (Jordan 2011) or no effect at all (Potrafke 2010). An alternative way of thinking about health spending is that it appears to fill a grey area between redistribution and "life-cycle" hardships (i.e., everyone eventually will need healthcare toward the end of his/her life) (Ross and Huber 1985; Jensen 2011c). Moreover, although both Jensen (2011c) and Lipsmeyer, Philips, and Whitten (2017) find that right parties may increase

---

[23] See Gift and Wibbels (2014) and Busemeyer and Trampusch (2011) for an overview of research in political science on education policy and preferences for education.

[24] Instead of modeling education as annual country years, Garritzmann and Seng (2016) use government years and find no partisan effect on education spending.

3.1 Ideology, Institutional Context, and Tradeoffs

healthcare spending, they argue that this is in order to further privatize healthcare.[25] The logic is that right parties can benefit their high income supporters by touting privatized healthcare, while they also expand public options for middle-class voters.

To summarize, in two policy areas – education and health – both left and right governments may prefer to reallocate budgetary funds to these areas. Therefore, we place checkmarks next to both education and healthcare for both government types in Table 3.1. Although there are plenty of reasons to expect differences in terms of what governments from the left and right will do within these areas of spending, the general expectation is that they will both prioritize these areas overall.

For one budget category, religion and culture, we do not have firm ideological expectations about whether this is a favored category for either left or right governments, as shown by the lack of checkmarks in this row in Table 3.1. While some evidence points to individuals who share a left ideology being more supportive of funding public arts (Brooks 2001), this budgetary category includes a range of activities with less obvious ideological leanings: from expenditures on public broadcasting and publishing, recreational and sporting expenditures, to cultural, religious and community services. The extant literature on ideological support for cultural activities is mixed, and the studies tend not to be cross-national. For example, when examining cultural expenditures in Italian municipalities, Dalle Nogare and Galizzi (2011) find no effect of ideology, nor do Getzner (2002), Lewis and Rushton (2007), or Werck, Heyndels, and Geys (2008) in the cases of Austria, the US states, or Flemish municipalities, respectively. In contrast, Schulze and Rose (1998) find that conservative and liberal German local governments support spending on orchestras more than the Social Democrats or the Green party. Based on these varied conclusions, although left and right governments certainly differ in terms of which areas *within* religion and cultural spending they are likely to prioritize – for instance, the former should prefer more expansive government intervention in broadcasting and publishing, while the latter should prefer more protection and recognition of a state's religion and culture – we do not have firm expectations that either side will prioritize this category in general.

---

[25] Jensen (2011c, p. 909) refers to this as "marketization vs. compensation."

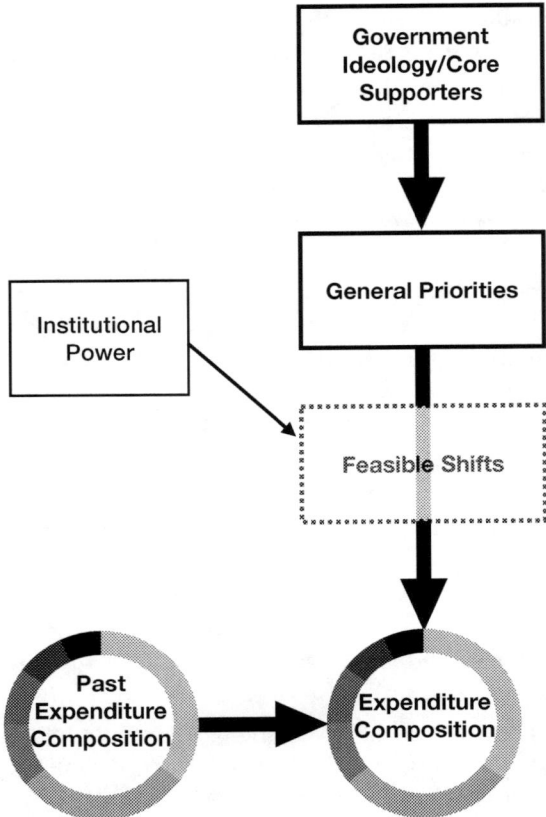

FIGURE 3.3. Taking into account institutional and electoral pressures on a government's general budgetary priorities

3.1.3 A Government Constrained

Although we have set out our expectations in Table 3.1 for how different policy areas will compete for resources depending on government ideology, a key part of our argument hinges on the idea that governments may not always be able to fulfil their ideological visions for reallocating budgets because of institutional constraints. In Figure 3.3, we illustrate how we expect institutional power to shape expenditure compositions by adding the "Feasible Shifts" box. In essence, we expect it to play a moderating role between general priorities and expenditure compositions by defining what types of shifts are feasible.

In the case of institutional power, our expectation is that governments will be more able to institute changes in line with their general priorities when they control a majority of the seats in the lower house of the legislature. Majority governments should be better suited to have budgetary tradeoffs reflect their ideological preferences along the lines shown in Table 3.1. In contrast, we anticipate that minority governments will be unable to substantially reallocate budgets to fit their preferences. While we expect divergences in spending allocations across ideological lines, this may only occur when governments have the ability to shift spending in a way that they see fit. Under a minority government, the pressure to please non-coalition partners combined with the fear of cabinet dissolution may serve as a powerful hindrance to change budgets to only fit their ideological preferences, especially when eyeing alterations that upset the balance of government support in parliament. Non-governmental parties pressure all governments to reallocate budgets toward their preferences, but the lack of a legislative majority means that minority governments must entertain, and possibly implement, at least some of these changes. There is more competition for resources under minority governments, leading to reallocations that may reflect a murkier ideological vision because of the influence of non-governmental parties.

To summarize our expectations for the moderating effect of institutions: budgetary tradeoffs for majority governments should reflect their ideological priorities, while minority governments lack the ability to hold their ideological lines. While we anticipate majority governments to behave along the ideological positions in Table 3.1, our expectations for minority governments only extend to their inability to fulfill their ideological visions. We do not have specific budgetary areas that we expect will shift under minority rule, since these depend on varying party support in the parliament.

3.2 POLITICS AND SPENDING TRADEOFFS: RESEARCH DESIGN AND MODELING STRATEGY

In order to test our theoretical expectations, we compiled data from as many developed democratic nations as possible over as long a time period as possible. As discussed in Section 2.5, we collected data on government spending from the International Monetary Fund's Classification of the Functions of Government, or COFOG database, because it offers the most comparable set of data on expenditure subcategories over the widest coverage of countries and years. We present broad brushstrokes of the data collection process for our independent variables in this section, but provide more details on these data in Section 3.5.

To capture the competition for funding between the various spending categories, we use a modeling strategy to estimate the impact of a change in each of our independent variables on all eight categories of the budget simultaneously. To do so, we take advantage of a series of papers written by the authors of this book and other members of the Dynamic Pie Group that focus on the analysis of compositional dependent variables measured over time (Philips, Rutherford, and Whitten 2015, 2016a, 2016b; Lipsmeyer, Philips, and Whitten 2017; Lipsmeyer et al. 2019; Jung et al. 2020). In Section 3.6, we provide more technical information about these models.

In order to test our initial theoretical claims (summarized in Table 3.1), we specify our model as:

$$\ln\left(\frac{y_{ijt}}{y_{i1t}}\right) = s_{ijt} = f(s_{ij,t-1} + \text{Ideology}_{it} + \text{Institutional}_{it} \\ + \text{Ideology}_{it} \times \text{Institutional}_{it} + \textbf{Controls}_{it}), \quad (3.1)$$

where the logged ratio between spending category j and reference spending category $j = 1$ is a function of its own lag and a number of theorized determinants of expenditure tradeoffs listed here.[26] Data sources and other specific details on these data can be found in Section 3.5.

- To account for ideology, we use a dichotomous variable, *Right*, that equals one if the government in country i in year t is right and zero otherwise. These data are from Seki and Williams (2014), who extended the government composition data of Woldendorp, Keman, and Budge (2000). As described in Section 3.5, we turned their original five point scale into a dichotomous measure; such an approach is common in the literature (c.f., Franzese 2002b; Lipsmeyer, Philips, and Whitten 2017).
- For the institutional variable, we use *Majority Government* that is equal to one if the government holds a majority and zero otherwise. We code a government as a majority if the government parties control

[26] Equation 3.1 results in $J - 1$ equations to be estimated. The choice of a "baseline" reference category is arbitrary, since we later untransform these compositions when presenting graphical results (c.f., Philips, Rutherford, and Whitten 2016a, 2016b). Note that the j subscripts are missing from the independent variables (excluding the lagged dependent variable), because these are fixed across the J categories (e.g., we observe the same level of GDP growth for country i in year t, no matter which budgetary category j we are modeling).

3.2 Politics and Tradeoffs: Research Design and Model 79

50 percent plus one of the seats in the lower house of the parliament. Governments with less than a majority receive a zero, and we code them as minority governments.
- Since we expect ideology to play a role only when the government is strong enough to push for their desired changes, we interact *Right* with *Majority Government*. Our expectation is that ideology will affect the composition of budgets only when parties in government command a majority.
- We also include a number of control variables:
  - *Growth* in the gross domestic product (GDP) of a country, expressed as the real annual percentage change, is a proxy for changes in economic development.
  - For demand-side drivers, we include: the percentage of the *Unemployed* and the *Age Dependency Ratio* to account for changes in social protection recipients. The former is expressed as the number of unemployed persons in a country as a percentage of the total labor force (the total labor force includes both the employed and unemployed), while the latter is the percentage of people younger than 15 or older than 64 relative to the total working age population (i.e., 15–65).
  - The economic *Openness* of a country is a proxy for globalization. It is the sum of exports and imports of goods and services as a share of a country's GDP.
  - We add a dichotomous variable equal to one if a country has either a legislative or executive *Election* in a given year, and zero otherwise.

To account for plausible rival explanations to our theory about compositional shifts, we include two additional variables. The first possibility is that, instead of reallocating expenditure categories based on ideological and institutional considerations, governments may increase the overall size of the budget. The idea here is that given a desire to increase a particular category, for example, defense, a government may instead increase the overall size of its spending budget and allocate more resources to that category. This will have the effect of making defense a larger share of the total (now enlarged) budget, at the cost of all categories equally, since retrenchment is not occurring in a particular category. To account for this alternative explanation, we add *Total Expenditures* as a percentage of GDP to our model. Second, we include the *Budget Deficit* as a percentage of GDP, since governments may decide to deficit spend as an alternative strategy to raising the spending budget or reallocating expenditures when they prefer to raise expenditures on specific policy areas. Therefore, the estimated effects of our variables are net of any effects of these two factors.

We also include a linear time trend variable to account for any consistent changes over time upward or downward that are shared among all units. For instance, globalization has affected nearly every country (and certainly every country in our sample), so while there may be periods of slow increases or minor declines, for the most part globalization has continuously increased across time. Including a time trend captures such continuous movement across time in the average value of a series. Its inclusion also has the added benefit of "de-trending" any mean non-stationary series in our models (Pickup 2014).[27] Since the time trend captures *any* observed or unobserved factor that has generally increased or decreased over time, it is mostly a nuisance parameter; therefore, we choose not to show any plots of this variable.

For this model – as well as those in Chapter 4 – we estimate the seven resulting compositional equations simultaneously in a system of equations known as a seemingly unrelated regression (SUR) (Zellner 1962). SUR models are similar to ordinary least squares (OLS) regressions, but they take advantage of the possibility of correlated errors between equations. In our case, since the dependent variable in each equation is the ratio between two compositional variables for unit i at time t (i.e., $\ln\left(\frac{y_{ijt}}{y_{iit}}\right)$), it is likely that an over- or under-estimate in one equation is correlated with an over- or under-estimate in another. SUR estimation allows us to gain leverage by taking advantage of these correlated residuals across correlations that typically result in more efficient estimates (Greene 2012).

The parameter estimates in the resulting models are difficult to interpret, because a coefficient represents the estimated effect of a one-unit increase in the relevant independent variable on the logged ratio between one category relative to the arbitrarily chosen baseline category. Therefore, we turn to graphical interpretations of the results, although our full set of results, as well as several robustness checks, can be found in Section 3.6. These "effects plots" show the predicted changes across all eight budgetary categories due to a one standard deviation increase in a particular independent variable.[28] Because we are estimating dynamic

---

[27] This is not to say that adding a trend term accounts for variance non-stationarity, such as a unit root. We perform unit root testing and show the results in Section 3.6.
[28] As we explain in Section 3.6, although estimates are linear in the parameters, these models lead to non-linear estimated predicted proportions of budgetary expenditures in

models, such changes have both short-run (i.e., the contemporaneous effect of a change in *x* at time *t* on the composition at time *t*) and long-run effects (i.e., the cumulative response in each part of the composition over a long time period, given a single change in *x* at time *t*) (c.f., Williams and Whitten 2012). We plot these estimated changes along with confidence intervals in figures we call "effects plots." We explain this process in greater detail in Section 3.6.

3.3 WHEN POLITICS MATTERS FOR EXPENDITURE TRADEOFFS

In order to understand how governments move around budgetary resources strategically, we begin by considering how governments of different ideological stripes alter expenditures under the different governing circumstances of having a majority versus a minority of seats in the national legislature.

3.3.1 Ideology and Expenditure Tradeoffs under Majority Governments

At the core of our theory is the argument that governments' ideologies and their core supporters drive their policy priorities. We expect that governments from the right and left of the ideological spectrum allocate resources differently to align with these priorities, as we showed in our theoretical table (Table 3.1). To illustrate the results from our budgetary compositional models, in Figure 3.4 we present an effects plot that shows the estimated reallocations of the budget when moving from a left majority to a right majority government (Figure 3.4a) and from a right majority to a left majority government (Figure 3.4b), while holding the values for all other variables in the model constant at their observed sample average values.[29]

In both graphs in Figure 3.4, the horizontal axis is the predicted change – expressed in terms of the percentage points of the total budget – for each of the budget categories resulting from the change in government

---

response to a change in an independent variable. In other words, the effect of a change in any independent variable *depends* on the starting point or the values of the dependent variables and independent variables before the change takes place. Throughout the book, we present effects plots calculated for a case in which the initial values for all variables including the dependent variables are held at their sample means.

[29] We hold the dichotomous election variable at zero.

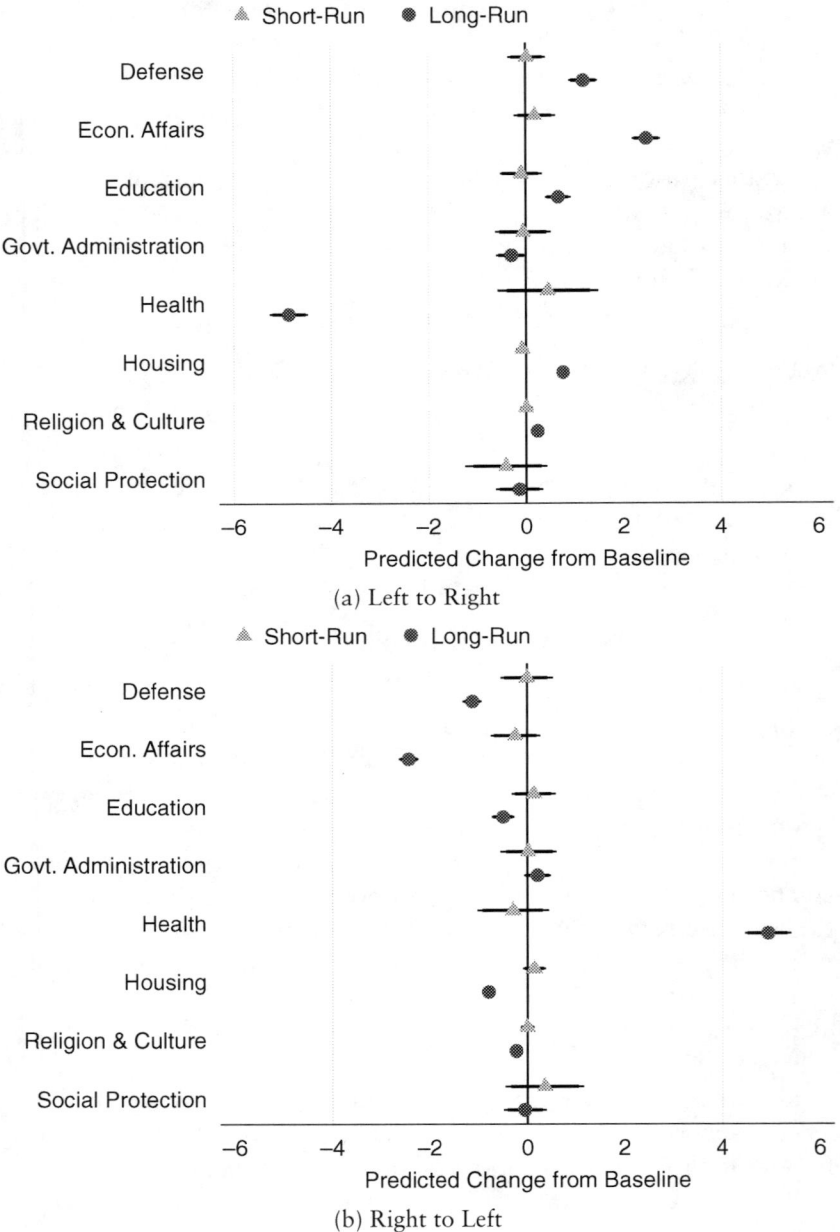

FIGURE 3.4. The effects of shifts in ideology on expenditures under a majority government
Note: Effects plots show the short- and long-run effects from a majority left to a majority right government (Figure 3.4a) and a majority right to a majority left government (Figure 3.4b) under otherwise average conditions; 90 (thick) and 95 (thin) percent confidence intervals shown.

3.3 When Politics Matters for Expenditure Tradeoffs

ideology. That is to say, these figures show the predicted percentage point spending difference between the value of each part of the spending composition as a result of an ideological shift. Note that when the confidence intervals for the predicted change for a particular policy category cross 0, this indicates that there is no statistically significant effect for the ideological change on that policy area.[30] We show both 90 (thick horizontal bar) and 95 percent (thin horizontal bar) confidence intervals throughout this book.[31] The short-run effects, depicted as triangles, indicate the instantaneous shift in budget compositions in response to a change in government ideology (left → right or right → left). The long-run changes, depicted as circles, show the predicted cumulative effect of such a shift, that is, after a sufficiently long period of time for values to settle to a new equilibrium level.[32]

Based on our estimates from the model presented in Equation (3.1), the results displayed in Figure 3.4 tell us several interesting things about political budgeting and our initial theory about the influence of ideology. First, we can see that, in both graphs in Figure 3.4, none of the short-run effects of an ideological shift (either left → right or right → left) are statistically significant. This indicates that holding all else constant, government ideological changes do not alter the reallocation of resources immediately. In contrast, over the long-run there are a number of statistically significant budgetary changes. These shifts vary in size across the eight budget categories, and many of them correspond with expected

---

[30] The interpretation of the results figures throughout the book will follow this pattern of displaying predicted percentage point changes in response to a specific shock or change in the value of an independent variable.

[31] For the vast majority of frequentist scholars, 95 percent confidence intervals represent the "sharp" determination of statistical significance of a p-value of less than .05 under a two-sided hypothesis test of no effect. We also show 90 percent confidence intervals for two reasons. First, effects that are significant at the 90 percent level could be seen as "likely," "plausible," or "weakly" statistically significant, and thus still of interest. Second, we have directional expectations for nearly all categories shown in the effects plots, so if still maintaining the sharp cutoff of .05, then a one-sided hypothesis test comports with a 90 percent confidence interval against the hypothesized direction of the effect.

[32] Typically, we would calculate these using equations for the long-run multiplier effects (e.g., De Boef and Keele 2008). Since the long-run effects in a model with a compositional dependent variable are more complex, we simulate a sufficient number of periods to see what the new, stable long-run equilibrium is and use these values to calculate our predicted changes from the baseline scenario. In doing so, we follow the lead of others by using simulations when analytical calculations are made difficult by a complex dynamic specification (c.f., Jordan and Philips 2018a, 2018b).

ideological priorities. Our finding that a change in government ideology does not lead to budgetary shifts in the short-run – although they do over the longer-term – echoes others in the literature on budgetary change (Brender and Drazen 2013), as well as the general conclusion that budgets are incremental and significant shifts only occur over several time periods (Dahl and Lindblom 1953; Wildavsky 1964).[33]

In Figure 3.4a, we can see how moving from a left majority government to a right majority government decreases the relative proportion of the budget devoted to health by a large amount, roughly five percentage points of the overall budget, over the long-run. The policies that benefit from this retrenchment are defense, economic affairs, education, housing, and religion and culture. The increases to defense and economic affairs are the largest shifts of one and just over two percentage points, respectively. Note that Figure 3.4b shows the predicted changes from an ideological shift in the opposite direction – from a right to a left government. In response to this shift, defense, economic affairs, education, housing, and religion and culture make up a smaller proportion of the budget, while government administration and health receive increases in relative shares. Interestingly, neither ideological change leads to a relative increase or decrease in allocations to social protection, indicating stable proportions. Both of these plots highlight how left and right governments trade off funding for policies in different ways, but the patterns suggest changes that mostly correspond to our theorized ideological preferences presented in Table 3.1.

In Figure 3.4b, we see some evidence that left governments reallocate resources to line up with their ideological visions of government responsibility. There is a slight and barely statistically significant shift toward increasing the expenditure share going to government administration and also a substantial increase in spending on health. In contrast, Figure 3.4a better reflects the priorities of right governments, where we see that they trade off funds to health spending for economic affairs and defense, indicating their emphasis on market-driven solutions, business interests, and international defense. While our expectations for education and health are ambiguous, with both left and right governments possibly considering them as priorities, in this context we observe a split. Right governments shift less than one percentage point to education, but the left reallocates a

---

[33] But see Tsebelis and Chang (2004), who find statistically significant budgetary changes in the short-run as the ideological distance between successive governments grows.

3.3 When Politics Matters for Expenditure Tradeoffs

much larger relative increase to health. Interestingly, these results contrast with the findings of Jensen (2011c), who argued the right increases health spending as a means of leading to privatization.

Overall, the results in Figure 3.4 tell an interesting story: under otherwise-average conditions, both left and right governments maneuver budgets strategically but not perfectly to fit their ideological visions. However, these shifts take time. Budgetary changes are not instantaneous; they take a number of years to occur. This supports the findings of Brender and Drazen (2013) that a few years under a new government are needed before budgets start to differ in significant ways from those of their predecessors. When tackling tradeoffs within the entire budget, this focus on long-term changes is more appropriate and in tune with realistic expectations.

3.3.2 Ideology and Expenditure Tradeoffs under Minority Governments

While governments want to shift budgetary resources between policy areas to match their ideological preferences, not all governments have the same ability to fulfil their policy goals. In Figure 3.4, we highlighted differences in budget allocations in response to shifts in ideology under majority governments, when they would have the most power to pass their preferred legislation. Do these ideological differences persist under a minority government, or will their need to cater to non-government parties in parliament diminish their own ideological priorities?

To test this, in Figure 3.5 we compare how governments behave under both majority and minority conditions with the expectation that budgetary allocations are more likely to reflect a government's ideology when it has a majority of seats in the lower house of parliament. The two graphs in Figure 3.5 illustrate the effects of an ideological shift under these two different levels of government power – majority (Figure 3.5a) and minority (Figure 3.5b). In both figures, we see the budgetary shifts that result from a change from a left to a right government.

As we saw previously in Figure 3.4a for majority governments, (reproduced here for reference purposes as Figure 3.5a), the reallocation of budgetary resources reflects shifts in government's ideologies. In a majority government, an ideological change from left to right results in tradeoffs from healthcare to economic affairs, education, housing, and defense. In contrast, under a minority government (Figure 3.5b), this same shift in government ideology results in long-run reallocations that are more of

(a) Left to Right (Majority)

(b) Left to Right (Minority)

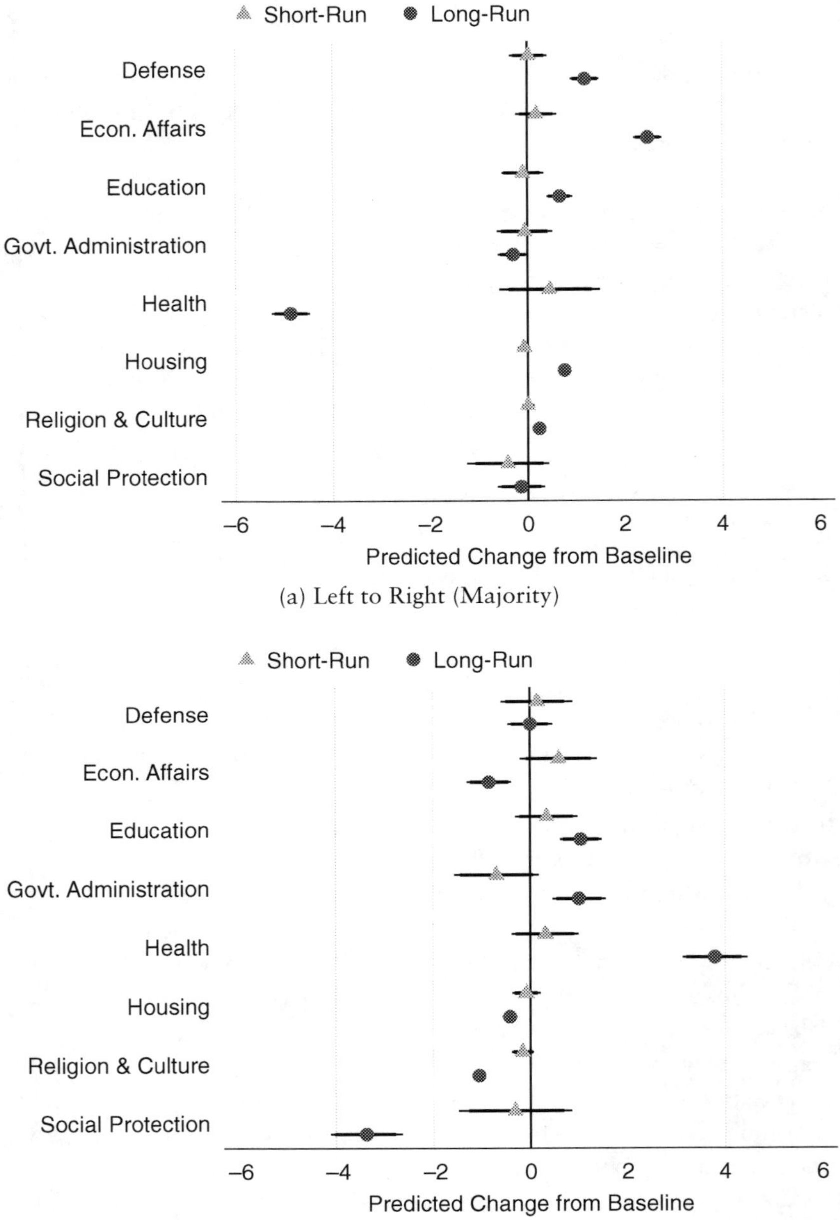

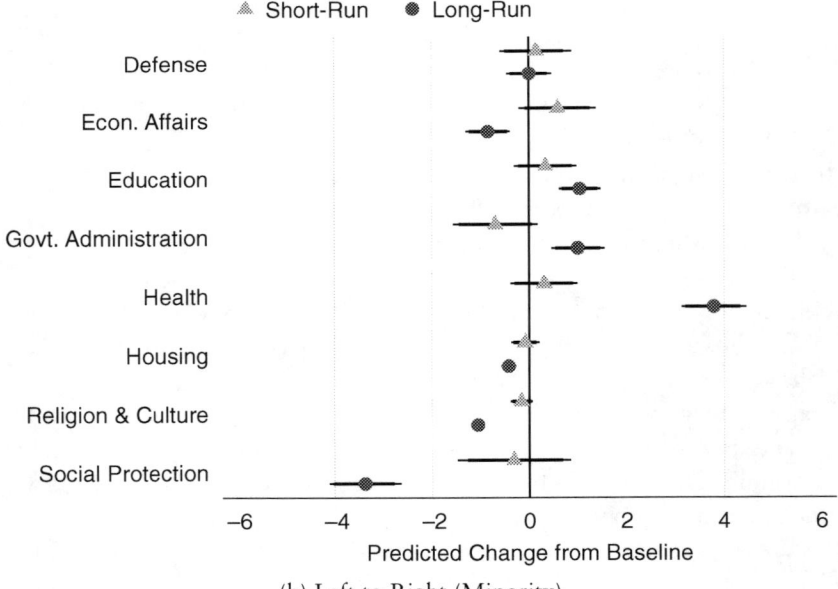

FIGURE 3.5. The effects of shifts from left to right government under majority versus minority government

Note: Effects plots show the short- and long-run effects for a majority left to a majority right government (Figure 3.5a) and a minority left to a minority right government (Figure 3.5b) under otherwise average conditions; 90 (thick) and 95 (thin) percent confidence intervals shown.

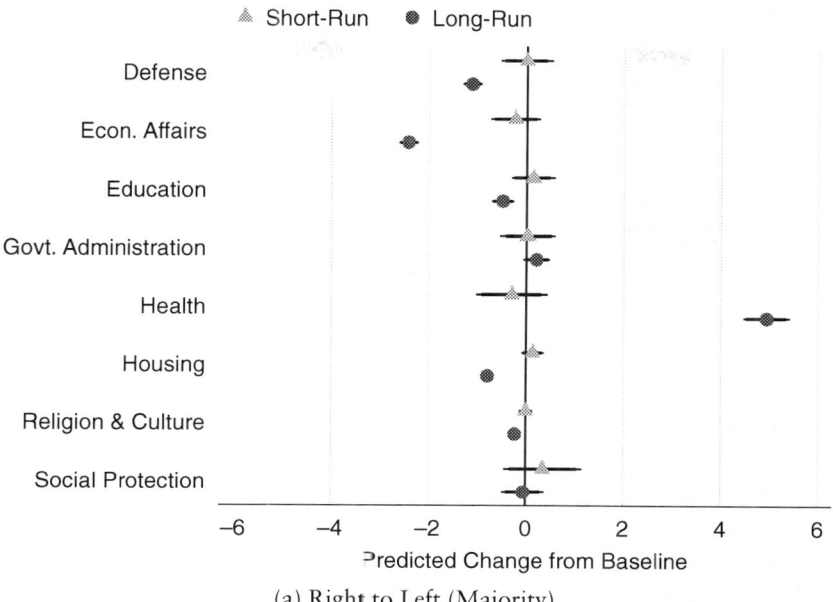

(a) Right to Left (Majority)

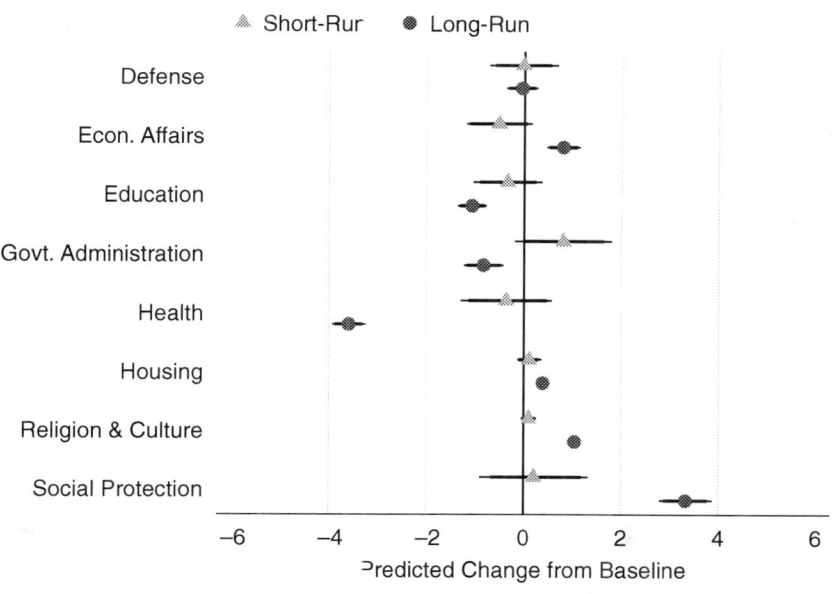

(b) Right to Left (Minority)

FIGURE 3.6. The effects of shifts from right to left government under majority versus minority government

Note: Effects plots show the short- and long-run effects for a majority right to a majority left government (Figure 3.6a) and a minority right to a minority left government (Figure 3.6b) under otherwise average conditions; 90 (thick) and 95 (thin) percent confidence intervals shown.

a mixture of ideological priorities: increasing allocations to education, government administration, and health, at the expense of economic affairs, housing, religion and culture, and social protection. The graphs in Figure 3.6 illustrate these same majority/minority differences in reverse when moving from right to left governments. In this case, moving from a right to left minority government results in an increased proportion of total expenditures going toward housing, economic affairs, religion and culture, and social protection, with retrenchments in government administration, education and health.

The shifts that occur in Figures 3.5b and 3.6b are ideologically muddled, suggesting that minority governments find it difficult to align budget allocations with their ideological preferences. These findings reinforce research that shows the limited ability of minority governments to institute their ideological preferences (Lijphart 1984; Strøm 1990a; Artés and Bustos 2008; Lipsmeyer 2011; Herwartz and Theilen 2014). Taken together, these results suggest that a government's budgetary behavior is dependent on its legislative power to pass its preferred legislation and control the policy agenda. Minority governments lack the legislative support to push their policies through parliament, so we would not expect their budgetary allocations to reflect only their ideological preferences. The results in both Figures 3.5 and 3.6 bear out these expectations. For minority governments, the passing of a budget requires deals with parties outside of the ideological fold and these can result in ideologically diverse tradeoffs. Considering only ideology supplies only part of the overall picture of government tradeoffs.

3.4 CONCLUSION

In this chapter, we developed a theory of how ideological and institutional factors influence the composition of government spending. While previous studies focused on either the entire budget (e.g., total spending) or a single category of the budget (e.g., spending on defense), we have shown that a compositional approach provides a richer understanding of how budgets compete for resources and when governments have the ability to make these strategic decisions.

Our theoretical argument centered around two key political factors – ideology and institutions – that influence budget allocations, and much of our results support our expectations. Relying on ideology as a driver of certain types of allocations, in Table 3.1, we laid out our expectations for the various pieces of the expenditure pie. This exercise went beyond previous work that focused on either total spending or select policy areas.

Policy areas compete for resources, and governments must decide how to allocate funds across the various pieces, typically with an eye on fulfilling their ideological vision.

Of course, not all governments are able to institute the budgetary allocations they prefer because of power dynamics between governments and parliaments. Our results highlighted that, while shifts in ideology led mostly to expected budgetary reallocations under majority governments, under minority governments, our budgetary findings were substantially different. In this latter scenario, we found more of a mixture of shifts in budgetary compositions with some that comported well with ideologically based expectations and some that did not. This suggests that minority governments are balancing their own budgetary preferences with those of non-governmental parties in order to continue in power.

To summarize our findings so far, holding all else equal, ideology does make a difference in expected ways for both relative increases and decreases in budgetary compositions under majority governments. This indicates that in the zero-sum game of budgets, policy areas compete for resources, and governments strategically make tradeoffs when they reallocate budgets. However, not all governments succeed in shifting budgets to fit their ideological visions. While budgetary outcomes for minority governments may not reflect their ideologies, these tradeoffs still suggest strategic behavior as they attempt to appease the various political parties necessary to stay in power. In Chapter 4, we relax the "all else equal" condition and look at how the combination of government ideology and external shocks – either in the form of electoral, economic, or international shifts – affect budgetary compositions.

3.5 DATA APPENDIX

In this section we provide more details about the variables that we use to test our theoretical expectations in Chapters 3 and 4 of this book. Statistical and modeling details, as well as robustness results, can be found in Section 3.6.

3.5.1 Details on the Dependent Variables

Note that specific details about the dependent variables we use in the models presented in Chapters 3 and 4 can be found in Section 2.5. These include measurement and sources.

3.5.2 Details on the Independent Variables

Details on each of our independent variables in the model:

- Throughout this book, we use the variable *Right*, which is a dichotomous variable equal to one if a government is right-leaning in country i in year t. These data are from Seki and Williams (2014), who extended the government composition data of Woldendorp, Keman, and Budge (2000).[34] Their coding results in a five-point scale equal to one for a government with "right-wing dominance," two for "right-center complexion," three for "balanced situation," four for "left-center complexion," and five for "left-wing dominance." We code our *Right* variable for each government in our data set as equal to one if the ideological complexion score for that government is less than or equal to two and zero otherwise. This avoids the strong functional form assumptions that would be imposed by using the original five-point scale as a continuous variable in interactive model specifications (Hainmueller, Mummolo, and Xu 2019). Following the lead of others (c.f., Franzese 2002b; Lipsmeyer, Philips, and Whitten 2017), for the years in which there were multiple governments, we calculated *Right* as a weighted average based on the proportion of days each government was in power.

- Data on majority/minority government status are also from Seki and Williams (2014). Given issues with there potentially being more than one government during a calendar year, we coded our variable as equal to one if a majority government was present in country i in year t – or if there was a majority government in place for over half the year – and zero otherwise. For the 778 country–years included in our analyses, 90 cases (11.5%) required rounding.

- Data on the *Age Dependency Ratio* are from the World Bank. This variable is the percentage of people younger than 15 or older than 64 relative to the total working age population (i.e., 15–64).[35]

- Data on economic *Openness* are from the World Bank (that come from both the World Bank's and OECD's national accounts data) and are expressed as the sum of exports and imports of goods and services as a share of a country's GDP. Due to very clear deterministic trend issues (discussed in Section 3.6.3), this variable always enters into our models in first-difference and lagged first-difference forms.

---

[34] Available at: https://doi.org/10.7910/DVN/0UNUAM. Last accessed September 27, 2017.
[35] From the World Bank's 2017 revision.

3.5 Data Appendix

- Data on the *Deficit* come from the World Bank.[36] The original variable is described as "surplus or deficit is revenue (including grants) minus expense, minus net acquisition of non-financial assets." We then use the negative of this variable, such that higher (lower) values indicate greater (lesser) deficits.
- Data on the *Unemployment* rate are mostly from the International Labor Organization (ILO). Different countries use different approaches to obtain the unemployment rate. We used the most common approach (a labor force survey), supplementing this with the second most common approach, third most common approach – and so on – where data were missing.[37] Where data were still missing, we supplemented using OECD and then World Bank unemployment rates. The variable is expressed as the number of unemployed persons in a country as a percentage of the total labor force (the total labor force includes both the employed and unemployed).
- Data on whether or not a country has an *Election* in a given year are from the Database of Political Institutions (Cruz, Keefer, and Scartascini 2016).[38] This variable is equal to one if a country has a legislative or executive election in year t and zero otherwise.
- Data on economic *Growth* are from the World Bank (and they come from both the World Bank and OECD national accounts). It is the real annual percentage growth rate of a country's Gross Domestic Product: "Annual percentage growth rate of GDP at market prices based on constant local currency. Aggregates are based on constant 2010 U.S. dollars. GDP is the sum of gross value added by all resident producers in the economy plus any product taxes and minus any subsidies not included in the value of the products. It is calculated without making deductions for depreciation of fabricated assets or for depletion and degradation of natural resources."[39]

---

[36] The World Bank obtained these data from the IMF's Government Finance Statistics Yearbook, as well as World Bank and OECD estimates.

[37] These other approaches are, respectively, employment office records, official estimates, the population census, "other" household surveys, household income or expenditure surveys, insurance records, "other" administrative records, other official sources, and a child labor survey.

[38] See https://datacatalog.worldbank.org/dataset/wps2283-database-political-institutions. Last accessed January 5, 2016.

[39] See https://data.worldbank.org/indicator/NY.GDP.MKTP.KD.ZG. Last accessed November 29, 2018.

3.6 STATISTICAL APPENDIX

Here, we provide technical details about the models we estimated and the construction of the figures we used to interpret the results from those models. We also provide results from several diagnostics and robustness checks.

3.6.1 Modeling Strategy and Simulation Approach

In this section, we offer a more detailed discussion of our statistical modeling approach. Although it is intuitive to think about budget compositions theoretically, testing theoretical propositions about compositions as they evolve over time is complex. In order to test our contextual theory of budgets, we make use of and extend recently developed strategies for the modeling of compositional dependent variables over time or what have come to be known as "dynamic pie" models (Philips, Rutherford, and Whitten 2016a). We can illustrate this approach by thinking of the expenditure proportions in a set of countries over years and across budgetary categories as a collection of y_{ijt} values, where $i = 1, 2, \ldots, N$ represents the different countries in the analysis, $j = 1, 2, \ldots, J$ represents the different budgetary categories, and $t = 1, 2, \ldots, T$ represents the different years.[40]

Compositions of this nature have four important characteristics (Philips, Rutherford, and Whitten 2016a). First, each spending proportion, y_{ijt}, must lie between 0 and 1:[41]

$$0 < y_{ijt} < 1. \tag{3.2}$$

Obviously, no j expenditure category would take up either all ($y_{ijt} = 1$) or none ($y_{ijt} = 0$) of the budget in any time point in a given country. Each of the categories will comprise a proportion of the budget somewhere in between.

The second characteristic is that, at any given point in time, in any single country, the categories *must* sum to 1:

$$\sum_{j=1}^{J} y_{ijt} = 1 \quad \forall\, i, t. \tag{3.3}$$

---

[40] In earlier work, we referenced such variables as "y_{itj}" (c.f., Lipsmeyer, Philips, and Whitten 2017). We found this order of triple indexing to be a bit clumsy when we referenced non-contemporaneous time periods (e.g., $t+1$ or $t-1$). Thus, we triple-index variables throughout this book as, for example, "y_{ijt}."

[41] Such proportions could also be expressed as values ranging between 0 and 100 (if expressed as a percentage).

3.6 Statistical Appendix

Put simply, all of the proportions of the budget must sum to the total budget, for any country–year observation.

Third, due to the [0, 1] boundedness restriction given in Equation (3.2) and the summation restriction in Equation (3.3), it is also the case that any change in a particular budgetary category in a given country–year must be bounded by -1 and 1:

$$-1 < \Delta y_{ijt} < 1. \quad (3.4)$$

Last, it follows that the sum of the changes across categories for any given year in a given country must be equal to zero:

$$\sum_{j=1}^{J} \Delta y_{ijt} = 0 \quad \forall \, i, t. \quad (3.5)$$

Positive changes in one (or more) categories must be completely offset by corresponding decreases in at least one other category.

In order to test our hypotheses about the drivers of tradeoffs within the expenditure pies that make up national budgets, we need a modeling strategy that accounts for the properties of compositional variables like y_{ijt}, as presented in Equations (3.2)–(3.5). Failure to acknowledge these properties has two consequences. First, as pointed out in political science by Katz and King (1999) and Tomz, Tucker, and Wittenberg (2002), employing standard multivariate regression techniques on compositional data can lead to nonsensical predictions that exceed 1 or fall below 0.[42] Second, an over- or under-estimate of one category, by definition, will lead to the opposite effect in at least one other category, as given by Equation (3.5). To better picture this, consider a composition made up of three budget categories, "A," "B," and "C." If "A" is predicted to include 30 percent of the budget, yet actually comprises only 25 percent, we have underestimated by 5 percentage points either "B," "C," or some combination of the two. Even in the most benign case, we have underestimated "B" and "C" by 2.5 percentage points each.

Due to this over-/under-estimation issue, it makes sense to use regression-based techniques, such as seemingly unrelated regression (SUR) or vector autoregressive (VAR) models that take into account the cross-category correlations. Such models have the advantage of using the covariance structure of the residuals across systems of equations to provide more efficient estimates. We use seemingly unrelated regressions

---

[42] A similar issue can occur when using linear probability models to estimate dichotomous dependent variables.

(SUR) for the compositional chapters of the book (Chapters 3 and 4) and vector autoregressive (VAR) models when examining the interrelationships between our four budgetary components in Chapter 5. As Zellner (1962) points out, while equation-by-equation OLS estimation of each of the budgetary categories separately is adequate, we can use FGLS to leverage cross-equation correlations in order to produce more efficient estimates.[43]

However, when modeling all J categories simultaneously in a system of equations, an indeterminacy or identification problem is created such that there is more than one set of parameters that will lead to the same values of the composition.[44] To both unbound the compositions off the [0,1] proportional space and to deal with the indeterminacy problem, we turn to additive logged ratios. This strategy was first pioneered in geology (Aitchison 1982, 1983). It involves taking the log of the ratio between *all but one* of the y_{ijt} categories and a "baseline" category:

$$s_{ijt} = \ln\left(\frac{y_{ijt}}{y_{i1t}}\right) \quad \forall\, j \neq 1. \tag{3.6}$$

This has the effect of creating $J-1$ series, since one series – y_{i1t} here – will always be in the denominator as the baseline category. In this exposition, we choose $j=1$ as the baseline category, although this choice is arbitrary and does not change the estimated predictions (Philips, Rutherford, and Whitten 2016a).[45]

There are several advantages to using the additive logged ratio strategy to model compositional data. First, the fact that there are now $J-1$ logged ratio compositions, which we reference as s_{ijt}, means that we are able to circumvent the indeterminancy issue. Moreover, by mapping the bounded compositional variables onto unbounded logged ratios, we can use standard regression techniques that assume a multivariate normal error

---

[43] SUR model results will be identical to OLS in two instances: if the cross-equation correlations truly are zero, and if the regressors are identical across equations. We find consistent evidence that there are strong cross-equation correlations (the Breusch and Pagan (1980) Lagrange multiplier test always rejects the null hypothesis that the cross-equation residuals are unrelated), and the former condition is not met, since the lagged dependent variable differs across equations.

[44] This indeterminacy or identification problem with compositional dependent variables is closely analogous to the indeterminacy or identification problems encountered with a multinomial logit model (Greene 2012, pp. 763–766).

[45] Such a choice is similar to a multinomial logit model, where the choice of excluded category will change how the estimates look but not affect the underlying predicted probabilities.

3.6 Statistical Appendix

distribution to estimate the marginal effects for independent variables on these new dependent variables.[46] Although alternatives exist to this additive logged ratio approach, we prefer it due to its relative ease of calculation, its similarity to multivariate choice models (e.g., multinomial logit and probit), and its use in political science (Katz and King 1999; Tomz, Tucker, and Wittenberg 2002; Breunig and Busemeyer 2012; Philips, Rutherford, and Whitten 2015, 2016a; Lipsmeyer, Philips, and Whitten 2017; Clayton and Zetterberg 2018; Funk and Philips 2019; Jung et al. 2020; Philips, Souza, and Whitten 2020; Kagalwala, Philips, and Whitten 2021).

Using an additive logged ratio approach does have several drawbacks. First, any time the value for a category is equal to zero, the composition s_{ijt} does not exist, either because we are taking the log of zero (the numerator $y_{ijt} = 0$ in Equation (3.6)) or dividing by zero (the denominator $y_{i1t} = 0$ in Equation (3.6)). There are a few proposed – and often quite technically involved – approaches for handling the "zero problem" in compositional data (Aitchison and Egozcue 2005), such as imputation or replacing both the zero and non-zero values observed for a given observation (Martín-Fernández, Barceló-Vidal, and Pawlowsky-Glahn 2003). For our purposes, we use a simple solution of adding a tiny (.00000001) value to any $y_{ijt} = 0$ values in order to allow us to take the additive logged ratio.[47] Fortunately, this comprises a minuscule amount of our data. Out of the eight budgetary categories used in our analysis, only one category (defense) had any zeros observed for the 778 country–years in our sample in Chapters 3 and 4 and even those only occurred for just four observations (comprising approximately .51 percent of our sample).

---

[46] There is some debate on this. In the context of multi-party election data, Katz and King (1999) advocate for a multivariate-t based model, while others advocate for estimating the equations in a seemingly unrelated regression model and assuming the residuals are multivariate normal (Jackson 2002; Mikhailov, Niemi, and Weimer 2002; Tomz, Tucker, and Wittenberg 2002). We use the latter due to its ease of computation and interpretation.

[47] One crucial assumption that needs to be made is the difference between essential zeros that are the "absolute absence of the part in the observation" (Martín-Fernández, Barceló-Vidal, and Pawlowsky-Glahn 2003, p. 255) and rounded zeros, which means that a category can be present, "but below detection limit" (Martín-Fernández, Barceló-Vidal, and Pawlowsky-Glahn 2003, p. 256). For our purposes, an essential zero would mean that a budget category of zeros may not be a suitable part of the budgetary composition. In other words, a country does not have, nor will it ever have, this expenditure category. In contrast, rounded zeros would indicate that, for a given country–year, governments have prioritized this category of the budget at zero or nearly-zero. This latter case is much more plausible given these data.

The second drawback of using additive logged ratios has to do with interpretation. While this approach enables us to model the entire composition of expenditures, interpreting coefficient sizes and making assessments of substantive significance become quite difficult using standard regression-based presentation approaches (i.e., tables of regression coefficients), since a coefficient now represents the estimated effect of a one-unit increase in an independent variable on the logged ratio of one spending category relative to another. In addition, just as with the results from multinomial choice models, interpreting these effects from tables of coefficients becomes quite unwieldy. This is the case, because we get $J-1$ sets of coefficients. Given that most variables appear more than once in the equation (e.g., in both levels and lagged form), this results in a substantial number of coefficients to compare across models.

To get around this disadvantage, we turn to graphical depictions of our statistical results. We use an adaptation of the approach first developed by Philips, Rutherford, and Whitten (2016a, 2016b).[48] These authors first estimate a seemingly unrelated regression which produces an estimated effect of each independent variable on each compositional dependent variable. They then use the Stata program Clarify (Tomz, Wittenberg, and King 2003) to produce 1,000 simulated parameter estimates from the empirical results using stochastic simulation. In this case, the parameter estimates for the regressors are drawn from a multivariate normal distribution, while the covariance matrix – since it relies on cross-correlated errors across equations in the SUR framework – is drawn from an inverse Wishart.

Next, the values of all independent variables are set to substantively interesting values – typically means if the variable is continuous, and modes if a variable is dichotomous – while the lagged dependent variables are set to their sample means. This will produce a stable "equilibrium" prediction of the composition at time $t = 1$. A stylized example of this is shown in Figure 3.7, that is based on a similar figure from Philips, Souza, and Whitten (2020, p. 13). We then move to $t = 2$, where all regressors still remain at their fixed values, while the value of the lagged dependent variable becomes the predicted value of the dependent variable from the previous period ($t = 1$).[49] Then, at a single point in time

---

[48] For a more recent extension, see Jung et al. (2020).
[49] Since there is a lagged dependent variable (of the logged-ratio composition) in the model, we set this to the mean in the first time period, and then estimate a number of "burn-in"

3.6 Statistical Appendix

$$\hat{s}_{ijt} = \hat{\beta}_{0j} + \hat{\phi}_j \hat{s}_{ij,t-1} + \hat{\bar{\beta}}_{1j} x^*_{it} + \hat{\beta}_2 x^*_{i,t-1} + \hat{\beta}_{Sj} \mathbf{x}_{it} + \hat{\beta}_{Mj} \mathbf{x}_{i,t-1} + \hat{\epsilon}_{ijt}$$

$t=1$	$\bar{s}_j$	$\bar{x}^*$	$\bar{x}^*$	$\bar{\mathbf{x}}$	$\bar{\mathbf{x}}$
$t=2$	$\hat{s}_{ij1}$	$\bar{x}^*$	$\bar{x}^*$	$\bar{\mathbf{x}}$	$\bar{\mathbf{x}}$
$t=3$	$\hat{s}_{ij2}$	$\bar{x}^*$	$\bar{x}^*$	$\bar{\mathbf{x}}$	$\bar{\mathbf{x}}$
$t=4$	$\hat{s}_{ij3}$	$\bar{x}^* + shock$	$\bar{x}^*$	$\bar{\mathbf{x}}$	$\bar{\mathbf{x}}$
$t=5$	$\hat{s}_{ij4}$	$\bar{x}^* + shock$	$\bar{x}^* + shock$	$\bar{\mathbf{x}}$	$\bar{\mathbf{x}}$
⋮					

FIGURE 3.7. Stylized example of our simulation approach to predicting compositions

($t = 4$ in Figure 3.7), we "shock" one of the independent variables of interest, x^*_{it}. By convention, we use an increase or decrease of one standard deviation. Since we are estimating autoregressive distributed lag models, this effect of the shock to the regressor will persist throughout future periods. Throughout the period of the simulation, the values of the other independent variables, which we reference as "$\bar{\mathbf{x}}$" in Figure 3.7, are held constant at their mean/modal values.

Note that, at every time point in the simulation, we create $B = 1,000$ predicted values of each part of the composition, $\hat{s}_{bijt}$ (recall that $B = 1,000$ was the number of stochastic simulation draws we took just after estimating the SUR model, indexed here with b). Thus, each $\hat{s}_{bijt}$ prediction for the same $\hat{s}_{ijt}$ scenario will differ slightly from one another, due to the nature of the random draws. Next, after allowing the movement into disequilibrium to play out over time, we then untransform the predictions using the following equation for all series in the composition except the baseline category, over all b simulations (Philips, Rutherford, and Whitten 2016a):

$$\hat{y}_{bijt} = \frac{exp(\hat{s}_{bijt})}{1 + \sum_{j=2}^{J} exp(\hat{s}_{bijt})}. \tag{3.7}$$

periods which we throw away in order to ensure that the model is at a stable equilibrium by $t = 1$.

For the baseline category, the following transformation is used:

$$\hat{y}_{bijt} = \frac{1}{1 + \sum_{j=2}^{J} exp(\hat{s}_{bijt})}. \tag{3.8}$$

From these final predictions of each budgetary category, $\hat{y}_{bijt}$, we are now able to obtain the average prediction (i.e., $\bar{\hat{y}}_{ijt} = \frac{\sum_{b=1}^{B} \hat{y}_{bijt}}{B}$), as well as 90 and 95 percent confidence intervals, which we calculate using percentiles of the distribution of the 1,000 simulated predictions (King, Tomz, and Wittenberg 2000). For our purposes, we are particularly interested in the changes to the predicted value of each category in the year in which the change in the relevant independent variable took place, as well as the long-run total change in the predicted values of each category. These predicted changes, known in the time series literature as the short-run or contemporaneous effect and the long-run effect, respectively (De Boef and Keele 2008), are depicted by figures such as Figure 3.4, together with 90 and 95 percent confidence intervals. We calculate the predicted short-run effects by subtracting the mean predicted value of each category in the time period before the change in the independent variable occurred from the predicted value for that category in the time period in which the change occurred. For the example in Figure 3.7, this calculation would be $\hat{s}_{bij3} - \bar{\hat{s}}_{ij2}$. We calculate the predicted long-run effects by subtracting the predicted value of each category in the time period before the change in the independent variable occurred from the predicted value for that category in a time period in which the series have settled into a new stable set of values. For the example in Figure 3.7, this calculation would be $\bar{\hat{s}}_{ijt_0} - \bar{\hat{s}}_{ij2}$ where $t = t_0$ is defined as a time point where $\bar{\hat{s}}_{ijt} - \bar{\hat{s}}_{ijt-1} \to 0$.

3.6.2 On Shock Sizes

Like many others, we prefer to use graphical depictions of our regression models. Such approaches typically show the effect of a counterfactual change in a variable, while holding all other variables at their means (if continuous) or modes (if dichotomous), and then plot predicted or expected values or changes in these values. One very common counterfactual change to depict is to show a plus or minus one standard deviation change from the mean.[50] One additional – and, we think,

---

[50] Although other alternatives exist (e.g., moving from the 10th to 90th percentiles).

3.6 Statistical Appendix

under-appreciated – aspect of cross-sectional time series (CSTS) data is that there are different forms of variability in these data that make thinking about counterfactual changes difficult. One form is overall or total variance, the standard deviation of which is given as (for some variable x_{it}):

$$\text{Total SD}(x_{i,t}) = \sqrt{\frac{\sum_{i=1}^{N} \sum_{t=1}^{T} (x_{it} - \bar{\bar{x}})^2}{N \cdot T - 1}}. \tag{3.9}$$

Such a measure describes the spread of the data around the grand mean, $\bar{\bar{x}}$, and is exactly the same as the standard deviation we would obtain in cross-sectional data. However, CSTS data has two additional forms of variation due to the structure of the data. The first is the within standard deviation:

$$\text{Within SD}(x_{i,t}) = \sqrt{\frac{\sum_{i=1}^{N} \sum_{t=1}^{T} (x_{it} - \bar{x}_i)^2}{N \cdot T - 1}}, \tag{3.10}$$

that effectively measures the average spread of x_{it} over time within a unit i. The other type is the between standard deviation:

$$\text{Between SD}(x_{i,t}) = \sqrt{\frac{\sum_{i=1}^{N} (\bar{x}_i - \bar{\bar{x}})^2}{N - 1}}, \tag{3.11}$$

that describes the spread of the unit-averages of x_{it} around the grand-mean (i.e., the variability across the units).

A naive strategy would be simply to use the total standard deviation as a counterfactual change. However, throughout this book, we did not want to run the risk of making counterfactual changes that *never* actually occurred in the data, specifically, movements in a variable from one year to the next in a country. To this end, we analyzed the three variability components described previously and compared them to the average year-to-year change in each variable, the overall standard deviation of this annual change, and the maximum year-to-year change (i.e., the most extreme value of an annual change observed in the data). In Chapters 4 and 6, we show plus one standard deviation changes from the mean using overall variance, since we found that such a change: (1) nearly always fell within two overall standard deviations of the year-to-year change and (2) was always smaller than the maximum annual change that occurred. In other words, our counterfactual changes show perhaps infrequent but entirely plausible shocks that have occurred in our data. Chapter 3 only uses dichotomous variables, so the within/between/overall concerns do not apply. In Chapter 5, we find that the overall standard deviation changes for expenditures, revenues, and deficits are rather large, so we instead show one standard deviation increases using the within formula described in Equation 3.10.[51]

3.6.3 Stationarity Diagnostics

Non-stationarity and the threat of spurious inferences is a concern for any model estimated with time series data (c.f., Newbold and Granger 1974; Philips 2021). This is also true with time series cross-sectional data where there are now a number of different tests for panel unit roots.[52] Tests for panel unit roots differ from each other on several important dimensions: the types of data structures that they can accommodate (i.e., whether they require that the data are balanced or not), asymptotic assumptions about the rates at which the number of units (countries for our data) and time points (years) are trending toward infinity, assumptions about whether or not the series has a drift or a trend component, and the specification of the null and alternative hypotheses.

Our data structure is unbalanced, meaning that, as is apparent in Table 2.2, we do not have data on exactly the same years for every country. We are thus, limited to tests that can accommodate unbalanced panel data. In terms of asymptotic assumptions, we are comfortable with tests that assume the number of time points is trending toward infinity, but less comfortable with tests that assume the number of countries is trending toward infinity.

Given the combination of the structure of our data and the asymptotic assumptions that we are willing to make, we have three different panel unit root tests available to us: the test developed by Im, Pesaran, and Shin (2003) and two variants of "Fisher-type" tests proposed by Choi (2001). All three of these tests have the additional advantage of relaxing the assumption of homogeneous time processes across units by estimating a panel-specific ρ term. As such, the null hypothesis is that all panels

---

[51] Within variation is always smaller than overall variance, sometimes appreciably so. Moreover, pooled intercept (what we use), random intercept (i.e., "random effects"), and fixed intercept ("fixed effects") models use different amounts of between and within variance: respectively, equal proportions, some optimally-determined proportion of between relative to within, and purely within variance (c.f., Mummolo and Peterson 2018; Jordan and Philips 2022).

[52] Pesaran (2015) and the documentation for StataCorp (2019) provide excellent discussions of these tests and the issues pertaining to them.

contain unit roots and the alternative hypothesis is that at least one panel is stationary. This is consistent with evidence presented by Phillips and Moon (1999) that, in data structured along the lines of ours (p. 1058), "the noise can be characterized as independent across individuals. Hence, by pooling the cross section and time series observations, we may attenuate the strong effect of the residuals in the regression while retaining the strength of the signal $X_{i,t}$."[53]

3.6.3.1 Stationarity Testing: Dependent Variables

As first noted by Philips, Rutherford, and Whitten (2016b), dynamic compositional variables present a rather unique challenge in terms of testing for unit roots. This is the case because the order of integration can vary across the vectors of data created by the log-ratio transformation displayed in Equation (3.6). In addition, the number of series found to be of different orders of integration has been demonstrated to vary depending on the choice of the baseline category (y_{i_1t} in Equation (3.6)). This is fairly remarkable, since the choice of baseline does not change model inferences. Regardless, we prefer to err on the side of caution and select a baseline category for which the findings from tests of the order of integration are fairly homogeneous. Based on our diagnostics, we settled on housing as the baseline category.

In Table 3.2, we report the results from our panel unit root tests using the three available tests with between one and three lags, as well as with and without a trend term. Across the board, and especially in tests with a

TABLE 3.2. *Panel unit root tests: dependent variables*

	No Trend			With Trend		
	1 lag	2 lags	3 lags	1 lag	2 lags	3 lags
Im Pesaran Shin	4/7	6/7	NA	2/7	7/7	NA
Fisher–Dickey-Fuller	10/14	12/14	9/14	7/14	14/14	14/14
Fisher–Phillips-Perron	14/14	14/14	14/14	14/14	14/14	14/14

Notes: Each cell reports the number of tests in which we are able to reject the null hypothesis that all panels contain unit roots at p<.05. Because the two Fisher-type tests report two different test statistics appropriate for our data structure, there are 14 tests reported for each lag level. Because of the short time coverage for some of our series, we were not able to estimate the Im, Pesaran, and Shin (2003) test with three lags.

---

[53] Phillips and Moon (1999) use the term "individuals" to represent "units" or the observations on which one has repeated observations across time.

TABLE 3.3. *Panel unit root tests: continuous independent variables*

Independent Variable	No Trend		Trend	
	F–DF	F–PP	F–DF	F–PP
GDP Growth	6/6	6/6	6/6	6/6
Δ Unemployment	6/6	6/6	4/6	6/6
Unemployment	2/6	0/6	3/6	0/6
Δ Openness	6/6	6/6	6/6	6/6
Δ Total Expenditures	6/6	6/6	6/6	6/6
Total Expenditures	6/6	6/6	6/6	6/6
Age Dependency Ratio	6/6	6/6	6/6	0/6
Deficit	6/6	6/6	4/6	6/6
Hostilities	6/6	6/6	6/6	6/6

Notes: Each cell reports the number of tests in which we are able to reject the null hypothesis that all panels contain unit roots at $p<.05$. Because the two Fisher-type tests (referenced in this table as "F–DF" for Fisher–Dickey-Fuller and "F–PP" for Fisher–Phillips-Perron) report two different test statistics appropriate for our data structure, and because we conducted each test with one, two, and three lags, we report for each test the results from six different tests estimated without trend and six different tests estimated with trend.

trend term and longer lag lengths, we are robustly able to reject the null hypothesis that all of our panels contain unit roots.

3.6.3.2 Stationarity Testing: Independent Variables

In Table 3.3, we display the results from panel unit root tests on our independent variables. Due to gaps in the time series for our independent variables, we were unable to estimate the Im Pesaran Shin test statistics. The overwhelming conclusion of the tests we presented in this table is that we were easily able to reject the null hypothesis that all of our panels contain unit roots. The one exception to this is for our measure of unemployment in levels. Given the preponderance of the evidence in Tables 3.2 and 3.3, we decided to proceed with models of all our variables in levels and to interpret the results for unemployment with added skepticism.

3.6.4 Autocorrelation Diagnostics

One common regression assumption violation in cross-sectional time series data to check for is residual autocorrelation, since – at best – it

3.6 Statistical Appendix

will lead to incorrect standard errors and, at worse, is a sign of model misspecification that could lead to incorrect estimates. While arguably much less of an issue than stationarity conditions (as discussed in Section 3.6.3), we still wanted to check whether our compositional models were well-specified in regard to residual autocorrelation.

In Table 3.4, we present the results of three relatively new autocorrelation tests across two different types of model specifications for each of the seven compositional models estimated in Chapters 3 and 4. These include the bias-corrected $Q(p)$ and $LM(k)$ tests of Born and Breitung (2016) that have been programmed for Stata by Wursten (2018). We also include a version that is robust to heteroskedasticity. In Monte Carlo simulations (see Wursten 2018), these tests have been shown to have good size and power relative to common alternative tests, such as that by Arellano and Bond (1991) or by Wooldridge (2010) and Drukker (2003).

All tests shown in Table 3.4 have a null hypothesis of no serial autocorrelation. One downside to these tests is that they cannot be used in the seemingly unrelated regression (SUR) framework. Instead, we estimate each equation separately, although we include results using both fixed and random intercepts models.[54] Across each of our different compositional dependent variables, we only once reject the null hypothesis of no AR(1) residual autocorrelation (and, even then, only at the .10 level).

Even given our findings in Table 3.4 that suggest there is no residual autocorrelation in any of the equations, it still may be the case that such unmodeled autocorrelation alters our findings. To test this, we estimated both single-equation random intercept and fixed intercept models. We show the estimates of ρ, the estimated value of the AR(1) parameter, in Table 3.5. As is clear from the table, the autoregressive parameter is quite small. The near-zero values suggest very little dependence in the errors between consecutive time periods. Second, we get near-identical results (at least out to three decimal places) no matter whether we use the random or fixed-intercept specifications. Last, comparisons of the coefficients from the two models in Table 3.5 and our main results show that the coefficients across models are nearly identical (these comparisons are not shown here).

---

[54] Moreover, we often find that in the latter estimates there is no quasi-demeaning, meaning that the random intercepts specification *is* the pooled intercept model that we show throughout Chapters 3 and 4.

TABLE 3.4. *No evidence of residual autocorrelation across our compositional seemingly unrelated regression*

Model	Bias-Corrected Born-Breitung $Q(p)$		Bias-Corrected Born-Breitung $LM(k)$		Heteroskedasticity-Robust Born-Breitung	
	RE	FE	RE	FE	RE	FE
$\ln\left(\frac{\text{Social Prot.}}{\text{Housing}}\right)$	1.18	.02	−1.08	−.14	−.67	−.12
$\ln\left(\frac{\text{Relig. \& Cult.}}{\text{Housing}}\right)$	.03	.64	−.25	.72	.82	1.11
$\ln\left(\frac{\text{Health}}{\text{Housing}}\right)$	1.66	.05	−1.32	−.26	−1.65*	−1.14
$\ln\left(\frac{\text{Education}}{\text{Housing}}\right)$	1.24	.03	−1.12	.14	−.92	−.34
$\ln\left(\frac{\text{Econ. Affairs}}{\text{Housing}}\right)$	.88	.10	−.95	.26	−.66	.32
$\ln\left(\frac{\text{Defense}}{\text{Housing}}\right)$	1.90	.12	−1.34	−.21	−.99	−.41
$\ln\left(\frac{\text{Govt. Admin.}}{\text{Housing}}\right)$	1.21	.07	−1.11	−.28	−.91	−.42

Note: $**: p < .05, *: p < .10$. All tests are for AR(1) residual autocorrelation where H_0: No autocorrelation. Tests are distributed $\sim N(0,1)$ for $LM(k)$ and heteroskedasticity-robust, and χ^2 with one degree of freedom for $Q(p)$.

TABLE 3.5. *Random and fixed effects estimates of ρ suggest it is extremely small*

Model	$\hat{\rho}$ (RE)	$\hat{\rho}$ (FE)
$\ln\left(\frac{\text{Social Prot.}}{\text{Housing}}\right)$	.028	.028
$\ln\left(\frac{\text{Relig. \& Cult.}}{\text{Housing}}\right)$	.0153	.153
$\ln\left(\frac{\text{Health}}{\text{Housing}}\right)$	−.013	−.013
$\ln\left(\frac{\text{Education}}{\text{Housing}}\right)$	.074	.074
$\ln\left(\frac{\text{Econ. Affairs}}{\text{Housing}}\right)$	.130	.130
$\ln\left(\frac{\text{Defense}}{\text{Housing}}\right)$	−.012	−.012
$\ln\left(\frac{\text{Govt. Admin.}}{\text{Housing}}\right)$	.012	.012

3.6.5 Additional Notes on Model Specification for Chapter 3

As discussed in Section 3.6.3, through our stationarity diagnostics, we concluded that our compositional dependent variable and most of our independent variables are either stationary or trend stationary. This allows us to use an autoregressive distributed lag (ADL) approach to test our expectations about the drivers of spending compositions. As

3.6 Statistical Appendix

explained in this chapter, our theoretical propositions involve interactions between government ideology and an institutional variable. In Chapter 4, we conduct analyses where the third variable in the interactions is a continuous variable. Here, our model specification for these analyses is a system of equations specified as

$$\ln\left(\frac{y_{ijt}}{y_{i1t}}\right) = s_{ijt} = \varphi s_{ij,t-1} + \delta_j t + \alpha_j + \beta_{jI0}I_{it} + \beta_{jM0}M_{it} + \beta_{jIM0}(I_{it} * M_{it})$$
$$+ \beta_{jI1}I_{i,t-1} + \beta_{jM1}M_{i,t-1} + \beta_{jIM1}(I_{i,t-1} * M_{i,t-1})$$
$$+ Z\beta_{jZ} + \varepsilon_{ijt},$$
$$(3.12)$$

where

- the subscript i is for countries, j is for budget categories, and t is for time,
- s_{ijt} are the seven dependent variables created by taking the log ratio of each of the other expenditure categories (y_{ijt}) relative to the baseline category of housing expenditures (y_{i1t}),
- $\delta_j t$ is a linear time trend, which we include in order to account for any series that consistently move upward or downward over time. This is plausible in several series, such as age dependency ratio or globalization,
- α_j is an intercept term that is allowed to vary across the seven equations but is currently pooled across countries and over time,[55]
- M_{it} is a dummy variable indicating whether or not the government in country i controlled a majority of the seats in the lower chamber of the legislature during year t,
- I_{it} is a dummy variable indicating whether or not the government in country i was from the ideological right during year t,
- Z is a matrix containing the contemporaneous (at time t) and lagged values (at time $t-1$) of all control variables in our models,
- δ_j, α_j, and all of the β_j terms, as well as the matrix β_{jZ} are parameters, and ε_{ijt} is an error term which are all estimated using seemingly unrelated regressions.

---

[55] In Section 3.6.6, we relax the assumption of a pooled intercept for each of these equations and probe the robustness of our results to country fixed and random effects.

TABLE 3.6. *Main compositional results*

	$\ln\left(\frac{\text{Social Prot.}}{\text{Housing}}\right)$	$\ln\left(\frac{\text{Relig. \& Cult.}}{\text{Housing}}\right)$	$\ln\left(\frac{\text{Health}}{\text{Housing}}\right)$	$\ln\left(\frac{\text{Education}}{\text{Housing}}\right)$	$\ln\left(\frac{\text{Econ. Affairs}}{\text{Housing}}\right)$	$\ln\left(\frac{\text{Defense}}{\text{Housing}}\right)$	$\ln\left(\frac{\text{Govt. Admin.}}{\text{Housing}}\right)$
Lagged DV	.914***	.914***	.916***	.923***	.909***	.848***	.915***
	(.007)	(.009)	(.009)	(.007)	(.009)	(.011)	(.008)
GDP Growth$_t$	−.013**	−.000	−.008	−.006	−.000	−.013	−.007
	(.006)	(.006)	(.007)	(.006)	(.007)	(.010)	(.007)
GDP Growth$_{t-1}$	−.003	.001	.003	.002	−.004	−.010	−.002
	(.006)	(.006)	(.007)	(.005)	(.006)	(.009)	(.006)
Δ Unemployment$_t$	.010	.008	.006	.004	.001	−.002	.017
	(.014)	(.014)	(.017)	(.014)	(.015)	(.023)	(.015)
Unemployment$_{t-1}$	.000	.002	.006	−.000	−.001	.000	.000
	(.003)	(.004)	(.004)	(.003)	(.004)	(.006)	(.004)
Δ Openness$_t$	−.001	.000	−.000	−.000	.001	−.001	.000
	(.002)	(.002)	(.002)	(.002)	(.002)	(.003)	(.002)
Δ Openness$_{t-1}$	.002	.002	.001	.001	−.001	.000	.003
	(.002)	(.002)	(.002)	(.002)	(.002)	(.003)	(.002)
Deficit$_t$	−.030***	−.025***	−.029***	−.027***	.004	−.016	−.033***
	(.007)	(.007)	(.009)	(.007)	(.007)	(.012)	(.008)
Deficit$_{t-1}$	.030***	.025***	.033***	.030***	−.001	.014	.036***
	(.007)	(.007)	(.009)	(.007)	(.008)	(.012)	(.008)
Δ Total Expenditures$_t$	.005**	.004*	.004**	.005***	.005***	.000	.006***
	(.002)	(.002)	(.002)	(.002)	(.002)	(.003)	(.002)
Total Expenditures$_{t-1}$	.005*	.003	.004	.005**	.004*	−.001	.007***
	(.002)	(.002)	(.003)	(.002)	(.002)	(.004)	(.003)
Age Dependency Ratio$_t$	−.026	−.001	−.048	−.016	−.047	−.075	−.042
	(.030)	(.030)	(.035)	(.029)	(.031)	(.049)	(.031)

Age Dependency Ratio$_{t-1}$	.028 (.029)	.002 (.030)	.054 (.035)	.019 (.028)	.048 (.030)	.078 (.049)	.046 (.031)
Election$_t$	-.021 (.032)	-.031 (.033)	-.030 (.038)	-.025 (.031)	-.038 (.033)	-.042 (.053)	-.011 (.034)
Election$_{t-1}$	-.029 (.032)	-.014 (.032)	-.023 (.038)	-.015 (.031)	-.042 (.033)	-.042 (.053)	-.028 (.033)
Right$_t$	.043 (.078)	-.005 (.080)	.084 (.092)	.076 (.076)	.094 (.081)	.067 (.129)	.009 (.082)
Right$_{t-1}$	-.029 (.078)	-.013 (.080)	-.029 (.093)	-.050 (.076)	-.078 (.081)	-.031 (.130)	.017 (.082)
Majority$_t$	-.052 (.057)	-.072 (.058)	-.043 (.067)	-.037 (.055)	-.042 (.059)	-.057 (.094)	-.050 (.059)
Majority$_{t-1}$	.089 (.057)	.083 (.058)	.146** (.068)	.072 (.055)	.053 (.059)	.082 (.095)	.075 (.060)
Right$_t$×Majority$_t$	.011 (.089)	.072 (.091)	.006 (.106)	-.023 (.087)	-.011 (.093)	.010 (.148)	.050 (.094)
Right$_{t-1}$×Majority$_{t-1}$	-.066 (.090)	-.086 (.092)	-.134 (.106)	-.038 (.087)	-.028 (.093)	-.067 (.149)	-.120 (.094)
Hostilities$_t$	-.003 (.005)	-.003 (.005)	.004 (.006)	.002 (.005)	.003 (.005)	-.003 (.008)	-.002 (.005)
Hostilities$_{t-1}$	.000 (.005)	.001 (.005)	-.001 (.006)	-.000 (.005)	-.004 (.005)	.013 (.008)	.001 (.005)
Year	.001 (.002)	.005*** (.002)	.005** (.002)	.004** (.002)	.003 (.002)	-.001 (.003)	.000 (.002)
Constant	-2.302 (3.450)	-9.901*** (3.680)	-1.512** (4.179)	-7.705** (3.393)	-5.016 (3.590)	2.201 (5.800)	-.532 (3.621)

Note: $N = 749$.

TABLE 3.7. *Compositional seemingly unrelated regression with fixed effects*

	$\ln\left(\frac{\text{Social Prot.}}{\text{Housing}}\right)$	$\ln\left(\frac{\text{Relig. \& Cult.}}{\text{Housing}}\right)$	$\ln\left(\frac{\text{Health}}{\text{Housing}}\right)$	$\ln\left(\frac{\text{Education}}{\text{Housing}}\right)$	$\ln\left(\frac{\text{Econ. Affairs}}{\text{Housing}}\right)$	$\ln\left(\frac{\text{Defense}}{\text{Housing}}\right)$	$\ln\left(\frac{\text{Govt. Admin.}}{\text{Housing}}\right)$
Lagged DV	.854***	.828***	.862***	.852***	.827***	.791***	.846***
	(.009)	(.013)	(.013)	(.011)	(.013)	(.016)	(.010)
GDP Growth$_t$	−.009	.004	−.003	−.004	.004	−.006	−.003
	(.006)	(.007)	(.008)	(.006)	(.007)	(.011)	(.007)
GDP Growth$_{t-1}$	−.002	.004	.007	.004	−.001	−.006	.003
	(.006)	(.006)	(.007)	(.006)	(.006)	(.010)	(.006)
Δ Unemployment$_t$	.010	.009	.012	.006	.001	.005	.024
	(.015)	(.015)	(.018)	(.014)	(.015)	(.025)	(.016)
Unemployment$_{t-1}$	−.006	−.001	.005	−.001	−.006	−.007	.004
	(.006)	(.006)	(.007)	(.006)	(.006)	(.010)	(.006)
Δ Openness$_t$	−.001	.000	−.000	−.000	.002	−.000	.000
	(.002)	(.002)	(.002)	(.002)	(.002)	(.003)	(.002)
Δ Openness$_{t-1}$	.002	.002	.001	.001	−.000	.001	.003
	(.002)	(.002)	(.002)	(.002)	(.002)	(.003)	(.002)
Deficit$_t$	−.026***	−.022***	−.026***	−.024***	.007	−.010	−.028***
	(.007)	(.007)	(.009)	(.007)	(.007)	(.012)	(.007)
Deficit$_{t-1}$	.034***	.029***	.035***	.032***	.005	.019	.041***
	(.007)	(.007)	(.009)	(.007)	(.008)	(.012)	(.008)
Δ Total Expenditures$_t$	.005***	.004**	.005**	.005***	.006***	.001	.006***
	(.002)	(.002)	(.002)	(.002)	(.002)	(.003)	(.002)
Total Expenditures$_{t-1}$	.005**	.004	.005	.005**	.005**	−.001	.007***
	(.002)	(.002)	(.003)	(.002)	(.002)	(.004)	(.002)
Age Dependency Ratio$_t$	−.091***	−.046	−.106***	−.056*	−.097***	−.154***	−.099***
	(.034)	(.034)	(.041)	(.032)	(.035)	(.057)	(.035)

	(1)	(2)	(3)	(4)	(5)	(6)
Age Dependency Ratio$_{t-1}$	.094*** (.033)	.049 (.034)	.113*** (.040)	.062* (.032)	.098*** (.034)	.155*** (.056)	.102*** (.035)
Election$_t$	−.017 (.032)	−.032 (.032)	−.040 (.038)	−.025 (.030)	−.038 (.033)	−.057 (.053)	−.013 (.033)
Election$_{t-1}$	−.030 (.031)	−.022 (.032)	−.038 (.037)	−.021 (.030)	−.048 (.032)	−.061 (.052)	−.036 (.033)
Right$_t$	.055 (.078)	.012 (.079)	.101 (.094)	.081 (.075)	.122 (.080)	.070 (.130)	.028 (.082)
Right$_{t-1}$	−.025 (.078)	−.011 (.079)	−.033 (.094)	−.047 (.075)	−.068 (.081)	−.043 (.131)	−.000 (.082)
majoritygovt	−.059 (.057)	−.072 (.058)	−.052 (.069)	−.037 (.055)	−.046 (.059)	−.060 (.096)	−.057 (.060)
lmajoritygovt	.090 (.058)	.097 (.059)	.145** (.070)	.083 (.056)	.053 (.060)	.061 (.097)	.088 (.061)
Right$_t$×Majority$_t$	.010 (.089)	.062 (.091)	.008 (.107)	−.020 (.086)	−.009 (.092)	.024 (.149)	.058 (.094)
Right$_{t-1}$×Majority$_{t-1}$	−.065 (.090)	−.104 (.092)	−.131 (.108)	−.043 (.087)	−.025 (.093)	−.055 (.151)	−.109 (.095)
Hostilities$_t$	.000 (.006)	.003 (.006)	.004 (.007)	.006 (.006)	.005 (.006)	−.010 (.010)	−.001 (.006)
Hostilities$_{t-1}$	.002 (.006)	.006 (.006)	−.002 (.007)	.003 (.005)	−.003 (.006)	.006 (.009)	.001 (.006)
Year	.004** (.002)	.012*** (.002)	.009*** (.002)	.008*** (.002)	.004** (.002)	−.000 (.003)	.002 (.002)
Constant	−8.266** (4.025)	−24.218*** (4.425)	−18.877*** (4.939)	−15.621*** (3.950)	−7.954* (4.148)	1.451 (6.746)	−3.805 (4.223)

Note: $N = 749$. Country fixed effects included but not shown.

TABLE 3.8. *Random effects compositional results*

	(1) $\ln\left(\frac{\text{Social Prot.}}{\text{Housing}}\right)$	(2) $\ln\left(\frac{\text{Relig. \& Cult.}}{\text{Housing}}\right)$	(3) $\ln\left(\frac{\text{Health}}{\text{Housing}}\right)$	(4) $\ln\left(\frac{\text{Education}}{\text{Housing}}\right)$	(5) $\ln\left(\frac{\text{Econ. Affairs}}{\text{Housing}}\right)$	(6) $\ln\left(\frac{\text{Defense}}{\text{Housing}}\right)$	(7) $\ln\left(\frac{\text{Govt. Admin.}}{\text{Housing}}\right)$
Lagged DV	.857*** (.018)	.879*** (.017)	.859*** (.017)	.843*** (.019)	.820*** (.021)	.837*** (.015)	.853*** (.019)
GDP Growth$_t$	−.016** (.006)	−.001 (.007)	−.011 (.008)	−.007 (.006)	−.002 (.007)	−.014 (.011)	−.010 (.007)
GDP Growth$_{t−1}$	−.006 (.006)	.000 (.006)	.001 (.007)	.000 (.005)	−.006 (.006)	−.010 (.009)	−.004 (.006)
Δ Unemployment$_t$	.006 (.014)	.007 (.015)	.001 (.017)	.002 (.014)	−.000 (.015)	−.002 (.024)	.011 (.015)
Unemployment$_{t−1}$	.001 (.004)	.002 (.004)	.007* (.004)	−.001 (.003)	−.000 (.004)	.001 (.006)	.002 (.004)
Δ Openness$_t$	−.001 (.002)	.000 (.002)	−.000 (.002)	−.000 (.002)	.002 (.002)	−.001 (.003)	−.000 (.002)
Δ Openness$_{t−1}$	.002 (.002)	.002 (.002)	.001 (.002)	.001 (.002)	−.000 (.002)	.000 (.003)	.003 (.002)
Deficit$_t$	−.032*** (.007)	−.027*** (.008)	−.031*** (.009)	−.029*** (.007)	.000 (.008)	−.017 (.012)	−.035*** (.008)
Deficit$_{t−1}$	.029*** (.007)	.025*** (.008)	.032*** (.009)	.029*** (.007)	−.000 (.008)	.014 (.012)	.036*** (.008)
Δ Total Expenditures$_t$	.004** (.002)	.004* (.002)	.004* (.002)	.005*** (.002)	.005*** (.002)	.000 (.003)	.006*** (.002)
Total Expenditures$_{t−1}$	.004* (.002)	.04 (.002)	.04 (.003)	.005** (.002)	.005* (.003)	−.001 (.004)	.006** (.003)
Age Dependency Ratio$_t$	−.028 (.030)	−.004 (.031)	−.069* (.036)	−.029 (.029)	−.058* (.031)	−.074 (.050)	−.048 (.032)

Age Dependency Ratio$_{t-1}$	.029 (.030)	.003 (.030)	.075** (.036)	.033 (.029)	.057* (.031)	.077 (.049)	.052* (.031)
Election$_t$	-.014 (.033)	-.028 (.033)	-.024 (.039)	-.014 (.032)	-.029 (.034)	-.040 (.054)	-.003 (.034)
Election$_{t-1}$	-.024 (.032)	-.011 (.033)	-.020 (.038)	-.006 (.031)	-.036 (.034)	-.042 (.053)	-.022 (.034)
Right$_t$	.033 (.079)	-.002 (.081)	.090 (.094)	.088 (.077)	.095 (.082)	.068 (.131)	.008 (.083)
Right$_{t-1}$	-.031 (.080)	-.014 (.081)	-.023 (.095)	-.044 (.077)	-.071 (.083)	-.030 (.132)	.018 (.084)
majoritygovt	-.053 (.058)	-.074 (.059)	-.031 (.068)	-.036 (.056)	-.041 (.060)	-.058 (.096)	-.053 (.060)
lmajoritygovt	.091 (.058)	.084 (.059)	.172** (.069)	.082 (.056)	.061 (.060)	.083 (.096)	.078 (.061)
Right$_t$ × Majority$_t$	.022 (.091)	.070 (.093)	-.002 (.108)	-.033 (.088)	-.006 (.095)	.008 (.151)	.058 (.095)
Right$_{t-1}$ × Majority$_{t-1}$	-.068 (.091)	-.083 (.093)	-.147 (.108)	-.048 (.089)	-.033 (.095)	-.070 (.151)	-.121 (.096)
Hostilities$_t$	-.003 (.005)	-.003 (.005)	.006 (.006)	.003 (.005)	.002 (.005)	-.003 (.008)	-.002 (.005)
Hostilities$_{t-1}$	-.000 (.005)	.001 (.005)	-.000 (.006)	.000 (.005)	-.005 (.005)	.013 (.008)	.001 (.005)
Year	.001 (.002)	.007*** (.002)	.008*** (.002)	.007*** (.002)	.003 (.002)	-.002 (.003)	.000 (.002)
Constant	-2.472 (3.510)	-14.142*** (4.134)	-15.409*** (4.429)	-13.368*** (3.667)	-5.170 (3.652)	3.076 (5.954)	.061 (3.686)

Note: $N = 749$. Results are from equation-by-equation random intercept FGLS.

TABLE 3.9. *Pooled seemingly unrelated regression, dropping imputed vars*

	$\ln\left(\frac{\text{Social Prot.}}{\text{Housing}}\right)$	$\ln\left(\frac{\text{Relig. \& Cult.}}{\text{Housing}}\right)$	$\ln\left(\frac{\text{Health}}{\text{Housing}}\right)$	$\ln\left(\frac{\text{Education}}{\text{Housing}}\right)$	$\ln\left(\frac{\text{Econ. Affairs}}{\text{Housing}}\right)$	$\ln\left(\frac{\text{Defense}}{\text{Housing}}\right)$	$\ln\left(\frac{\text{Govt. Admin.}}{\text{Housing}}\right)$
Lagged DV	.916***	.917***	.919***	.925***	.911***	.848***	.919***
	(.007)	(.009)	(.009)	(.007)	(.009)	(.011)	(.008)
GDP Growth$_t$	−.013*	.000	−.007	−.004	.002	−.012	−.006
	(.006)	(.007)	(.008)	(.006)	(.007)	(.011)	(.007)
GDP Growth$_{t-1}$	−.003	.001	.003	.002	−.004	−.010	−.002
	(.006)	(.006)	(.007)	(.005)	(.006)	(.009)	(.006)
Δ Unemployment$_t$	.012	.010	.009	.007	.002	.000	.019
	(.014)	(.014)	(.017)	(.014)	(.015)	(.024)	(.015)
Unemployment$_{t-1}$	−.000	.002	.007	−.001	−.001	−.000	.000
	(.004)	(.004)	(.004)	(.003)	(.004)	(.006)	(.004)
Δ Openness$_t$	−.001	.000	−.001	−.000	.002	−.001	−.000
	(.002)	(.002)	(.002)	(.002)	(.002)	(.003)	(.002)
Δ Openness$_{t-1}$	.002	.002	.001	.001	−.001	.001	.003
	(.002)	(.002)	(.002)	(.002)	(.002)	(.003)	(.002)
Deficit$_t$	−.032***	−.027***	−.030***	−.028***	.005	−.018	−.035***
	(.008)	(.008)	(.009)	(.007)	(.008)	(.013)	(.008)
Deficit$_{t-1}$	.032***	.026***	.034***	.031***	−.003	.015	.039***
	(.008)	(.008)	(.009)	(.007)	(.008)	(.013)	(.008)
Δ Total Expenditures$_t$	.005***	.004**	.005**	.006***	.006***	.001	.006***
	(.002)	(.002)	(.002)	(.002)	(.002)	(.003)	(.002)
Total Expenditures$_{t-1}$	.005**	.004*	.005	.006**	.005*	−.001	.007***
	(.002)	(.003)	(.003)	(.002)	(.003)	(.004)	(.003)
Age Dependency Ratio$_t$	−.028	−.013	−.052	−.018	−.049	−.074	−.043
	(.030)	(.031)	(.036)	(.029)	(.031)	(.050)	(.031)

Age Dependency Ratio$_{t-1}$	.030 (.030)	.013 (.030)	.058 (.035)	.021 (.029)	.049 (.031)	.077 (.049)	.047 (.031)
Election$_t$	-.018 (.033)	-.021 (.033)	-.030 (.039)	-.024 (.032)	-.038 (.034)	-.042 (.054)	-.012 (.034)
Election$_{t-1}$	-.025 (.032)	-.010 (.033)	-.017 (.038)	-.009 (.031)	-.037 (.033)	-.037 (.054)	-.025 (.034)
Right$_t$	.042 (.079)	-.001 (.080)	.085 (.093)	.077 (.076)	.098 (.082)	.066 (.131)	.012 (.082)
Right$_{t-1}$	.027 (.079)	-.008 (.080)	-.025 (.094)	-.046 (.077)	-.077 (.082)	-.030 (.132)	.022 (.083)
Majority$_t$	-.053 (.057)	-.073 (.058)	-.042 (.068)	-.036 (.056)	-.038 (.059)	-.057 (.095)	-.047 (.060)
Majority$_{t-1}$	.089 (.058)	.087 (.059)	.150** (.069)	.074 (.056)	.051 (.060)	.080 (.096)	.080 (.060)
Right$_t$ × Majority$_t$	.014 (.090)	.065 (.092)	.000 (.107)	-.027 (.087)	-.009 (.094)	.016 (.150)	.048 (.094)
Right$_{t-1}$ × Majority$_{t-1}$	-.067 (.090)	-.101 (.092)	-.138 (.107)	-.042 (.088)	-.028 (.094)	-.063 (.150)	-.121 (.094)
Hostilities$_t$	-.003 (.005)	-.002 (.005)	.004 (.006)	.002 (.005)	.004 (.005)	-.003 (.008)	-.002 (.005)
Hostilities$_{t-1}$	.001 (.005)	.000 (.005)	-.000 (.006)	-.000 (.005)	-.004 (.005)	.013 (.009)	.002 (.005)
Year	.002 (.002)	.005*** (.002)	.005** (.002)	.004** (.002)	.003 (.002)	-.001 (.003)	.001 (.002)
Constant	-2.945 (3.508)	-1.896*** (3.707)	-1.754** (4.239)	-7.970** (3.439)	-5.434 (3.637)	1.750 (5.900)	-1.133 (3.665)

Note: $N = 733$.

3.6.6 Tabular Results from Chapter 3 and Robustness

While we prefer showing graphical depictions of our results, in this section, we show a series of tables that depict both our main results and several robustness checks:

- In Table 3.6, we show the tabular results of the basic model specification used throughout this chapter and in Chapter 4.
- Since our main set of results come from a fully pooled SUR model, in Table 3.7, we show the same SUR model but also include country fixed effects.
- In Table 3.8, we show equation-by-equation random effects models.[56]
- In Section 2.5, we discussed how we imputed a small number of observations: United Kingdom (1995–1996), France (1994), Luxembourg (1996–1997), Norway (1978–1979), Greece (1978–1979), Spain (1986), New Zealand (2003 and 2008), Bulgaria (1995–1997), and Slovenia (1997–1998). In Table 3.9, we show the robustness of our results to dropping these country–years.

---

[56] Estimating both SUR models and random intercepts is computationally intensive, and the SUR model realistically only provides more efficient estimates, so these results can be considered conservative.

4

The Effects of Elections, Economics, and International Shocks on the Expenditure Pie

We will do what we need to get through this. And then at the end we will look at what that means for our budget. The other thing comes first now.
German Chancellor Angela Merkel, talking about the COVID-19 pandemic.[1]

When explaining budgetary tradeoffs, what governments prefer is key. However, they may find it easier to accomplish their ideologically driven goals under certain conditions rather than others. In Chapter 3, we established that government ideology is a key determinant of budgetary tradeoffs, but we also showed that the power conferred on majority governments helps them to accomplish their ideologically driven goals. In this chapter, we further investigate the role of context in shaping budgetary compositions by developing and testing a series of competing theoretical propositions about how election timing, economic conditions, and international circumstances may change how governments allocate funds.

From the perspective of governments, in an ideal world, they would see their ideological visions seamlessly become reality. But, as we witnessed in Chapter 3, the context that surrounds governments can, at certain times, moderate this. To some extent, groups of scholars have explored the relationships between budgets and contextual conditions – elections, economics, and international factors – but two important factors have

---

[1] www.reuters.com/article/us-health-coronavirus-germany-debt/merkel-distances-herself-from-fiscal-policy-of-no-new-borrowing-idUSKBN20Y1SC. Last accessed October 8, 2021.

remained in the shadows (and, at times, been completely ignored). First, while scholars have acknowledged that conditions, such as a downward sliding economy, may influence budgets directly, we know less about how such factors constrain or liberate government decision-making. Second, they have largely ignored the compositional nature of budgets, those tradeoffs between categories. As Dreher, Sturm, and Ursprung (2008) point out, there is little research that considers how one part of the budget may shift in response to the opening of an economy on a global scale, while other budgetary categories may not move at all. We argue that a similar logic may hold for other types of shifts. Analyses that ignore the compositional nature of budgets may thus obscure important political and economic relationships between policy areas.

While the idea that circumstances can make the implementation of ideological visions easier or harder is uncontroversial, the mechanisms through which electoral, economic, and international conditions affect government decision-making remain a bit murky. In this chapter, we consider a variety of arguments about how these factors influence when we are more or less likely to see the effects of governments' ideological preferences on the composition of budgets. We focus on five major factors that have been thought to shape political budgeting: elections, unemployment, economic growth, globalization, and international hostilities. In Figure 4.1, we incorporate these five factors into our theoretical framework as "Electoral Considerations," "Economic Circumstances," and "International Circumstances."[2] As shown in the theoretical figure, we expect that these conditions, at times, will alter the ability of governments to follow through on their ideological priorities in budgetary compositions (i.e., they will help determine the "Feasible Shifts").

For each condition, we develop expectations about how and when we will see electoral, economic, and international factors shape the influence of ideology on budgetary compositions. We discuss our expectations as "tournaments," because, for each contextual factor, we allow two sets of possibilities to compete against each other. The first, which we

---

[2] Other major factors that might exert similar influences include societal changes such as demographic shifts and public opinion (McGann, Dellepiane-Avellaneda, and Bartle 2022). The former are such slow-moving processes that we cannot include them in the study as interactions, but we do add them as controls. The latter would be informative to include, but we cannot because of data limitations.

The Effects of Contexts on the Expenditure Pie

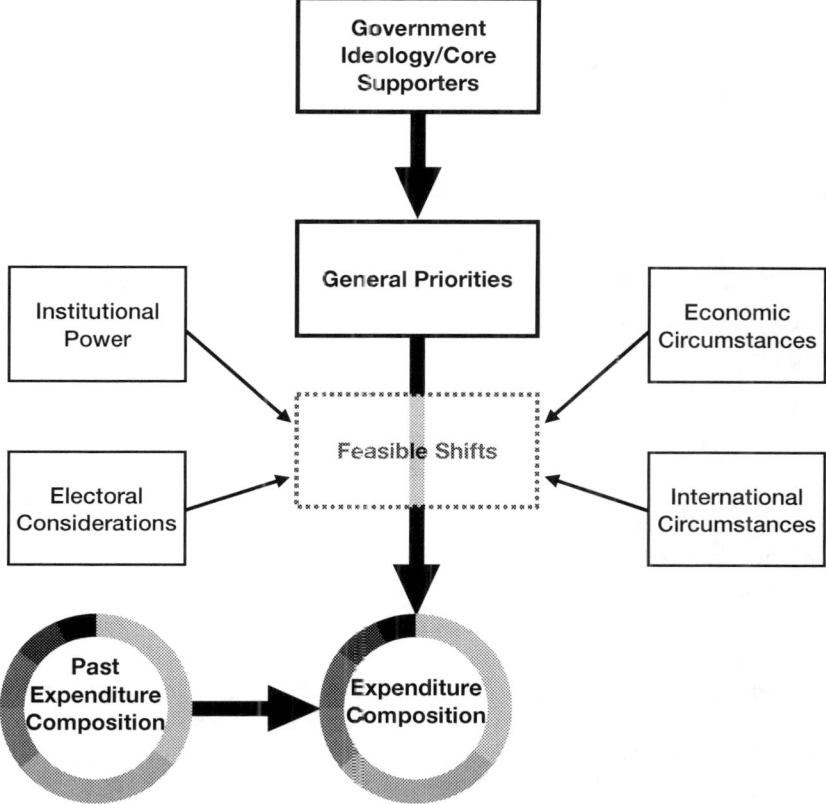

FIGURE 4.1. Summary diagram

reference throughout this chapter as "Expect 1," is our set of expectations where ideology will be the main driver, but the context will combine with ideology to shape our expectations. Under these circumstances, we expect that some, but not all, of a government's ideological preferences will be achieved. The second competing theoretical expectation, which we reference as "Expect 2," is a set of expectations where the context mostly overwhelms ideology. We anticipate that, unlike the previous scenario, governments will sometimes go against their ideological priorities because of contextual conditions. We test our tournaments of competing expectations using dynamic pie models that include interactions between these changing circumstances, government majority status, and government ideology. As we discuss briefly in Section 4.4, the modeling strategy that we use to test our theoretical expectations in this chapter is very similar to the one we use in Chapter 3.[3]

4.1 ELECTORAL CONSIDERATIONS AND SPENDING TRADEOFFS

One of the defining characteristics of democracies is that governing policymakers always have one eye on the next electoral campaign. Given the implicit success of a government's last campaign, scholars expect ideological visions to exert a strong influence on budgetary behavior.[4] However, electoral pressures may affect the timing of budgetary changes and perhaps even influence whether they occur at all. For instance, in the lead up to an election, governments may find it beneficial to shift resources to budget categories that boost the economy or benefit larger groups of people as a means to gain some electoral ground (Franzese 2002a; Dubois 2016; Philips 2016). *The Economist* has highlighted this relationship: "[i]ncumbent politicians know that if the economy is doing well, they are much more likely to be re-elected ... [s]mall wonder, then, that many governments attempt to manipulate the economy to boost their political fortunes."[5]

As for discussing contexts that can affect government success when reallocating budgets, elections may influence the timing of these changes. For incumbents, elections usually represent the largest hurdle to remaining in office, but these events involve two priorities that are often at odds with one another. On the one hand, parties must seek to maintain their base of electoral support (Cox and McCubbins 1986; Calvo and Murillo 2004; Nichter 2008). However, on the other hand, they need to look to broaden their voting bloc by attracting voters beyond their typical support base (Dixit and Londregan 1996; Kwon 2005). Due to these competing electoral pressures, incumbents face a strong incentive to pursue a mixture of strategies to win the support of voters (Rogoff and Sibert 1988; Alesina and Roubini 1992). These tactics have been theorized to lead to increasing expenditures – typically by running budget deficits – just prior to elections. While the beneficial electoral boost from increased expenditures

---

[3] The only real difference is an additional interaction term, as we show in Equation (4.2).
[4] Although it is possible for political parties to lose votes and seats and still end up in governing coalitions, Martin and Stevenson (2010) demonstrate that parties and groups of parties that gain seats are more likely to enter into coalitions.
[5] Source: www.economist.com/finance-and-economics/2015/04/18/string-pushers. Last accessed October 24, 2021.

4.1 Electoral Considerations and Spending Tradeoffs

may come just before the election, the painful process of paying off these increased deficits, through slashed expenditures or increases in revenues, would occur right at the start of a new legislative term, allowing the cycle to repeat again at the next election (Nordhaus 1975).[6] These periodic swings in expenditures have become known as "political budget cycles."

If and how governments use the budget for electoral gain has led to a large body of research in political economy on political budget cycles (for reviews of the literature, see Franzese and Jusko 2005; Dubois 2016; Philips 2016).[7] The focus varies, with some scholars demonstrating that parties in government may increase total expenditures during elections (Alt and Lassen 2006), while others uncover increases in specific categories of spending (Vergne 2009; Brender and Drazen 2013) such as infrastructure (Aidt, Veiga, and Veiga 2011), grants to subnational entities (John and Ward 2001; Padovano 2012), or administrative expenditures (Enkelmann and Leibrecht 2013). When highlighting specific policy areas, the approach has been to think in terms of pairwise tradeoffs (for instance, manipulation of capital versus current expenditures or vice versa) rather than as budgetary compositions and allocations, as we do in this book.

A growing body of research has delved further into the issue of political budget cycles, focusing less on if governments use them and more on how they use them to build support. This line of reasoning looks into whether context influences how governments rely on budgetary spending for electoral gains (Dubois 2016). One of the most important contextual factors is ideology. If governments pursue political budget cycles, parties of the right and left may differ in what they choose to manipulate around elections (Hibbs 1977). Recent research has argued that incumbents will increase spending on visible areas, though there is little agreement on what actually constitutes a "visible" expenditure area (Philips 2016, 2017). They may spend in areas most salient to their supporters, while cutting back expenditures in other areas; however, empirical evidence for ideological differences in shifts in spending allocations during elections is some-

---

[6] Note that such deficit increases must be paid off by whoever wins the election – either the (successful) incumbent party or the opposition. As such, governments may increase deficits in order to fiscally "tie the hands" of future opposition governments (Persson and Svensson 1989; Weisstanner 2017).

[7] A related literature involves the manipulation of monetary policy (e.g., interest rates or the money supply) around elections and is known as "political business cycles" (Hibbs 1977; Tufte 1978). Other less common terms include "partisan" or "opportunistic" cycles (Philips 2017).

what mixed. For instance, Saez and Sinha (2010) find no evidence that ideology has an influence on the type of spending that occurs in Indian states. In contrast, Veiga and Veiga (2007) find that left parties tend to spend more than right ones during elections in Portuguese municipalities. Recent work on established democracies of the OECD show some support for political budget cycles, highlighting the use of increased spending on visible and short-term policies (Castro and Martins 2018), as well as on social spending compared to "non-social" spending (Herwartz and Theilen 2017).

If governments do engage in political budget cycles, the action may be at the level of expenditure categories, not the overall budget. The 2016 Australian election highlights this, because while "The budget [was] unusual for pre-election budgets in that it contain[ed] few sweeteners," the Liberal Party did allocate extra funds to the defense budget as a means to appease voters in a region of the country with a submarine industry where other budgetary decisions had been unpopular (*The Economist*; Australia Government delivers a lackluster pre-election budget).[8] This move by a center-right party in government illustrates how governments of various ideological stripes may shift resources to different policy areas in order to shore up their supporters and/or to build new electoral coalitions. These reallocations may not affect total expenditures or may change them only slightly. Suggestive evidence for this comes from Castro and Martins (2018), who, in a study of spending at both the aggregate and disaggregate policy area levels, emphasize hidden decisions where governments strategically use spending on specific policies to bolster their electoral chances.

While prior work has shown the importance of political budget cycles – even if the evidence for ideological-based manipulation is weak – it has been limited by examining single expenditure areas separately. For instance, researchers have separately considered grants (John and Ward 2001), administrative (Enkelmann and Leibrecht 2013), and social welfare expenditures (Chang 2008) as candidates for pre-electoral manipulation. While this helps to answer the question of whether or not expenditures (or a particular expenditure category) increase around elections, it does not facilitate our understanding of the political budgeting tradeoffs that governments may undertake.

---

[8] http://country.eiu.com.srv-proxy1.library.tamu.edu/article.aspx?articleid=1744194758. Last accessed May 26, 2021.

4.1 Electoral Considerations and Spending Tradeoffs

Even research that goes beyond individual allocations by exploring a range of multiple policy areas is limited in what it can say about budgetary tradeoffs. For example, Saez and Sinha (2010) analyze state expenditures in India across six budgetary categories separately and find evidence that health, agriculture, and social security expenditures decrease in state election years, while expenditures on irrigation increase. Bove, Efthyvoulou, and Navas (2017, p. 584) find that "governments tend to bias outlays towards social expenditure and away from military expenditure at election times." While these works that model electoral effects for multiple (but individual) policy areas move us one step closer to budgetary reality (Dreher, Sturm, and Ursprung 2008; Gemmell, Kneller, and Sanz 2008; Vergne 2009; De Haan and Klomp 2013), they still cannot explain where relative changes occur. Might there be an "electoral portfolio" of budgetary allocations that correspond with visible and/or short-term gains that governments prefer prior to an election, perhaps even regardless of ideology? Our compositional approach can help answer these questions.

4.1.1 Expectations

Elections are often seen as the time when it is *most* important for governments to emphasize their constituents' preferred policy areas, since they need to motivate their base of support in order to win re-election. In Figure 4.2, we highlight the role of elections in influencing government behavior on budgetary tradeoffs. While we do not expect there to be differences in terms of overall spending between right and left governments – both have an incentive to spend more during elections – we may see different budgetary categories emphasized during elections, depending on whether a right or left government is running for re-election. Indeed, much of the prior research on the ideological conditioning of political budget cycles suggests that there is *no* difference between left and right governments in terms of overall spending during elections (c.f., Philips 2016). However, there may be budgetary allocation differences based on our ideological expectations, which we presented in Table 3.1.

We present our competing set of theoretical expectations for electoral considerations in Table 4.1. Each ideological priority is indicated by a "✓," and our expectations as to the direction of the budgetary change is given by either a "+" (budgetary category will increase) or a "−" (budgetary category will decrease). Categories for which we do not have a theoretical expectation or those which we theorize will neither increase

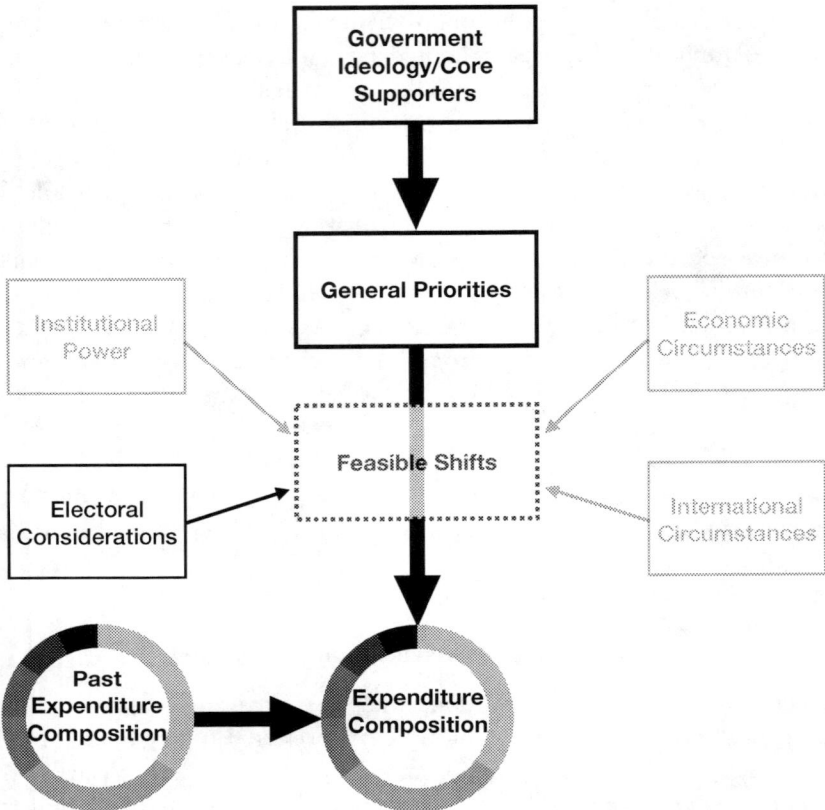

FIGURE 4.2. Highlighting how election considerations affect the budgetary composition

nor decrease in response to the shock are left blank. For Expect 1, we argue that left and right governments will pursue their general ideological priorities that offer the most in terms of short-term visible gains, so we expect left governments to reallocate budgets toward government administration, housing, and social protection. All of these offer immediate results that appeal to their supporters through public sector jobs and/or targeted assistance.[9] In contrast, when right governments follow an ideologically driven strategy during elections, we anticipate a shift in resources to defense and economic affairs. These offer visible support through subsidies that benefit their core supporters.

---

[9] Aaskoven (2019) finds a partisan effect for public employment during election years.

4.2 Domestic Economic Circumstances and Tradeoffs

TABLE 4.1. *Expected reactions to an election shock*

	Left Government			Right Government		
Policy Area	Priority	Ideologically Consistent (Expect 1)	Context Overwhelms (Expect 2)	Priority	Ideologically Consistent (Expect 1)	Context Overwhelms (Expect 2)
Defense				✓	+	
Economic Affairs				✓	+	
Education	✓			✓		
Govt Admin	✓	+				
Health	✓			✓		
Housing	✓	+				
Religion & Culture						
Social Protection	✓	+	−			+

Note: ✓ indicates a government priority. + government will increase share of policy area.

In Expect 2, where electoral considerations overwhelm ideological priorities, we expect governments to act more opportunistically, with both the left and right deciding to move resources to the main policy area that offers visible and immediate results during an election: social protection. While governments may target the funds within social assistance to benefit different groups (the lower class versus the middle class, for example), both the left and right should find this shift to be the most electorally beneficial. Now that we have considered elections, we turn to our expectations about the domestic economy in Section 4.2.

4.2 DOMESTIC ECONOMIC CIRCUMSTANCES: HOW UNEMPLOYMENT AND GROWTH AFFECT SPENDING TRADEOFFS

Depending on the health of the economy, domestic economic circumstances can shape budgets in various ways. A thriving economy can produce more revenue for governments to allocate and also provide more jobs and opportunities for people who are relying less on government assistance. Therefore, favorable economic conditions can offer opportunities for governments to shift resources among budgetary policy areas with less fear of political backlash. Governments can focus on reallocating

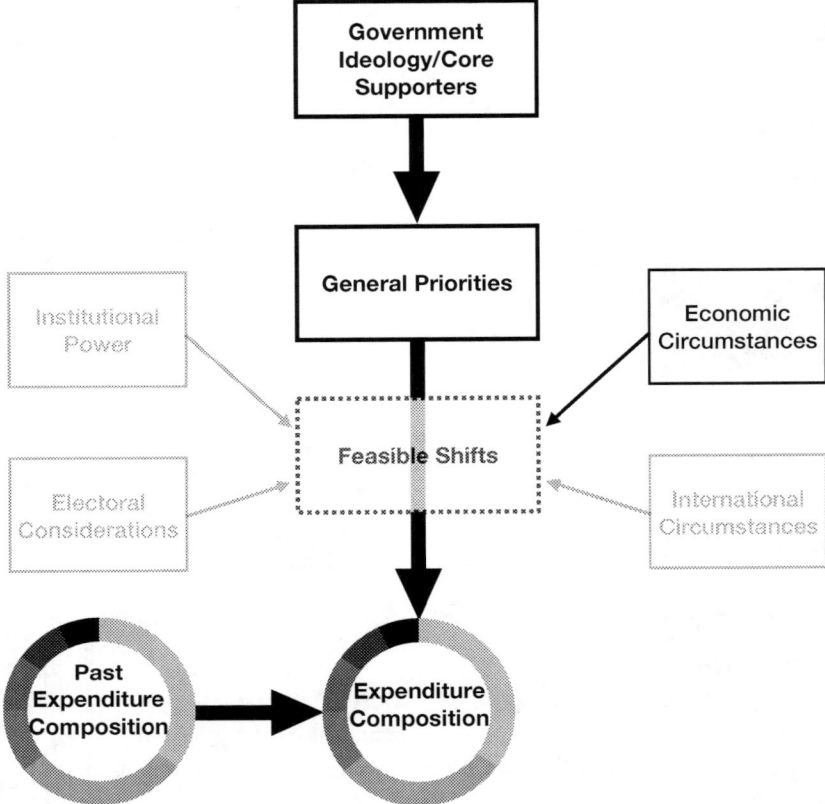

FIGURE 4.3. Highlighting how economic factors affect the budgetary composition

funds without the pressure of necessary decreases. Quite the opposite can occur during economic downturns. With reduced revenues and more people relying on government assistance because of lost employment, lower wages, etc., budgetary wiggle-room for governments may diminish and lead to politically challenging times (Cameron 2012). But the extent to which these changing economic conditions affect government budgetary tradeoffs remains an open question.

In this section, we present competing arguments for how economic conditions can affect governments' budgetary behavior. Keeping in mind our overarching argument, we highlight how economic circumstances play into our theoretical diagram, as shown in Figure 4.3. Varying economic contexts can present opportunities or challenges to governments' abilities to alter budgetary compositions, so we present a tournament of

4.2 Domestic Economic Circumstances and Tradeoffs 125

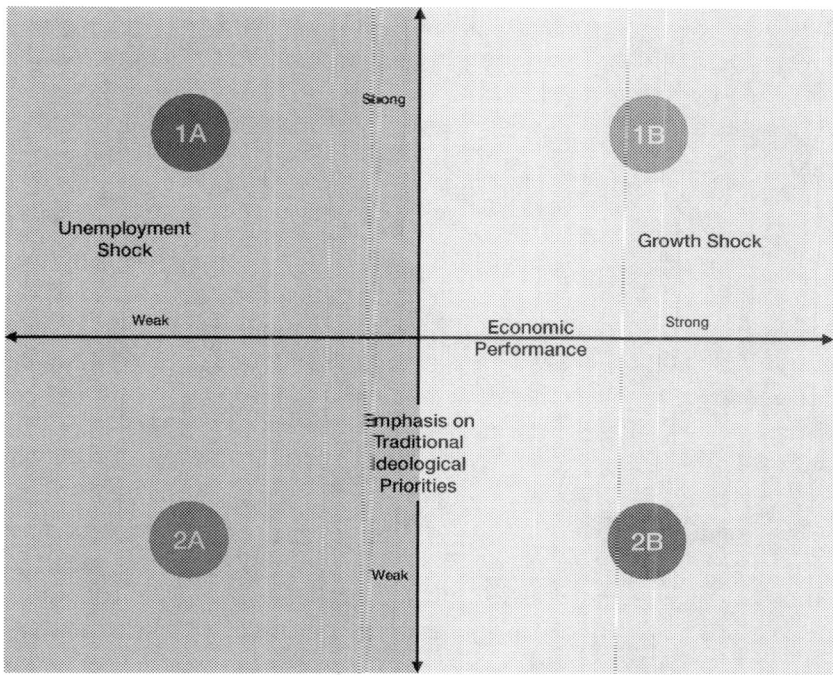

FIGURE 4.4. Competing expectations about economic performance and policy priorities

arguments to explain budgetary reallocations under both good and bad economic conditions.

In Figure 4.4, we present a visual summary of our competing expectations about economic performance and policy priorities. The horizontal arrow depicts the health of the economy, with the right-hand side of the figure representing strong economic performance with a positive shock to growth, while the left-hand side indicates a weak economy with a rising unemployment rate. The vertical arrow depicts the varying emphasis on governments' ideological priorities. The top of the figure (quadrants 1A and 1B) illustrates a strong emphasis on ideology, with governments preferring to shift budgetary resources to suit their ideological preferences, and the bottom cells of the figure (quadrants 2A and 2B) indicate when ideological priorities are weaker. This figure highlights competing arguments for what drives budgetary compositions during varying economic performances. Some previous research has argued that more positive economic conditions allow governments extra room to please their core supporters, while less favorable conditions constrain governments' spending choices, leading to policy budgets that are farther from their ideals (Lipsmeyer 2011). Alternatively, governments may react to economic performance measures in the opposite way. They may interpret favorable conditions as opportunities to expand their support by allocating funds to secondary policy areas but react to unfavorable environments by shoring up their preferred policy areas.

We begin with the stronger economic outlook, a Growth Shock, on the right side of the figure. Cell 1B represents a scenario in which rosier economic conditions make for easier times for governments to reallocate expenditures on policy areas based on their ideologies. This cell reflects the argument that governments may have more room to maneuver during a robust economy versus economically tight times. According to this logic, economically favorable conditions offer governments an environment where their own partisan or ideological priorities can take center stage. For left governments, they will shore up spending on social and employment-related benefits, while trading off relative spending on defense. Right governments, in contrast, should take the opportunity to shift responsibility for social policies away from the government by allocating relatively fewer resources to those policies and, instead, prioritize defense and economic policy areas.[10] For example, in 2015, when the Irish coalition government of the larger center-right party, Fine Gael, and the smaller center-left Labour Party projected an improving economic outlook, government ministers hinted that they would "cut taxes and protect public spending levels" to appease their supporters (*The Economist*; Ireland approaching election shapes economic decisions).[11] With lower unemployment rates, increasing job numbers, and rising revenue, governments have the budgetary and electoral leeway to worry less about automatic stabilizers (e.g., unemployment or retirement benefits) eating into budgets and, instead, can follow through on shifting resources to their preferred policy areas.

---

[10] As we discussed in Chapter 3, we include measures of changes to budget size in our models, so these theoretical considerations are the effects of economics and government ideology holding constant the size of the budget.

[11] http://country.eiu.com.srv-proxy1.library.tamu.edu/article.aspx?articleid=152686599. Last accessed November 11, 2016.

4.2 Domestic Economic Circumstances and Tradeoffs

Under a strong economy, the competing story in quadrant 2B in Figure 4.4 focuses on the context mostly overwhelming ideology. Governments will view healthier economic conditions as opportunities to seek out new budgetary reallocations that do not necessarily match up with their electoral support groups and ideological visions. Through increased relative spending to areas outside of their traditional budgetary priorities, governments may be able to attract new voters and extend their electoral support. The logic of the argument in 2B is that, in times of strong economic performance, governments have more room to make policy and budgetary changes without the electoral fallout. They can continue the status quo budgets for their main goals, while increasing relative amounts to secondary policy areas, such as education or health.

Turning now to economically difficult times, on the left side of Figure 4.4, we focus on budgetary behavior during rising unemployment. Under these circumstances, our competing expectations are between 1A and 2A. In quadrant 1A, ideology is a key driver of budgetary allocations, with governments emphasizing their core preferences and shoring-up the budgets of their primary policy areas at the expense of less important areas. They focus on retaining their core supporters by shifting relative budgetary decreases to non-ideologically significant areas in order to relatively increase, or at least retain status quo levels of, the budgets of their policy priorities. The story in 1A highlights how government ideology might drive budgetary decisions, even under adverse economic conditions.

The alternative budgetary story for economically difficult times emphasizes economic hardship rather than ideological priorities. In quadrant 2A, bad economic conditions may lead to budgetary divergence from a government's ideological ideal. Governments have fewer resources at a time when reliance on government assistance increases, so this requires decisions to maneuver spending to policy areas that may be outside of their ideological preferences. Rising unemployment and falling government revenues squeeze governments' abilities to spend as they wish, meaning that the ideological visions that separate parties on budgetary priorities take a backseat to socio-economic pressures (Lipsmeyer 2011). These can lead to fewer apparent ideological differences in relative spending behavior, with parties of different ideological stripes behaving in similar fashions when setting budgets. Competing with the argument in 1A, the outlook in 2A focuses on how economic hardship will push budgetary allocations in a uniform way, even at the expense of ideological priorities.

TABLE 4.2. *Expected reactions to an unemployment shock*

	Left Government			Right Government		
Policy Area	Priority	Ideologically Consistent (Expect 1A)	Context Overwhelms (Expect 2A)	Priority	Ideologically Consistent (Expect 1A)	Context Overwhelms (Expect 2A)
Defense		−		✓	+	
Economic Affairs		−		✓	+	+
Education	✓		+	✓		+
Govt Admin	✓	+	+		−	
Health	✓		+	✓		+
Housing	✓	+	+			
Religion & Culture						
Social Protection	✓	+	+		−	+

Note: ✓ indicates a government priority, + government will increase share of policy area, − government will decrease share of policy area.

4.2.1 Expectations

Combining these four competing arguments from Figure 4.4 with the general priorities of left and right governments summarized in Chapter 3 (and listed under the "Priority" column in Table 4.2), we explain our theoretical expectations of how left and right governments will react to different economic conditions in Table 4.2. We discuss the particulars of two different types of economic shocks: first in the form of an increase in unemployment and, second, in the form of an increase in economic growth.

Our expectations for when government ideology takes precedence during rising unemployment correspond with "Expect 1A." Left governments react to an increase in unemployment by shifting resources to social protection, housing, and government administration at the expense of areas that are not among their general priorities: defense and economic affairs. This expectation follows from the idea that left governments will want to use government resources to take care of those individuals most affected by the increase in unemployment. This can best be accomplished by shifting funds toward social protection, which includes unemployment benefits, as well as other benefits for the more disadvantaged members of society (e.g., housing). We also anticipate a shift toward government adminis-

4.2 Domestic Economic Circumstances and Tradeoffs

tration in an effort to increase the effectiveness and scope of government services in reaction to what is likely to be an increase in their activity levels. Note that the cells for education and health are blank. We do not expect left governments to shift spending in these areas, because they offer fewer short-term benefits in response to an unemployment shock.

Turning to Expect 1A that posits ideologically driven budgetary change for right governments in the face of a shock to unemployment, we expect that they will increase relative spending on defense and economic affairs. These expectations follow from previous research that contends that governments can use defense allocations as welfare projects, thereby shoring up core areas of the economy through increased relative spending on economic affairs (Whitten and Williams 2011). These responses are more consistent with right governments' ideological visions of the role of government in the economy (Boix 1998). We also anticipate that right governments will offset the increases to defense and economic affairs with relative decreases in budgets for government administration and social protection. Left and right governments, then, will make different compositional choices to benefit their supporters during an economic downturn.

In reaction to an unemployment shock, governments from the left and right may choose budgetary shifts that fit an alternative expectation. Expect 2A in Table 4.2 reflects the argument that economic hardship will play a larger role than ideology in influencing their behavior. In some ways, governments from both sides will react similarly to the hardship by shifting resources to social protection in order to buffer society from economic loss. Education and health could also be a common area when attempting to use government funds to assist their supporters and society. We also anticipate some differences based on the use of government power. The left will use funding for government administration and housing to buttress public employment and subsidize living conditions, and the right will continue to buffer industries by shifting funds to economic affairs. Overall, these expectations rely more on economic necessity and less on ideological priorities.

What if, instead of an economic downturn, governments had the luxury of a robust economy? With a positive shock in growth, we consider government budgetary behavior during good times with a focus again on whether governments decide to reward their supporters or wish to expand their electoral base. In Table 4.3, we summarize these competing expectations by explaining how governments may reallocate their budgets across policy areas. Similar to the unemployment shock discussed in

TABLE 4.3. *Expected reactions to a growth shock*

Policy Area	Left Government			Right Government		
	Priority	Ideologically Consistent (Expect 1B)	Context Overwhelms (Expect 2B)	Priority	Ideologically Consistent (Expect 1B)	Context Overwhelms (Expect 2B)
Defense		−	−	✓	+	
Economic Affairs		−	−	✓	+	
Education	✓	+	+	✓	+	+
Govt Admin	✓	+			−	−
Health	✓	+	+	✓	+	+
Housing	✓	+			−	−
Religion & Culture			+			+
Social Protection	✓	+			−	−

Note: ✓ indicates a government priority, + government will increase share of policy area, − government will decrease share of policy area.

Table 4.2, our first expectation here (Expect 1B) relies on governments' ideological priorities to explain their budgetary behavior. In the face of economic good news, both left and right governments should find the political space to reallocate funds to their preferred policies, culminating in relative increases for those areas. In the Expect 1B columns, the relative increases ("+") correspond with the Priority columns, while the relative decreases ("−") come from those areas prioritized by the other type of government.[12] With positive economic growth, governments will take the opportunity to reward their supporters through funding of those policy priorities.

What if governments decide to use the extra breathing room created by a healthy economy to expand their electoral base and political clout? Unlike the ideological argument of Expect 1B, in Expect 2B we argue that the context offers governments the latitude to move beyond their typical priorities. Rather than reallocate budgets to fit their policy preferences, we would expect them to relatively increase funds to secondary policy areas that offer possibilities of attracting new supporters. The striking

---

[12] Since Religion & Culture is not a priority for either the left or right, it is left blank for Expect 1B.

point of these columns is the similarity in our expectations across left and right governments; we argue for the same relative increases across secondary policy areas – education, health, and religion and culture.[13] The differences between the left and right appear in the areas where they decrease relative spending. Under this scenario, left governments will take from defense and economic affairs, and the right from government administration, housing, and social protection. Note that we do not expect governments to relatively decrease funds to their prioritized policy areas. With less of a need for social assistance, left governments may stay with the status quo, but we expect right governments to make relative cuts to government assistance type programs, where positive growth makes them less controversial. With a healthy economy, governments can retain status quo funding for key prioritized policy areas, while reaching out to shift funds to new areas and potentially new supporters.[14]

4.3 INTERNATIONAL CIRCUMSTANCES

Domestic contexts are not the only pressures on the budgetary behavior of governments. Countries can find it difficult to exist in a solitary bubble, so governments must consider the pressure of international forces on budgetary decisions. While there are many theories and much research debating the influence of globalization (Dreher 2006; Shelton 2007; Dreher, Sturm, and Ursprung 2008; Gemmell, Kneller, and Sanz 2008; Jensen 2011b; Lipsmeyer, Philips, and Whitten 2017) and international conflict (Russett 1982; Mintz 1989; Narizny 2003; Whitten and Williams 2011; Töngür, Hsu, and Elveren 2015) on specific policy budgets, we are interested in understanding how these pressures affect governments' abilities to reallocate budgets.

As shown in Figure 4.5, our theoretical argument highlights how international circumstances can affect governments' abilities to achieve their policy goals, and we expect that changes in countries' global situations can alter government behavior when making budgetary tradeoffs. In tackling the question of internationalization's influence on budgetary expenditures, we move beyond research that focuses on the direct influence of

---

[13] Our expectation about religion and culture comes from our classification of most spending in this category as being a luxury good.

[14] While we propose that these categories are the same across governments, we do not expect that the left and right will employ those relative increases similarly for education, health, or religion and culture.

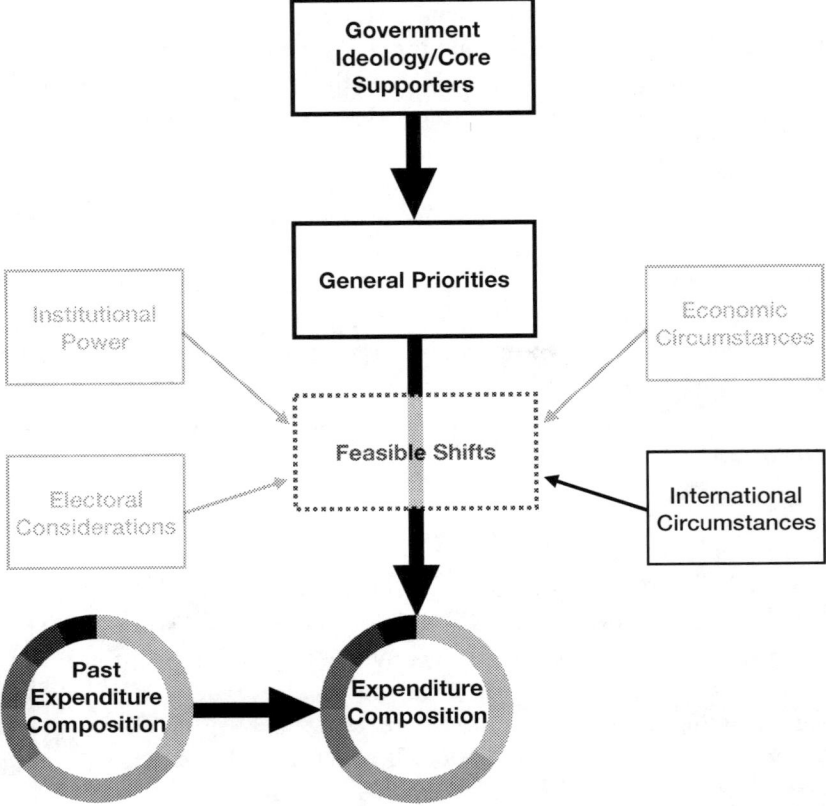

FIGURE 4.5. How international factors affect expenditure compositions

international forces and, instead, emphasize how these pressures change the budgetary calculations of governments. To this end, we are interested in how globalization and conflict involvement affect governments' allocations of budgetary resources – the policy areas that governments reinforce versus those that they cut.

4.3.1 International Economic Circumstances: How Globalization Affects Spending Tradeoffs

Focusing on international conditions, we first look to the opening of domestic economies to globalizing forces. The effects of globalization can be wide-ranging and complex because of, for example, increased competition, changes in the factors of production, or pressures for regulatory and protectionist policies (Tanzi 2002).[15] When considering the relationship between governments, international pressures, and budgetary compositions, we argue that globalization can alter what we consider "typical" ideological expectations.

Research on globalization and budgetary behavior has emphasized two main theories to explain governments' reactions to opening their economies. With a focus on welfare and redistributive policies, some scholars have emphasized how economic pressures from international trade and capital mobility can push governments to spend more to *compensate* their domestic populations (Rodrik 1998), while others point to an *efficiency* argument, whereby, because of tightening revenues, governments need to decrease their budgetary bottom-line (Bretschger and Hettich 2002).[16]

While in the long-run all members of society may benefit from the lower costs of goods and services in an increasingly integrated world, in the short-run, globalization may adversely affect some members of society more than others through increased inequality and lower job market security (Quinn 1997; Garrett 2001).[17] In response to this, there is an expectation that governments will play an active role in compensating those who "lose out" to globalization (Rodrik 1998; Garrett and Mitchell 2001; Swank 2002; Hays 2009; Leibrecht, Klien, and Onaran 2011).[18] Illustrating this, in the post-war era, a deal was struck, "implying social insurance in exchange for foreign trade liberalization" (Schulze and Ursprung 1999, p. 296). This pressure to compensate may be particularly acute for left governments, who have traditionally drawn support from

---

[15] Scholars have theorized that globalization can affect a myriad of factors outside of budgets as well, including inequality (Philips, Souza, and Whitten 2020), taxation (Dreher 2006; Plümper, Troeger, and Winner 2009), unemployment benefits (Lipsmeyer and Zhu 2011), just to name a few. Similarly, they have argued that international conflict influences a range of things, such as the popularity of governing parties (Norpoth 1987; Clarke, Mishler, and Whiteley 1990) or economic growth and inflation (Gupta et al. 2004).

[16] A third possibility exists – that globalization does not directly affect government spending (Dreher 2006; Dreher, Sturm, and Ursprung 2008).

[17] Perhaps paradoxically, increased globalization – in the form of increased capital mobility – may allow governments to issue debt in order to spend in these compensatory areas. Quinn (1997) finds evidence of a positive relationship between capital account liberalization and government spending.

[18] The compensation hypothesis is sometimes referred to as "embedded liberalism" (Meinhard and Potrafke 2012).

the working class, although empirical findings on this have been mixed (Dreher 2006; Potrafke 2009).

Government compensation for globalizing markets is at odds with the efficiency argument that focuses on the changes in revenue rather than the spending element of the budget. Opening borders can cause a race-to-the-bottom in corporate taxation as governments attempt to retain increasingly mobile factors of production. This drop in revenue would result in reducing the government's ability to spend, leading to an emphasis on more market and business driven government policies (Garrett 2001; Bretschger and Hettich 2002; Devereux, Lockwood, and Redoano 2008; Meinhard and Potrafke 2012).[19] To summarize these competing hypotheses, the efficiency argument emphasizes the reduced footprint of the state in order to remain competitive in an increasingly globalized world, while the compensatory argument focuses on government welfare expansion to protect those who lose out from globalization.

In terms of research that studies the effect of globalization on budgets, the findings are mixed with evidence for and against both the compensation and efficiency hypotheses (Gemmell, Kneller, and Sanz 2008; Plümper, Troeger, and Winner 2009; Rickard 2012).[20] Increased trade openness has often been found to be associated with larger-sized governments, which is at odds with the efficiency hypothesis (Garrett 1995; Rodrik 1998; Burgoon 2001; Garrett and Mitchell 2001).[21] In contrast, while the compensatory hypothesis predicts that increased trade openness will lead to increased economic volatility (and, thus, a greater need for governments to step in and insulate segments of society from these economic changes), the evidence for this is relatively weak (Kim 2007).[22] Interestingly, Garrett (2001) finds that greater trade openness is associated with higher levels of spending, while also uncovering that increased trade growth is associated with a *decreased* rate of growth in government spending. Ultimately, the relationships between globalization and government expenditures remain unclear.

---

[19] But see Plümper, Troeger, and Winner (2009) on why there is a paucity of evidence of a race-to-the-bottom situation in terms of capital taxation.

[20] Hays (2009) makes a case for why we might not observe support for either the efficiency or compensatory hypotheses and points to a group of scholars (e.g., Iversen and Cusack 2000; Pierson 2001) who argue that globalization does not affect government spending.

[21] But see Gemmell, Kneller, and Sanz (2008).

[22] This is not to say that other types of openness – such as trade and exchange rate risk – do not cause increased domestic economic volatility (Rodrik 1998; Kim 2007).

4.3 *International Circumstances*

While the literature we have discussed so far focuses mostly on the size of government, scholars have also explored the effects of globalization on spending for particular policies, typically social welfare. The focus here has tended to be on the compensation hypothesis, whereby the expectation is that the opening of economies should lead to increased government assistance. Earlier studies found that welfare states expanded as a result of increased market openness, particularly when left parties were in power (Cusack 1999; Iversen and Cusack 2000; Hall and Soskice 2004). More recently, the findings have been less clear. Although Ha (2008) concludes that globalization has increased welfare expenditures, Dreher (2006) finds no relationship between globalization and general or social spending. Other researchers have even found evidence of a negative relationship. In a meta-analysis of the literature on the effects of globalization on government spending, Heimberger (2020) finds that "globalization has a small-to-moderate negative impact on social spending." Interestingly, Jensen (2011b) also hypothesizes that there will be a decrease in welfare service provision as a result of increased globalization. While he finds that healthcare spending may have decreased as a result of increased trade openness after 1990, results are inconclusive for expenditures on social care. Although the research focuses on developing countries, Rickard (2012) finds evidence that increases in globalization lead to decreased welfare spending but an increase in education subsidies.

At times, this focus on exploring the links between globalization and welfare policy has overshadowed more comprehensive research that attempts to uncover which policy areas governments protect under globalizing pressures. Much of this work analyzes multiple policy areas and tends to find evidence in support of a compensatory argument more broadly. For instance, Gemmell, Kneller, and Sanz (2008) find associations between increased FDI flows and social welfare and public services, while Shelton (2007) notes that, in developed democracies, more trade openness is associated with increased spending on public transfers (social security being the largest portion) and infrastructure/transportation.[23] Considering globalization as integration in the European Union setting, Lipsmeyer, Philips, and Whitten (2017) examine several budgetary

---

[23] Both Gemmell, Kneller, and Sanz (2008) and Shelton (2007) studied government expenditures as compositions using equations for each policy budget either yearly or averaged over five years, respectively. Also note that Gemmell, Kneller, and Sanz (2008) found no significant effects for openness, only FDI.

categories in 15 developed countries and find that, in response to increased labor market integration, governments tend to devote a larger share of their budgets to health and education, with smaller proportions going toward public services, defense, and social protection. Overall, they conclude that budgetary changes are much larger for right governments than for left ones.

Nevertheless, this question of whether government ideology and globalization work together to affect budgets remains unanswered. The interlinking of markets and the openness of trade create environments in which governments may have less freedom to make their preferred ideological tradeoffs. Potrafke (2009) points out that much of the research tying globalization to macroeconomic policies has found little partisan influence. Globalization, thus, may alter governments' abilities to focus only on their desired policy areas, highlighting how forces outside of domestic partisan differences can shape the compositions of budgets. As Ha (2008) highlights, while globalization has increased demand for welfare expenditures, powerful domestic political forces in the form of veto players have affected whether a government can respond to such pressures.[24] Studies focusing on whether or not globalization has a direct effect on overall budgets have overlooked the possibility that governments react to these global pressures in different ways depending on their policy preferences. Researchers do not consider the possibility that these reactions might lead to changing allocations across budgetary areas, in addition to – or instead of – changes in aggregated budgets.

4.3.1.1 Expectations

To answer questions about how globalization may alter government behavior on budgetary tradeoffs, we combine expectations about government ideology with insights from both the compensation and efficiency arguments.[25] We build a tournament of expectations that considers the possibility that globalization pressures may reinforce ideological priorities, while acknowledging that these international forces may leave less room for government maneuvering.

In Table 4.4, we summarize our expectations of how left and right governments will reallocate budgets in response to an increase in

---

[24] Ha (2008) also finds that ideology does not have a direct effect on welfare spending.
[25] While our focus is on relative expenditure shifts, note that this may not be the only policy tool used by governments; regulations and changes in revenues may also offer opportunities to shield supporters from the effects of globalization (Tanzi 2002).

4.3 International Circumstances

TABLE 4.4. *Expected reactions to a globalization shock*

Policy Area	Left Government Priority	Left Ideologically Consistent (Expect 1)	Left Context Overwhelms (Expect 2)	Right Government Priority	Right Ideologically Consistent (Expect 1)	Right Context Overwhelms (Expect 2)
Defense				✓		
Economic Affairs			+	✓	+	
Education	✓	+	+	✓	+	+
Govt Admin	✓	+				+
Health	✓	+		✓		+
Housing	✓	+				+
Religion & Culture						
Social Protection	✓	+				+

Note: ✓ indicates a government priority, + government will increase share of policy area.

globalization. Because of their ideological visions, governments attract different segments of society, so an ideologically consistent response to increased globalization depends on the groups that are their core supporters. We see these differences reflected in their differing priorities (as set out in Chapter 3 and presented again here). Right party support generally comes from higher-skilled workers, capital and business, and retirees (i.e., citizens relying less on compensation). Under globalization, an ideologically consistent reaction from these governments would be to shift resources away from redistributive policies and toward those that promote smaller government and efficiency. For left governments, however, an ideologically consistent response would mean shoring up their support from lower skilled workers and labor, leading to the shifting of budgetary resources toward redistributive policies and government administration with its ties to public employment. The expectations listed under the two Expect 1 columns in Table 4.4 reflect governments of the left emphasizing compensation, and governments of the right emphasizing efficiency. Continuing our logic of Expect 1 and Expect 2 throughout this chapter, Expect 2 puts an emphasis on context overwhelming ideology. For the left, this means responding to an increase in globalization with changes in line with an efficiency argument. For the right, this means responding with changes in line with a compensation argument.

For the compensation argument (Expect 1 for left governments and Expect 2 for right governments), we expect to see governments shifting budgetary resources toward government assistance programs that benefit those harmed by the opening of markets: education, government administration, health, housing, and social protection. Since our expectations are for relative budgetary increases, left governments may still allot more of their budgets to these policy areas than right governments; however, the compensation expectation would predict relative increases to these areas for all governments.

For the efficiency argument (Expect 2 for left governments and Expect 1 for right governments), we expect that governments will move budgetary resources to policy areas that benefit the competitiveness of domestic markets and businesses: economic affairs and education. Relative increases to these policy areas reflect investment in human capital, while supporting core areas of the economy. Rather than shift resources to compensating for the negative externalities of globalization, the efficiency explanation emphasizes policy areas that maximize the market productivity of the nation. Similar to the compensation expectations, the expectations for efficiency are the same across government ideology.

4.3.2 International Political Circumstances: How Conflict Involvement Affects Spending Tradeoffs

In addition to globalization, international situations may arise when governments are faced with military conflicts that force changes to their budgetary calculations. With increased hostilities, one initially reasonable expectation would be that governments of all ideological persuasions would increase relative spending on defense. This should be especially true when the nation is facing an existential threat that overrides ideological or partisan considerations. However, for the time period and the set of nations that we are studying, there are no such scenarios. Instead, the period that we are studying is one in which countries were involved, to varying degrees, in lower-level and/or far away conflicts that have been demonstrated to have effects on military spending (Whitten and Williams 2011). Given these circumstances, the question of how international conflict affects government budgetary behavior remains unanswered. Do governments make similar, strategic budgetary tradeoffs in response to increased hostilities, or are budgetary reactions more likely to be shaped by more ideological concerns?

Not surprisingly, research on military spending tends to conclude that conflict can drive funding. For instance, examining 37 countries between 1988 and 2003, Töngür, Hsu, and Elveren (2015) find that conflict is a strong determinant of increased military expenditures, as is increased military spending by foes. Whitten and Williams (2011) report a similar result: increased conflict involvement leads to increased defense spending by all types of governments (in their analysis, hawkish versus dovish and generous versus austere governments).[26] Putting a slightly different spin on this argument, Bove, Efthyvoulou, and Navas (2017) note that, although governments tend to prioritize social spending rather than defense expenditures during election periods, this difference is much more muted for countries involved in conflict. This expectation of reallocating resources between defense and welfare spending has become a common tradeoff mentioned by researchers looking for strategic budgetary behavior: "guns versus butter." Governments face a fundamental constraint between increasing defense spending ("guns") and raising social/domestic expenditures ("butter") (Russett 1982; Mintz 1989; Narizny 2003; Whitten and Williams 2011).[27] Empirical studies, for the most part, have found little evidence of such a tradeoff. For instance, Mintz (1989) finds no evidence of any tradeoff occurring in the United States before the 1980s (a finding echoed by Russett 1982), although he does find evidence of a tradeoff between military investment in weapons systems and education expenditures during the Reagan era.

A reason for a lack of empirical evidence in support of a guns versus butter tradeoff may be researchers' emphases on government ideology, with expectations that right governments will tend to favor defense spending, while governments of the left will prefer social spending (Narizny 2003; Whitten and Williams 2011; Bove, Efthyvoulou, and Navas 2017).[28] Whitten and Williams (2011), however, present an argument that scholars should conceptualize government ideology as it pertains to

---

[26] This effect is even stronger for more hawkish governments, but there is no such interactive relationship between hostility involvement and government positions on welfare.

[27] See Hwang (2012) and Alesina and Spolaore (2005, 2006) for more formal theorizing of parts of this theory.

[28] An alternative explanation is that there *is* a guns versus butter tradeoff, but the mechanism is indirect. Increased defense expenditures crowd out investment or increase fiscal deficits, reducing growth that, in turn, leads to smaller revenues to allocate to welfare (Mintz and Huang 1991; Gupta et al. 2004).

military spending along two different dimensions: a hawk versus dove international dimension and a generous versus austere welfare dimension. They advance a theory in which both more hawkish and more generous governments will spend more on defense, because military spending has employment and other economic benefits that appeal to more welfare-generous governments.[29] Consistent with their expectations, they find that both hawkish and more generous governments spend more on defense, and more dovish and austere governments spend less. This suggests that government ideology may not be as strong a driver as previously thought, which supports previous studies that argue left governments might be more likely to devote resources to the military since it typically goes along with greater state intervention in the economy (Narizny 2003).[30]

Of course, in this book, we emphasize the examination of tradeoffs among all expenditure categories. Surprisingly, for a theory whose name *is* an explicit tradeoff ("guns versus butter"), the literature has seldom modeled it as such. Typically, researchers express the dependent variable – most often military or social expenditures – as a share of GDP (Whitten and Williams 2011; Töngür, Hsu, and Elveren 2015) or as a percentage of the total budget (Gupta et al. 2004). Alternatively, they have directly regressed one expenditure category on one or more of the other categories (Russett 1982; Mintz 1989; Mintz and Huang 1991).[31] More recently, there has been interest in exploring these relationships more compositionally by considering multiple categories of expenditures simultaneously. For instance, Bove, Efthyvoulou, and Navas (2017) operationalize this tradeoff as the ratio between military and social expenditures. In their analysis of five budget categories in the United States, Philips, Rutherford, and Whitten (2016a) hypothesize (and model) directly the compositional tradeoffs between these categories with the expectation that increased conflict involvement will lead to increases in defense spending relative to all other categories (i.e., welfare, social security, debt repayments, and an "other" category). By approaching the relationship between conflict

---

[29] Alternatively, see Dunne (2012), who finds that increased military spending is associated with a decline in GDP per capita in the short run – especially for low-income countries – and negative or no effect over the long run.

[30] For instance, Narizny (2003, p. 204) notes that, "in the presidential election of 2000, the Democrat Al Gore proposed higher defense spending and a more actively interventionist foreign policy than the Republican George W. Bush."

[31] For example, Mintz (1989) examines subcategories of military expenditures (e.g., spending on personnel, procurement, and research and development), while regressing these categories on the growth rates of two social expenditure categories: health and housing.

4.3 *International Circumstances* 141

TABLE 4.5. *Expected reactions to a hostilities shock*

	Left Government			Right Government		
Policy Area	Priority	Ideologically Consistent (Expect 1)	Context Overwhelms (Expect 2)	Priority	Ideologically Consistent (Expect 1)	Context Overwhelms (Expect 2)
Defense		+	+	✓	+	+
Economic Affairs		−	−	✓		
Education	✓	+		✓	+	
Govt Admin	✓	+				−
Health	✓	+		✓	+	
Housing	✓	+				−
Religion & Culture						
Social Protection	✓	+			−	−

Note: ✓ indicates a government priority, + government will increase share of policy area, − government will decrease share of policy area.

and budgets from a contextual framing, we argue that the hostility environment may influence how governments reallocate their budgets in a broader context rather than emphasizing only two policy areas.

4.3.2.1 *Expectations*

Keeping this in mind when examining the entire composition of expenditures, in Table 4.5, we present our expectations for how governments of the left and the right will adjust their relative spending budgets in reaction to an increase in hostilities. Like our previous expectation tables, we start by including columns with ideological priorities for left and right governments that correspond with our discussion in Chapter 3. Then, we distinguish between two competing arguments, where Expect 1 is an ideologically consistent set of expectations, and Expect 2 is a set of expectations where context mostly overwhelms ideology.

Expect 1 in Table 4.5 reflects an ideologically driven "guns yield butter" argument. In the face of increased hostilities, both the left and right relatively increase spending to defense and to some redistributive policy areas (i.e., education or health). But left governments extend the relative increases to other redistributive areas – housing and social protection – in accordance with their preference for government action, and right governments tradeoff their relative increases in education and health with a decrease in social protection. Note that, since our ideologically driven expectation is that left governments will retrench in economic affairs, we also expect them to lower relative spending in this area in response to increased hostilities.

Expect 2 reflects a more traditional "guns versus butter" story. Following from Whitten and Williams (2011), we expect governments from both the left and the right to react to a hostilities shock with an increase in the relative share of spending on defense. But the governments will differ on where the offsetting relative decreases fall based on their ideological priorities. Left governments will retain stable relative funding for redistributive policy areas, instead, trading off economic affairs resources for defense funds. Under this scenario, we expect right governments to cut relative spending on government administration, housing, and social protection to fund the increase to defense.

Without looking at these relationships compositionally, these various tradeoffs and what they mean for understanding government decision-making during conflict situations would remain hidden. In this tournament of scenarios, we offer one common theme: all governments are expected to increase relative military spending in the face of hostilities. The question remains how and if redistributive policies (the "butter" side) fit into the story.

4.4 CONTEXTS AND EXPENDITURE TRADEOFFS: RESEARCH DESIGN

4.4.1 Data and Modeling Strategy

To test our competing theoretical expectations across all of these contexts, we use the same data as in Chapter 3. However, unlike in Chapter 3, we have the added complexity of testing whether ideology and institutional considerations (majority/minority government) both work to condition electoral, economic, and international effects. Given our conclusions about majority government power in Chapter 3, we only show the results for majority governments in this chapter. We summarize our model for this chapter as:[32]

---

[32] Our actual model is slightly more complicated, since we include all of the constituent parts of the three-way interaction, that is,

$$\ln\left(\frac{y_{ijt}}{y_{i1t}}\right) = s_{ijt} = f(s_{ijt-1} + \text{Ideology}_{it} + \text{Institutional}_{it} + \text{Elect/Econ/Intl Factor}_{it}$$
$$+ \text{Ideology}_{it} \times \text{Institutional}_{it} + \text{Ideology}_{it} \times \text{Elect/Econ/Intl Factor}_{it} \quad (4.1)$$
$$+ \text{Institutional}_{it} \times \text{Elect/Econ/Intl Factor}_{it}$$
$$+ \text{Ideology}_{it} \times \text{Institutional}_{it} \times \text{Elect/Econ/Intl Factor}_{it} + \mathbf{Controls}_{it}).$$

4.5 Results: When Contexts Influence Tradeoffs

$$\ln\left(\frac{y_{ijt}}{y_{iIt}}\right) = s_{ijt} = f(s_{ijt-1} + \text{Ideology}_{it} + \text{Institutional}_{it}$$
$$+ \text{Elect/Econ/Intl Factor}_{it} + \text{Ideology}_{it} \times \text{Institutional}_{it}$$
$$\times \text{Elect/Econ/Intl Factor}_{it} + \textbf{Controls}_{it}),$$

(4.2)

where the budgetary compositional variable, s_{ijt}, is a function of its lag, a left–right ideology variable, a majority–minority institutional variable, one of the electoral, economic, or international factors discussed in Sections 4.1–4.3, an interaction between these three variables, and a host of controls that are the same as in Chapter 3. To avoid an over-parameterized model, we interact only one of the electoral, economic, or international conditions with ideology and majority government at a time. Note that the control variables from Chapter 3 are total expenditures, the budget deficit (both expressed as a percentage of GDP), and the age dependency ratio. If one of the key theoretical independent variables – election year, unemployment rate, economic openness, GDP growth rate, or hostility index – is *not* being interacted with the institutional and ideological variables, we include it as a control variable. As with the model for Chapter 3, we also include a linear time trend.

4.5 WHEN ELECTORAL, ECONOMIC, AND INTERNATIONAL CONDITIONS INFLUENCE SPENDING TRADEOFFS

Governments do not make budgetary decisions in an economic or political vacuum. Domestic or international conditions can create situations where governments may find it easier or more difficult to make tradeoffs that suit their ideological visions. Here, we present the results from models that test our theoretical tournaments of expectations about how these various contexts that surround governments affect their budgetary actions by modeling relative spending tradeoffs in the face of changing conditions. Throughout this section, it is useful to keep in mind that theoretical ideas labeled "Expect 1" reflect our ideologically consistent expectations, while "Expect 2" reflects expectations when context mostly overwhelms ideology.

4.5.1 Elections and Expenditure Tradeoffs

We begin by analyzing how election timing may influence governments' budgetary behavior. Our competing expectations, summarized in Table 4.1, are that governments attempt to energize their core supporters by shifting resources to those policies best suited to benefit them in the short-run (Expect 1) versus the idea that all governments attempt to increase their overall electoral support by moving funds into short-term social policies in an effort to maximize support from all types of voters (Expect 2).

In Figure 4.6, we show the results for both left and right majority governments. In Figure 4.6a, we present the estimated effects of an election year on budget compositions when there is a left majority government. The fact that every confidence interval, both those for short-run and long-run effects, crosses zero tells us that there are no statistically significant changes to budgetary compositions in reaction to electoral conditions under left governments. In Figure 4.6b, showing the effect of the election year on budget compositions when there is a right majority government, there are only two statistically significant short-run effects, an increase in spending on government administration and a decrease in spending on religion and culture, both of which are not consistent with either Expect 1 or Expect 2. The overall lack of effects for elections fits with neither of our expectations, although it does correspond with research that finds essentially no political budget cycle effects (Remmer 2007; Enkelmann and Leibrecht 2013).[33]

In terms of spending tradeoffs, we have found no evidence of political budget cycle effects; neither type of majority government – left or right – appears to manipulate budgetary categories in any meaningful way during legislative elections. Governments do not shift their budgets in election years for either ideological or short-term electoral gains. While such findings are not surprising given the very mixed results on political budget cycles in the literature (Dubois 2016; Philips 2016), this is not to say that *no* increases in these categories are occurring. Instead, systematic relative tradeoffs appear to be absent. Components of the budget may be changing simultaneously during elections (e.g., deficit or total expenditures may be increasing or total revenues may be decreasing), and we test these conjectures in Chapter 6.

---

[33] In Section 4.7, we also present results where we do not interact ideology and majority status with elections. We similarly find little-to-no effect of elections on the budgetary composition.

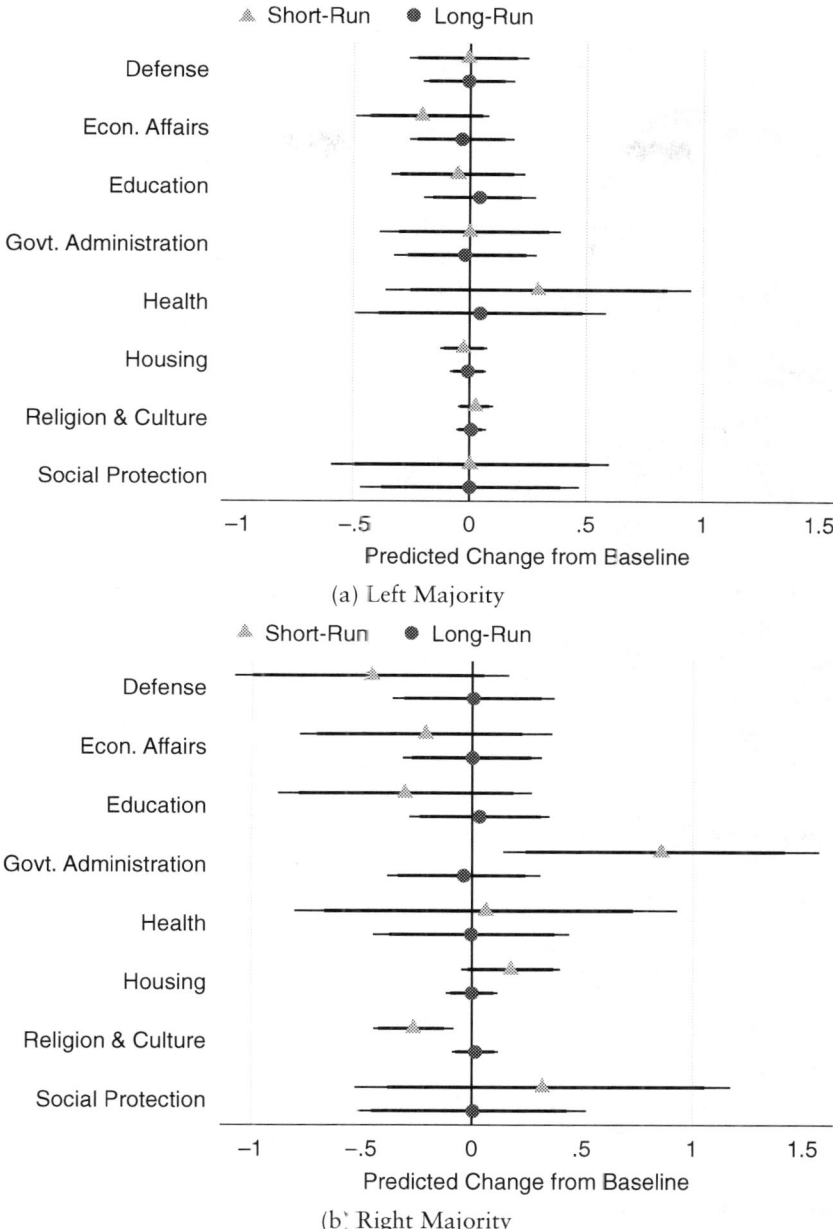

FIGURE 4.6. The effects of elections on expenditures
Note: Effects plots show the short- and long-run effects for an election cycle in a left majority government (Figure 4.6a) and a right majority government (Figure 4.6b) under otherwise average conditions; 90 (thick) and 95 (thin) percent confidence intervals shown.

4.5.2 Domestic Economic Circumstances

To test our rival arguments about the influence of both negative and positive economic conditions from Tables 4.2 and 4.3, we incorporate two shocks (separately) into our model – an increase in unemployment and an increase in economic growth.

Although a shock to unemployment can increase the numbers of those relying on social assistance, results in Figure 4.7a indicate that, contrary to our expectations (both Expect 1A and 2A predict increases in relative spending on social protection), left governments do not shift further resources to that policy area in reaction to such a shock. They hold steady on that priority, while reallocating funds in the short-run to government administration and away from almost all other policy areas. This relative increase in funds to government administration that was expected under both Expect 1A and 2A suggests that left governments are using public resources to maximize service efficiency and for job creation during an unemployment shock. In addition, this reallocation is at the expense of both defense and economic affairs. But we did not anticipate the additional statistically significant cuts to relative spending on education and health care.

While right majority governments do react differently from the left when faced with an increase in unemployment, these results do not neatly fit with Expect 1A or 2A. Results in Figure 4.7b indicate that they reallocate the budget away from social protection and health in favor of education and housing. The large cut to relative spending on social protection is consistent with our more ideologically driven expectations (1A), and the increase in spending on education is consistent with our more context-driven expectations (2A).

Taken together, the findings in Figure 4.7 indicate that ideology makes a substantial difference to how governments respond to these less favorable economic conditions. Returning to our competing expectations in Table 4.2, we see that these findings are somewhat mixed but offer some support for our expectations. The left turns to government action in the form of government administration, while the right shifts to market-driven solutions to assist the labor market (education). Here, we see both sides protecting their main policy areas – government administration and social protection for the left and defense and economic affairs for the right – while imposing relative decreases on the opposing side's preferred areas. We can summarize these results by saying that harsh economic

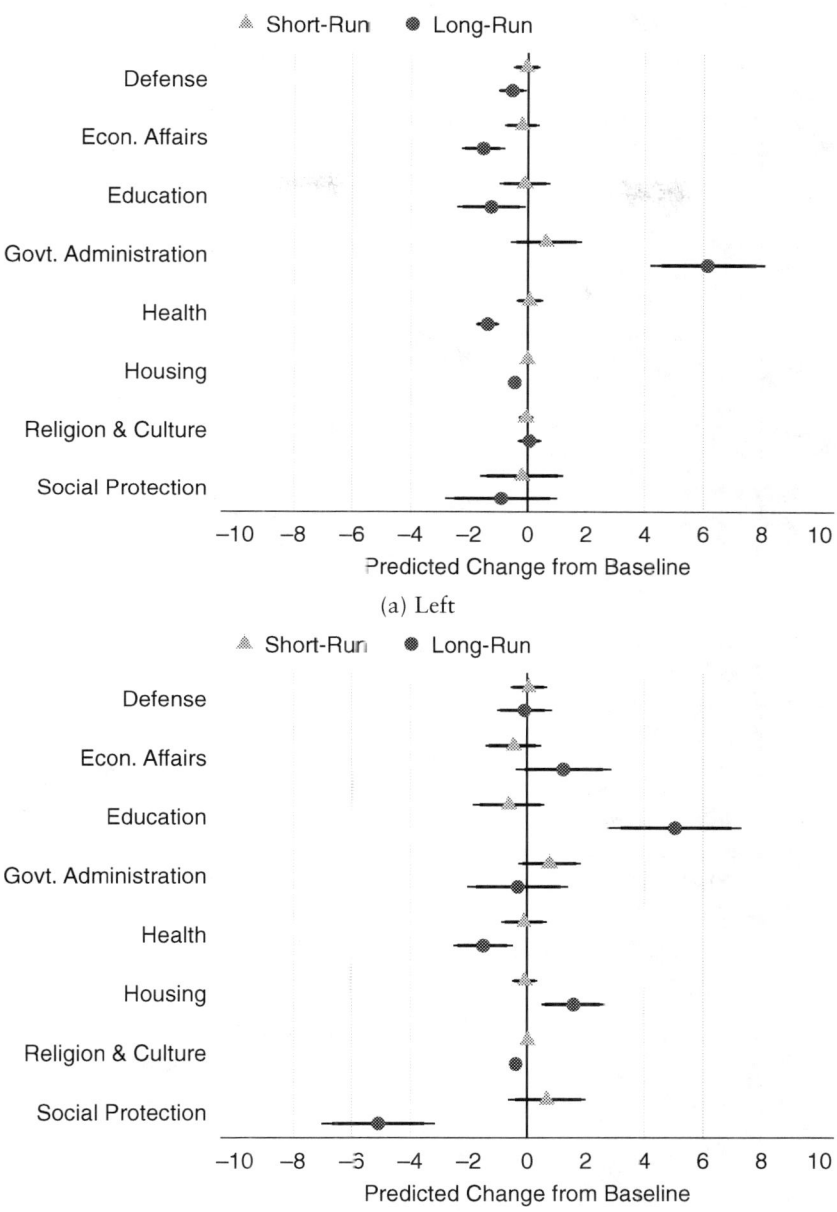

FIGURE 4.7. The effects of ideology on expenditures under an increase to unemployment

Note: Effects plots show the short- and long-run effects for a majority left government (Figure 4.7a) and a majority right government (Figure 4.7b); 90 (thick) and 95 (thin) percent confidence intervals shown.

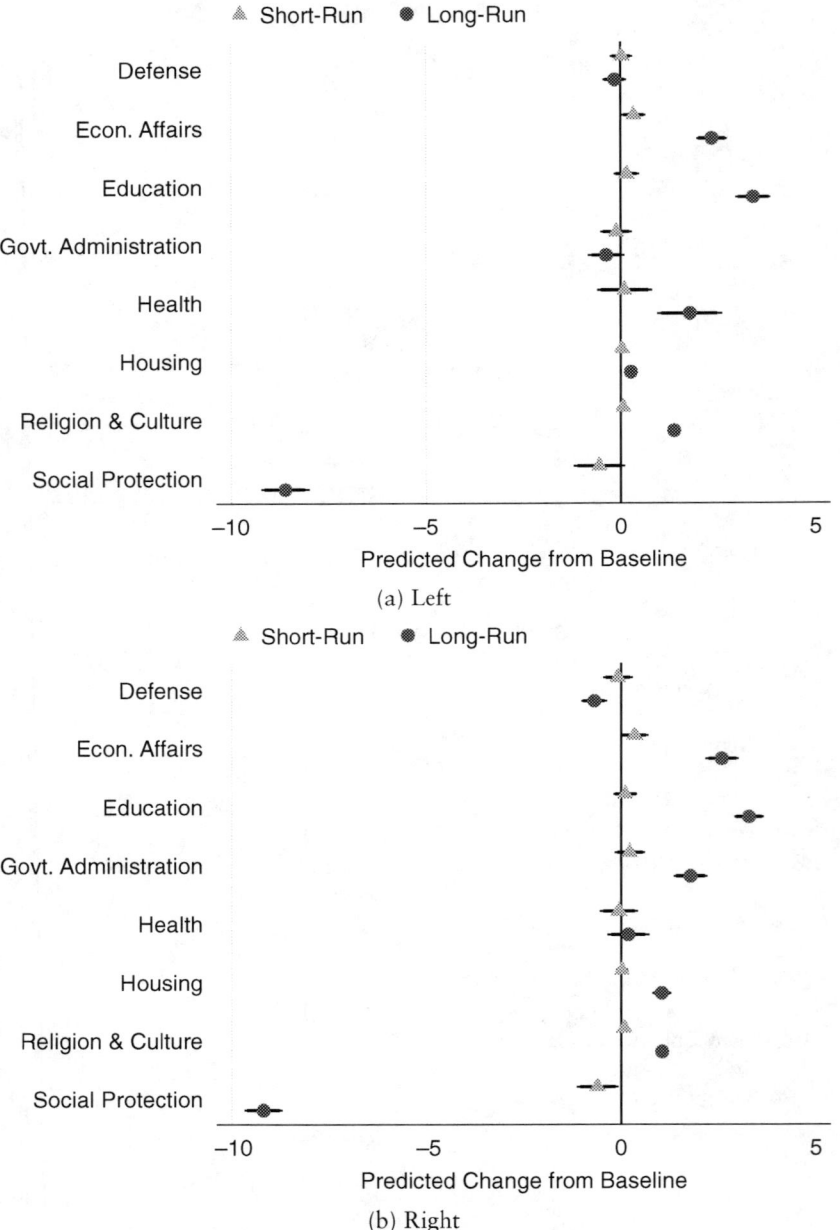

FIGURE 4.8. The effects of ideology on expenditures under a positive shock to growth
Note: Effects plots show the short- and long-run effects for a majority left government (Figure 4.8a) and a majority right government (Figure 4.8b); 90 (thick) and 95 (thin) percent confidence intervals shown.

4.5 Results: When Contexts Influence Tradeoffs 149

conditions in the form of an increase in unemployment appear to lead to a mixture of ideological and strategic tradeoff decisions.

How do governments react when the economy is doing well? In Figure 4.8, we show how left and right majority governments respond to an increase in real GDP growth. Our competing expectations in Table 4.3 offered either a reinforcement of ideological priorities (Expect 1B) or an emphasis by both left and right governments on secondary priority areas at the expense of areas supported by the other side (Expect 2B). We find that governments do branch out and reallocate resources to secondary areas. The biggest budgetary shift is a large (eight-to-nine point) relative long-run decrease in social protection for both government types. This reallocation allows for some of the same long-run relative increases for both left and right governments: to economic affairs, education, housing, and religion and culture. We also find that the left increases relative spending on health. With the more positive economic context, governments from both sides appear to tradeoff social protection policies for secondary areas that offer them opportunities to expand their electoral reach, while still appeasing supporters. These results support Expect 2, where a positive context allows governments the space to go beyond ideological priorities.

4.5.3 International Contexts

While domestic contexts can influence governments' budgetary choices, international situations may also affect their behavior. Both economic relationships beyond domestic borders and international conflicts can shape domestic budgetary decisions. In the face of these international circumstances, we anticipate that governments may find themselves constrained to change relative spending for some policy areas regardless of their preferred allocations.

Considering globalization first, Table 4.4 sets out a tournament of expectations that correspond with the compensation and efficiency hypotheses from previous research. Given the conflicting ideological priorities of left and right governments, our expectations are that, in reaction to an increase in globalization, the left will follow a compensation pattern, while the right will pursue efficiency when reallocating spending. However, if this globalization context overwhelms ideological preferences, then we would anticipate relationships in line with Expect 2, where the left would make more efficient changes and the right would

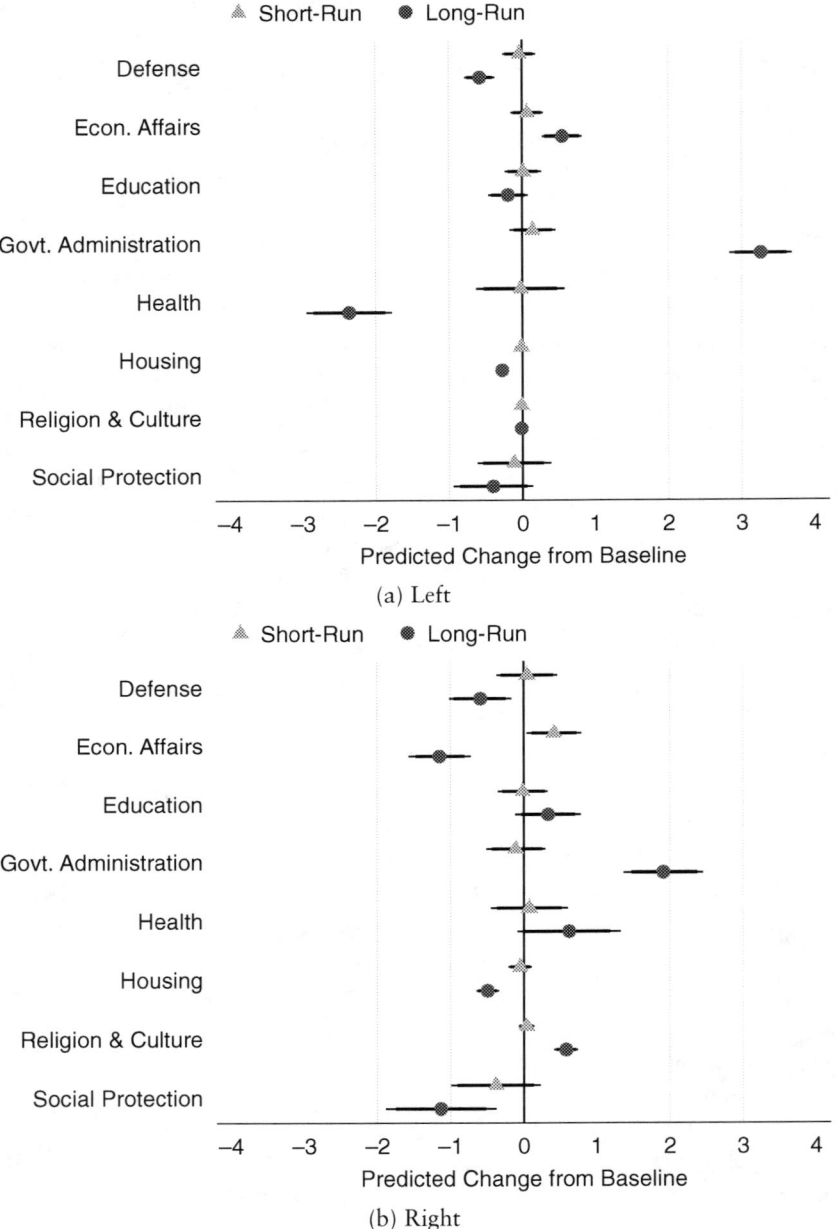

FIGURE 4.9. The effects of ideology on expenditures under a positive shock to openness
Note: Effects plots show the short- and long-run effects for a majority left government (Figure 4.9a) and a majority right government (Figure 4.9b); 90 (thick) and 95 (thin) percent confidence intervals shown.

4.5 Results: When Contexts Influence Tradeoffs

compensate. In Figure 4.9, we present the tradeoff patterns of these two government types, and they both show some ideological priorities and some overlap in their behavior. Left governments (Figure 4.9a) and right governments (Figure 4.9b) respond to an increase in economic openness with significant relative shifts to spending on government administration. While this corresponds with the compensation argument, a slightly different spin is that, in the face of greater exposure to international markets, governments of all stripes need increased capacities to improve conditions and compete in the international arena. This still accords with compensating domestic groups, albeit with a broader interpretation.

The tradeoffs where the relative budgets decrease, however, differ for the left and right. Here, governments take aim at their opponents most prized policies, with left governments targeting defense, and right governments diminishing relative spending on social protection. Left governments appear to keep the status quo for social protection; instead, they diminish their relative priority on a secondary policy area, health. The ideological distinction on social protection is not surprising, and it illustrates that governments tend to remain ideologically consistent. The left argues for using government resources to protect those harmed by globalization, and the right would prefer to enforce market-oriented approaches through its budgetary decisions. While increasing funds for government administration can be seen as supporting the compensation argument, the tradeoff side of the budget points to ideologically driven choices. For the efficiency expectations, left governments increase the relative allocation on economic affairs, which offers some support to the argument that governments react to globalization through channels that benefit economic streamlining and market practices, but the behavior of right governments offers little support for such an argument.

When considering international conditions and budgets, another key factor is how governments allocate resources during international military conflict. How will governments tradeoff between defense and other policy areas? Previous research on defense spending discusses various options for governments – tradeoffs between welfare and defense spending or the use of defense spending as a means of redistributive policy. In our theoretical expectations in Table 4.5, we created a tournament of rival expectations: whether guns yield butter (Expect 1) or guns compete with butter (Expect 2). In terms of our results, the graphs in Figure 4.10

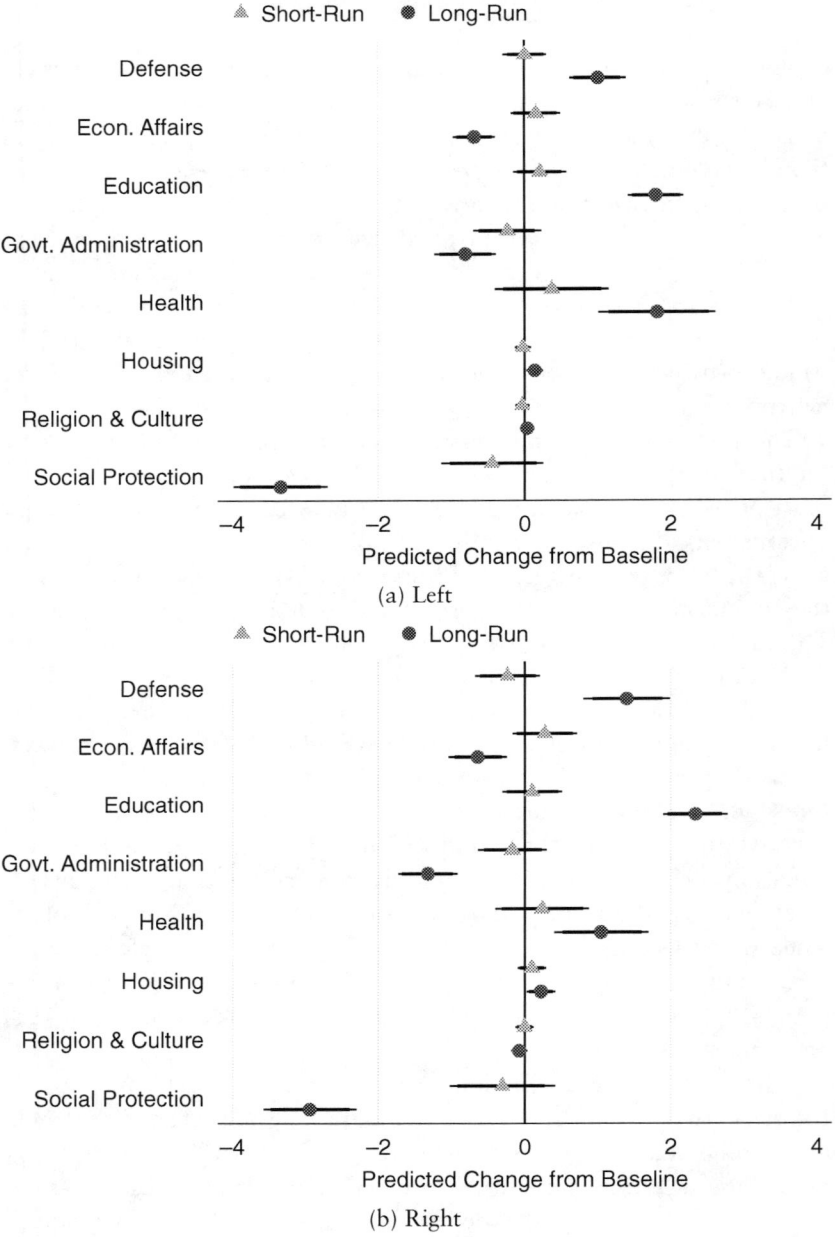

FIGURE 4.10. The effects of ideology on expenditures under a positive shock to hostilities
Note: Effects plots show the short- and long-run effects for a majority left government (Figure 4.10a) and a majority right government (Figure 4.10b); 90 (thick) and 95 (thin) percent confidence intervals shown.

point to some intriguing findings. Unsurprisingly, in the face of increased hostilities, governments from both the left and the right increase relative spending on defense (both Expect 1 and 2). As expected, governments of the right make relative cuts to social protection, but, unexpectedly, governments of the left also make relative cuts to social protection. While these results certainly support an argument for guns versus butter, other results muddy the waters and suggest a guns yield butter story.

In the face of increased hostilities, both governments of the left and right make relative increases to spending on health and education, aligning with the argument that an emphasis on defense can lead to benefits for secondary policy areas that feed into it. We also see that both types of governments make relative cuts to spending on government administration. While this is consistent with our expectations for the right, we did not anticipate this shift on behalf of the left. We find a similar but reverse pattern for economic affairs, where both types of governments make relative cuts to spending. This is consistent with our expectations for left governments, but we did not have this expectation for right governments.

Overall, the results in Figure 4.10 show quite similar tradeoff reactions by left and right governments in the face of increased military conflict, and these patterns offer some support for both of our theoretical arguments. Governments do appear to trade off guns for butter, but the kind of butter matters. Previous research that highlighted defense versus social welfare spending misses this more complex story that not all "butter" policy areas see relative cuts.

4.6 CONCLUSION: CONTEXT, IDEOLOGY, AND TRADEOFFS

When discussing how governments shape budgets in order to correspond with their ideological visions, the domestic and international contexts in which they find themselves can shape those decisions. In this chapter, we have explored how electoral, economic, and international forces can affect the reallocation of budgetary resources. While previous research has mostly emphasized how these factors influence the total budget or a single category of expenditures – such as how hostilities might affect defense spending – our focus has been to paint a more complete picture of how relative budgetary tradeoffs are occurring in response to domestic and international shifts. We have theorized about various relationships between governments, contexts, and budgetary pieces, and created "tournaments" of expectations between ideologically consistent reactions to shocks and reactions in which context plays a larger role. At times, our evidence points to governments making ideologically driven tradeoffs, while at others, they prioritize policy areas outside of their typical ideological priorities. Particularly interesting was our ability to see how both positive and negative contexts, as well as domestic and international contexts affect governments in different ways. A main take away is how some environments constrain, while others facilitate governments' decision-making on budgetary tradeoffs.

When considering the domestic conditions under which governments make budgetary choices, we find that they do not always alter budgetary allocations in response to these changes. Does election timing push left and right governments to make strategic spending tradeoffs that will benefit their electoral chances? Our answer to this question is a resounding "no." While the theories that attempt to explain this strategic behavior offer clear expectations that governments *should* shift budgets for election-year benefits, just how they should move resources is less clear. While we consider two possibilities in our theoretical expectations, we find no evidence that governments make budgetary tradeoffs because of elections. Since we look at the tradeoffs that include both relative increases and decreases across policy areas, these findings add a significant contribution to the already mixed evidence on electoral budget cycles.

Turning to the domestic economic situations surrounding governments, we evaluated both positive and negative economic conditions, theorizing about how they should affect budgetary behavior in different ways. Once again, we showcased two possible expectations, one in which reactions are driven more by ideological priorities and another where context was more important. We observe the biggest differences between ideologically opposed governments with regard to their reactions to an increase in unemployment. The different tradeoffs undertaken by left and right governments in the face of such a negative economic shock are generally consistent with differences in terms of fundamental ideas about the role of government in employment markets. Our results point to a situation where governments attempt to alleviate the economic downturn in varying ways, relying on their ideological preferences to guide their spending shifts. The left chooses public services and administration, while the right moves relatively more funds into education. Our approach also allows us to see the relative decreases and these appear to be ideologically driven, with governments defunding areas prized by their opponents. In the face of rising unemployment, we see a common need for governments to fund redistributive policies at the expense of their oppositions' priorities.

A different picture emerges when governments shift budgets during an economic upswing with a positive shock in real economic growth. Our two competing expectations called for governments to either boost funding for their prized policy areas or to seize the opportunity to shift resources into secondary priorities as a way to expand their electoral bases. What we find is evidence in support of the latter. Similar outcomes arise for left and right governments, both in their relative spending increases and in their decisions on where to cut. Governments appear to take the opportunities available during economically good times to expand into secondary policy areas, although left and right governments may use the resources for these policies in ways that suit their different ideological visions.

Section 4.3 focuses on international conditions, where globalization and conflict may affect governments' behavior on budgetary compositions. With globalization, previous literature is relatively mixed on whether governments will seek to compensate workers for the ill effects of increased economic openness by prioritizing social services and social protection or if they will focus on creating a more efficient and promising business environment to attract investment and capital. Our theoretical tournament includes these two arguments. We find that the tradeoffs governments make under these circumstances lack a coherent ideological bent. For example, right governments relatively decrease spending on social policies, but they also cut back on defense. Our results point to a story of both left and right governments expanding government administrative capacity in the face of rising globalization. We can interpret this as both increasing public sector jobs, as well as on relying on government resources to oversee the open markets and competition. Globalization appears to be a context in which budgetary reallocations fall along mixed ideological lines.

Finally, research on how international conflict affects budgets relies heavily on a "guns versus butter" dichotomy, although, as we discussed, tradeoffs may be more complex in the real world. We offered competing expectations, but a commonality for both is the expectation that increased hostilities will result in governments prioritizing defense expenditures, regardless of ideology. This relative increase in spending was expected to come at the expense of different policy areas for the left and right, emphasizing their ideological differences. Additionally, we offered a second possibility where defense spending may yield spending on redistributive policies; however, left and right governments would be expected to differ on their preferred policies that fall under that heading, emphasizing again their ideological priorities. Interestingly, our findings suggest that governments from both sides trade off butter for guns. In the face of increased hostilities, the evidence points to governments relatively increasing budgets on some redistributive policy areas that fit their respective ideological visions. It is striking how similarly governments reallocate their budgets in the context of international conflict.

While our overall findings in this chapter do not offer a clear verdict in favor of either purely ideologically driven reactions to contexts or to contexts taking center stage, we do see greater evidence of ideologically driven tradeoffs in reaction to domestic economic shocks than we see in response to international environments. Within domestic situations, we find that economic conditions can both help and hinder governments to make ideologically distinct budgetary tradeoffs. Our results suggest that governments are most constrained under adverse conditions, such as economic downturns and international conflict, while an economic boom can facilitate their abilities to fulfil their ideological priorities. Globalization, with its combination of international and economic conditions, appears to be both a help and hindrance to both left and right governments with their mix of similar and different budgetary tradeoffs. Across all of these contexts, except elections, we find evidence that they lead to substantial long-run relative budgetary tradeoffs. Whether these contexts also affect broader budgetary pieces, such as total expenditures and deficits, is the subject of Chapter 6.

4.7 APPENDIX

Perhaps a surprising finding in the main results in this chapter is that we found little evidence of electoral effects on budget compositions. However, most political budget cycle models include elections without interacting the variable with ideology or institutional factors. If researchers show results for interaction models, typically, they are performed as robustness checks. To relate more closely to the empirical literature, in Figure 4.11 we show the results of an election shock *without* interacting the election variable with either ideology or majority government. We find very little

4.7 Appendix

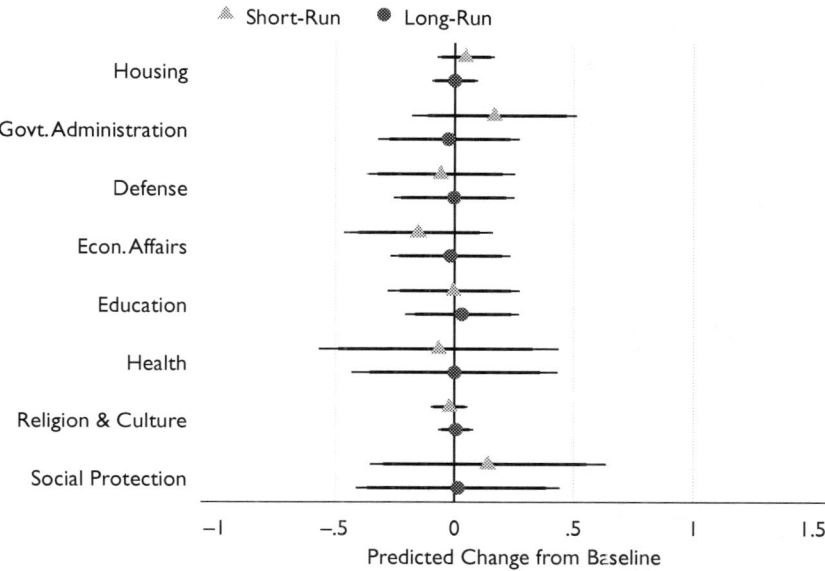

FIGURE 4.11. Further evidence of a lack of a political budget cycle effect

movement as a result of the electoral shock, and none of the short- or long-run effects are statistically significant. This indicates that our earlier findings of little to no electoral effects are robust, regardless of the model specification.

5

Four Sides of the Budgetary Ledger

Brazil is broke, boss, I cannot do anything
Brazilian President, Jair Bolsonaro[1]

The idea that governments make tradeoffs across the broader components of the budgetary ledger – between revenues, expenditures, deficits, and budgetary volatility – resonates with how people think about budgets. Media accounts from countries across the globe rely on such "tradeoff" language to explain government budgetary decisions. Take, for instance, the case of the United Kingdom. When Chancellor of the Exchequer George Osborne presented his budget in 2016, *The Economist* explained: "Mr Osborne's move towards the centre went only so far. Cuts to disability benefits will raise almost enough money to pay for an increase in the personal tax-allowance, from which the middle class will benefit more than the poor."[2]

Not surprisingly, politicians and governments frame their budgetary decisions using tradeoff language as well. When President Donald Trump announced his 2018 budget plan for the United States, he relied on a framework of tradeoffs: "The defense and public safety spending increases in this Budget are offset and paid for by finding greater savings and efficiencies across the Federal Government. Our Blueprint insists

---

[1] www.marketwatch.com/story/brazilian-president-says-his-country-is-broke-heres-why-11609949590. Last accessed October 8, 2021.
[2] *The Economist*; "Britain's budget: The fiddler's charter." www.economist.com/leaders/2016/03/17/the-fiddlers-charter. Last accessed November 12, 2020.

Four Sides of the Budgetary Ledger

on $54 billion in reductions to non-Defense programs."[3] In addition, consider the process of enacting deficit reduction in the 2013 French budget, "The good news is that it demonstrates a firm commitment by President François Hollande and his Socialist government to keep to its deficit-reduction promises. The less good news lies in the balance of taxes and spending that it uses to get there."[4] Each of these examples highlight the interplay between budgetary tools.

Previously, we have shown that politicians speak of expenditure categories as a "pie," where they can allocate more resources to one category at the cost of reductions in other categories and that they react in this manner when confronted with domestic and international stimuli. In this chapter, we turn our theoretical argument to questions about the larger components of the budget in our framework: expenditures, revenues, deficits, and budgetary volatility. We focus on the inter-workings of the components of the budgetary ledger to answer a series of questions. How and when do governments tradeoff spending, revenues, and deficits? For instance, do they offset expenditure increases with a corresponding rise in revenues, or do they pursue deficit spending in response to these various situations? With all of these questions, we are interested in how the components relate to each other and explore whether left and right governments rely on different tools.

In this chapter, we bring together these four components. First, we investigate if and how they affect each other. Then, relying on inferences about the causal relationships between expenditures, revenues, deficits, and budgetary volatility, we explore if and how politics affects these budgetary components. We contend that ideology and power status may lead governments to choose changes in some budgetary components over others. Thinking back to our overall theoretical argument, we ask: do right and left majority governments influence these components in different ways? In Chapter 6, we will further explore how governments may behave differently regarding these components by evaluating varying domestic and international contexts.

Another contribution of this chapter is a methodological one. Accounting for feedback effects between budgetary components is not

---

[3] Budget FY 2018, America First: A budget blueprint to make America great again. Budget of the United States government, Office of Management and Budget, p. 2. Published March 16, 2017. www.budget.gov. Last accessed January 17, 2020.

[4] *The Economist*; "The French budget: One cheer". www.economist.com/charlemagne/2012/09/28/one-cheer. Last accessed November 12, 2020.

straightforward. We rely on a panel vector autoregressive model (Holtz-Eakin, Newey, and Rosen 1988) that allows us to avoid imposing causal orderings on our four budgetary components. This is perfect for our analysis, since we do not have strong expectations about the directions of the arrows in these causal relationships. For example, we do not know whether government expenditures drive revenues, revenues drive expenditures, or whether both or neither of these relationships exist. This methodological approach has seldom been used in political science research to date.[5] Here, it allows us to conduct causality tests, which we use in order to specify our models in Chapter 6.

Specifically, in this chapter we begin by investigating the causal relationships between expenditures, revenues, deficits, and budgetary volatility. This knowledge then informs our model specification when we move onto testing our theoretical ideas about how governments' ideologies and institutional power influence their budgetary decisions. In Chapter 6, we continue to use the evidence of causality that we find in this chapter when we turn to explore how political, economic, and international factors shape these main budgetary components.

5.1 THE BIG PICTURE: AN OVERVIEW OF BUDGETARY COMPONENTS

Since we have not discussed in detail the broader budgetary components, we briefly describe each component here. We acknowledge that there is much research on each one of these pieces, but, for space considerations, we offer only a short overview of how each fits into the larger picture of our causal, budgetary frame.[6]

5.1.1 Introduction to Expenditures

A central role of governments is to spend. Governments use expenditures to fund everything from public housing to highways to naval vessels.

---

[5] The only examples using this approach that we could find are Davies (2016) and Coutts et al. (2019); there are more examples from the economics literature. Our approach also builds on many simple panel VAR estimation strategies by overcoming dynamic bias imposed by controlling for time-invariant country-specific unobserved factors in the context of small-T dynamics through the use of a Generalized Methods of Moments estimator.

[6] Scholars have written entire books on each of these pieces, so we recognize the inadequacies of these sections to those researchers.

5.1 The Big Picture: Overview of Budgetary Components

In the previous chapters, we emphasized the disaggregated categories of spending; here, we focus on total expenditures as a component of the overall budget. Although this approach more closely matches previous research on spending and expenditures (e.g., Persson and Tabellini 2004; Bawn and Rosenbluth 2006; Potrafke 2017), our goal is to take into consideration how expenditures fit into the larger budget and model them more realistically.

How expenditures relate to budget deficits, revenues, and budgetary volatility tends to be straightforward. As governments spend funds, they need to offset this increase with either a rise in revenues or an increase in the deficit (or a combination of the two). Should expenditures fall, governments may cut revenue or run a surplus. As Roubini and Sachs (1989a) note, throughout most of the second half of the twentieth century, both expenditures and revenues – as well as deficits – have tended to increase. The relationship between expenditures and budgetary volatility also appears straightforward, with spending increases or decreases leading to more volatility. But governments may find themselves needing to shift expenditures (see Chapters 3 and 4), even without a change in spending levels, so the link between total spending and volatility may not be as straightforward as first imagined.

Research on budgets tends to be more focused on the associations between expenditures and other components. Whether expenditures are driving these other budgetary components or whether they themselves drive expenditures remains an open question. While it is not uncommon to model multiple budgetary components in a single article – for instance, Katsimi and Sarantices (2012) focus on deficits, expenditures, and revenues – it is uncommon to see all four components modeled simultaneously. Instead, each component is a dependent variable in a separate model. In addition, we are not aware of efforts to uncover the underlying causal relationships between these aggregate components of the budget. While expenditures receive much attention in the budgetary causal game, the empirical research to ground this assumption has been missing.

5.1.2 Introduction to Revenues

All governments require some level of funds to function, so revenues are a vital budgetary component. Discussions about increasing or decreasing taxes on specific groups are commonly debated by politicians around the world, and, while there is much attention on tax systems, our focus here is on total revenues, rather than from where the revenue flows.[7] Previous research has differed in the way revenues are operationalized, ranging from analyzing tax rates (Cusack and Beramendi 2006) and exploring types of revenue (Hollenbach, Lipsmeyer, and Whitten 2021) to understanding tax reforms.[8] For our purposes, we focus on the level of revenues in the aggregate, emphasizing when changes in this total amount occur and exploring how shifts in revenues relate to the other budgetary components. Do they lead to changes in expenditures, deficits, or volatility, or are these components driving revenues?

Thinking of revenues through a lens of government responsibility and size, we next ask if governments' ideologies help shape their revenue decisions. While governments' ideological visions and electoral supporters can play roles in shaping their preferred revenue levels, our theoretical framework emphasizes the political contexts that may affect their abilities to fulfil these goals. As we discussed in earlier chapters, a government's ideology may not influence policy-making if it lacks the power to push its policy agenda through the legislature. We witnessed the influence of institutional relationships on expenditures in Chapter 3, and previous research points to this possibility for revenues as well (Tsebelis and Chang 2004). In other words, we expect that a majority government will be better able to pursue their ideological preferences for more or less revenues.

5.1.3 Introduction to Deficits

With a balanced budget, spending and revenues will result in a zero balance, but governments budgeting decisions, realistically, will result in

---

[7] Indeed, the notion of "who pays" has been the subject of a substantial amount of research in economics and political science. Scholars have studied changes in revenue streams over time, with some using a more historical lens to look at the development of progressive tax states (e.g., relying on income and capital taxation) in the nineteenth and early twentieth centuries (Scheve and Stasavage 2016). Others have focused on the latter half of the 1900s, and the shift from more progressive to more regressive regimes that rely on consumption and insurance taxes (Kato 2003; Ganghof 2006). Much of this historically based research also highlights the various pressures that led to more progressive tax systems before the early 1900s, such as democratization and war (Kiser and Karceski 2017). As Gould and Baker (2002, p. 96) note, "In practice, policy makers consider multiple tax instruments and multiple tax bases. Tax incidence involves multiple dimensions as well, especially the balance between regressivity and progressivity of the tax system, in addition to the overall burden of taxation."

[8] Researchers, for instance, have compared effective tax rates on labor versus capital (Swank and Steinmo 2002) and investigated the timing of the introduction of certain types of taxes (Seelkopf, Lierse, and Schmitt 2016; Seelkopf et al. 2021).

5.1 The Big Picture: Overview of Budgetary Components

TABLE 5.1. *Percentage of years in deficit spending, 1960–2011 for a sample of OECD countries*

Country	% of Years with a Deficit	Country	% of Years with a Deficit
Italy	100	Ireland	80
Portugal	100	Germany	78
Belgium	96	Spain	78
United States	92	Canada	76
France	90	Japan	68
The Netherlands	88	Denmark	48
United Kingdom	84	New Zealand	46
Austria	82	Sweden	42
Australia	80	Finland	20
Greece	80	Norway	4

Source: Wyplosz (2012, p. 496)

either a deficit or a surplus. In this chapter, we investigate how the other budgetary components affect this fiscal tool, and we ask if right or left governments are more likely to rely on deficits.

Table 5.1 illustrates how common budgetary deficits have been in the last 50 years. Between 1960 and 2011, Italy and Portugal ran deficits during the entire time period, and almost 75 percent of these OECD countries ran deficits at least 75 percent of the time. Only the Scandinavian and Nordic countries – plus New Zealand – had deficits less than half the time during this time period. Therefore, deficits are a vital part of the budgetary picture in developed democracies.

The size of deficits can vary, depending on economic and political factors, but if and when these factors will matter remains less clear. For example, the debate over if left or right governments use deficits more often has yet to be resolved (Cameron 1985; Volkerink and De Haan 2001), with the discussion highlighting the left's propensity to raise expenditures and the right's desire to cut taxes as possible causes of ideological differences on deficits. Previous work has also debated whether and how fragmentation in governments (particularly, coalition governments) can result in higher deficits and debt because of collective action problems and/or time horizon issues (Roubini and Sachs 1989a; De Haan and Sturm 1997; Franzese 1999; Persson and Tabellini 2004; Bäck and Lindvall 2015; Weissstanner 2017).

Deficits can offer governments leeway for balancing their spending and revenues, although governments' ideological stances on fiscal budgets may affect their willingness or ability to use these budgetary tools. With majority governments having more sway over budgetary decisions, we are interested in whether left and right majority governments rely on deficits in varying ways.

5.1.4 Introduction to Budgetary Volatility

In Chapter 2, we introduced the notion of budgetary volatility, whereby we may observe more or less movement between expenditure categories at certain times (Tsebelis and Chang 2004; Brender and Drazen 2013).[9] Although expenditures, revenues, and deficits are the traditional components of a budgetary equation, volatility captures how much expenditure categories are moving and shifting, even when aggregate spending may not be changing. How much governments are able to alter budgetary components to fit their preferences remains debatable, but governments should want to make policy changes, leading to more budgetary volatility.

There may be situations where governments feel constrained in terms of the *total* size of expenditures, but they still find enough room to tinker with the various subcomponents (i.e., those analyzed in Chapters 3 and 4). Whether or not we should expect governments on the left and right to move budgets more or less remains unclear. Since budgetary volatility does not indicate shifts in the amount of expenditures, only the changes, government ideology by itself may not influence it. However, these governments may react differently to the economic and international contexts introduced in Chapter 6. With few exceptions (Tsebelis and Chang 2004; Brender and Drazen 2013), volatility measures that analyze total movement in budgets over time have remained understudied in the budgetary literature, but we argue that including this volatility under the "hood" of budgets is the final piece to understanding the political competition at an aggregated level.

5.1.5 Putting the Components Together

In Figure 5.1, we show a visual depiction of how these four budgetary components might fit together. While scholars have studied each one

---

[9] Equation (2.2) showed this as $I_{it} = \frac{\sum_{j=1}^{J} |e_{jit} - e_{ji,t-n}|}{2}$, where budgetary volatility, I_{it}, is the sum of the change between all budgetary categories e_j, observed for country i at time point t and time $t - n$, divided by two.

5.2 Research Design and Modeling Strategy

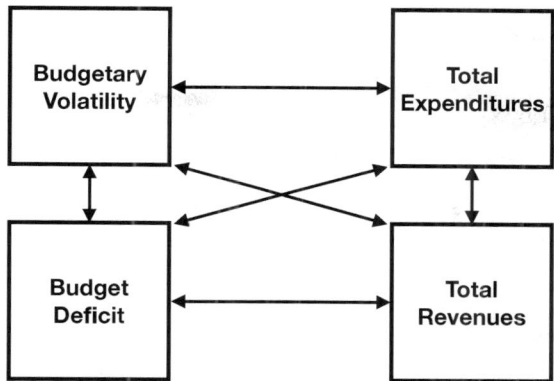

FIGURE 5.1. Possible causal relationships between the four budgetary components

individually (and in some cases two or three together), there is little research that acknowledges the possible interconnectedness of these pieces. How do these components fit together? We argue that understanding which of these causal arrows are empirically supported is an important first step in piecing together a clearer budgetary picture. Once we understand the causal relationships between the four components, we will use that knowledge to update the traditional models about budgets and incorporate the various pieces.

Using our newly specified models, we will explore if governments on the left and right rely on these components in different ways. We recognize that governments must have the ability to enact change, so we will focus on majority governments in our models. Ultimately, our question remains: Do we find varying budgetary outcomes for different governments?

5.2 RESEARCH DESIGN AND MODELING STRATEGY

Unlike Chapters 3 and 4, that focused on compositional expenditures, in this chapter, we are explaining macro-budgetary variables (with the exception of budgetary volatility, that is a single summary measure of expenditure change). Our interest is in exploring the causal relationships between total expenditures, total revenues, budget deficits, and budgetary volatility before we shift to creating a model of each one using our causality-test findings. Further information about the creation of and sources for these variables are in Section 5.7.

To account for economic, political, international, and demographic factors, we also include a series of independent variables in our models.

These are the same as those used in Chapters 3 and 4: GDP growth, unemployment, economic openness, age dependency ratio, a legislative election dummy, hostility level, right government dummy, majority government dummy, and a linear trend term. We discuss their measurements and sources in Section 3.5.

5.2.1 Modeling Strategy

Since we are interested in how changes in expenditures, revenues, deficits, and budgetary volatility affect each other, we have four dependent variables. A straightforward way to model multiple dependent variables simultaneously is to estimate a system of equations known as a vector autoregressive (VAR) model, because it allows each of the variables to be potentially endogenous to one another. For instance, VARs permit past changes in expenditures to affect changes in revenues that in turn might have a feedback effect of affecting expenditures in the future and so on. While in standard models we run the risk of endogeneity if we suspect reverse causality, VARs allow for such feedback effects using fewer assumptions. Such a notion of feedback fits with Figure 5.1, where one budgetary component could affect another that might go on to further affect yet another component (perhaps even spilling back into the original component) and so on.

One complication is that, since we have cross-sectional time series data, we need to estimate a panel VAR or pVAR (Holtz-Eakin, Newey, and Rosen 1988). Abrigo and Love (2016) propose estimating a pVAR using a Generalized Methods of Moments (GMM) framework to both remove unobservable heterogeneity common to each unit and the dynamic bias that results from including lagged dependent variables when the number of total time points is small. For brevity, we do not describe in detail this estimation strategy here, although we offer a full description of this approach in Section 5.8.

In addition to modeling the four possibly endogenous variables described in Section 5.1, we include a host of other variables assumed to be exogenous. As mentioned at the beginning of Section 5.2, these are the GDP growth rate, unemployment rate, change in the level of economic openness, age dependency ratio, an election year dummy, hostility level, a right government dummy, and a majority government dummy. We also include a trend term. Also note that, to ensure stability of the pVAR – something we discuss in Section 5.8 but that essentially ensures the results

5.2 Research Design and Modeling Strategy

are reliable – three of the dependent variables, expenditures, revenues, and deficits, are first-differenced when appearing in the model.[10]

We can represent the resulting system of four equations in our pVAR model as:

Budget Component $A_{it} = f$(Budget Components B,C,D$_{it}$
$\qquad$ + L.Budget Components A,B,C,D + Controls),
$\hfill$ (5.1)

where Budget Component A_{it} is the dependent variable which we specified to be a function of the contemporaneous values of the other three budgetary components, lagged values of itself, and the other three budgetary components (L.Budget Components A,B,C,D), and the control variables listed in the previous paragraph (Controls). We chose the lag structure of L.Budget Components A,B,C,D using a set of model selection criteria explained in Section 5.8.

To uncover the causal relationships between these components, we use the results from our pVAR model to conduct Granger causality tests (Granger 1969). Relying on these test results, we specify separate reduced-form models for each of our budget component variables, which we then use to test for the role of different determinants of each budgetary aggregate in the remainder of this chapter and in Chapter 6. We specify these models as:

Budget Component $A_{it} = f$(Budget Component A_{it-1} + (Budget Component B,C, or D$_{it}$)
$\qquad \times (1 + \text{Right}_{it} + \text{Majority}_{it} + \text{Right}_{it} \times \text{Majority}_{it})$
$\qquad +$ (Budget Component B,C, or D$_{it-1}$)
$\qquad \times (1 + \text{Right}_{it-1} + \text{Majority}_{it-1} + \text{Right}_{it-1} \times \text{Majority}_{it-1})$
$\qquad + \text{Right}_{it} + \text{Majority}_{it} + \text{Right}_{it} \times \text{Majority}_{it}$
$\qquad + \text{Right}_{it-1} + \text{Majority}_{it-1} + \text{Right}_{it-1} \times \text{Majority}_{it-1}$
$\qquad + \text{Controls}_i.$
$\hfill$ (5.2)

where Budget Component A_{it} is the dependent variable for each separate model that is a function of its lagged value, Budget Component A_{it-1}, and only those other budgetary components identified through the Granger causality tests to cause Budget Component A_{it} are included as "Budget Components B,C, or D$_{it}$" and "Budget Components B,C, or

---

[10] We do not first-difference the budgetary volatility measure since it is already effectively in changes.

D_{it-1}." We include dummy variables for right governments, Right$_{it}$, and majority status, Majority$_{it}$, and an interaction between them to test the impact of these variables on each budgetary component. These variables are also interacted with the other relevant budget components at both time t and $t-1$ to allow us to test for differences in the impact of the relevant budgetary components across government ideology and majority status.[11] Based on unit root diagnostics, discussed in Section 5.8, we specify the models of expenditures, revenues, and deficit in levels. Budgetary volatility, which we also found to be stationary, is the only one of our budgetary components that we specify the same way in both the pVAR and the reduced-form models in this chapter.

5.3 BUDGETARY COMPONENT RESULTS

5.3.1 Assessing the Relationship between Expenditures, Revenues, Deficits, and Budgetary Volatility

As in the other chapters in this book, we turn to graphical representations of our models to assess the substantive and statistical significance of our results. One difficulty with our pVAR setup arises from the relaxation of the usual exogeneity assumptions, because this makes it arduous to show the effect of any variable in the pVAR on the endogenous variables.[12] To overcome this issue, we present a series of impulse–response functions (IRFs) that show the effect of a one standard deviation shock – or "impulse" – to the error term for one of the equations and the corresponding "response" across time for all of the equations. Since, by definition, the error term is assumed to be independent from the right-hand side variables in the pVAR, we can think of the impulse as something exogenous and not caused by changes in any of the four budgetary dependent variables.[13]

---

[11] As with our analyses in Chapter 4, we include these interactions sequentially instead of all together for the one budget component that we find to be caused by two others.

[12] Of course, we do not have this difficulty with the variables in the equation that we assumed were exogenous, such as GDP growth. We examine these in Chapter 6.

[13] It is worth noting that shocking one variable and seeing how it affects the others still lacks a strictly causal interpretation. Readers looking for a more technical discussion of IRFs, as well as approaches to establishing stronger causal interpretations of the results, can find it in Section 5.8. An additional issue with this is that the residuals themselves may be correlated across equations, making a single impulse to a single residual less realistic. As is standard practice in the interpretation of VAR models, we show the effects of

5.3 Budgetary Component Results

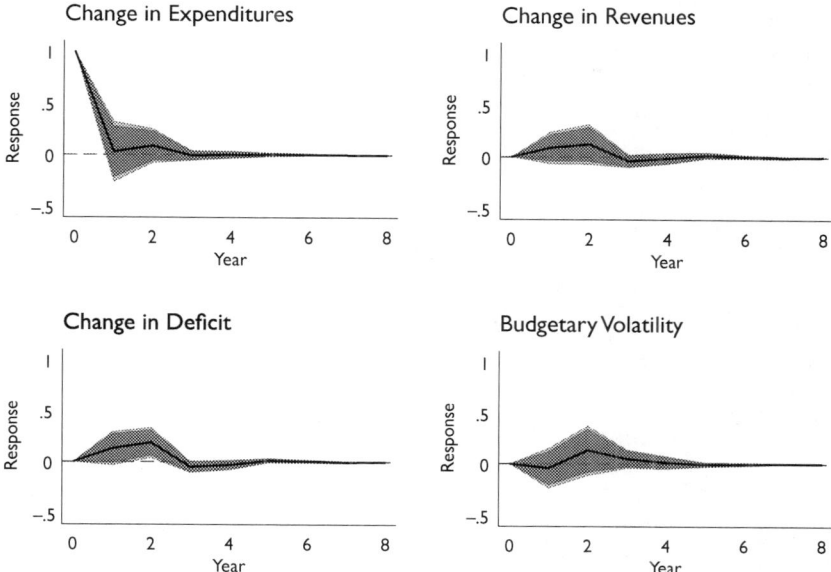

FIGURE 5.2. The effects of an expenditure change impulse

Note: Predicted response in each variable in response to a one standard deviation increase in expenditure change at time $t = 0$ shown in black. Darker and lighter shaded areas show 90 and 95 percent confidence intervals, respectively.

In Figure 5.2, we show the impulse–response function for a one standard deviation increase in expenditure change at time $t = 0$.[14] This acceleration in the rate at which expenditures are changing can clearly be seen in the top-left plot in Figure 5.2 ("Change in Expenditures"), where the shock effectively dissipates to zero by the next year. However, for the other three budgetary aggregates – revenues, deficits, and budgetary volatility – the shock is much more persistent, although the impacts are not typically statistically significant. For instance, changes to both revenues and deficits experience a positive shift of between .1 and .2 standard deviations over the first two years, given a one standard deviation increase in expenditure

---

independent residuals through the creation of orthogonalized impulse response functions in Section 5.8.

[14] Note that, for all of the plots shown in this section, the results are for a one standard deviation increase to ensure comparability between plots and to keep the shock sizes relatively consistent across chapters. We calculate confidence intervals using a parametric bootstrap with 500 simulations.

change. For deficits, this positive change is statistically significant in year two, indicating that an increase in a change in expenditures leads to rising deficits. Budgetary volatility also appears to increase the most two years after a large increase in the change in expenditures, although this effect is not statistically significant. Across all four variables, movements in response to a one standard deviation increase in the change in expenditures are effectively zero after three years, indicating that there is not much persistence, at least in terms of the change in each of the series.

We illustrate the impulse–response function for a one standard deviation increase in the change in revenues in Figure 5.3. This shock dissipates quickly in revenues itself and has effectively no effect on either the change in expenditures or budgetary volatility. However, an increase in revenue change appears to decrease the change in deficits; this effect is statistically significant at the 90 percent level. In other words, given an increase in revenues, deficits are likely to fall one year later. This decline in the rate at which deficits are changing becomes effectively zero after three years. To summarize Figure 5.3, we find that revenues and deficits appear to

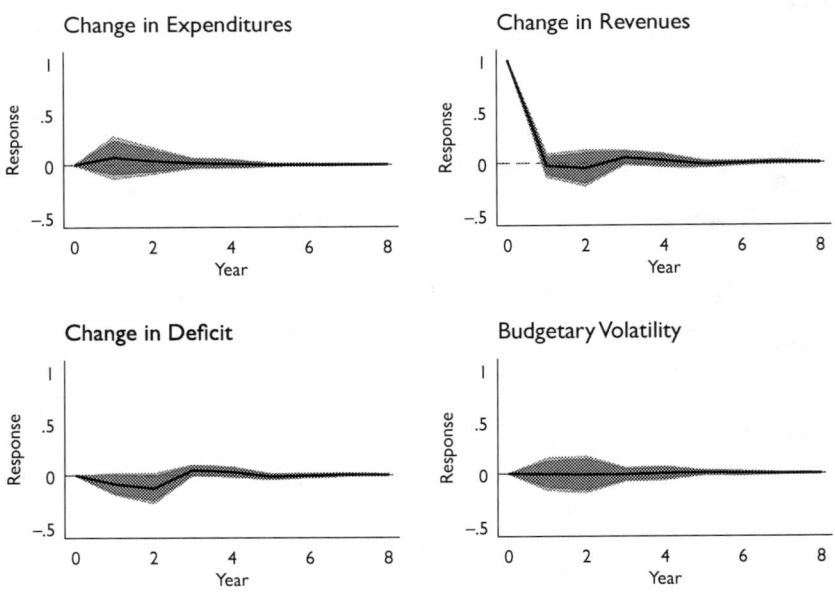

FIGURE 5.3. The effects of a revenue change impulse

Note: Predicted response in each variable in response to a one standard deviation increase in revenue change at time $t = 0$ shown in black. Darker and lighter shaded areas show 90 and 95 percent confidence intervals, respectively.

5.3 Budgetary Component Results

be substitutes. Change in revenues decreases change in deficits, but revenue changes have no effect on either change in expenditures or on the rate at which subcomponents of expenditures are reallocated (budgetary volatility).

Turning to a shock in deficits, we show the impulse–response function for a one standard deviation increase in the change in deficits in Figure 5.4. Deficits themselves quickly dissipate in response to this increase at $t = 0$, but positive changes in deficits are associated with a negative and statistically significant change two years later. While expenditure change does not appear to respond at all to deficits, in contrast, the change in revenues declines by about .2 standard deviations one year after the shock. This effect is statistically significantly different from zero and lasts about one year. Similar to the results in Figure 5.3, this suggests that revenues and deficits are compliments to one another; when deficits rise, revenues fall, and vice versa. We find that the effect on budgetary volatility is also positive but not statistically significant one period after a change in deficits occurs. This implies that sudden increases in deficits are associated with more reallocations of expenditure categories, albeit only weakly.

Last, in Figure 5.5, we display the impulse–response function for a one standard deviation increase in the budgetary volatility measure. Following this shift, the change in expenditures does not increase or decrease, similar to the results in the other IRF figures. Deficit change decreases only slightly, and this effect is not statistically significantly different from zero. In response to the increase in volatility, change in revenue rises one year later, although this effect is not statistically significant. This suggests that, as governments reallocate the spending budget, they also bring in more revenue. Particularly interesting is the persistent effect of budgetary volatility over time in response to a budgetary volatility shock. One year after a one standard deviation shock, budgetary volatility is still slightly increasing, and this effect is statistically significant; it is only two years after a positive shock to budgetary volatility that the change goes back down to zero. This suggests that, once governments begin to reallocate their budgets, they continue to do so.

5.3.2 Which Aggregate Budgetary Components Are Driving the Others?

Similar to the compositional models used in Chapters 3 and 4, tables of VAR results do not lend themselves to easy interpretation due to their

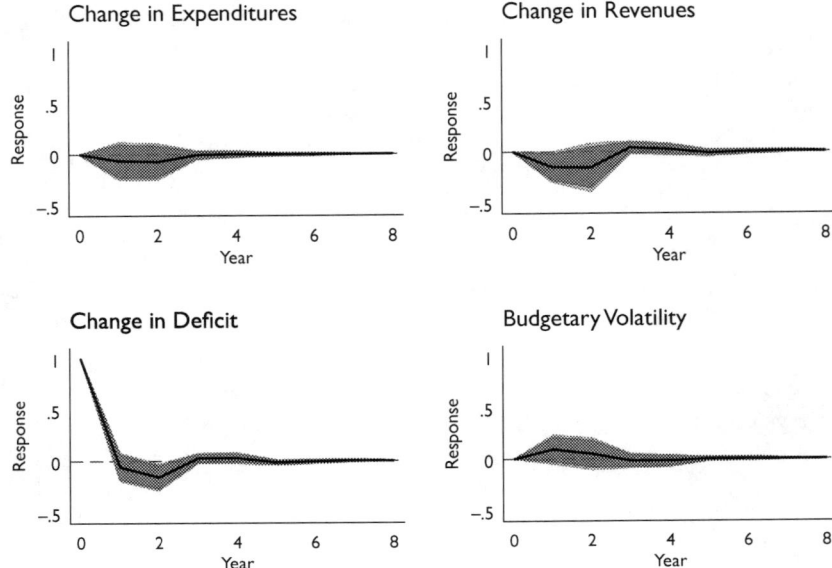

FIGURE 5.4. The effects of a deficit change impulse

Note: Predicted response in each variable in response to a one standard deviation increase in deficit change at time $t = 0$ shown in black. Darker and lighter shaded areas show 90 and 95 percent confidence intervals, respectively.

multiple lags and large number of estimated parameters. Instead, we choose to show figures and simplified tables of results rather than a table of estimates (although the latter can be found in Table 5.4 in Section 5.8).

Since pVARs allow for feedback effects between variables assumed to be endogenous, they are far less restrictive than standard models, but it still can be difficult to establish whether one variable is *causing* movements in another, or vice versa. One common approach to determine these relationships is through Granger causality tests. These are a type of block-exogeneity test that assesses whether lagged values of one variable are statistically significant predictors of another variable, even when accounting for the past history of the latter variable.[15] For brevity, we

---

[15] For instance, given two variables, X_t and Y_t, we would conclude that X_t "Granger-causes" Y_t if, after regressing Y_t on past lags of itself, as well as past lags of X_t, the coefficients on lags of X_t are jointly statistically significant.

5.3 Budgetary Component Results

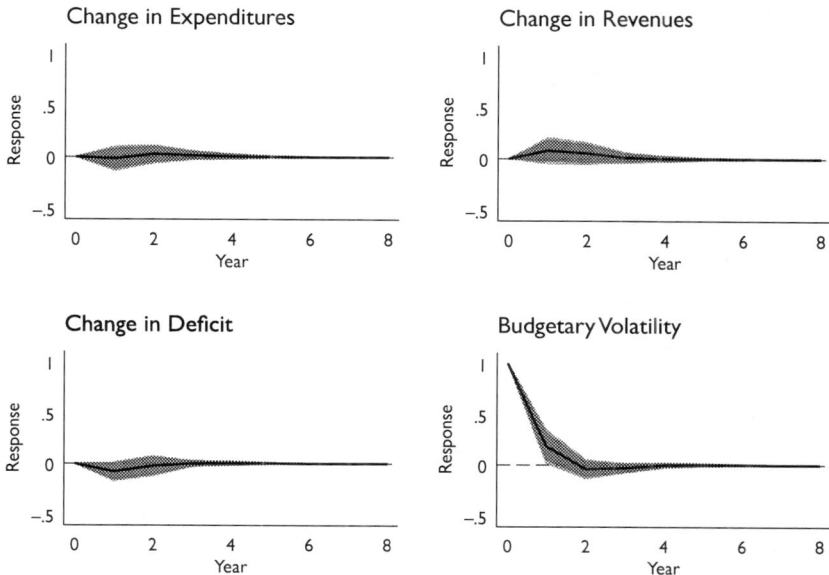

FIGURE 5.5. The effects of a budgetary volatility impulse

Note: Predicted response in each variable in response to a one standard deviation increase in budgetary volatility at time $t = 0$ shown in black. Darker and lighter shaded areas show 90 and 95 percent confidence intervals, respectively.

show a simplified version of the Granger causality tests in Table 5.2 with the full set of results – as well as a more thorough description of these tests – available in Section 5.8 (Table 5.5).

As shown in Table 5.2, Granger causality tests provide evidence that changes in deficits cause changes in revenues. In addition, they indicate that changes in both expenditures and revenues cause deficit changes, although the effect of the latter is only weakly statistically significant. Interestingly, we find no evidence of causality from the other factors to changes in either expenditures or the budgetary volatility measure. Nor do we find evidence that budgetary volatility causes changes to any of the other three variables. The lack of a relationship between change in total expenditures and budgetary volatility is particularly noteworthy and suggests that the budgetary action with spending is at a disaggregated level. We summarize the findings presented in Table 5.2 in Figure 5.6, where the solid arrows indicate evidence of Granger causality at the .05 level or lower, and the arrow with the dashed line reflects evidence of Granger causality at the .10 level.

TABLE 5.2. *Summary of the results from Granger causality tests*

b "Granger-Causes" $\longrightarrow a$	Findings
Δ Expenditures $\longrightarrow$ Δ Revenue	No
Δ Expenditures $\longrightarrow$ Δ Deficit	Yes
Δ Expenditures $\longrightarrow$ Budgetary Volatility	No
Δ Revenue $\longrightarrow$ Δ Expenditures	No
Δ Revenue $\longrightarrow$ Δ Deficit	Weak Support
Δ Revenue $\longrightarrow$ Budgetary Volatility	No
Δ Deficit $\longrightarrow$ Δ Expenditures	No
Δ Deficit $\longrightarrow$ Δ Revenue	Yes
Δ Deficit $\longrightarrow$ Budgetary Volatility	No
Budgetary Volatility $\longrightarrow$ Δ Expenditures	No
Budgetary Volatility $\longrightarrow$ Δ Revenue	No
Budgetary Volatility $\longrightarrow$ Deficit	No

Note: "Weak Support" means that a Wald test for Granger causality is significant at the .10 level, and "Yes" indicates significance at the .05 level. "No" shows a failure to find Granger causality at conventionally accepted levels of statistical significance. We make available the full results in Table 5.5 in Section 5.8. All dependent variables are standardized.

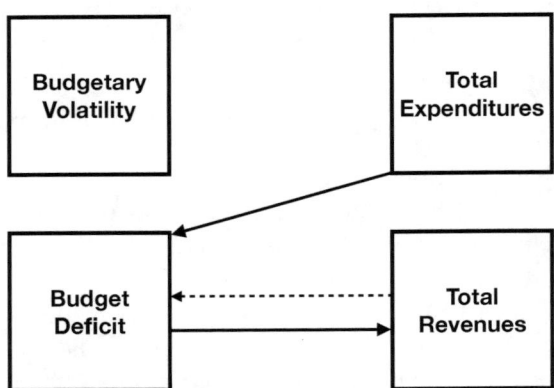

FIGURE 5.6. Updated illustration of how each of the four budgetary components affect one another

5.4 IDEOLOGICAL INFLUENCES AND THE ROLE OF INSTITUTIONAL CONTEXT

When considering ideological differences, in general, right governments would prefer a smaller role of government in the economy compared to

5.4 Ideological Influences and Institutional Context

left governments who would advocate for using government power and resources in the market. These varying ideals of the relationship between government and the economy may translate into how governments use the budgetary components discussed in this chapter – expenditures, revenues, budget deficits, and budgetary volatility. Given their overarching preferences on government responsibility, left and right governments may differ in their reliance on these budgetary tools.

As we have stressed throughout this book, how left and right governments behave on budgets may depend on other factors, such as their political status or power. Because governments rely on the legislature to pass their preferred policies, when governments can draw on a majority of votes, their ability to institute change is considerably stronger (Laver and Shepsle 1996). At the heart of this argument is the link between governments and their level of parliamentary support. By definition, minority governments must rely on non-government parties to ensure the necessary votes for their policy agendas (Strøm 1990a), while majority governments have simply to rely on their own party members. Under a minority government, we can consider the non-government parties in the lower house that are necessary for passing bills as veto players (Tsebelis and Chang 2004), who have the ability to slow down, alter, or even stop legislation desired by the government. Minority governments may not find it as easy to use budgetary tools or make budgetary changes to fit their desired ideological preferences.

5.4.1 Ideology on Expenditures

A sizable literature exists on ideology and the size of government, and researchers tend to start with similar assumptions. The general expectation is that, during periods of left government, government expenditures, typically expressed as a percentage of national output (e.g., GDP), will grow, because they generally favor more government involvement in markets and the economy (Boix 1998). Since right governments favor the opposite, they should oversee lower government expenditures.

Despite such straightforward theoretical characterizations of left versus right government differences, empirical evidence as to whether right and left governments actually differ in terms of total expenditures is more mixed (e.g., Blais, Blake, and Dion 1993; Garrett 2001; Bräuninger 2005; Martin and Vanberg 2013; Herwartz and Theilen 2017). For example, Herwartz and Theilen (2020) do not find a statistically significant difference across ideology on the trajectory of public spending, while others (c.f., Bawn and Rosenbluth 2006) find ideological distinctions under specific circumstances. What explains this lack of differences? Do governments of different ideological stripes use expenditures in similar ways? One explanation might be a convergence of party positions over time. For instance, in the context of Sweden, Blyth and Katz (2005, pp. 51–52) point out that, "the discourse of downsizing has been a recurrent feature of Swedish public debate since the early 1980s, so much so that by the 1998 elections both major parties' policy proposals had converged to the extent that neo-liberal restructuring was universally 'in' while the defense of the welfare state was very much 'out'."

But might the circumstances that surround these decisions matter? Scholars have shown how both the number of government parties (Bawn and Rosenbluth 2006) and the power of finance ministers (Martin and Vanberg 2013) can alter the ability of governments to institute ideological changes to expenditures. Blais, Blake, and Dion (1993) argue that majority governments are better able to implement their ideological changes when it comes to overall government spending. They find that majority status determines whether left governments are actually able to increase total expenditures, while Lipsmeyer (2011) finds a similar conditioning effect of majority power on government ideology for the subset of social expenditures. In contrast, De Haan and Sturm (1997) argue that such a majority–minority distinction does not matter for determining total expenditures. However, in most of this research, and as we will see with all of these budgetary components, the emphasis has been on the individual component rather than considering its position within the larger budgetary picture.

5.4.2 Ideology on Revenues

Similar to expenditures, there is reason to believe that the politics of revenues and taxation is a competitive game. With decisions about raising or lowering taxes – while of course recognizing that no one would like to foot the bill – governments must balance their need for revenues with their ideological preferences and their desire for electoral support.[16]

---

[16] Scholars have investigated how government ideology relates to tax rates, tax bases, and tax systems (Garrett 1998; Basinger and Hallerberg 2004; Cusack and Beramendi 2006; Sakamoto 2008; Plümper, Troeger, and Winner 2009; Angelopoulos, Economides, and

5.4 Ideological Influences and Institutional Context

Ideology has the potential to influence the amount of total revenue a government has at its disposal. We would expect a need for larger amounts of revenue under left governments in order to fund their larger public sectors and more generous government policies, while we would assume that right governments rely on smaller revenues to support a reduced public realm that aligns with their ideological preference for less government involvement in the economy and society (Huber, Ragin, and Stephens 1993; Cusack and Beramendi 2006).[17] If we consider the mix of budgetary components, left and right governments may rely on different components, resulting in ideological distinctions. For example, governments may pursue fiscal adjustments – such as reducing deficits – in different ways, with the left increasing revenues and right governments decreasing expenditures (Tavares 2004).

The extant research also highlights the possibility that government ideology does not play a role in revenue amounts. Potrafke (2017, p.738) points out that "governments certainly have less means to influence tax revenues (which depend on the business cycle) than expenditures," and Harrinvirta and Mattila (2001), for example, find no ideological differences in terms of changes to total revenues for 17 OECD countries.[18] Therefore, how much governments can affect revenues remains unclear.

In the realm of taxation and revenues, institutional contexts may come into play on whether governments achieve their goals. More veto players or diminishing the power of the government is related to an inability by governments to make changes in taxes that translate into more stability in the tax mix (Ashworth and Heyndels 2002). This may alter the effect of ideology on certain types of tax revenues, such as taxes on labor (Cusack and Beramendi 2006). By extension, these constraints may cause a decrease in overall tax revenues over time (and higher debt) (Alesina and Drazen 1989). Dash and Raja (2014) also argue that unstable gov-

---

Kammas 2012), but we note here that our interest is in total revenue as a budgetary component.

[17] Interestingly, research has highlighted the inconsistencies of left and social democratic parties when supporting more regressive taxes to fund the welfare state in the latter part of the 1900s (Swank 2002; Kato 2003; Beramendi and Rueda 2007). One proposed explanation of these often unexpected findings is akin to the Nixon-to-China theory, "if a left-wing cabinet adjusts by increasing taxes it may be perceived as partisan, whereas if the same cabinet cuts spending it signals to economic agents the urgency and benefits of the fiscal adjustment" (Tavares 2004, p. 2451).

[18] Interestingly, research also shows that left governments tend to be more optimistic in their revenue forecasts than their right counterparts (Jochimsen and Lehmann 2017).

ernments (e.g., those without majority status) are more likely to discount the future, so they expect these types of governments to decrease taxes, resulting in decreasing total revenue, to attract electoral support.

As the previous paragraph highlights, researchers have focused on the possible direct effects of institutions on revenues with an expectation that minority governments will decrease taxes and revenues, regardless of their ideologies. However, we are more interested in how these ideological and institutional dynamics affect the budgetary behavior of governments. As Tavits (2004) shows, governments with more dispersed power (or consensus governments such as Belgium or Switzerland, per Lijphart (1999)) are associated with higher total revenues, and this effect increases with rising left party cabinet seats, highlighting how left parties are associated with larger governments (in this case, total revenues). A similar logic may hold here. With minority governments needing to consider and appease more non-government parties in the legislature, these types of governments may not be able to alter their preferred revenue levels based on ideological preferences. Instead, they will negotiate a compromise that ultimately will diminish the effect of ideology on revenues. For majority governments, their higher level of political power should lead to changes that reflect the ideological vision of the government. To summarize, we expect to find that right majority governments will decrease revenues, while left majorities will increase revenues. Under minority governments, we do not expect ideology to have an impact on revenues.

5.4.3 Ideology on Deficits

Just as with revenues and expenditures, governments' ideological leanings may influence the timing and size of deficits. The general expectations are that right governments, with their general tendency toward fiscal austerity, will find it less palatable to run a deficit rather than cut spending on government programs, while left governments will be more willing to fund public policies with future funds.

Previous research on the effects of these ideological differences includes work that provides evidence in support of ideologically driven deficits (Alesina and Roubini 1993; Boix 2000), as well as research that questions ideological differences on deficits (Hahm, Kamlet, and Mowery 1995; Potrafke 2017). Researchers also discuss the underlying causes of deficits with an eye on possible left and right distinctions. Some explanations focus on left governments' propensities to both spend and tax more than the right, resulting in lower deficits and no ideological differences on

5.4 Ideological Influences and Institutional Context

deficits (Hahm, Kamlet, and Mowery 1995; Volkerink and De Haan 2001), while both types of governments are "equally likely to make successful fiscal adjustments" (Alesina and Perotti 1995, p. 234).[19] Tavares (2004) argues that left governments raise revenues to keep deficits in check, while others argue that the right decreases spending for the same reason; this results in no ideologically significant differences in deficits. Müller, Storesletten, and Zilibotti (2016, p. 253) illustrate the mixed findings regarding ideology and fiscal balance in the context of Europe:

> ...postwar European history is full of instances in which the right has been less fiscally responsible than the left. In Sweden, the debt–GDP ratio increased during the conservative governments of Fälldin and Bildt, and was reduced by the subsequent Social Democratic governments. In Italy, debt expanded first under the center coalition governments of the 1980s, and remained thereafter high under the right-wing governments of Berlusconi, while falling during Prodi's left-leaning cabinets.

Another reason for the mixed findings might be uncertainty over whether the next government will be of the same ideological orientation as the current government, producing a time-inconsistency problem (Persson and Svensson 1989). For instance, Seiferling (2019, pp. 8–9) finds that, although budget surpluses are generally higher under right governments than left (or center) governments, "a right-wing government, who believes that their most likely successor is of a similar ideology, will tend to run a .73 percent surplus, while a right-wing government who believes that their successor is of a left-leaning ideology will tend to run a .07 percent surplus." Therefore, a government may behave in a fiscally irresponsible manner – regardless of ideology – if it looks like taking on increased debt to finance the deficits will be passed along to governments of a different ideology.[20] Running deficits might even be used by governments as a way to fiscally "tie the hands" of future governments (Alesina and Passalacqua 2016).

In shifting away from ideology, previous research has also focused on institutional reasons for why governments run deficits. Here, the institutional argument emphasizes the possibility that governments with more

---

[19] Hahm, Kamlet, and Mowery (1995) find that, although larger governments tend to spend more, they also tax more, and thus deficits remain largely unchanged. Nor are there ideological differences between left and right government with regard to the latter budgetary instrument.

[20] This increased tendency of taking on debt has been found to be mitigated by coalitions that, in some instances, may produce a longer time-horizon and, thus, may be adverse to increased debt (Bäck and Lindvall 2015; Weisstanner 2017).

actors (such as coalition governments) or those with less power (such as minority governments) lack the ability to keep spending contained and revenues high (Roubini and Sachs 1989b; Edin and Ohlsson 1991; Grilli, Masciandaro, and Tabellini 1991; Hahm, Kamlet, and Mowery 1995; Tsebelis and Chang 2004; Bawn and Rosenbluth 2006). However, the empirical results have been mixed in terms of whether or not fragmented governments are really more likely to run higher deficits (Potrafke 2019). Some research finds that coalitions do not increase deficits; instead, they raise both expenditures and revenues, keeping deficits in line with less fractured governments (Harrinvirta and Mattila 2001). Alternatively, Roubini and Sachs (1989b) argue that coalition governments lack the consensus necessary to stabilize budgets. Edin and Ohlsson (1991), in a re-analysis of this work by Roubini and Sachs (1989b), find that the latter's conclusions that coalitions are unable to reduce budget deficits is due to minority governments, rather than coalitions more broadly. However, building off these prior findings, in another re-analysis, De Haan, Sturm, and Beekhuis (1999) find no support for either the "power dispersion" hypothesis of Roubini and Sachs (1989b), or the effect of minority (not majority coalition) governments as suggested by Edin and Ohlsson (1991). In yet another view of the issue, others have come to the conclusion that holding a majority of the seats in parliament is associated with lower deficits (Volkerink and De Haan 2001).

For the most part, these institutional arguments do not take into consideration that government configurations and power (i.e., majority versus minority governments) may have varying effects on deficits depending on ideological preferences. The exploration of government ideology and government power separately offers only limited insights into political competition on deficits. Here, we are interested in analyzing whether institutions affect governments' abilities to use deficits in varying ways.

5.4.4 Ideology on Budgetary Volatility

Sections 5.4.1–5.4.3 have offered brief surveys of how government ideology and minority–majority status may affect expenditures, revenues, and deficits. Our fourth component, budgetary volatility, has attracted much less attention. While ideological influences on budgetary volatility may be possible, we do not have assumptions that lead us to expect that a left or right government may be more or less "active" from a budgetary perspective. Indeed, as Brender and Drazen (2013) point out, most academic articles focus on ideology's effects on a particular piece of an entire spending composition, not on how much change is taking place. The existing literature is largely silent on budgetary volatility itself, including how coalitions or ideology may affect such volatility.

If we consider what political circumstances may affect volatility, then we can see how government power may be a key factor. Once they gain power, both left and right governments will set out to alter expenditures to fit their own preferences, so the amount of change may not vary across ideological differences. But, as we witnessed in Chapter 3, majority status can benefit governments in their pursuit of reallocating budgets. When it comes to overall budgetary volatility, then, majority status will likely have a direct effect, regardless of the ideology of the government. There is an alternative scenario, whereby minority governments rival their majority counterparts in altering budgets with the result that majority–minority status has no effect on budgetary volatility. Since minority governments must negotiate and appease more political parties than their own members, they may find themselves making a multitude of changes to ensure that all interested actors receive their due.

Because there are so few studies of budgetary volatility, empirical evidence on these claims is limited. Brender and Drazen's (2013) finding that the vote shares of the largest party in parliament (as well as the vote share of the incumbent party in presidential systems) are largely unassociated with budgetary volatility suggests that volatility may not shift as a result of a majority government coming to power. Using their measure of budgetary volatility, Tsebelis and Chang (2004) specifically find no difference between majority and minority governments on volatility. While we do not expect ideology to alter budget volatility, we acknowledge that government power in the form of majority governments may be better positioned to enact more changes, although the alternative that minority governments will reallocate more to appease nongovernment parties is also plausible. Given these competing arguments and the general lack of previous work on the effects of majority status and ideology on budgetary volatility, we have competing expectations of what we will see in these models.

5.5 THE EFFECTS OF IDEOLOGY AND INSTITUTIONS ON BUDGETARY COMPONENTS

Recall that the Granger causality diagnostics from our pVAR model indicated that deficits cause total revenues and that both total revenues and total expenditures cause deficits. In addition, we did not find that the other components caused either total expenditures or budgetary volatility. Using these findings as a guide, we specify the budgetary component part of a series of reduced-form single-equation models in which we can test our theoretical ideas about the influence of ideology and institutions on individual budgetary components, as presented in Equation (5.2). Next, we will show the effects of expenditures and then revenues on deficits across right and left (majority and minority) governments. Following that, we will see the effect of deficits on revenues also across these government types. Since these models involve a large number of interactive terms, it is difficult to glean much information from the numeric presentation of the results.[21] For this reason, we present a series of graphical figures to assess the degree to which inferences from these models comport with our theoretical expectations discussed in Section 5.4 and present the full numerical tables from these models in the Section 5.8.

5.5.1 How Budgetary Components Affect Each Other under Governments with Different Ideologies and Majority Status

Much of our argument throughout the book has been that ideological *and* institutional contexts will work together to affect the influence of other factors on budgets. In this section, we present a series of graphs to interpret the results from the highly interactive models that involve ideology, majority–minority status, and the aggregate budgetary components deemed relevant to cause each other from our pVAR model.

Beginning by modeling deficits, in Figure 5.7, we show the effects of a one standard deviation increase in expenditures on deficits across ideology and minority–majority status.[22] Since we estimate an autoregressive distributed lag model, we show both the short- and long-run effects. Across all combinations of majority status and ideology, we can see that an increase in expenditures leads to a substantial short-run increase in the deficit. Although the size of the resulting increase declines, it is still statistically significant and positive in the long run. There are, however, no statistically significant differences across ideology and majority status, suggesting that different government types respond in a similar

---

[21] We include the numeric results for these models in Section 6.7 in Tables 6.1–6.4.
[22] As discussed in Section 3.6.2, we found that the overall standard deviation changes for expenditures, revenues, and deficits were rather large, so we instead show one standard deviation increases using the within formula. In the case of expenditures, this means an increase of 6.62 percent of GDP, 5.84 percent for revenues, and 3.49 percent for deficit.

5.5 Effects of Ideology and Institutions

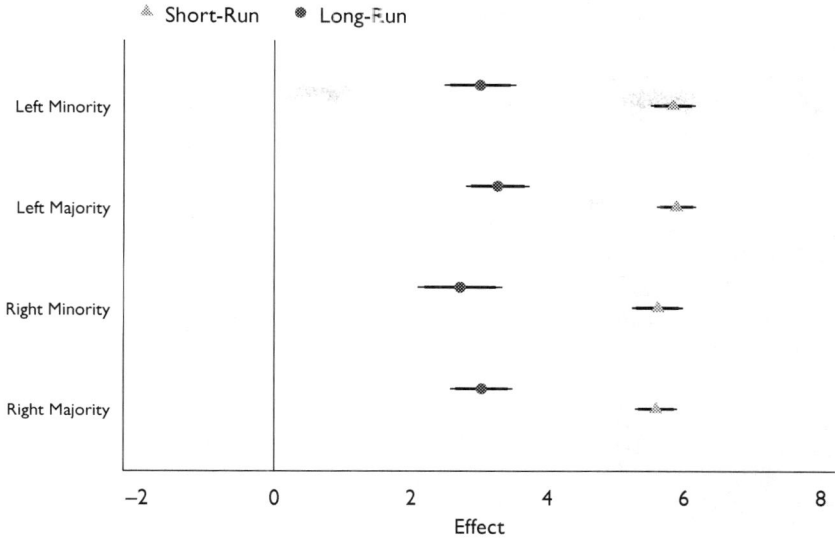

FIGURE 5.7. The effects of a one standard deviation (within) increase in expenditures on the deficit

manner. When expenditures increase, deficits increase substantially in the short-run, followed by a smaller, positive, and significant change in the long-run.

In Figure 5.8, we see the marginal effects of a one standard deviation increase in revenues on the deficit. In all cases, both the short-run and long-run effects are statistically significant and negative. As we saw with expenditures, the effects of an increase in revenues are larger in the short-run than in the long-run. Once again, we do not find that this pattern differs across the four government types.

Switching to our model of revenues, in Figure 5.9, we show the marginal effects of a one standard deviation increase in the deficit. Here, we see somewhat different results from what we observed in our models of deficits. For both left and right minority governments, as well as for majority right governments, there are no statistically significant effects for an increase in the deficit on revenues. However, for left majority governments, there are statistically significant borderline results indicating that in both the short- and long-run an increase in the deficit leads to an increase in revenues. The short-run change is significant at the 90 percent level, while the long-run effect is significant at the 95 percent level.

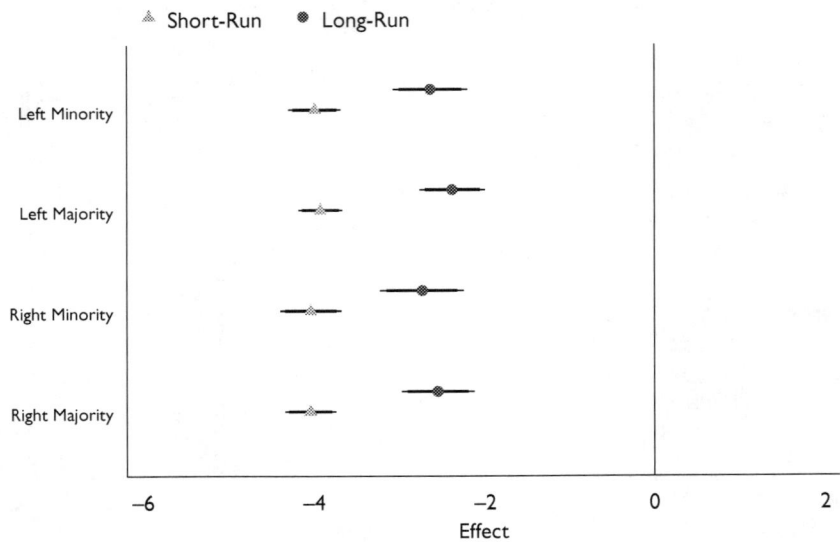

FIGURE 5.8. The effects of a one standard deviation (within) increase in revenues on the deficit

5.5.2 Results of Ideology and Institutions on Individual Budgetary Components

Section 5.5.1 showed that, with only one exception, the influence of the budgetary components on each other did not vary across the different ideological and institutional government types. One last question remains: Do government ideology and majority or minority status interact with one another to affect certain aggregate components of the budget? To test for this possibility, we interact ideology and our majority–minority indicator and analyze our four budgetary components individually.

Starting with total expenditures, in Figure 5.10a, we show the effect of moving from a left to right government for both majority and minority government status. This first figure indicates that there are no statistically significant effects across ideology in the short- or long-run for either majority or minority governments when it comes to spending. We see a similar pattern for revenues in Figure 5.10b: no significant political effects. For both deficits (Figure 5.10c) and budgetary volatility (Figure 5.10d), we observe no effects for government ideology and minority governments. However, we do find that, for deficits, a shift from a left majority to a right majority government has a significant negative long-run

5.6 Conclusion: Four Components of the Budget

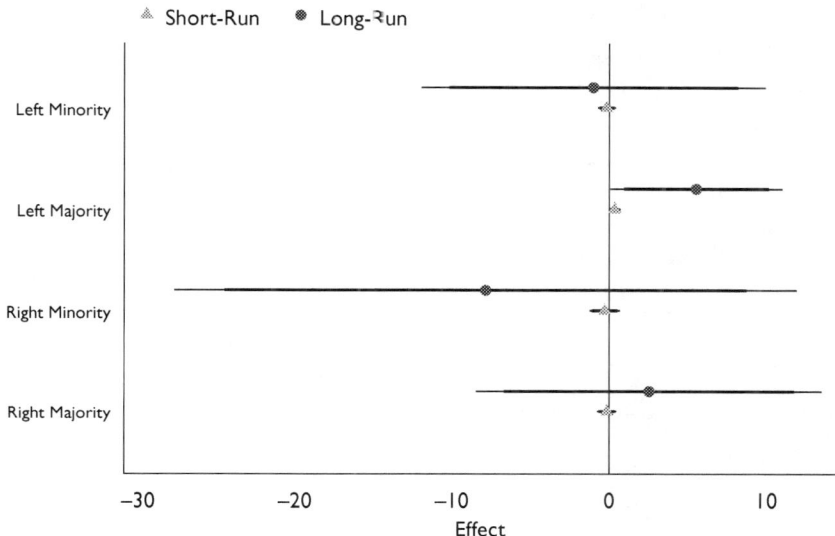

FIGURE 5.9. The effects of a one standard deviation (within) increase in the deficit on revenues

effect at the 90 percent confidence level. For budgetary volatility, we also see that a shift from a left to a right majority government is associated with a positive effect at the 90 percent confidence level. In both of these cases, then, the results are suggestive that, over the long-run, moving from a left to a right government leads to a decrease in deficit spending and an increase in budgetary volatility.

5.6 CONCLUSION: FOUR COMPONENTS OF THE LARGER BUDGET

How do governments make tradeoffs across the broader budgetary ledger? We asked this question throughout this chapter, building a theoretical framework that tied together revenues, expenditures, deficits, and budgetary volatility. We contended that analyzing all four budgetary components fits closer with how governments, politicians, and the media discuss budgets.

Because of a lack of previous work that links all of these pieces together, we started this chapter without many preconceived notions, other than that these components would be related. Our first job was to investigate the causal relationships between these budgetary pieces. Therefore, we

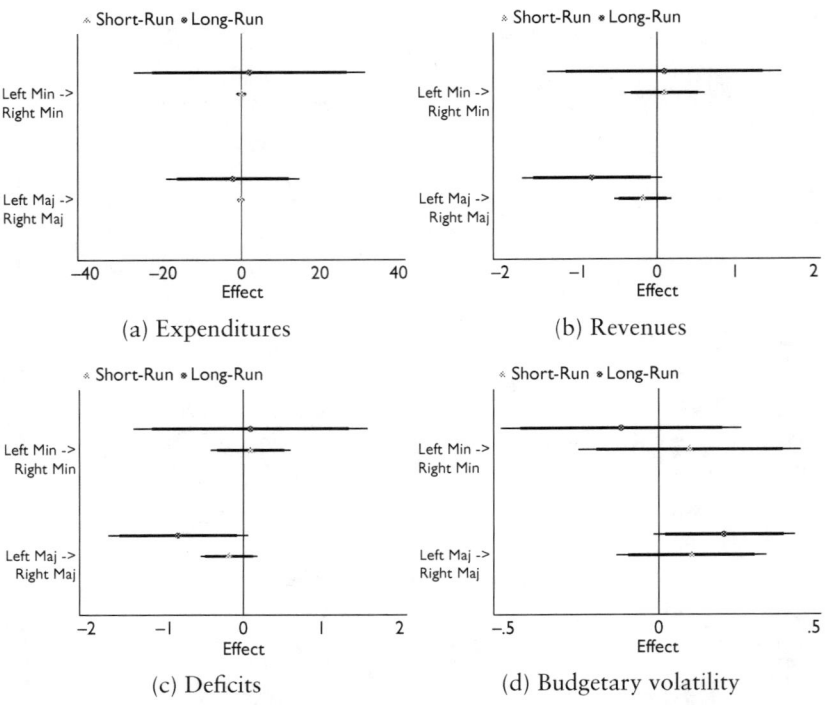

FIGURE 5.10. The effects of moving from left to right government

Note: 95 (thin) and 90 percent (thick) confidence intervals shown.

started our analyses in this chapter by estimating flexible models that made few assumptions about causality, before narrowing our specification and estimating single-equation models, particularly for deficits and revenues (since we found that other budgetary components affected those two categories, but not the reverse). Relying on assumptions from our previous theoretical argument, we examined whether these causal relationships between the pieces differed across left and right governments of majority and minority status, but we found that these big budgetary areas do not vary across governments types.

This chapter also offered a substantial methodological contribution to the study of budgets, because we acknowledge that the budgetary components are not determined in isolation from one another. While in previous chapters – and in much of the extant literature – we can account for this by controlling for the other budgetary aggregates, this still requires the assumption that we know which component is affecting the other, and that there are no feedback effects. This is an assumption unlikely to be met in the real-world. Our approach of using panel vector autoregressive models is one way of relaxing unrealistic assumptions and turning them into testable propositions. Interested readers are encouraged to consult Section 5.8 for a more technical discussion of this approach.

A number of important findings from this chapter are worth restating here. We found strong evidence that expenditures are positively related to budget deficits, and this relationship holds up regardless of the ideology and majority status of the government. Also, we highlight the similarly strong results for the negative relationship between revenues and deficits, again, regardless of government ideology and majority status. The one place where we found ideological and institutional effects for these relationships was for the effect of an increase of the deficit on revenues. Under a left majority government, there was a positive relationship between these two budgetary components.

However, we do find that our results suggest political competition within the interactive analyses of the budgetary components. Government ideology and status do not appear to alter either expenditures or revenues, indicating that moving from a left to right government does not significantly influence those budgetary pieces. But, as we would have expected, a shift from a left to a right majority government is associated with a long-run decrease in deficits, and we do not see this relationship for the same shift with minority governments. While we did not have an ideological expectation for budgetary volatility, our results suggest an outcome that does fit with our story. A move from a left to a right majority government corresponds with a positive significant increase in volatility, and, once again, we do not find that result for minority governments. This finding fits our expectations that it is political competition that shifts budgets, with government ideology driving these differences.[23] In Chapter 6, we relax the "holding all else constant" idea and explore the interactive effects of government ideology and majority status under different political, economic, and international circumstances.

5.7 DATA APPENDIX

Data on expenditures, revenues, and deficits are from the World Bank World Development Indicators.[24] Expenditures (or "expense" as the

---

[23] Also see Brender and Drazen (2013) for their argument about regime change and volatility.
[24] Indicators that appear on the World Bank's website commonly are sourced from a variety of places, including the International Monetary Fund, the Organization for Economic Cooperation and Development, and the World Bank itself.

World Bank calls it) are "cash payments for operating activities of the government in providing goods and services. This includes compensation of employees (such as wages and salaries), interest and subsidies, grants, social benefits, and other expenses such as rent and dividends."[25] In other words, it is the broadest measure of government spending. Revenues data are "cash receipts from taxes, social contributions, and other revenues such as fines, fees, rent, and income from property or sales."[26] As is commonly done, this measure excludes grants. Both expenditures and revenues are expressed as percentages of GDP, and we reformulate each measure as the annual percentage change relative to the previous year so that positive values for our expenditure measure indicate that expenditures are growing relative to last year.

Data on deficits are the difference between revenues and expenditures (also subtracting the net acquisition of non-financial assets).[27] We use the negative of this series, such that positive values mean that there is a deficit and negative values indicate a budgetary surplus. One distinction to make is that deficits – a measure of budgetary balance – and debt – a measure of the total amount a government owes – are often used interchangeably. We prefer the former for several reasons. First, it speaks more to our annual "balance sheet" approach where expenditures and revenues directly affect government balance, and, second, the use of deficits appears to be more common in the literature.

We discussed the creation of budgetary volatility measures in Section 2.1.2. Using a similar measure to that in Brender and Drazen (2013),[28] we specify budgetary volatility as:

$$I_{it} = \frac{\sum_{j=1}^{8} |e_{jit} - e_{ji,t-1}|}{2}, \qquad (5.3)$$

---

[25] Source: https://data.worldbank.org/indicator/GC.XPN.TOTL.GD.ZS. Last accessed November 19, 2020. Similar to the COFOG expenditure compositional data we used in Chapters 3 and 4, for expenditures and revenues, we first used central government finance data. If these series were not available, budgetary central government data were used, although it may omit certain types of spending, such as on pensions. Countries that are highly decentralized may also appear to have lower central government finances than centralized ones, even though local governments might be substantially involved in the economy.

[26] Source: https://data.worldbank.org/indicator/GC.REV.XGRT.GD.ZS. Last accessed November 19, 2020.

[27] Source: https://datacatalog.worldbank.org/cash-surplusdeficit-gdp. Last accessed November 19, 2020.

[28] As Brender and Drazen (2013) point out, in their measure, they use absolute values, rather than the Euclidean distance employed by Tsebelis and Chang (2004).

where I_{it}, the measure of budgetary volatility in country i in year t, is the absolute change between expenditure category, e_j, and the prior year, summed across all $J = 8$ categories, divided by two.[29] The expenditure categories are the same as in Chapters 3 and 4: government administration, defense, economic affairs, education, health, religion and culture, social protection, and housing. Bounded by 0 and 100, larger values indicate greater absolute shifts in the budget.

5.8 STATISTICAL APPENDIX

5.8.1 Stationarity Testing: Budget Components

In Section 3.6.3.1, we presented the results from panel unit root tests for the variables analyzed in Chapters 3 and 4. Similarly, in Table 5.3, we present the results from panel unit root tests for our four budget components. Across the board, we can see that we are able to reject the null hypothesis at the .05 or lower level for lag lengths of unit root tests conducted without a trend term. Oddly enough, though, the results are more mixed, especially for revenues when we repeat these same tests with a trend term. Visual inspection of these series does not indicate the presence of a general trend in any of these series, so we are comfortable analyzing these variables in levels for the single equation models discussed in Section 5.5.

5.8.2 Panel Vector Autoregressive Models

As discussed in this chapter, we make use of a panel vector autoregressive model to help identify which of our budget components are endogenous to each other. This involves estimating a system of equations, allowing certain variables to be potentially endogenous, as well as – for our purposes – accounting for unobservable unit heterogeneity and eliminating coefficient bias introduced by having small T time periods through the use of generalized methods of moments (GMM).

In Equation (5.2.1), we presented a simplified representation of our model specification. In more detailed terms, the dependent variables are

---

[29] In their article, Brender and Drazen (2013) examine different temporal changes in budgets. We looked at two- and four-year changes as well. While the results were similar (they correlate with the measure in Equation (5.3) at .71 and .52, respectively), there was a substantial loss of data due to taking so many lags.

TABLE 5.3. *Panel unit root tests: budgetary component*

Budget Component	No Trend			Trend		
	IPS	F-DF	F-PP	IPS	F-DF	F-PP
Expenditures	3/3	6/6	6/6	3/3	2/6	6/6
Revenues	3/3	6/6	6/6	1/3	0/6	0/6
Deficit	NA	6/6	6/6	NA	4/6	6/6
Budgetary Volatility	3/3	6/6	6/6	3/3	6/6	6/6

Note: Each cell reports the number of tests in which we are able to reject the null hypothesis that all panels contain unit roots at $p < .05$. For the Im Pesaran Shin tests (referenced in this table as "IPS"), we report the results from three tests without a trend term and three tests with a trend term, each with zero, one, and two lags. Because the two Fisher-type tests (referenced in this table as "F-DF" for Fisher–Dickey-Fuller and "F-PP" for Fisher–Phillips-Perron) report two different test statistics appropriate for our data structure, and because we conducted each test with one, two, and three lags, we report for each test the results from six different tests estimated without trend and six different tests estimated with trend. Due to gaps in the time series for our measure of deficit, we were unable to estimate the Im Pesaran Shin test statistics, thus the "NA" in those cells indicating that these results are not available.

specified as Y_{it}, a 4×1 vector observed for each country i in year t of the following (potentially) endogenous variables:

$$Y_{it} = \begin{bmatrix} \Delta \text{Expenditures}_{it} \\ \Delta \text{Revenues}_{it} \\ \Delta \text{Deficit}_{it} \\ \text{Budgetary Volatility}_{it} \end{bmatrix}. \quad (5.4)$$

Thus, our four dependent variables of interest are the change in total government expenditures (as a percentage of GDP), the change in total government revenues (as a percentage of GDP), the change in a country's debt (as a percentage of GDP), and the one-year budgetary volatility measure for expenditures used by Brender and Drazen (2013) and discussed in Chapter 2 (Equation (2.2)):

$$I_{it} = \frac{\sum_{j=1}^{J} |e_{jit} - e_{ji,t-1}|}{2}. \quad (5.5)$$

In other words, I_{it} is a measure of year-to-year total budgetary volatility across all J categories of the budget (e.g., health, defense, public services, ...). Since this variable is analogous to a first-difference, we do not difference I_{it} like the other variables in Equation (5.4). We take the change of the other three series for two reasons. First, it helps to ensure model stability, as we discuss in more detail in Section 5.8.4. The second reason is because instruments in GMM models tend to be weak when the series are near-unit roots (Blundell and Bond 1998) and the estimators have been shown to have poor performance (Pickup et al. 2017).[30] Thus, we can think of them as being near-unit roots.

We model vector $\mathbf{Y}_{it}$ as a function of its prior p lags, $\mathbf{X}_{it}$, which is a $k \times 1$ vector of control variables that are assumed to be exogenous, $\mathbf{u}_i$, which is a 4×1 vector of country intercepts, and ε_{it}, which is an error term that may be correlated across the equations for $\mathbf{Y}_{it}$:[31]

$$\mathbf{Y}_{it} = \mathbf{A}_1 \mathbf{Y}_{i,t-1} + \mathbf{A}_2 \mathbf{Y}_{i,t-2} + \cdots + \mathbf{A}_p \mathbf{Y}_{i,t-p} + \mathbf{B}\mathbf{X}_{it} + \mathbf{u}_i + \varepsilon_{it}. \quad (5.6)$$

While Equation (5.6) is straightforward to estimate, adding successive lags in the presence of the unit fixed effects produces the well-known Nickell (1981) bias in small T and large N (Nerlove 1967).[32] To overcome this issue, we start with Equation (5.6) and, assuming that the transformed residuals $\Delta \varepsilon_{it}$ are not autocorrelated, estimation in first-differences will remove the unit intercepts from the equation:

$$\Delta \mathbf{Y}_{it} = \mathbf{A}_1 \Delta \mathbf{Y}_{i,t-1} + \mathbf{A}_2 \Delta \mathbf{Y}_{i,t-2} + \cdots + \mathbf{A}_p \Delta \mathbf{Y}_{i,t-p} + \mathbf{B}\Delta \mathbf{X}_{it} + \Delta \varepsilon_{it}. \quad (5.7)$$

A further problem arises in Equation (5.7) in that, due to taking first-differences, by construction $\Delta \mathbf{Y}_{i,t-1}$ and $\Delta \varepsilon_{it}$ will no longer be independent.[33] To overcome this form of endogeneity, a number of scholars have advocated using prior lags of the right-hand side variables (both in level and first-difference form) as instruments (Arellano and Bond 1991; Arellano and Bover 1995; Blundell and Bond 1998). Since the number of instruments tends to be larger than the number of regressors, generalized methods of moments are used; these are often known as level- or system-GMM estimators for panel data. In Equation (5.7), we can obtain

---

[30] Although, as we discuss in Section 5.8.1, we found all series to be I(0); we also found them to have high levels of temporal persistence. We present the numeric results for these models in Tables 6.1–6.4.

[31] We also assume that the effects are constant across units. That is, $\mathbf{A}_p$ and $\mathbf{B}$ are fixed for all i and all time points t. Of course, coefficients will differ across each of the four equations.

[32] In our model, there are $N = 33$ countries, and the average number of years per country is 21.

[33] Since $\Delta \mathbf{Y}_{i,t-1} = \mathbf{Y}_{i,t-1} - \mathbf{Y}_{i,t-2}$ and $\Delta \varepsilon_{it} = \varepsilon_{it} - \varepsilon_{i,t-1}$, the two terms are non-independent, because $\varepsilon_{i,t-1}$ is the unexplained portion of variance in $\mathbf{Y}_{i,t-1}$. This dependence could be considered the "best-case" scenario; more issues would arise in the presence of autocorrelated residuals.

$(4 \times p) + k$ instruments. We could obtain further instruments by taking lags farther back (e.g., $y_{i,t-(p+1)}$), but this starts to sharply reduce the estimation sample, since N (the total number of countries) observations are lost for every additional lag taken. An approach that preserves more data than first-differencing – and the one that we use – is to take forward orthogonal deviations (Arellano and Bover 1995) that "subtract the average of all available future observations, thereby minimizing data loss" (Abrigo and Love 2016, p. 780). This also removes individual effects from the model, and forward orthogonal deviation has been shown to outperform first-differencing in the context of panel-data GMM models (Hayakawa 2009). The full table of pVAR results is shown in Table 5.4.

5.8.3 Lag Length Selection

In order to choose the correct lag length of our pVAR, we used several selection criteria. Andrews and Lu (2001) propose using "model and moment selection criteria" (MMSC) when choosing the correct lag length in the GMM context that are similar to more familiar information criteria like AIC and BIC but "include bonus terms that reward the use of more moment conditions for a given number of parameters and the use of less parameters for a given number of moment conditions" (Andrews and Lu 2001, p. 125). The two we use are MMSC for BIC and MMSC for AIC (Andrews and Lu 2001; Abrigo and Love 2016):

$$\text{MMSC}_{BIC} = J_n(k^2 p, k^2 q) - (|q| - |p|)k^2 \ln(n), \quad (5.8)$$

$$\text{MMSC}_{AIC} = J_n(k^2 p, k^2 q) - 2k^2(|q| - |p|), \quad (5.9)$$

where $J_n(k^2 p, k^2 q)$ is the Hansen (1982) J-statistic of overidentifying restrictions, k is the number of variables, p is the number of lags of the endogenous variables, q is the order of the number of lags to use as instruments, and n is the number of observations. We tested for up to four lags (i.e., $p = 4$, meaning A_1, A_2 and A_3 in Equation (5.7)) using up to $q = 5$ instrumenting lags. While MMSC_{BIC} suggests using $p = 1$, MMSC_{AIC} indicates that $p = 2$ is the preferred lag length. Given these mixed conclusions, another factor to consider is the value of the Hansen (1982) J-statistic of overidentifying restrictions. The system is "overidentified" since we have more instruments than endogenous variables, and this test serves as a way to determine if the instruments are exogenous. We find that $J = 100.89$ and is statistically significant when $p = 1$ and $J = 53.00$

TABLE 5.4. *Panel VAR results*

	Δ Expenditures$_{it}$		Δ Revenue$_{it}$		Δ Deficit$_{it}$		Budgetary Volatility$_{it}$	
Δ Expenditures$_{i,t-1}$	.030	(.144)	.089	(.076)	.129	(.086)	-.042	(.100)
Δ Expenditures$_{i,t-2}$	.087	(.086)	.147	(.100)	.194*	(.081)	.130	(.130)
Δ Revenue$_{i,t-1}$	.069	(.099)	-.026	(.054)	-.085	(.053)	-.005	(.077)
Δ Revenue$_{i,t-2}$	.033	(.062)	-.069	(.089)	-.144*	(.073)	.002	(.086)
Δ Deficit$_{i,t-1}$	-.064	(.095)	-.149	(.077)	-.057	(.073)	.094	(.070)
Δ Deficit$_{i,t-2}$	-.063	(.095)	-.170	(.126)	-.158*	(.067)	.035	(.076)
Budgetary Volatility$_{i,t-1}$	-.016	(.059)	.081	(.064)	-.078	(.045)	.184*	(.081)
Budgetary Volatility$_{i,t-2}$	.020	(.041)	.032	(.044)	-.004	(.049)	-.066	(.038)
GDP Growth$_t$	-.255***	(.058)	.095	(.056)	-.397***	(.060)	-.140**	(.052)
Unemployment$_t$	-.315**	(.107)	-.270*	(.108)	-.039	(.103)	.277	(.163)
Δ Openness$_t$	-.064	(.079)	.028	(.085)	-.111*	(.048)	.038	(.035)
Age Dependency Ratio$_t$	.038	(.162)	-.072	(.170)	.112	(.154)	-.184	(.160)
Election$_t$	.144	(.080)	-.101	(.085)	.213**	(.080)	-.028	(.068)
Hostilities$_t$	-.021	(.075)	-.083	(.084)	-.072	(.099)	.059	(.081)
Right$_t$	-.106	(.119)	-.171	(.121)	-.041	(.127)	.041	(.113)
Majority$_t$	.131	(.130)	.198	(.146)	-.066	(.151)	-.403*	(.159)
Year	-.001	(.008)	-.010	(.009)	-.008	(.009)	-.012	(.009)
Hansen's J			11.78					
Observations			697					
Countries (N)			33					

Note: Panel vector autoregressive model estimated using GMM, with two lags ($p = 2$) of the endogenous variables. Instruments include the first through third lag of all endogenous variables, along with all independent variables. Coefficients with standard errors in parentheses. All continuous variables are standardized. Two-tailed tests: * $p < .10$, ** $p < .05$, *** $p < .01$.

and is not statistically significant when $p = 2$. Based on this – along with the MMSC results – we chose to use a lag length of $p = 2$.

5.8.4 Stability and Instruments

Another important component with VAR models is ensuring stability since, without it, statistical inferences are not plausible. Stability in VAR models requires not only that the series are covariance stationary, but also that the VAR is invertible, meaning it can be written as an infinite-order vector moving average representation (Lütkepohl 2005). In our model, we found that first-differencing the dependent variables helped ensure that the resulting estimates were stable; although keep in mind that the budgetary volatility measure is already effectively first-differenced since it measures year-to-year change (see Equation (5.5)), so we did not first difference it. As shown in Figure 5.11, the roots of the companion matrix of the estimated parameters all lie well within the unit circle, meaning we can proceed forward with inference.

An additional issue has to do with the use of instruments in GMM estimation. Too many instruments can overfit and bias the instrumented variables (c.f., Roodman 2009). We used the Hansen (1982) J-statistic of

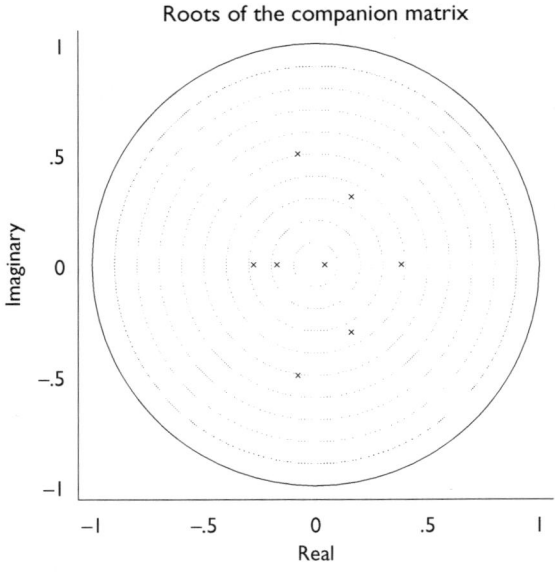

FIGURE 5.11. The pVAR is stable

5.8 Statistical Appendix

overidentifying restrictions to help determine the correct lag length (see Section 5.8.3) and found that, by including the first through the third lags of the dependent variables, along with all the independent variables – for a total of 21 instruments – we failed to reject the null hypothesis of the Hansen test that the over-identifying restrictions are valid (see Table 5.4). This suggests that the instruments are exogenous. We also use the suggestion of Holtz-Eakin, Newey, and Rosen (1988) of augmenting the instruments by replacing any missing observations with zero, since in panel settings the number of time points is generally smaller than classic VAR datasets.[34]

5.8.5 Granger Causality

Parsing out cause-and-effect in time series, especially VAR models, is typically performed using Granger causality tests (Granger 1969). This differs from other common notions of causality, such as the potential outcomes framework, due to the inability to find different counterfactual units, one treated and the other nontreated. Under Granger causality, a variable b is said to Granger-cause variable a if, after conditioning on past values of a, past values of b are still useful in predicting current values of a. In pVAR models, testing for Granger causality consists of estimating joint Wald tests that the coefficients of past values of b are jointly equal to zero, where failing to reject the null hypothesis that the coefficients on all lags of b are equal to zero leads us to conclude that b *does not* Granger-cause a.[35]

We show the results for the Granger causality tests in Table 5.5. Note that these are the same as the results shown in Table 5.2, but these include the actual χ^2 values and levels of statistical significance. At the bottom of Table 5.5, we also include combined tests of the null hypothesis that all lags of all other variables do not Granger-cause the fourth variable; for instance, to test whether revenue, deficit, and budgetary volatility combined may Granger-cause expenditures. We labeled them as "All Variables" in Table 5.5. The only combined Granger causality test that is statistically significant at conventional levels is that expenditures, revenues, and deficit changes together appear to Granger-cause budgetary volatility. Slightly weaker evidence suggests that expenditure change, rev-

---

[34] Without this augmentation, the results are similar, although the number of observations is reduced from 697 to 661.

[35] In our models, the Wald tests have two degrees of freedom since the lag length for all endogenous variables is $p = 2$.

TABLE 5.5. *Granger causality tests*

b "Granger Causes" $\longrightarrow a$	χ^2
Δ Expenditures $\longrightarrow$ Δ Revenue	2.80
Δ Expenditures $\longrightarrow$ Δ Deficit	6.58**
Δ Expenditures $\longrightarrow$ Budgetary Volatility	1.03
Δ Revenue $\longrightarrow$ Δ Expenditures	.63
Δ Revenue $\longrightarrow$ Δ Deficit	5.85*
Δ Revenue $\longrightarrow$ Budgetary Volatility	.01
Δ Deficit $\longrightarrow$ Δ Expenditures	.87
Δ Deficit $\longrightarrow$ Δ Revenue	6.37**
Δ Deficit $\longrightarrow$ Budgetary Volatility	2.28
Budgetary Volatility $\longrightarrow$ Δ Expenditures	.32
Budgetary Volatility $\longrightarrow$ Δ Revenue	1.78
Budgetary Volatility $\longrightarrow$ Δ Deficit	3.07
All Variables $\longrightarrow$ Δ Expenditures	6.52
All Variables $\longrightarrow$ Δ Revenue	6.90
All Variables $\longrightarrow$ Δ Deficit	10.75*
All Variables $\longrightarrow$ Budgetary Volatility	15.61**

Note: Results from Wald tests shown with two degrees of freedom for single variable causality tests, and six degrees of freedom for "All Variables".
*$p < .10$, **$p < .05$, ***$p < .01$. All dependent variables are standardized.

enue change, and budgetary volatility together Granger-cause changes in deficits, although this effect is statistically significant only at the 10 percent level.

5.8.6 Impulse–Response Functions

pVAR models do not lend themselves to easy interpretation. However, once we have ensured that the model is stable, we can use impulse–response functions to examine the dynamic effect that a shock in one series has on the others. If the pVAR is stable, then we can write it as an infinite-order vector moving average representation (VMAR):

$$\mathbf{Y}_{it} - \boldsymbol{\mu}_{it} = \sum_{s=0}^{\infty} \boldsymbol{\varphi}_s \mathbf{u}_{i,t-s}. \qquad (5.10)$$

Where $\mathbf{Y}_{it}$ is the vector of dependent variables shown in Equation (5.4), $\boldsymbol{\mu}_{it}$ is the unconditional expected value of each of the four endogenous variables $\mathbf{Y}_{it}$, and $\boldsymbol{\varphi}_s$ is a matrix equal to:

5.8 Statistical Appendix

$$\varphi_s = \begin{cases} I_K, & \text{if } s = 0 \\ \sum_{q=1}^{s} \varphi_{s-q} A_q, & \forall\, s > 0, \end{cases} \quad (5.11)$$

where $K = 4$. In other words, the q,k'th element of φ_s shows the effect of a one-time unit increase in the k'th element of u_t on the q'th entry of Y_{it} after s periods have passed, holding everything else constant.[36] Thus, we can shock the errors – sometimes called an innovation or impulse – of one of the series and plot the effects – typically called the response, but really the elements of φ_s – across time to create the impulse response functions. Note that, since all of the Y_{it} variables are standardized, the "one-unit" increase represents a one standard deviation increase. We then plot the predicted response of each of the endogenous variables over time with 90 and 95 percent confidence intervals created using a bootstrapping procedure (Abrigo and Love 2016) with 500 draws from a multivariate normal parametric bootstrap with variance equal to the estimated variance–covariance matrix, $\hat{\Sigma}_{u_t}$.

5.8.7 Orthogonalized Impulse–Response Functions and Additional Results

One drawback of IRFs is that we can only assume innovations – the "impulse" that occurs in the dependent variable of interest – are uncorrelated with the residuals in the other equations at $t = 0$. If this is not the case, then an innovation in one equation might occur simultaneously with innovations in other equations, and this would make causal inferences difficult, since IRFs have the convenient interpretation that an innovation in equation A goes on to affect equation B, C, etc. We find some evidence that the off-diagonals of the estimated variance–covariance matrix, $\hat{\Sigma}_{u_t}$ for the four equations are not zero, meaning that an innovation in one series at time t is likely correlated with innovations in other series at time t.

One way to relax this assumption is to estimate orthogonalized impulse response functions, or OIRFs. These orthogonalize the residuals by finding some matrix P, such that it equals the variance–covariance matrix of the equation residuals when post-multiplied by its transpose: $\hat{\Sigma}_{u_{it}} = PP'$. We can then orthogonalize the innovations by post-multiplying them by the inverse of P: $u_{it}P^{-1}$. The VMAR parameters are also transformed: $P\varphi_s$. The resulting VMAR is:

---

[36] Note, too, that $A_q = 0 \,\forall\, q > p$.

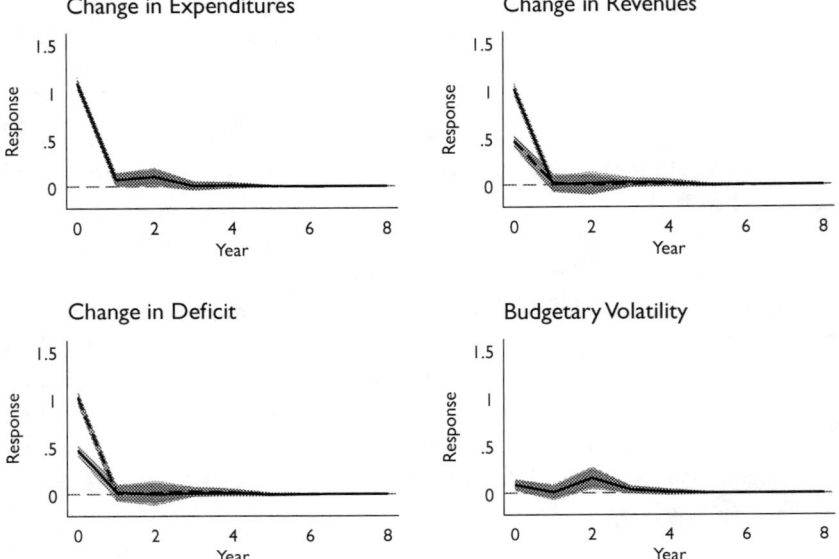

FIGURE 5.12. Orthogonalized impulse response function for change in expenditure shock

Note: Predicted response in each variable in response to a one standard deviation increase to expenditure change at time $t = 0$. Solid line: causal ordering 1 (ΔExpenditures→ ΔRevenues→ ΔDeficits→ Budgetary Volatility); dashed line: causal ordering 2 (ΔExpenditures→ ΔDeficits→ ΔRevenues→ Budgetary Volatility). Darker to lighter shaded areas indicate 90 and 95 percent confidence intervals, respectively.

$$Y_{it} - \mu_{it} = \sum_{s=0}^{\infty} \theta_s \gamma_{i,t-s}. \quad (5.12)$$

The only way to identify **P** is to assume a causal ordering of the variables in the contemporaneous period (i.e., at $t = 0$). Fortunately, we can use Granger causality tests from the pVAR results to suggest likely causal orderings. In Figures 5.12 and 5.13, we show OIRFs for our four endogenous variables. As described at the beginning of this section, impulses are only orthogonal after assuming a causal ordering in **P**. Given the Granger causality results, we use two potential causal orderings:

1. ΔExpenditures→ ΔRevenues→ ΔDeficits→ Budgetary Volatility.
2. ΔExpenditures→ ΔDeficits→ ΔRevenues→ Budgetary Volatility.

Since expenditure change seemed to not be dependent on the other three series (if anything, it causes deficit change), we put it in first. Budgetary

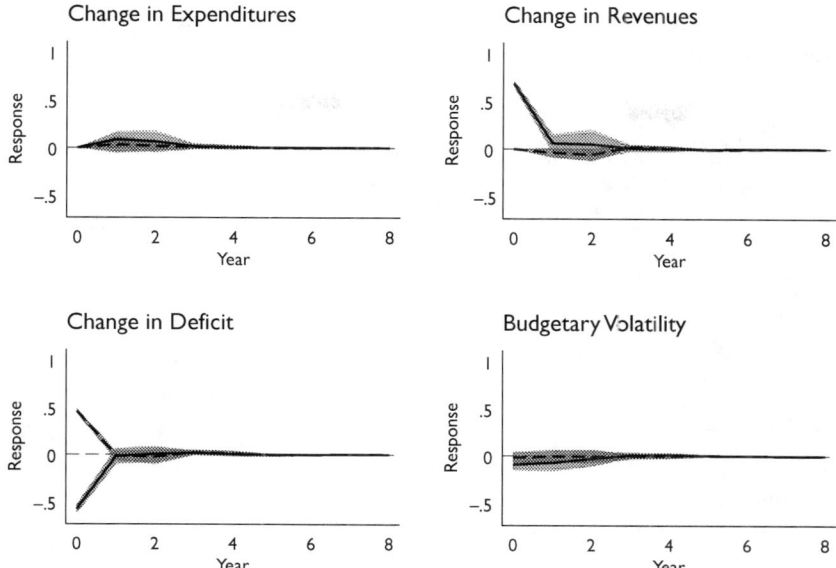

FIGURE 5.13. Orthogonalized impulse response function for revenue change shock

Note: Predicted response in each variable in response to a one standard deviation increase to revenue change at time $t = 0$. Solid line: causal ordering 1 (ΔExpenditures→ ΔRevenues→ ΔDeficits→ Budgetary Volatility); dashed line: causal ordering 2 (ΔExpenditures→ ΔDeficits→ ΔRevenues→ Budgetary Volatility). Darker to lighter shaded areas indicate 90 and 95 percent confidence intervals, respectively.

volatility, in contrast, while not affected by any particular variable, jointly appeared to be caused by all of them (see the "All Variables" result at the bottom of Table 5.5). Thus, it goes last in our causal ordering. In the middle, we show two sets of results. In the first, we assume that revenues cause deficits, and in the second, deficits cause revenues. We show these two orderings, since Table 5.5 indicated that while deficits are probably causing revenues, the reverse may also be true.

In Figure 5.12, we show the OIRF given a one standard deviation shock increase in expenditures. The solid line shows the predictions assuming causal ordering 1 (i.e., assume that ΔRevenues→ ΔDeficits), while the dashed line shows causal ordering 2. The OIRFs suggest that all variables are affected by a shock to expenditures and that every component shows an increase. This is temporary (just a single year) for deficits and revenues and differs in magnitude depending on the assumed causal ordering. To emphasize, the impact on deficits and revenues is very large. A one standard deviation increase in expenditure change results in a one standard deviation increase in revenue change and a .5 standard deviation increase change in deficits (assuming that ΔRevenues→ ΔDeficits), and a similar, though flipped, effect if we assume that ΔDeficits→ΔRevenues. Interestingly, the effect on budgetary volatility (an increase) appears only two years after the shock.

We illustrate the OIRF results for a shock increase to revenue change in Figure 5.13. Revenue has no statistically significant effect on either expenditure change or budgetary volatility, regardless of the causal ordering. In contrast, the different causal assumptions determine the response to deficits, as well as to revenues themselves. If we assume that revenues cause deficits, then there is a positive and declining response in revenues and a strong, immediate negative shock in deficits that goes away one year later. In contrast, if we assume that deficits cause revenues, there is virtually no response in revenues, unlike for deficits, where we see a large positive shock that goes away after one year.

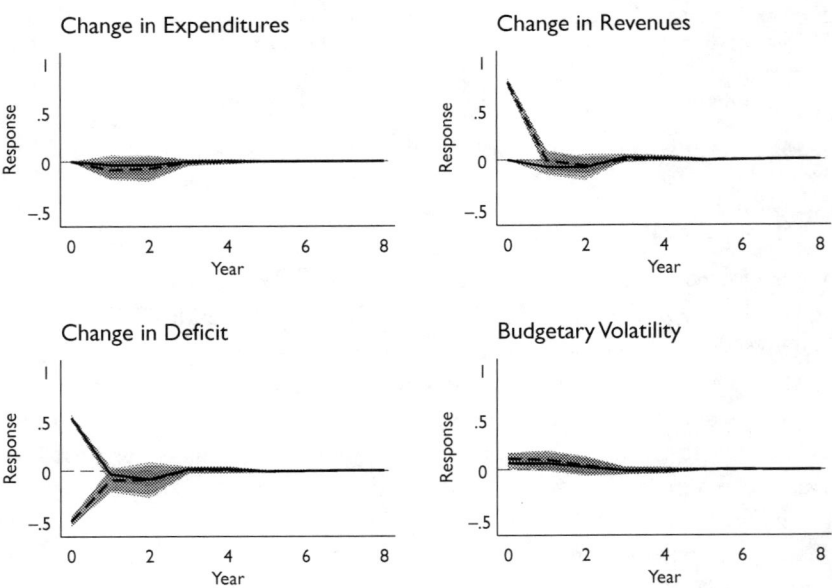

FIGURE 5.14. Orthogonalized impulse response function for deficit change shock

Note: Predicted response in each variable in response to a one standard deviation increase to deficit change at time $t = 0$. Solid line: causal ordering 1 (ΔExpenditures→ ΔRevenues→ ΔDeficits→ Budgetary Volatility); dashed line: causal ordering 2 (ΔExpenditures→ ΔDeficits→ ΔRevenues→ Budgetary Volatility). Darker to lighter shaded areas indicate 90 and 95 percent confidence intervals, respectively.

5.8 Statistical Appendix

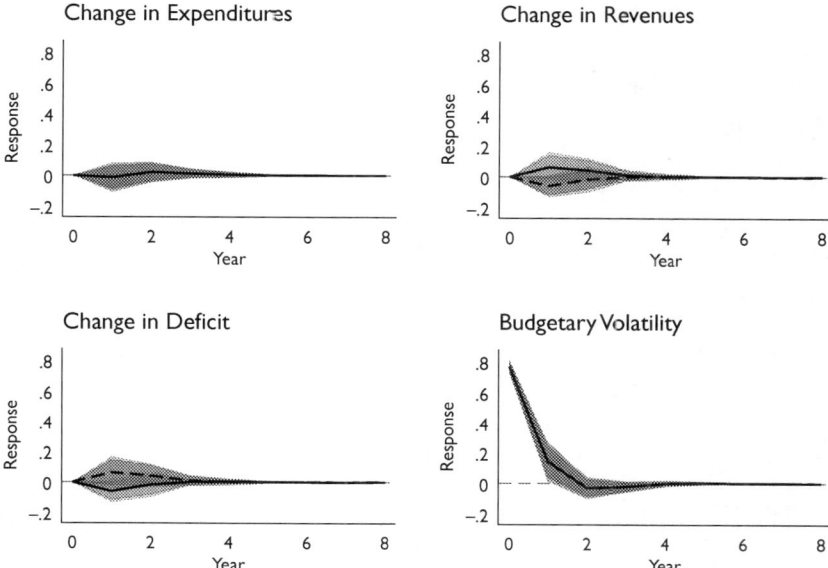

FIGURE 5.15. Orthogonalized impulse response function for budgetary volatility shock

Note: Predicted response in each variable in response to a one standard deviation increase to the budgetary volatility measure at time $t = 0$. Solid line: causal ordering 1 (ΔExpenditures→ΔRevenues→ΔDeficits→Budgetary Volatility); dashed line: causal ordering 2 (ΔExpenditures→ΔDeficits→ΔRevenues→Budgetary Volatility). Darker to lighter shaded areas indicate 90 and 95 percent confidence intervals, respectively.

In Figure 5.14, we show OIRF results for a shock increase to deficit change. While there is no statistically significant effect on expenditure change caused by this shock to deficit change, there is a small, weakly statistically significant effect on budgetary volatility. The response for deficits and revenues differs based on our assumptions about the causal ordering. If we assume that revenues cause deficits, then there is a positive and diminishing response to deficits (in response to a positive shock in deficit change) and a slight negative effect for revenues change. If we assume the opposite (i.e., deficits cause revenues), then there is an immediate large positive response in revenues and a negative effect can be seen in deficits.

Last, in Figure 5.15, we shock budgetary volatility and plot the resulting OIRF responses. The results are nearly identical to those in Section 5.3 when we look at both expenditure change and budgetary volatility, as well as for deficits and revenues when we assume causal ordering 1. With the other causal ordering, only deficits and revenues are affected. Although their effects flip signs (budgetary volatility has a positive effect on deficits and a negative effect on revenues), neither are statistically significant.

To summarize, in this section we use OIRFs that, unlike IRFs, allow for more "all else equal" causal comparisons. The downside is that they force users to make assumptions about causality in the contemporaneous period. We used our Granger tests to guide us and find that our resulting OIRFs are extremely similar to the IRFs we showed for expenditures and budgetary volatility. For deficits and revenues, OIRF results differ based on whether we assume deficits cause revenues or vice versa, but, regardless, this helps us clearly establish that those two budgetary categories are closely linked to one another. This highlights why we specify our single-equation models in this chapter (as well as Chapter 6) to account for this.

6

The Effects of Elections, Economics, and External Shocks on the Budgetary Ledger

Events, dear boy, events
  UK Prime Minister Harold Macmillan, when asked by a reporter
  what the most difficult problem of his time in office was[1]

Danish politicians know all too well that the politics of budgets can be deadly. Since 1945, "six Danish governments have fallen during the Christmas period due to major disagreements over fiscal policy," and, by late 2016, the rumblings of yet another government to add to the list had increased because of tax and revenue policy.[2] This Danish example illustrates how the choices surrounding expenditures, revenues, and deficits, as well as budgetary volatility can make or break governments. Government longevity and electoral outcomes hinge on the interplay between these budgetary pieces, highlighting the competition and tradeoffs inherent in politics and policymaking. However, we know little about how governments use these various components when making fiscal policy, and we know even less about how the contexts surrounding governments affect these decisions. In this chapter, we investigate whether electoral, economic, and international conditions alter the ways in which governments use these budgetary components.

As we discussed in Chapter 5, there are good reasons to think that budgetary policy differs depending on the government in power, but we found that governments of all types similarly used budgetary components.

---

[1] See Ayto and Crofton (2011).
[2] www.irishexaminer.com/archives/2016/1108/business/electionriskoverdanishbudget429535.html. Last accessed February 1, 2017.

However, we also have good reasons to expect that contexts affect how governments make budgetary policy. As we witnessed in Chapter 4, in the face of changing conditions, governments may not behave as expected based on ideology alone. Instead, ideologically different governments may react similarly when confronted with the same shocks. In this chapter, we broaden our window of budgetary analysis by examining the contextual determinants of expenditures, revenues, deficits, and budgetary volatility. While Chapter 5 discussed the interplay between these components, together with ideology and power, in this chapter we focus on the conditioning role of other factors. Although we expect that governments: (1) have different ideological priorities about the role of government, and (2) propose different solutions when faced with domestic or international changes, they may be forced to behave similarly when confronted with the same political, economic, and international challenges. Whether this is indeed the case – regarding expenditures, deficits, revenues, and budgetary volatility – is the subject of this chapter.

Here we ask a similar question to that first posed in Chapter 4: how do domestic and international factors affect budgets? Our starting point relies on models informed by the causality results from Chapter 5. From there, we create the same ideological–institutional interactions with domestic and international factors as we did in Chapter 4. In doing so, we answer two questions central to expenditures, revenues, deficits, and budgetary volatility. First, how might these domestic and international factors affect governments' use of these budgetary tools? In thinking about answers to this question, we are able to draw from a large body of existing literature on the subject (although substantially less so in regard to budgetary volatility). Second, how might ideology and institutions condition these relationships? Here, the literature is much quieter on how government characteristics (ideology and majority status) may interact with domestic and international contexts to affect the broader components of the budget.

Similar to Chapter 4, we tend to have competing expectations about these relationships: Do urgent domestic and international factors force governments to behave the same, regardless of ideology? Or does ideology win out with governments enforcing their political visions, regardless of external factors? To answer these questions, we use a common research design across our four dependent variables, which we explain in Section 6.1. We then present separate sections on the contextual influences of elections, domestic economic circumstances, international openness, and international conflict on our four budgetary components. For each contextual factor, we review the extant literature and then present results from our analyses. To preview our findings, although the results vary somewhat across the range of contextual factors and budgetary components, we generally find little evidence of an impact of government ideology on shaping budgetary behavior. As we discuss in the conclusion of this chapter, the contrast between the richness of the findings from our examination of contexts in Chapter 4 and the relatively meager nature of our findings in this chapter is quite remarkable and speaks to the difficulties of understanding budgetary entanglements.

6.1 MODELING STRATEGY

In the latter half of Chapter 5, we used the results from Granger causality tests to specify separate reduced-form models for each of our budget component variables. We then used these reduced-form models to test for the influence of government ideology and majority status, and, where appropriate, other budgetary components on each of our four budgetary components. To test for the influence of contextual factors in this chapter, we use a slightly modified version of the specification from Chapter 5:

$$\begin{aligned}
\text{Budget Component } A_{it} = f(&\text{Budget Component } A_{it-1} \\
&+ (\text{Context}_{it}) \times (1 + \text{Right}_{it} + \text{Majority}_{it} + \text{Right}_{it} \times \text{Majority}_{it}) \\
&+ (\text{Context}_{it-1}) \times (1 + \text{Right}_{it-1} + \text{Majority}_{it-1} + \text{Right}_{it-1} \\
&\quad \times \text{Majority}_{it-1}) + \text{Right}_{it} + \text{Majority}_{it} + \text{Right}_{it} \times \text{Majority}_{it} \\
&+ \text{Right}_{it-1} + \text{Majority}_{it-1} + \text{Right}_{it-1} \times \text{Majority}_{it-1} \\
&+ \text{Budget Component B,C, or } D_{it} + \text{Budget Component B,C,} \\
&\quad \text{or } D_{it-1} + \text{Controls}),
\end{aligned} \qquad (6.1)$$

where Budget Component A_{it} is the dependent variable for each separate model and is a function of its lagged value (Budget Component A_{it-1}), our contextual variables (Context$_{it}$), our political variables (Right$_{it}$ and Majority$_{it}$), the other budgetary components identified through the Granger causality tests to cause Budget Component A_{it} (Budget Components B, C, or D_{it}), and a set of control variables.[3] We interact the

---

[3] Recall that, in Chapter 5, we found that expenditures cause deficits, while revenues and deficits appear to be caused by one another.

political variables with the context, and we include all of our variables contemporaneously (at time t) and lagged (at time $t-1$).[4]

In addition to the highly interactive model dictated by our theory of how context and politics work together, we also specify a more restrictive, mostly additive, version of each of our reduced-form models of budgetary components:

$$\begin{aligned}
\text{Budget Component } A_{it} = f(&\text{Budget Component } A_{it-1} \\
&+ \text{Context}_{it} + \text{Right}_{it} + \text{Majority}_{it} + \text{Right}_{it} \times \text{Majority}_{it} \\
&+ \text{Context}_{it-1} + \text{Right}_{it-1} + \text{Majority}_{it-1} + \text{Right}_{it-1} \\
&\times \text{Majority}_{it-1} + \text{Budget Component B,C, or } D_{it} \\
&+ \text{Budget Component B,C, or } D_{it-1} + \text{Controls}).
\end{aligned} \quad (6.2)$$

From these models, we obtain a single estimate of the effect of each contextual variable on each of our budgetary components. In other words, it is the estimated effect of each contextual variable – say unemployment or hostility level – across all government types. This calculation is useful as a baseline for comparison with the results from our interactive models. In the sections that follow, for each of our contextual variables, we explore the theoretical literature, develop expectations about how they will affect each of the four budgetary components, and present results.

6.2 THE EFFECTS OF ELECTIONS

Scholars have developed a vast literature on how elections may influence expenditures, revenues, and deficits, and this work on political budget cycles focuses on links between electoral support and public policy timing (Nordhaus 1975). The general idea is that governments will raise spending just before an election to win voter support, with the costs resulting in increased post-election deficits. This cycle can appeal to governments. While raising revenues before elections would be electorally unpopular, these budgetary shortfalls do not necessarily need to be paid off immediately (Schuknecht 2000; John and Ward 2001; Alt and Lassen 2006; O'Mahony 2011; Philips 2017). Therefore, we focus on budgetary components such as expenditures or deficits to see if politicians might try

---

[4] As with our analyses in Chapter 4, we include these interactions sequentially for each contextual measure instead of all together.

6.2 The Effects of Elections

to "have it all." In reality, what governments do remains an open question. Do governments use budgetary tools during electoral cycles, and is their use dependent on their ideological preferences and majority power?

6.2.1 The Effect of Elections on Expenditures

In Chapter 4, we presented a theory of how elections might affect the composition of expenditures. There were two contrasting forces that led to differing ideological expectations. On the one hand, parties may try to allocate greater shares of expenditures to their ideologically preferred policy areas, in order to shore up their levels of support among their base. On the other hand, they may choose electorally advantageous policy areas that appeal to the largest share of voters. For instance, Bove, Efthyvoulou, and Navas (2017) find that governments spend less on military expenditures and more on social expenditures around elections, since the latter likely affect a broader swath of the electorate. This secondary view holds that, during elections, parties with different ideological dispositions may spend more on similar policies as a way to attract groups of voters.

We illustrated these contrasting theoretical expectations in Table 4.1, but our findings indicated that there was largely no political budget cycle effect on the composition of expenditures. While such a result is in line with others' findings, it lacks strong evidence for electorally motivated spending (Remmer 2007; Enkelmann and Leibrecht 2013). However, if governments are increasing expenditures without reallocating funds across policy areas, then total spending would be ideal for seeing this strategic behavior.

Based on the extant literature on political budget cycles (Alesina, Cohen and Roubini 1999; Persson and Tabellini 2000; Dubois 2016), we expect that government expenditures will increase during elections as parties in government attempt to win over voters. Whether left or right governments differ in their amount of electoral manipulation of expenditures is a less-clear question. Taken at face value, political budget cycles, regardless of a government's ideology, would be an instrument to help ensure re-election. While an older literature on political budget cycles made the distinction between left and right governments – see articles on "partisan" business cycles (Hibbs 1977; Alesina and Roubini 1992) – most scholars today do not make such a distinction, although they *do* typically control for partisan effects. Alternatively, there is some evidence that runs contrary to the claim that governments will raise expenditures before elections. The argument here rests on the point that voters are aware of and likely to punish heavy spenders near elections (Drazen and Eslava 2010; De Haan and Klomp 2013).

6.2.2 The Effect of Elections on Revenues

We also investigate the possibility that governments change revenue levels during election season as a means of appeasing their supporters and garnering new voters. Why would this matter? Take the apocryphal story of George H. W. Bush, who lost the 1988 US presidential election due in part to going against his election promise of "read my lips: no new taxes;" voters do not like tax hikes. This tact may be especially risky for governments to pursue around elections, when voters do not have the time to forgive and forget their actions.[5] Thus, we may expect both left and right governments to pursue the strategy of not increasing revenues around elections, in order to keep voters appeased.

If governments choose not to raise revenues around elections, because of the possibility of an electoral backlash, then is the implication that governments *decreasing* revenues would be a good strategy? In this scenario, governments use revenues as an electoral tool to attract votes, so we would expect to see revenue levels decreasing during election years (or possibly the year after an election, depending on the timing of the policy changes). Although the electoral cycle literature has mostly focused on expenditure increases (either total expenditures or particular expenditure categories) as a means to attract favorable attention (Franzese 2002a; Brender and Drazen 2005; Vergne 2009; Drazen and Eslava 2010; Philips 2016), governments may also use the revenue side of the budget as an electoral incentive (Barberia and Avelino 2011; Katsimi and Sarantides 2012; Aidt and Mooney 2014). Realistically we expect that governments will only benefit from a decrease in taxes at election time due to "myopic" voters, those who only take into account government performance in the election year (Tufte 1978; Campbell 2008; Kayser and Wlezien 2011, but see Wlezien 2015). Moreover, we expect that governments of all ideological stripes, both right and left, will take advantage of this potential electoral boost.[6]

---

[5] Since voters are likely to evaluate the incumbent on what has happened to them recently rather than in the more-distant past (Tufte 1978; Campbell 2008; Kayser and Wlezien 2011, but see Wlezien 2015), pursuing fiscal adjustments near an election can be a risky strategy.

[6] As we will discuss with deficits later in this chapter, decreasing revenues may not necessarily result in a corresponding decrease in expenditures, so voters may view this as a "win" with decreasing taxes and stable spending.

6.2.3 The Effect of Elections on Deficits

Since the shifts in spending and revenues do not always balance, it is not surprising that there is also some debate about the timing of deficits in relation to the election cycle. Elections can pressure governments to alter their budgetary policies – increasing spending or decreasing revenues – in order to appease supporters or attract swing voters. Given the asymmetries between government policy actions and the fiscal consequences voters observe, governments may choose to pursue budget deficits. Voters may not realize that these deficits from overspending and/or tax cuts will need to be repaid until later, with "later" being after the election (Rogoff and Sibert 1988; Rogoff 1990). Running budget deficits, then, allows governments to use political budget cycle instruments: increase expenditures, while temporarily shielding voters from a corresponding increase in revenue.[7]

There is fairly strong evidence that deficits rise during elections.[8] Aggregating 234 study-model results on whether elections affect the fiscal balance, Philips (2016) finds by using a meta-analysis that the strength of evidence in favor of deficits increasing during election years is about double that for all other variables commonly analyzed in the political budget cycle literature (e.g., expenditures, debt, and revenues). More specifically, Harrinvirta and Mattila (2001) conclude that deficits increase during election years because of lower tax revenue (and no changes to expenditures).

Yet whether governments of different ideological stripes increase deficits during elections to differing extents is far less clear. Examining West Germany, Galli and Rossi (2002) find no evidence of an ideological difference but do find that expenditures in German Länder increase around elections, mostly from increased deficit spending, not increased tax revenues. In contrast, other work finds that right-leaning governments are more likely to run a deficit before an election (Alt and Lassen 2006). Overall, it remains unclear as to how – or even if – government ideology should have a different effect on deficits depending on electoral timing, since neither party may find it advantageous to raise taxes or cut spending on government programs in an election year. This may limit their budgetary choices, resulting in both left- and right-wing governments

---

[7] Additionally, even if expenditures do not rise, revenues may fall, which could also appeal to voters.
[8] Perhaps surprisingly, Brender and Drazen (2008) find no evidence that increasing fiscal deficits actually helps the incumbent win re-election.

turning to deficit spending around elections.[9] In addition, majority versus minority status may play a role in how elections shape deficits, since government power may affect governments' abilities. Potrafke (2019) finds no difference between minority and majority governments, while Harrinvirta and Mattila (2001) also find no effect between coalition and single-party governments, likely because coalitions tend to increase both revenues and expenditures.

6.2.4 The Effect of Elections on Budgetary Volatility

According to the political budget cycle literature, elections should be a time of active shifts and increased volatility in the budget composition. While the total level of expenditures may increase during elections (Alesina, Cohen and Roubini 1999; Persson and Tabellini 2000), as we discussed in Chapter 4, there are many reasons to expect that particular subcategories of expenditures might increase while others decrease. For instance, social expenditures may increase at the cost of "non-social" expenditures, such as defense (Bove, Efthyvoulou, and Navas 2017; Herwartz and Theilen 2017). Health (Potrafke 2010; Herwartz and Theilen 2014), grants (John and Ward 2001), or administrative expenditures (Enkelmann and Leibrecht 2013) are just some of the other categories of government spending that have been shown to increase during elections. This would lead us to expect that, all else equal, budgetary volatility would increase during elections years. However, in Chapter 4, we found evidence of only small shifts in budgetary compositions and that most of these shifts were not statistically distinguishable from zero. In fact, the only significant shifts that we saw for majority governments in Chapter 4 were for right governments that increased spending on government administration and decreased spending on religion and culture, both in the short run. Therefore, our expectation for volatility around elections remains mixed.

6.2.5 Results of Elections on the Budgetary Ledger

We show the results of elections on all four budgetary components through a series of graphs in Figure 6.1. First, we consider Figure 6.1a, that shows the results of elections on expenditures. We find no evidence that elections affect total expenditures across all government types (this

---

[9] Moreover, other institutional effects such as divided government (Streb and Torrens 2013) or balanced budget requirements (Rose 2006) may also limit increases in deficits around elections.

6.2 The Effects of Elections

is the "No Interaction" scenario, which we estimate using Equation (6.2)). Moreover, this effect is not statistically significant, even once we account for the fact that left and/or right majority governments might have a greater tendency to raise expenditures around elections (these are the Left Majority and Right Majority results, which we estimate using Equation (6.1)).

In Figure 6.1b, we show the effect of elections on total revenues. Here, we observe two statistically significant short-run effects in the expected negative direction, since revenues are expected to decline as governments seek to win greater voter support. These results are from the model without interactions and for the left majority in the interactive model, estimated at −.93 and −.62, respectively. The metric for these estimated effects is as a percentage of GDP, so these effects are substantively large. But they are obscured by the large confidence intervals around the long-run effects, all of which are far from statistically significant.

We show the effect of elections on deficits in Figure 6.1c. Without taking into account ideology or majority context, there appears to be no effect of elections on deficit spending. However, from the results in Figure 6.1c we can see a more complicated story once we consider that various types of governments may respond differently to electoral manipulation. It appears that right majority governments, not left majority ones, increase deficits in an election year, and this effect is weakly (at the 90 percent level) statistically significant, over the long run. We note that we do not find this difference for budgetary volatility in Figure 6.1d. As is clear from that figure, there appear to be no statistically significant effects of elections on budgetary volatility, either directly or for different types of governments.

To summarize our results in Figure 6.1, when it comes to electoral cycles and budgetary tools, we find little to substantiate the expectations that governments manipulate components for electoral gain or behave differently because of their ideological inclinations. Neither the left nor the right appears systematically to use expenditures to retain their supporters or to expand their electoral coalitions. We find some evidence that left governments cut revenues in the short-run. While right governments come closest to using deficits around elections, this result is not statistically significant, at least at conventional levels, in the short-run. Governments also do not appear to be making substantial changes to the budgetary composition just before elections. In sum, we find only weak evidence that ideology, power status, and budgetary components come together during

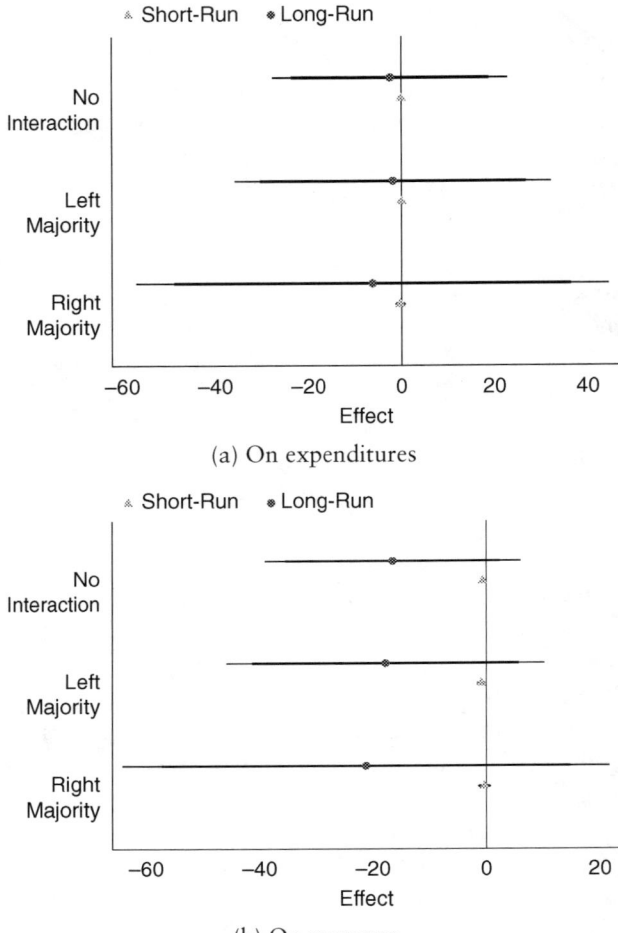

FIGURE 6.1. The effects of elections on the budgetary ledger

Note: 95 (thin) and 90 percent (thick) confidence intervals shown.

elections to create ideologically distinct outcomes. However, elections are just one factor; other domestic characteristics may matter, as we explore in Section 6.3.

6.3 THE EFFECTS OF THE DOMESTIC ECONOMY

The relationship between economic conditions and government behavior can be loaded with potholes, as *The Economist* noted when it framed the

6.3 The Effects of the Domestic Economy

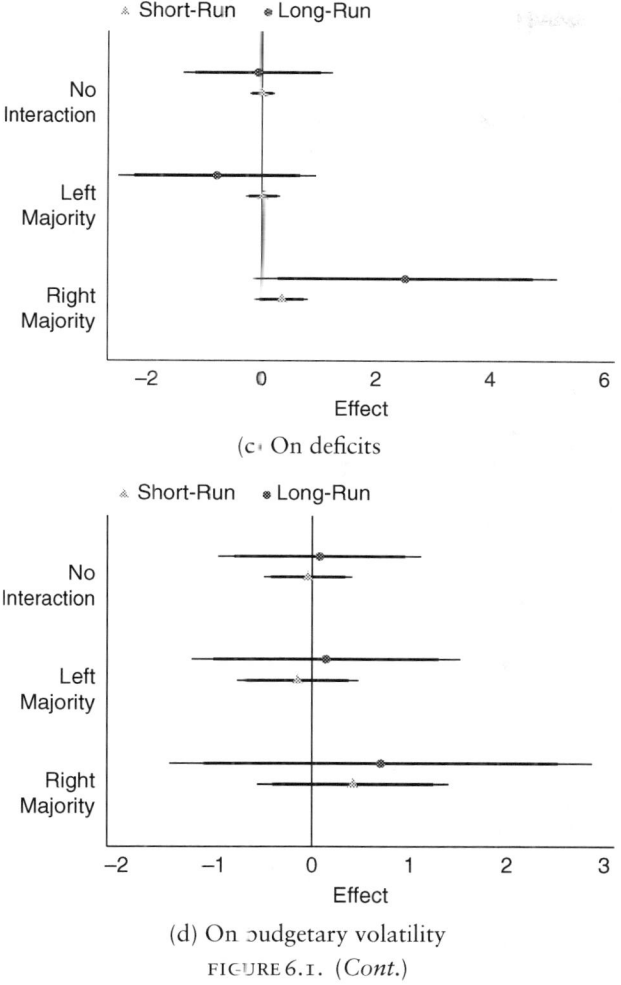

(c) On deficits

(d) On budgetary volatility

FIGURE 6.1. (Cont.)

attempts by the government led by John Major to cut back expenditures just as the UK economy was leaving a recession as a "cheerless recovery."[10] The health of the economy can affect the budgetary options from which governments have to choose. From the size of the government's

---

[10] "Fairness and the coalition: Great aspirations." www.economist.com/node/16847696/print. Last accessed August 23, 2016.

purse to decisions about taxes, the economic environment affects how much room governments have to maneuver when making budgetary decisions. Positive economic conditions offer the rosiest scenarios for governments, while more negative economic situations may restrict their options. While we have previously examined how such economic conditions affect the composition of expenditures, here we form a series of expectations on how domestic conditions may affect the overall size of budgets.

6.3.1 The Effects of the Domestic Economy on Expenditures

Given that the domestic economy can influence the supply and demand of government resources, governments with different ideological visions may react to these changes in economic fortunes in varying ways. While, in Chapter 3, we discussed the possibilities of governments shifting funds within the budget, here we investigate how governments increase or decrease total expenditures in the face of positive or negative economic shocks. How does the economic context constrain or enable governments to change total government spending?

Although scholars expect economic situations to have an effect on government expenditures, the actual relationships between governments, spending decisions, and economic conditions remain unresolved. As we discussed in Chapter 5, research on whether government ideology influences total expenditures (or expenditures as a percentage of GDP) is voluminous. From Hibbs (1977) and Cameron (1978) to Alesina (1988) and Potrafke (2017), scholars have continued the search to explain the relationship between partisan politics and government spending. Although the theoretical expectations about how ideology should drive government spending decisions appear straightforward, the empirical evidence remains largely inconclusive. The effect of government ideology may in reality be more complicated than the direct influence that scholars have assumed.

Starting with total expenditures and then turning to two subcomponents of spending (social and non-social spending), Herwartz and Theilen (2017) find that right governments tend to increase redistributive spending when the economy is performing well, while left governments raise spending when the economy is performing poorly or in reaction to rising unemployment and demographic shifts. However, Lipsmeyer (2011) argues that poor economic conditions push governments into supporting redistributive policies, thus, diluting the ideological differences between

6.3 The Effects of the Domestic Economy

governments. Her findings appear to support this contention. During economic downturns, both left and right governments tend to increase welfare spending, and only when the economy is on an upswing does ideology seem to matter with left governments increasing welfare spending and right governments retrenching. Along these same lines, times of economic crisis are likely to tie the hands of governments in terms of pleasing their domestic constituents, instead making them beholden to international credit markets (Lierse and Seelkopf 2016). All of these arguments highlight how governments may react to economic conditions in different ways depending on their ideological positions, although research indicates that the reverse may hold, whereby governments may instead behave similarly depending on the constraints put on them by the economy.

6.3.2 The Effect of the Domestic Economy on Revenues

Changing economic fortunes can also influence a government's revenues. Take the economic slowdown in Romania in 2009, for example, that pushed the government to revise its budget to "take into account the expected deterioration in revenues from income taxes, profit taxes and value-added tax (VAT)."[11] Domestic economic pressures in the form of changing unemployment, growth, or inflation can affect governments' behavior on revenues. Negative economic conditions may constrain governments' abilities to increase or even stabilize revenues, while more positive economic situations may offer governments opportunities to alter revenues in order to fit their ideological preferences.

Much social science research has focused on the interplay between the economy and budgetary spending, although how such economic changes relate to government behavior on revenues remains less explored. Some scholars have found little evidence to support a link between government ideology and tax systems (Swank and Steinmo 2002; Cusack and Beramendi 2006). However, others looking to revenues more broadly argue that economic downturns may cause governments to enact tax cuts in order to create more demand in the economy (Raess and Pontusson 2015), a phenomenon referred to as "expansionary fiscal contraction" (Giavazzi and Pagano 1990; Dellepiane-Avellaneda 2015).

---

[11] http://country.eiu.com/article.aspx?articleid=1204447305#. Last accessed September 28, 2017.

During economically difficult times, governments may feel pressure to reassure their electoral supporters, but these circumstances may also make it less likely that governments can fall back on their ideological preferences. Increasing unemployment, for example, can diminish both personal income taxes (because of lost jobs) and consumption taxes (through lost consumer purchases) (Dolls, Fuest, and Peichl 2012). Although these declines in taxes may be viewed as "automatic" and fall outside of direct government intervention, how governments react to these economic pressures lies at the core of the politics of budgets. Since taxes from labor comprise a large share of revenues in most developed economies – around 50 percent of all revenues on average by the end of the twentieth century (Cusack and Beramendi 2006) – such declines can have substantial impacts on revenues. Economic downturns may diminish the room that governments have to maneuver. Do they shift their preferences under varying economic conditions in order to insulate their supporters, or is government behavior as it relates to revenues under these pressures the same, regardless of ideological preferences?

Economic downturns should decrease revenues regardless of the types of taxes employed. For one, a rise in unemployment is usually coupled with a decline in consumer confidence (thus reducing consumption revenues, and there should also be a corresponding decline in revenues from corporate taxes, as growth slows. Under such conditions, governments may find it difficult to alter revenue levels, with the result that governments of all ideologies will stay the course and behave similarly. Alternatively, left and right governments may view economic slowdowns in comparatively different ways. Left governments may prefer to stabilize revenues in order to continue to fund government programs during the hardship, while right governments may view the economic hardship as an opportunity to allow revenues to fall and public programs to diminish. Alternatively, right-leaning governments may argue for tax breaks for businesses as a means to boost the economy through job creation, with the result being a decrease in government revenues.

While scholars have investigated a connection between governments and taxes and revenue streams, studies of how these relationships might change depending on the economy remain somewhat limited. An example of this research comes from Huber, Ragin, and Stephens (1993), who find that being a social democratic government is the most important predictor of government revenues, and that Christian democratic governments tend to prefer lower levels of revenue (although relatively high levels of social redistributive policies, like the social democrats)

6.3 The Effects of the Domestic Economy

(see also Esping-Anderson 1990). However, further research finds that governments, especially left governments, use a mixed strategy of visible and less visible taxes to appease both partisan supporters and capital interests (Basinger and Hallerberg 2004; Plümper, Troeger, and Winner 2009; Shin 2017). With the addition of economic context, whether government ideology matters for taxes and revenue becomes even murkier. Examining four international recessions among OECD countries, Raess and Pontusson (2015) find that in more recent recessions, governments of all ideological stripes have tended to rely more on tax cuts to boost demand in the economy, although left governments appear to have relied more on revenue increases (in order to enact fiscal stimulus packages) than right governments.[12] Many of the anecdotes and much of the research point to situations whereby economic conditions affect governments' fiscal behavior. Whether the economy is booming or in a nosedive, governments make fiscal decisions in the environment around them.

6.3.3 The Effect of the Domestic Economy on Deficits

Previously, we have asked: how do economic situations influence the ability of governments to shape expenditures or revenues in their preferred ways? Since all of these budgetary components are interlinked, we are also interested in whether left or right governments are more likely to run deficits in the face of economic changes. Our question enters quite a long-running debate about government ideology, deficits, and fiscal prudence in the literature.[13]

There remain questions about whether governments employ deficits differently because of their ideological leanings. We argue that part of this confusion relates to the issue of when different governments rely on deficit spending. Governments may turn to deficits as an option when economic conditions warrant fiscal changes. For instance, in the face of higher or increasing unemployment, Carlsen (1997) finds that left-leaning

---

[12] Sometimes governments change tact. Dellepiane-Avellaneda (2015, p. 408) notes that, during the Great Recession, Spain's socialist government initially pursued a fiscal stimulus: "once the severity of the economic crisis became clear, the government phased out fiscal stimulus and adopted a gradual, revenue-based consolidation strategy. The intention was to protect core social spending, sheltering welfare beneficiaries from the economic downturn. Yet, this gradual, tax-focused approach was abandoned."

[13] See Hahm, Kamlet, and Mowery (1995) for a theoretical overview of six possible reasons behind variation in deficits across countries and time.

governments run higher deficits compared to right governments. This example shows how left- or right-wing governments may react to economic conditions in similar or different ways, depending on their expectations, outlooks, or the preferences of their supporters (Hibbs 1977). Alesina and Drazen (1989) argue that parties react to economic shocks differently because of their underlying distributional preferences, resulting in a waiting game on tax policy and ultimately in higher deficits. Governments' reactions to economic shocks, and their use of deficits, could then vary depending on their ideological preferences for altering revenue and/or spending.

The alternative is that, in times of economic hardship, left and right governments may instead rely on deficits in a similar fashion. Finding it difficult to rein in spending when automatic stabilizers (e.g., unemployment benefits and other types of government assistance) kick-in during higher unemployment or declining growth, governments are left to run deficits or increase revenues at a time when the economy is cooling off.[14] Regardless of ideological preferences, governments may turn to deficit spending during times of hardship rather than increase taxes or other forms of revenue to offset the increased spending. Müller, Storesletten, and Zilibotti (2016) explain that left-leaning governments will tend to aggressively pursue countercyclical policies during economic downturns (accumulating a lot of debt during these periods), while right-leaning governments will be less aggressive, but still accumulate debt. While economic changes may result in similar outcomes across governments, the underlying behavioral reasons may differ. Left governments may choose not to decrease spending or raise taxes, resulting in rising deficits; right governments may decide to alter spending, while also decreasing taxes, leading to higher deficits.

6.3.4 The Effect of the Domestic Economy on Budgetary Volatility

The domestic economy also has the potential to affect budgetary volatility, although whether or not left and right governments differ on how much they change expenditures in the face of such challenges is less clear. Economic shocks may push all governments, both left and right, to change budgets, leading to more volatility. In addition, both left and right govern-

---

[14] Darby and Melitz (2008) find that not only do unemployment benefits appear to be an automatic stabilizer; health, retirement, disability, and illness benefits also appear to behave cyclically.

ments may find that automatic stabilizers lead to more volatility (Darby and Melitz 2008).

We might expect that, during poor economic conditions, budgetary volatility would rise as governments either automatically or manually shift expenditures toward certain areas. Of course, when economic times are good – increasing economic growth, for instance – governments may move policy spending more toward their desired spending categories, resulting in greater budgetary volatility. As a result, unless governments reallocate more during one of these periods and not the other, the overall effect may be that there is no real difference in budgetary volatility between good domestic economic times and bad ones. The only real difference may be that, in the former, governments choose their budgetary allocations, while, in the latter, poor economic conditions force their hands. Additionally, left and right governments also may behave similarly, since conditions will pressure them to make changes (although the changes themselves may be different across ideologies – as we saw in Chapter 4).

6.3.5 Results of the Domestic Economy on the Budgetary Ledger

Similar to Chapter 4, we are interested in how governments behave fiscally during both positive and negative domestic economic shocks. Taking each part of the budgetary ledger individually, we compare the effect of an increase in growth (a positive shock) or an increase in unemployment (a negative shock) on each component for both left and right majority governments.

Focusing first on expenditures, in Figure 6.2a, we show the effect of an unemployment shock under left majority, right majority, and all government types. All results point to a positive effect in the short-run, and perhaps a negative effect of increased unemployment on expenditures in the long-run. The non-interacted short-run effect is statistically significant at conventional levels with a substantial .43 percentage points of GDP. We see a similar statistically significant effect for left majority governments, although the effect falls just short of conventional standards for statistical significance for the right majority governments. Ultimately, this suggests that left and right governments do not behave in substantively different ways during economic shocks. In Figure 6.2b, we show the effect of GDP growth on government expenditures. Although there are no statistically significant long-run changes in expenditures in response to increased

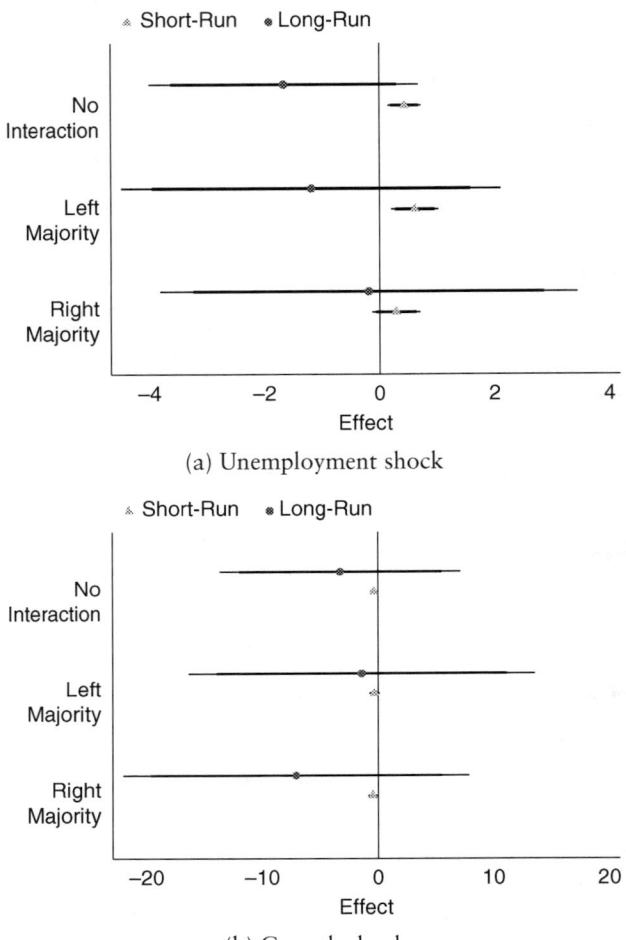

(a) Unemployment shock

(b) Growth shock

FIGURE 6.2. The effects of the domestic economy on expenditures

Note: 95 (thin) and 90 percent (thick) confidence intervals shown.

economic growth, both the non-interacted and right-majority short-run effects are negative and statistically significant. These effects are moderate, with a short-run decline of −.38 for no interaction and −.46 for right majority governments.

What about the effect of unemployment on government revenues? As shown in Figure 6.3a, there appear to be no statistically significant effects across all three scenarios considered. Governments do not increase revenues in response to increased unemployment, nor do left-majority or

6.3 The Effects of the Domestic Economy

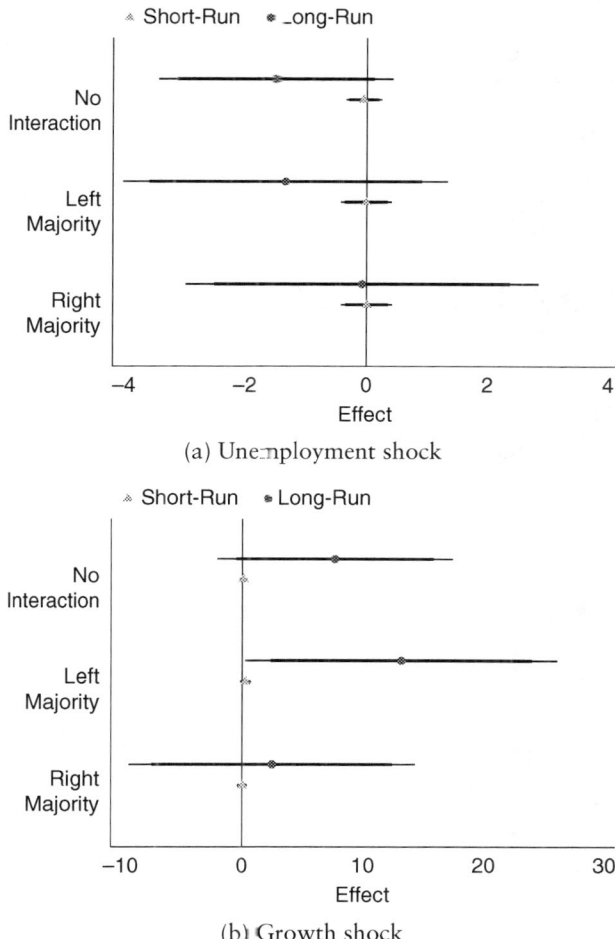

FIGURE 6.3. The effects of the domestic economy on revenues

Note: 95 (thin) and 90 percent (thick) confidence intervals shown.

right-majority governments pursue differing strategies. In Figure 6.3b, we can see the effect of a shock to economic growth. While we find no evidence that economic growth on its own affects revenues (i.e., the no interaction effects are positive but do not achieve statistical significance), left majority governments increase revenues over the long-run in response to increased economic growth, and this increase is substantial at about a 13 percentage point increase. In contrast, right majority governments do not alter revenues in response to a growth shock.

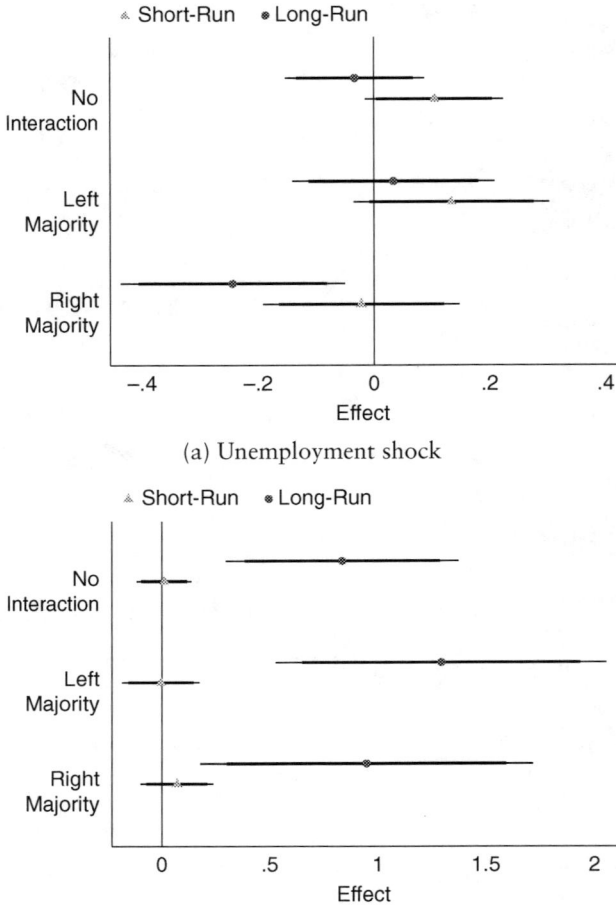

FIGURE 6.4. The effects of the domestic economy on deficits

Note: 95 (thin) and 90 percent (thick) confidence intervals shown.

We show the effect of unemployment on government deficits in Figure 6.4a. Turning first to the results from the noninteractive model, there is a weakly statistically significant short-run increase – and no long-run change – in deficits in response to an increase in unemployment. Yet this story becomes far more complex when we condition unemployment on ideology and majority status. In Figure 6.4a, we see that left-majority governments increase deficits in the short-run, although this effect is not statistically significant. In contrast, right majority governments do not change deficit spending in the short-run in response to an increase in unemployment, but they do decrease the deficit by a little over .2 percentage points over the long-run. Moreover, this latter effect is statistically significant.

To see how a positive domestic economy affects deficits, in Figure 6.4b, we show both the noninteracted and conditional effects of economic growth on deficits. Although there are no statistically significant short-run effects across all three scenarios, over the long-run, deficits increase between .75 and 1.3 percentage points. This is perhaps a surprising finding. As economic growth becomes more favorable, most governments tend to (slightly) increase deficit spending over the long-run rather than increase taxes, as evidenced by the lack of increased revenues in Figure 6.3b (with the large exception of left majority governments, who *do* increase revenues).

In Figure 6.5a, we test whether unemployment alters the composition of expenditures (in terms of budgetary volatility), as well as if this effect is conditional on ideology and majority status. Interestingly, when we look at all governments in the noninteracted results, there are small positive short- and long-run increases in budgetary volatility that suggest governments shift their budgets around when the domestic economy worsens. This pattern continues for left majority governments, where worrying economic conditions appear to significantly increase volatility in the short- and long-runs. In contrast, we find no evidence that right majority governments change budgetary volatility in response to an unemployment shock. In Figure 6.5b, we find no evidence that all governments, or governments with the ability to allocate expenditures to their ideological goals (e.g., left and right majority governments), significantly change their budgetary volatility as economic growth increases.

6.4 THE EFFECTS OF THE INTERNATIONAL ECONOMY

6.4.1 The Effect of the International Economy on Expenditures

Scholars have long discussed if or how international economic conditions affect domestic expenditures. Hearkening back to Chapter 4, the main debate has been focused on the divide between labor and capital, with one side arguing that governments will compensate workers who are adversely affected by the increased competition of opening markets (Rodrik 1998; Garrett and Mitchell 2001; Swank 2002; Hays 2009), while the other side suggests that, since countries desire to remain

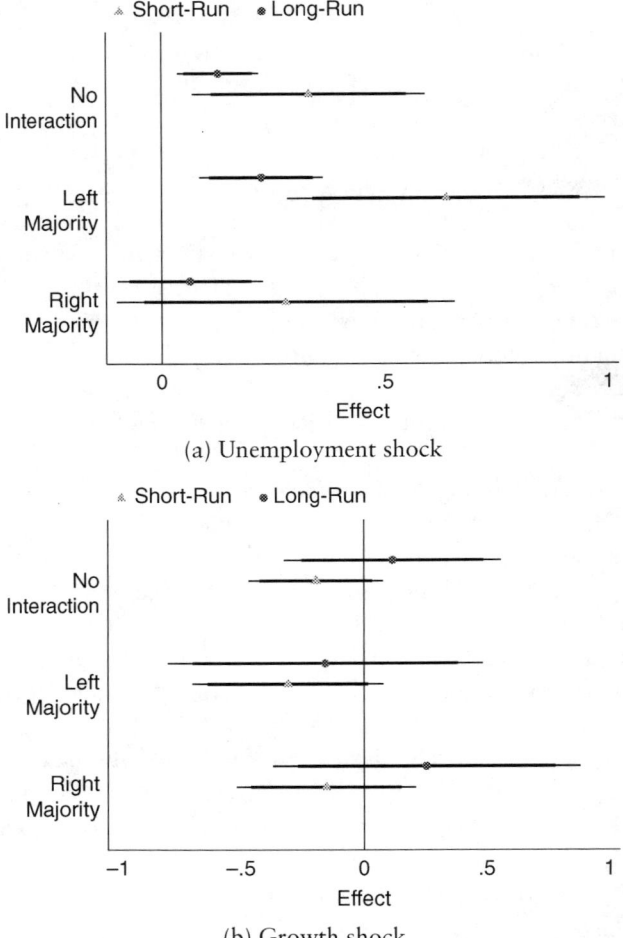

FIGURE 6.5. The effects of the domestic economy on budgetary volatility

Note: 95 (thin) and 90 percent (thick) confidence intervals shown.

competitive and attract international capital, they will tend to keep corporate taxes low, meaning expenditures will also remain low in order to make the government more efficient (Garrett 2001; Bretschger and Hettich 2002; Devereux, Lockwood, and Redoano 2008). Another possibility does exist: that there is no effect from globalization on domestic spending (Iversen and Cusack 2000; Swank and Steinmo 2002; Dreher, Sturm, and Ursprung 2008). Of course, the point of this chapter

6.4 The Effects of the International Economy

is to see whether global economic conditions influence left and right governments' behavior on the various parts of the budget.

When it comes to total expenditures, governments' ideologies can suggest how they will respond when opening their markets to external forces. Given left governments' priority to protect their electoral supporters (domestic workers) through government action, we could expect that these governments would align themselves with the compensatory argument and support government assistance, thus raising total expenditures. In contrast, assuming that right governments hold more of a pro-market stance (and less preference for expanded government), they should decrease overall expenditures as their economies become increasingly exposed to globalization, as the efficiency argument would predict.

From Cusack (1999) to Bergh (2021), there have been researchers who have argued that globalization has diminished the room available for governments to make ideological changes to spending budgets. For example, while left governments expanded the size of government substantially in the 1980s, by the 1990s those left-versus-right ideological differences were small and appeared to not be linked to globalization. Instead, Potrafke (2009) argues they were due to left parties shifting rightward toward less involvement in the economy (see also, Blyth and Katz 2005). If we consider the possibility that government ideology has little-to-no effect, then several outcomes are possible. First, *both* left and right governments may behave the same way in compensating workers through increased social protection (and thus possibly raising total expenditures). Second, they might both conform to the desire for efficiency and decrease overall expenditures in the face of global competition. Third, as much of the literature would suggest, left governments may choose to compensate by increasing expenditures, while right governments decrease them, as the efficiency hypothesis would suggest. A final possibility is that perhaps globalization has no effect on expenditures, regardless of ideology, providing no evidence for either the compensatory or efficiency theories.

6.4.2 The Effect of the International Economy on Revenues

When discussing the ramifications of globalization for governments' behavior on increasing or decreasing government spending, many arguments rely on assumptions about shifting taxes and revenue streams. But research on this aspect of the budgetary relationship is less clear. We argue that such international economic changes may affect governments' abilities to achieve their preferred levels of revenues.[15]

How globalization affects revenues includes both supply and demand concerns. Much of the research that ties together revenues and globalization starts with the premise that opening markets would have a direct effect on tax burdens. As competition for portable capital increased, countries were expected to mimic the reduced taxation rates set by other countries, leading to a domino effect and producing a race-to-the-bottom in international taxation rates on mobile capital (Garrett 2001; Bretschger and Hettich 2002; Devereux, Lockwood, and Redoano 2008; Meinhard and Potrafke 2012).

While the logic about taxes and globalization has been attractive to researchers, the evidence for this behavior has been less persuasive. The empirical research on whether governments shift the tax burden away from capital and toward labor has been mixed. For example, Swank and Steinmo (2002, p. 651) conclude that "[i]nternationalization has not resulted in a shift of the tax burden to labor and consumption as conventional globalization theory predicts." Quinn (1997) even finds that increasing financial liberalization is associated with a reduction in taxation on labor and an increase in a reliance on corporate taxation. While governments may desire to decrease capital taxation relative to taxes on labor to compete with global competition, current research highlights how they face budgetary constraints, political factors, and fairness norms that can counteract these tendencies (Plümper, Troeger, and Winner 2009; Kiser and Karceski 2017). These questions about altering taxation leave changes in the revenue bottom-line in question, since researchers tend to assume that, once governments cut tax rates on one group, they increase taxes on another.

Despite the debate over the shifting of taxation, expectations that governments play a role in determining total revenue levels remain. As compensatory theories of globalization contend, citizens will increasingly demand protection as global competition intensifies, and governments may pay for these programs in various ways. As Chapter 4 reminds us,

---

[15] As the world's economies have become more integrated, scholars have focused on debating if and how factors such as economic integration, trade, and financial liberalization, or other globalizing forces have affected various aspects of domestic tax systems – tax rates, tax reforms, and the introduction of different types of taxes (Garrett 1995; Quinn 1997; Garrett and Mitchell 2001; Bretschger and Hettich 2002; Ashworth and Heyndels 2002; Seelkopf, Lierse, and Schmitt 2016; Seelkopf et al. 2021). This focus on taxes is outside of the scope of our interest in total revenue.

6.4 The Effects of the International Economy

governments can keep the costs of globalization within expenditures by reshuffling budget allocations among a fixed total amount. Another option would be to pay for the extra costs by running deficits to offset the increased spending, while raising revenues in order to pay for increased compensatory policies for workers offers another possibility. Unlike the story that emphasizes "supply-side" factors, where capital would likely flee unless tax rates decline, leading to decreased revenues, another version of the story would highlight the possibility that the "demand-side" might lead. Here, in order to offset increased compensatory spending, governments will not engage in lowering taxes but instead will increase revenues.

While the push and pull relationship between globalization and revenues remains murky, this complexity also makes it difficult to find clear ideological expectations for governments. We could expect left governments to feel the pressure from labor to compensate for more open economies, leading to increased revenues. Paralleling that expectation, we should see right governments bowing to capital (both domestic and foreign) by lowering taxes and, by extension, decreasing revenues. However, governments may find it difficult to implement policies to match their ideological preferences, given the multiple pressures, institutions, and fairness issues. Thus, we expect that, under increasing globalization, there may be less of an ideological effect on changes in revenues.

6.4.3 The Effect of the International Economy on Deficits

In our discussions about how globalization may influence government behavior on expenditures and revenues, an underlying assumption has been a tradeoff between these two components of the budget. Here, we acknowledge that deficits offer governments another budgetary option when faced with international economic pressures. Previous research that has studied government fiscal behavior has found mixed results when analyzing ideological distinctions and deficits. While the conventional wisdom has argued that left governments will run higher deficits than right governments, who are seen as more fiscally prudent (Alesina and Roubini 1993), this debate has continued. Some researchers find no relationship between government ideology and deficits (Hahm, Kamlet, and Mowery 1995; De Haan and Sturm 1997), while others find the opposite (Cameron 1985). In yet another turn of events, others contend that our expectations should be updated, saying that "[i]n anything but the short run, the fiscal and monetary policies of governments of the left and the right should converge" Garrett and Lange (1991, p. 543). While, under normal conditions, left and right governments may behave similarly when it comes to deficits, how they react when faced with international economic pressures remains an open question.

Therefore, does globalization alter left and right governments' use of deficits? In the case of worrying economic conditions, researchers have found that ideological or partisan differences can matter for deficits. For example, Carlsen (1997) finds that left governments are more likely to run a deficit when unemployment is high, while Oatley (1999) contends that domestic governments continue to play a role when explaining deficits. He notes that, even under recessionary conditions and tightening European Union conditions, these partisan differences matter, although the size of the effects on deficits starts to decrease in the 1990s. A similar point about the changing constraints of the international context comes from Boix (2000), who notes that capital mobility constrains governments' choices and their behavior. While some previous research has pointed to the lingering power of government ideology on deficits, even when economic conditions are not ideal, scholars have acknowledged the constraints placed on all governments by globalization. There may be little room remaining for left and right governments to implement their chosen fiscal preferences.

6.4.4 The Effect of the International Economy on Budgetary Volatility

Although expenditures, revenues, and deficits capture most of the movement in budgets, budgetary volatility offers a slightly different perspective on how government behavior may react to international economic shocks. Governments may find it necessary to shift resources when faced with changing market conditions, so we consider whether left and right governments will respond differently – will one or the other move expenditures more?

We could expect that there will be more volatility associated with left governments if they shift funds in an attempt to compensate those most adversely affected by globalization. The shifting (both increasing and decreasing) of resources may involve a number of budgetary areas, resulting in increased volatility. However, it is easy to picture a similar outcome for right governments, because of two reasons. First, they too may move funds, leading to more volatility, but this may be to decrease expenditures and offset their adjustment with lower taxes and revenue.

6.4 The Effects of the International Economy

Alternatively, if we consider a scenario without a "race to the bottom" in taxation, then right governments may move around their expenditures just as much as the left in order to create a more efficient situation for capital. In both of these cases, we would expect budgetary volatility to increase for both left and right governments when faced with increasing globalization.

By including this fourth component of budgets in our investigation, we can explain movement in expenditures without relying on specific policy areas. Instead, we are able to discuss issues about the volatility of budgets that touch on budgetary equilibrium and stability. Are left or right governments more likely to react to globalization by shifting resources, or might they behave similarly?

6.4.5 Results of the International Economy on the Budgetary Ledger

In Figure 6.6, we show the results of a one standard deviation increase in international economic openness on each of the four budgetary components. Turning first to the expenditure results shown in Figure 6.6a, although there is some suggestive evidence that, over the long-run, left majority governments spend more, while right majorities spend less, neither effect achieves statistical significance. Nor do we find that overall (i.e., the "no interaction" scenario) governments respond in any meaningful way by altering expenditures in response to increased globalization. Additionally, the short-run effects are not statistically significant, leading us to conclude that governments of all types fail to respond to increasing international openness by altering their overall expenditures.

Next, we show how increased globalization affects government revenue in Figure 6.6b. Overall, the effects are again suggestive but never statistically significant. When we look at right majority governments, there is a positive long-run increase, while for left majority governments, revenue falls over the long-run in response to increased international openness. For all government types, this negative long-run effect appears to be slightly smaller, although none of the short- or long-run effects achieve statistical significance.

In Figure 6.6c, we show the effects of increased international openness on deficits. When we examine all governments, we do not observe any short-run changes, although there is a weakly statistically significant long-run increase of a little less than .5 percentage points in deficits in response to increased globalization. When we limit this to left majority governments, this effect is even stronger (although once again only significant

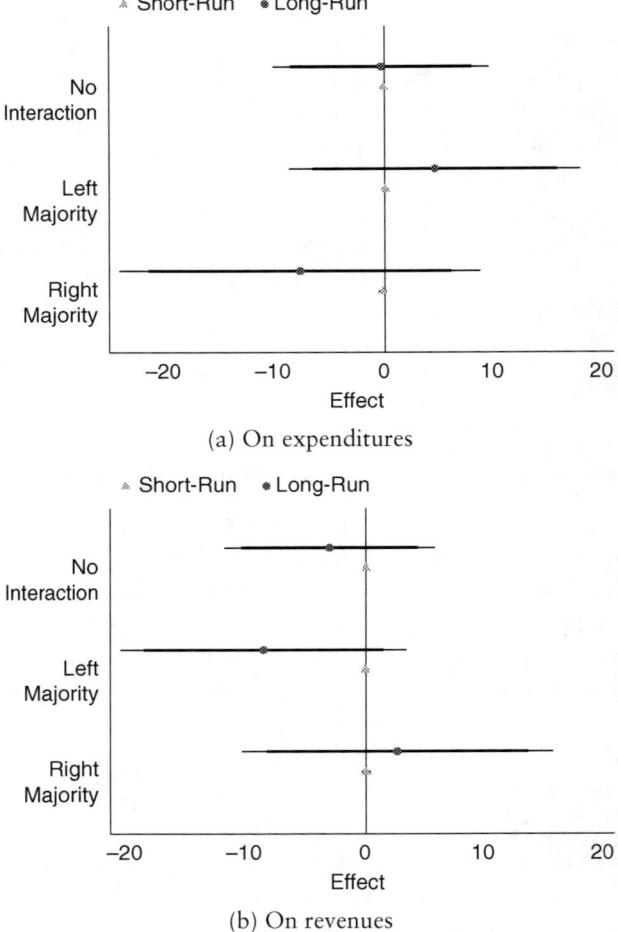

FIGURE 6.6. The effects of openness on the budgetary ledger

Note: 95 (thin) and 90 percent (thick) confidence intervals shown.

at the 90 percent level). Left majority governments increase their deficits by slightly more than .5 percentage points over the long-run in response to increased international openness. In contrast, we find no evidence that right majority governments alter deficits in any meaningful way.

We show the effect of increased globalization on budgetary volatility in Figure 6.6d. Across all government types, as shown in the "no interaction" scenario, we find that, in the short-run, budgetary volatility increases by around .32 in response to increased international openness. Given that

6.4 The Effects of the International Economy

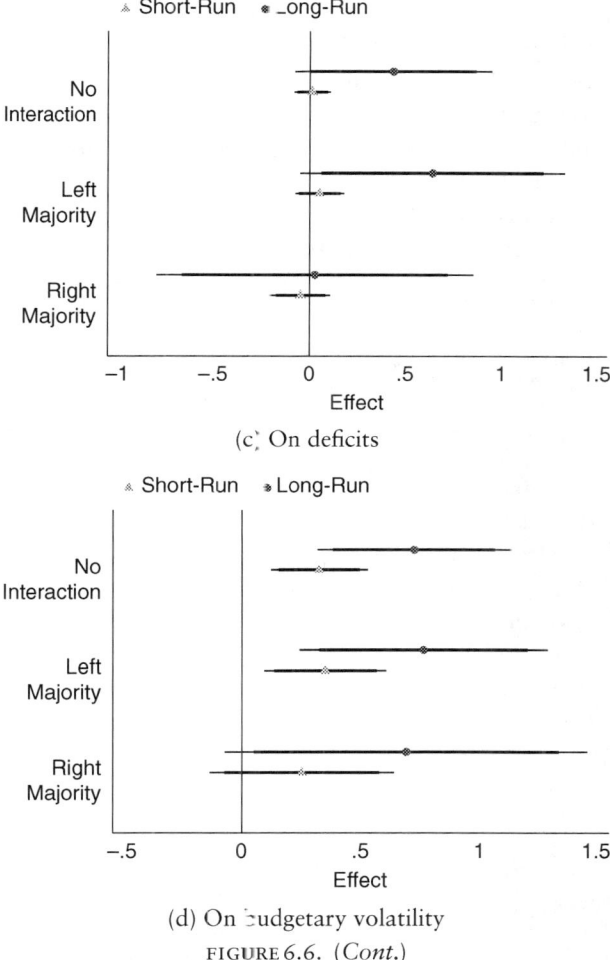

(c) On deficits

(d) On budgetary volatility

FIGURE 6.6. (Cont.)

the average budgetary volatility in our sample is about 2.78, an increase of .32 from the mean would represent roughly an 11.5 percent increase.[16]

Moreover, over the long-run, this effect is even larger, with just over a .70 increase in budgetary volatility. This suggests that, looking across all government types, budgetary volatility does increase with increased

---

[16] We note, however, that an increase of .32 is far smaller than an overall standard deviation of this measure (approximately 2.36) or even the "within-country" standard deviation (2.65).

globalization. When we restrict ourselves to seeing how left majority governments only respond to globalization, we see a similar effect, which is perhaps even slightly larger. In contrast, when we look only at right majority governments, there is no statistically significant increase in budgetary volatility in the short-run, and only a weakly statistically significant increase of just over .2 in the long-run. Thus, we conclude that all government types shift their expenditure allocations in response to globalization, although right majority governments do this to a smaller extent than their left majority counterparts.

6.5 THE EFFECTS OF INTERNATIONAL CONFLICT

6.5.1 The Effect of International Conflict on Expenditures

International conflicts may not offer governments much space to make budgetary decisions. At times, they are funding ongoing or escalating situations, rather than making original decisions. In Chapter 4, we concluded that left and right governments react to international conflict by reallocating expenditures in similar ways. However, it is also important to understand if governments make similar choices across budgetary components when faced with these situations. Might left and right governments differ in the overall resources that they allocate to the country when faced with increasing military conflict?[17]

As discussed in Chapter 4, when it comes to budgetary behavior in an environment of international conflict, governments from all ideological camps may find it politically prudent to increase funding for defense. Since right governments have an ideological preference to increase spending on the military, such environments reinforce their vision. For left governments, the public saliency of international conflict may pressure them to increase military spending, leading to an overall increase in expenditures. Alternatively, raising spending on the military may not always lead to increased overall levels of expenditures.

As Chapter 4 emphasized, governments may choose to tradeoff military spending with decreases in other policy areas, thereby preventing an overall increase in budgetary expenditures. Looking to the broader

---

[17] As we discussed in Chapter 4, researchers tend to approach military spending from a "guns versus butter" framework (Russett 1982; Mintz 1989; Narizny 2003; Whitten and Williams 2011; Bove, Efthyvoulou, and Navas 2017). Here, we are interested in total spending.

6.5 The Effects of International Conflict

budgetary components, governments also have options that offset raising military funds. As other parts of this section will highlight, raising revenues or running deficits could offer right and left governments options that allow them to increase funds in response to the international conflict environment.

6.5.2 The Effect of International Conflict on Revenues

Similar to the relationship with expenditures, the ways in which international conflict may affect governments' abilities to alter revenues might be more about how these external pressures tie the hands of governments, rather than how ideological differences shape revenues. International conflict may constrain government behavior by requiring governments to allocate resources to fund a military conflict. Deciding to decrease funding to the military during an international conflict is rarely an option for any government. Therefore, regardless of their ideological stance on defense, governments will require revenues.[18]

Empirical research on how international conflicts might affect revenues remains limited and work that theorizes about how this context affects governments' behavior on revenues even more so. Hostilities may change governments' calculations for raising revenues. War may make citizens more likely to agree to a higher tax burden to pay for the increased costs of defense expenditures (Tilly 1990), although this may be more true during conflict (especially less intense ones) rather than the years preceding it (van den Boogaard et al. 2018).[19] Post-conflict and long-term effects of hostilities on revenues also remain unclear. For instance, van den Boogaard et al. (2018) found evidence to support the notion that revenues probably increase in the post-conflict environment; out of the 18 conflicts they analyzed, post-conflict revenues increased in two-thirds of them. Overall, the literature would seem to suggest that, if anything, revenues might stay the same or even rise – mostly due to citizens' increased willingness to fund conflict – certainly over the short-run, but perhaps even in the long-run as increased revenues pivot toward other spending categories. Therefore, we argue that, in reaction to an international

---

[18] Of course, governments may choose to increase deficits rather than revenues, something we take up in Section 6.5.3.

[19] Conflict may have other side-effects tied to revenues, namely, the argument that conflict during the twentieth century led to increasingly progressive taxation policies (Scheve and Stasavage 2010, 2012).

military event, governments will not decrease revenues. More specifically, we expect that governments, regardless of ideology, will either increase revenues or keep the status quo in order to fund the military operation without decreasing funds for other preferred policy areas.

6.5.3 The Effect of International Conflict on Deficits

International conflict also has the potential to affect how governments use deficits. Given that government expenditures on defense should increase in response to greater conflict involvement (Whitten and Williams 2011; Töngür, Hsu, and Elveren 2015; Bove, Efthyvoulou, and Navas 2017), governments may choose deficit spending over increasing revenues. Narizny (2003, p. 204) explains this logic: "governments can also borrow the funds needed to build up their militaries, then gradually pay off the debt once the international crisis has passed. Since voters tend to discount future costs and benefits, this option may be less politically painful to the right than sudden increases in taxation."

Empirical evidence suggests that deficit increases in response to conflicts may indeed be more palatable than either revenue increases or budgetary cuts to other expenditure areas; the latter representing the "guns versus butter" tradeoff. Moreover, deficit increases may be more popular than reallocating the expenditure budget. Gupta et al. (2004, p. 409) find that governments will choose to finance greater military expenditures by growing deficits, "rather than at the cost of lower spending on education and health."[20] Given the overall paucity of evidence in support of the "guns versus butter" hypothesis (Russett 1982; Mintz 1989; Mintz and Huang 1991), it is clear that, since increased defense expenditures do not necessarily come at the cost of social policies, governments are either increasing revenues or are taking on increased deficits in order to finance these changes.

As we demonstrated in Chapter 4, right and left governments make similar changes to budgetary tradeoffs in the face of increasing hostilities, so they may turn to deficits to help fund the military during these conflicts. Both types of governments require revenue, but neither desires to raise taxes during difficult times. Left governments may be more prone

---

[20] These authors also note that, in real terms, expenditures on education and health are actually decreasing (as a percentage of GDP), since a country's growth rate slows during the conflict.

to deficit spending, but right governments may have some latitude when the reason is a key ideological priority.

6.5.4 The Effect of International Conflict on Budgetary Volatility

International conflict has the potential to reshape budgets. As we saw in Chapter 4, both right and left governments reallocated their spending budgets in response to increased hostilities. While we can debate the merits of discussing a "guns versus butter" tradeoff, these types of expenditure changes should be expected to increase the volatility of budgets. Whether governments move funds between policy areas, increase revenues, or deficit spend, the result should be increased changes to budgets resulting in more volatility.

While we argue that budgetary volatility will increase with an international conflict environment, we find little reason to expect that right and left governments will differ in their behavior. They shift policy budgets in similar ways, although they may be reallocating varying amounts of resources among policy areas, but the relative volatility may be similar across left and right governments. For example, while left governments tend to be associated with larger government sizes compared to right governments, the relative movement of funds between policy areas, leading to increased volatility, may be similar in times of conflict. Although increased international conflict should lead to more shifting of resources, the overall volatility may not differ by ideology.

6.5.5 Results of International Conflict on the Budgetary Ledger

How might hostilities influence overall government expenditures? We investigate this in Figure 6.7a, where we show the effect of a one standard deviation increase in the international hostility level on expenditures. Perhaps surprisingly, all scenarios we examine in Figure 6.7a suggest that expenditures decrease over the long-run, although none of the effects are statistically significant. Moreover, there appears to be no statistically significant change in the short-run regarding expenditures either.

In Figure 6.7b, we test whether increased hostilities shape government revenue. Similar to our results for expenditures, over the long-run, revenues slightly decrease across all government types, although no effects are statistically significantly different from zero.

Contrast this with Figure 6.7c, in which we show the effect of increased hostilities on government deficits. Here the story is more interesting.

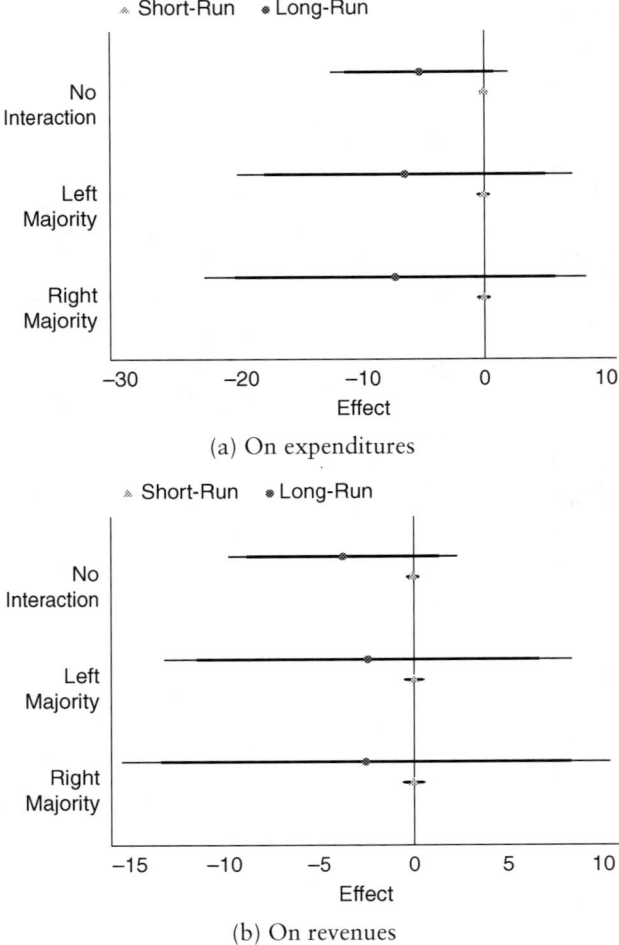

FIGURE 6.7. The effects of international conflict on the budgetary ledger

Note: 95 (thin) and 90 percent (thick) confidence intervals shown.

As hostilities increase, over the long-run, there appears to be a small increase in deficit spending when we look across all government types, although this effect is only statistically significant at the 90 percent level. We see a similar, slightly stronger effect when we examine how right majority governments respond to increased hostilities, although once again the effect is only weakly statistically significant over the long-run (and not significant in the short-run). In contrast, left majority

6.5 The Effects of International Conflict

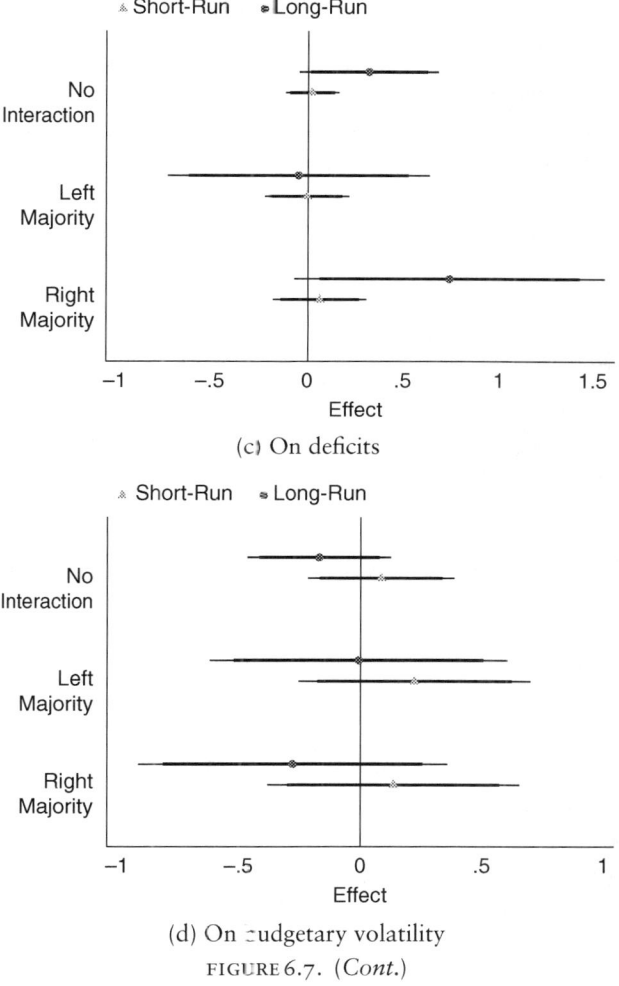

(c) On deficits

(d) On budgetary volatility

FIGURE 6.7. (Cont.)

governments do not change deficits at all in response to increased hostilities.

In Figure 6.7d, we show the effect of an increase in hostilities on budgetary volatility. While we expect volatility to increase as expenditures are reallocated toward defense, in the short-run, the positive effect does not achieve statistical significance for all government types. For left or right majority governments, where we would expect governments to have the greatest budgetary leeway, we also find no significant results for hostilities.

6.6 CONCLUSION

In this chapter, we have used our knowledge (and basic model specifications) from Chapter 5 to tie together the components of the budget with the behavior of governments in response to domestic and international factors. At the center of this chapter is an assumption that governments with varying policy preferences and ideologies will behave differently on budgetary decisions when they encounter situations that alter their political calculations. How these electoral, economic, and international shocks affect budgetary components may depend on the government driving those fiscal decisions.

One striking element across the results we presented in this chapter is the lack of statistically significant effects, especially in terms of long-run effects, on these budgetary components. While the lack of differences across left and right majority governments stands out, our findings for how contexts affect governments' behavior on overall expenditures indicates some ideological movement. We did find evidence that unemployment leads to short-run increases in total spending for all governments, and these increases are also significant for left majority governments but not for right majorities. Economic growth leads to short-run decreases in total spending for all governments, with left and right majorities behaving similarly. This lends some evidence to the notion that both good and bad domestic economic situations affect government expenditures. But, otherwise, we found no effects for overall expenditures. Contrast this with Chapter 4, where we examined the effects of these same contextual factors on the composition of budgetary expenditures. There, we found numerous statistically significant relationships, many of which were long-run effects, and many of which differed significantly across left and right majority governments. Together, the findings from Chapter 4 and this chapter suggest that the main political action of how governments respond to external factors in terms of expenditures are by reallocating across spending categories rather than on overall spending as a percentage of GDP.

In terms of our findings for revenues, we also saw very little of note. Elections seem to drive governments to collect less revenue in the short-run, especially for left majority governments. The only long-run effect that we found on revenues is a substantial increase in revenues under left majority governments in reaction to an increase in economic growth. One explanation for this overall dearth of evidence for revenues might be governments' unwillingness to raise taxes in the face of nearly any contextual shock, likely because doing so would prove unpopular and electorally unwise, at least in the short-run.

In fact, this lack of evidence for altering revenues may explain why we found relatively more effects for deficits, though many of these results were on the borderline of conventional standards of statistical significance. Deficits, unlike revenues, can alleviate budgetary shortfalls without raising additional revenues.[21] In terms of findings, our results indicate that right majority governments do increase deficits in the long-run during elections. Our strongest – and perhaps most surprising – results for deficits are for domestic economic factors, with unemployment leading to a long-run decrease in the deficit under a right majority. In contrast, increased economic growth results in a long-run increase in the deficit for all types of governments.[22] With regard to economic openness, we found borderline significant results, indicating that, for all governments, as well as left majority governments specifically, greater openness leads to increases in the deficit. Moreover, we found similarly borderline results for international conflict, indicating that, for all governments, especially right majority governments, greater conflict leads to increases in the deficit.

Across the four budgetary components, we observed our strongest results for the influence of contextual factors on budgetary volatility. These results all come in reaction to increasing unemployment and economic openness, evidence that governments are responding (by shifting their expenditure allocations) mostly to domestic shocks. For unemployment, all governments increase budgetary volatility in the short- and long-run, and the effect exists in the long-run for left majority governments as well. Similarly, we found that an increase in economic openness results in significant short- and long-run increases in budgetary volatility for all governments and, in particular, for left governments.

Ultimately, this chapter has highlighted how complicated government budgetary behavior can be. Governments have various budgetary tools at their disposal, but, in the real world, they may not be able to use them. In the face of electoral, economic, and international contexts, left and right governments can struggle to make their preferred budgetary changes. At times, conditions influence budgetary components under governments

---

[21] As discussed at the beginning of this conclusion, we found little evidence that governments are increasing expenditures during these shocks, so the changes in deficits seem to be coupled more with rises and falls in revenues than changes in expenditures themselves.

[22] Whether this is due to difficulties in cutting spending once the good times of increased growth are over remains an interesting question.

of all ideological stripes, while, at others, left and right majority governments show slight differences. Therefore, context and conditions can matter for budgetary decision-making, overwhelming the ideological side of budgets.

6.7 APPENDIX

The results in this chapter showed estimates from pooled OLS models. These have fairly strong assumptions about unobservable heterogeneity common to a given unit (c.f. Clark and Linzer 2015). Tables 6.1–6.4 present the numerical results for each of the four dependent variables analyzed in this chapter. The figures of the results presented in this chapter are all from the models displayed in the first two columns of numeric output in each table under the heading "Pooled." We also include the results from two alternative model specifications. The fixed effects model (under the

TABLE 6.1. *Expenditure single-equation results*

	Pooled		RE		FE	
	Coef.	(S.E.)	Coef.	(S.E.)	Coef.	(S.E.)
Expenditures$_{i,t-1}$	.967***	(.009)	.967***	(.009)	.850***	(.019)
GDP Growth$_{i,t}$	−.124*	(.052)	−.124*	(.051)	−.163**	(.054)
GDP Growth$_{i,t-1}$	.088	(.045)	.088*	(.045)	.027	(.048)
ΔUnemployment$_{i,t}$	.330**	(.112)	.330**	(.110)	.304*	(.121)
Unemployment$_{i,t-1}$	−.043	(.028)	−.043	(.028)	.010	(.049)
ΔOpenness$_{i,t}$	−.012	(.016)	−.012	(.016)	−.013	(.016)
ΔOpenness$_{i,t-1}$	.010	(.017)	.010	(.017)	.009	(.017)
Age Dependency Ratio$_{i,t}$	.323	(.247)	.323	(.244)	.275	(.274)
Age Dependency Ratio$_{i,t-1}$	−.270	(.246)	−.270	(.243)	−.234	(.274)
Election$_{i,t}$	−.072	(.265)	−.072	(.262)	.049	(.266)
Election$_{i,t-1}$	−.009	(.264)	−.009	(.261)	.119	(.264)
Hostilities$_{i,t}$	−.013	(.042)	−.013	(.042)	−.006	(.048)
Hostilities$_{i,t-1}$	−.030	(.042)	−.030	(.041)	−.021	(.047)
Right$_{i,t}$	−.015	(.643)	−.015	(.636)	−.251	(.647)
Right$_{i,t-1}$	.085	(.652)	.085	(.645)	−.025	(.662)
Majority$_{i,t}$	.113	(.478)	.113	(.472)	.025	(.487)
Majority$_{i,t-1}$	.256	(.478)	.256	(.472)	.315	(.496)
Right$_{i,t}$×Majority$_{i,t}$	−.126	(.729)	−.126	(.720)	.143	(.734)
Right$_{i,t-1}$×Majority$_{i,t-1}$	−.016	(.738)	−.016	(.729)	.070	(.749)
Year	−.007	(.014)	−.007	(.014)	.005	(.017)
Constant	13.649	(28.846)	13.649	(28.505)	−7.462	(33.985)

Note: $N = 893$. Coefficients with standard errors in parentheses shown from OLS (Pooled/FE models) or maximum likelihood (RE) estimators. Dependent variable is expenditures. Two-tailed tests. ***$p < .01$; **$p < .05$; *$p < .10$.

6.7 Appendix

TABLE 6.2. *Revenues single-equation results*

	Pooled		RE		FE	
	Coef.	(S.E.)	Coef.	(S.E.)	Coef.	(S.E.)
Revenues$_{i,t-1}$	.961***	(.010)	.961***	(.010)	.818***	(.021)
Deficits$_{i,t}$	.046	(.049)	.046	(.048)	.056	(.050)
Deficits$_{i,t-1}$	−.007	(.051)	−.007	(.050)	.048	(.053)
GDP Growth$_{i,t}$	.033	(.052)	.033	(.051)	.024	(.054)
GDP Growth$_{i,t-1}$	.066	(.045)	.066	(.044)	.089	(.048)
ΔUnemployment$_{i,t}$	−.037	(.113)	−.037	(.111)	.026	(.121)
Unemployment$_{i,t-1}$	−.044	(.029)	−.044	(.029)	.004	(.049)
ΔOpenness$_{i,t}$	.002	(.016)	.002	(.016)	.001	(.016)
ΔOpenness$_{i,t-1}$	−.018	(.017)	−.018	(.016)	−.020	(.017)
Age Dependency Ratio$_{i,t}$	.294	(.246)	.294	(.243)	−.143	(.277)
Age Dependency Ratio$_{i,t-1}$	−.243	(.245)	−.243	(.241)	.208	(.276)
Election$_{i,t}$	−.620*	(.266)	−.620*	(.262)	−.468	(.266)
Election$_{i,t-1}$	−.028	(.264)	−.028	(.261)	.044	(.263)
Hostilities$_{i,t}$	−.011	(.043)	−.011	(.042)	.026	(.049)
Hostilities$_{i,t-1}$	−.025	(.042)	−.025	(.042)	.011	(.048)
Right$_{i,t}$	−.087	(.642)	−.087	(.633)	−.052	(.648)
Right$_{i,t-1}$	−.184	(.649)	−.184	(.640)	−.201	(.657)
Majority$_{i,t}$	.083	(.470)	.083	(.464)	.194	(.481)
Majority$_{i,t-1}$	−.098	(.472)	−.098	(.466)	.085	(.490)
Right$_{i,t}$×Majority$_{i,t}$	.063	(.732)	.063	(.722)	.046	(.738)
Right$_{i,t-1}$×Majority$_{i,t-1}$	.151	(.738)	.151	(.728)	.169	(.750)
Year	−.016	(.014)	−.016	(.014)	.026	(.017)
Constant	30.400	(28.702)	30.400	(28.316)	−49.787	(34.560)

Note: $N = 861$. Coefficients with standard errors in parentheses shown from OLS (Pooled/FE models) or maximum likelihood (RE) estimators. Dependent variable is revenues. Two-tailed tests. ***$p < .01$; **$p < .05$; *$p < .10$.

heading "FE" in the tables) add unit intercepts to the model – that is, going from α to α_i – that have the effect of soaking up all time-invariant factors common to a country (e.g., culture, geography). We find that, even after we account for such unobservable time-invariant heterogeneity, the results are very similar to those of the fully pooled models. We also test robustness by estimating a random effects model (under the heading "RE") that assumes country intercepts come from draws from a normal distribution with some global average, α, as well as some variance around it which we estimate, σ_α^2.[23] In this sense, it can be seen as somewhere between ignoring heterogeneity completely (the pooled model) and fully

---

[23] Unlike the pooled and fixed effects estimators that are estimated using OLS, we use maximum likelihood when estimating the random effects model.

TABLE 6.3. *Deficit single-equation results*

	Pooled		RE		FE	
	Coef.	(S.E.)	Coef.	(S.E.)	Coef.	(S.E.)
Deficits$_{i,t-1}$	.735***	(.022)	.624***	(.034)	.531***	(.029)
Expenditures$_{i,t}$	.876***	(.021)	.882***	(.021)	.890***	(.021)
Expenditures$_{i,t-1}$	−.621***	(.029)	−.529***	(.035)	−.451***	(.033)
Revenues$_{i,t}$	−.675***	(.022)	−.679***	(.022)	−.678***	(.022)
Revenue$_{i,t-1}$	.442***	(.028)	.361***	(.033)	.300***	(.031)
GDP Growth$_{i,t}$	.004	(.021)	.001	(.021)	.003	(.022)
GDP Growth$_{i,t-1}$	.069***	(.018)	.060**	(.018)	.054**	(.019)
ΔUnemployment$_{i,t}$	.079	(.046)	.062	(.046)	.049	(.048)
Unemployment$_{i,t-1}$	−.007	(.012)	−.013	(.016)	−.022	(.020)
ΔOpenness$_{i,t}$	.002	(.007)	.000	(.006)	−.000	(.006)
ΔOpenness$_{i,t-1}$	.014*	(.007)	.012	(.007)	.012	(.007)
Age Dependency Ratio$_{i,t}$	.095	(.100)	.118	(.104)	.164	(.109)
Age Dependency Ratio$_{i,t-1}$	−.099	(.100)	−.127	(.104)	−.180	(.109)
Election$_{i,t}$	.000	(.109)	.004	(.104)	−.010	(.106)
Election$_{i,t-1}$	−.020	(.107)	−.018	(.103)	−.032	(.104)
Hostilities$_{i,t}$	.005	(.017)	.001	(.018)	−.010	(.019)
Hostilities$_{i,t-1}$	.016	(.017)	.011	(.018)	−.001	(.019)
Right$_{i,t}$	.098	(.261)	.074	(.253)	.044	(.257)
Right$_{i,t-1}$	−.073	(.264)	−.129	(.256)	−.195	(.260)
Majority$_{i,t}$	−.055	(.191)	−.040	(.187)	−.043	(.191)
Majority$_{i,t-1}$	.248	(.192)	.216	(.190)	.151	(.194)
Right$_{i,t}$×Majority$_{i,t}$	−.280	(.298)	−.266	(.288)	−.240	(.292)
Right$_{i,t-1}$×Majority$_{i,t-1}$	.035	(.300)	.077	(.292)	.142	(.297)
Year	.011	(.006)	.014*	(.006)	.012	(.007)
Constant	−22.031	(11.940)	−27.831*	(12.943)	−25.530	(13.895)

Note: N = 861. Coefficients with standard errors in parentheses shown from OLS (Pooled/FE models) or maximum likelihood (RE) estimators. Dependent variable is deficits. Two-tailed tests. ***$p < .01$; **$p < .05$; *$p < .10$.

removing unit heterogeneity from the model (fixed effects). We find that the results remain robust to using this estimator as well.

6.7.1 Residual Autocorrelation Tests

Similar to the residual autocorrelation tests we performed in Section 3.6.4 for the Chapter 3 and 4 compositional models, it is important to check for serial correlation in the models presented in this chapter. Using the same Born–Breitung tests described in Chapter 3, in Table 6.5, we show that, with the exception of revenue models under the fixed effects specification, there is no evidence of residual autocorrelation across our dependent

6.7 Appendix

TABLE 6.4. *Budgetary volatility single-equation results*

	Pooled		RE		FE	
	Coef.	(S.E.)	Coef.	(S.E.)	Coef.	(S.E.)
Budgetary Volatility$_{i,t-1}$	.294***	(.034)	.273***	(.042)	.182***	(.037)
GDP Growth$_{i,t}$	−.064	(.045)	−.070	(.046)	−.105*	(.048)
GDP Growth$_{i,t-1}$	.090*	(.040)	.086*	(.040)	.057	(.042)
ΔUnemployment$_{i,t}$	.245*	(.099)	.238*	(.099)	.179	(.107)
Unemployment$_{i,t-1}$	.067**	(.024)	.075**	(.028)	.097*	(.039)
ΔOpenness$_{i,t}$	.046**	(.015)	.045**	(.014)	.041**	(.015)
ΔOpenness$_{i,t-1}$	.026	(.015)	.026	(.015)	.026	(.015)
Age Dependency Ratio$_{i,t}$	.064	(.215)	.144	(.238)	.527*	(.244)
Age Dependency Ratio$_{i,t-1}$	−.098	(.212)	−.186	(.239)	−.583*	(.240)
Election$_{i,t}$	−.044	(.231)	−.037	(.228)	.017	(.231)
Election$_{i,t-1}$	.097	(.231)	.106	(.227)	.156	(.230)
Hostilities$_{i,t}$	.020	(.037)	.025	(.037)	.083*	(.042)
Hostilities$_{i,t-1}$	−.049	(.037)	−.041	(.038)	.028	(.042)
Right$_{it}$	.315	(.576)	.334	(.568)	.367	(.581)
Right$_{t-1}$	−.584	(.579)	−.577	(.571)	−.527	(.587)
Majority$_{i,t}$	−.572	(.412)	−.558	(.407)	−.560	(.421)
Majority$_{i,t-1}$	.426	(.410)	.455	(.409)	.563	(.428)
Right$_{i,t}$ × Majority$_{i,t}$	.018	(.654)	−.022	(.647)	−.180	(.659)
Right$_{i,t-1}$ × Majority$_{i,t-1}$	.723	(.654)	.690	(.647)	.487	(.668)
Year	−.011	(.012)	−.017	(.014)	−.041**	(.014)
Constant	24.497	(24.525)	36.997	(29.165)	85.194**	(29.794)

Note: $N = 782$. Coefficients with standard errors in parentheses shown from OLS (Pooled/FE models) or maximum likelihood (RE) estimators. Dependent variable is budgetary volatility. Two-tailed tests. ***$p < .01$; **$p < .05$; *$p < .10$.

TABLE 6.5. *Very weak evidence of residual autocorrelation across our Chapter 6 models*

	Bias-Corrected Born-Breitung $Q(p)$		Bias-Corrected Born-Breitung $LM(k)$		Heteroskedasticity-Robust Born-Breitung	
Model	RE	FE	RE	FE	RE	FE
Expenditures	.07	.99	.27	.98	−1.57	.56
Revenues	.00	10.60**	−.14	3.26**	.72	2.27**
Deficits	1.31	1.71	−1.16	1.25	.34	1.88*
Budgetary Volatility	.01	2.22	−.09	1.47	−.18	.86

Note: **$p < .05$; *$p < .10$. All tests are for AR(1) residual autocorrelation where H_0: No autocorrelation. Tests are distributed $\sim N(0, 1)$ for $LM(k)$ and heteroskedasticity-robust, and χ^2 with one degree of freedom for $Q(p)$.

variables analyzed throughout the chapter, since we nearly always fail to reject the null hypothesis of no residual autocorrelation.

7

Conclusion: The Budgetary Mix

> *Your mission is to pick from a menu of tax and spending options to reduce the debt from projected levels over the next 25 years. But budget decisions aren't only about fiscal sustainability. To win the game, you also must find a combination of policies that match your values and priorities.*
> Directions from the game, *Fiscal Ship*.[1]

At the beginning of this book, we highlighted two online games – *Budget Hero* and *Fiscal Ship* – that showed how complicated it can be to understand the moving parts of government budgets. As the title (and the graphics) of *Fiscal Ship* allude, trying to manipulate all of these interconnected pieces can seem as challenging as trying to save a foundering vessel lost at sea. Yet if online games can attempt to educate people about the politics behind all of these budgetary moving parts, then social scientists should also seek to better explain how they fit together.

In this book, we have argued for an explanation of government budgets that focuses on competition between parties, governments, policies, and even budgetary components. We have waded through the compositions of expenditures, the causal relationships of budgetary components, and the various economic and international contexts that can plague government decision-making. What we have uncovered is a complicated story of government budgeting. Considering the opening quote, if governments played *Fiscal Ship*, then they may very well lose often, since we have found

---

[1] *Fiscal Ship*: The Woodrow Wilson International Center for Scholars' Serious Games Initiative and The Brookings Institute's Hutchins Center on Fiscal & Monetary Policy, https://fiscalship.org/. Last accessed June 15, 2021.

that they do not always succeed in matching their budgetary decisions to their ideological priorities.

As we have stressed throughout this book, much of the research on government budgets has focused on specific parts in isolation – deficits, tax revenue, total spending, or on individual policies – rather than acknowledge the interconnectedness and messiness of budgets. In his review of *Fiscal Ship* on FiveThirtyEight, Ben Casselman explained: "But entertainment value aside (and it's more fun than it sounds), the simulation does an admirable job of illustrating the tradeoffs that policymakers face."[2] And tradeoffs are the backbone of budgets. Increasing spending in one policy area means taking funding from another area or areas, while raising the overall level of spending will require increasing revenue or running a deficit. All of these decisions involve some form of tradeoff. In this book, we have emphasized, as well as modeled these tradeoffs, both at the expenditure level (with a compositional approach, as done in Chapters 3 and 4) and at the overall budgetary level, by considering the causal relationships between the various budgetary components (i.e., expenditures, revenues, deficits, and volatility, in Chapters 5 and 6).

While we conclude this book by placing both our theoretical and methodological contributions within the wider literature, we also discuss our thoughts on how research on budgets, compositions, and competition can move forward. As we have mentioned throughout this book, budgets have knock-on effects on all things political, from elections and political parties to representation and news media. Tradeoffs, competition, context, and policy resonate well beyond budgets, so we take a wide-angle view in the remainder of this chapter.

7.1 THEORETICAL CONTRIBUTIONS

Our book began by analyzing both how researchers have studied budgets and the previous conclusions they have reached. We grouped these approaches to budgetary research into three main types: studies focusing on single budgetary categories, studies of budgetary changes, and studies of aggregate budgetary components. Regardless of the approach used, we identified that the missing elements in much of this work were two-fold. First, research designs typically failed to appreciate the fact that increasing

---

[2] https://fivethirtyeight.com/features/the-economys-crisis-ended-under-obama-but-its-long-term-problems-didnt/. Last accessed May 27, 2021.

one category of spending (relative to some total budget) will necessarily result in a simultaneous decrease in at least one other category. Therefore, when a government chooses (or is forced automatically) to raise spending on one category, it must offset this increase with a corresponding decrease somewhere else in the budget. Second, research has largely focused on one component of the budget rather than studying the multiple components as interconnected pieces, leading to a compartmentalization of much of the budgetary research.

Much has been written about the role of government ideology and partisanship in reference to policy and budgetary outcomes. In a nutshell, this research has asked some version of the "Does ideology matter for [insert budgetary component here – total spending, policy spending, budget deficits, tax systems, etc.]?" question. More realistically, there are times when scholars should expect governments to accomplish their ideological goals, but there are other times when they should consider that governments might actively choose to sideline their ideological goals. We set out to include these more complicated possibilities in our expectations and contribute to the understanding of politics and budgets.

Acknowledging the competitiveness of budgets is key to understanding how politics influences spending, revenues, deficits, and volatility. Political parties offer the electorate choices, and the governments that result from these electoral contests have opportunities to implement their agendas. In this book, we have been interested in relating these different policy visions to the resulting budgetary outcomes, but realistically, governments may encounter help and hindrances along the way when attempting to fulfil their aspirations. Our argument that electoral, economic, political, and international contexts affect governments' desires and abilities to alter budgets remains key to our theoretical contribution. We have kept a common theoretical framework throughout this book as we have tackled two different aspects of budgets – the competition in spending tradeoffs and the competition between budgetary components.

Core to our theoretical argument has been the assumption that government ideology, which itself is typically a function of parties' core supporters, drives the general budgetary priorities of governments. In other words, with a blank slate, how would budgets look under a right versus a left government? Of course, governments seldom have the ability to enact large-scale changes to fulfill their ideological agendas. Contexts and environments in which governments make these decisions influence whether they can reshape budgets. Throughout this book, we focused on how four main circumstances – institutional power, electoral considerations, domestic economic circumstances, and international pressures – can affect governments' behavior on budgets. We also noted that budgets are incremental across time, so previous budgets and policies can hinder governments' attempts to begin with a blank slate. While arguments about representative government would have us expect that governments with different ideological leanings would oversee varying budgets and choose different budgetary tools in response to similar shocks, our findings throughout this book point to a complicated story of ideology, political strategy, and overwhelming circumstances. Politics does not always win the day in our theoretical tournaments. In fact, contexts are likely to overrule partisan visions, pointing to government strategic behavior that transcends left and right priorities.

While our compositional, broad-picture approach is novel, we realize it may not be a one-size-fits-all approach for every budgetary research question. Scholars may find that their research interests require a specific expenditure category (e.g., defense or welfare spending) or that a focus on a particular component of the budget (e.g., deficits or volatility) is most appropriate for their question. While the first half of this book (Chapters 3 and 4) focused on budget areas as a proportion of total expenditures, we acknowledge that, for some research questions, it might be more appropriate to describe budgets relative to other factors, such as expressing them as a percentage of GDP (closer to the research in Chapters 5 and 6). As with all social science research, the questions should largely dictate the research design.

For those attempting to explain budgetary behavior in a broader sense, however, we believe our theoretical approach offers a more inclusive picture of how changes in one portion of the government budget are not independent of others. In particular, we agree with the warning by Kramon and Posner (2013, p. 467) when discussing discrepancies in findings by distributive politics scholars that any article's conclusions, "will as much be a function of the outcome they happen to select as of the general patterns of political behavior that they are trying to understand." Our approach helps to guard against this by forcing scholars to consider, or at least acknowledge, theoretical expectations among *all* potential outcomes that could be considered.

7.2 METHODOLOGICAL CONTRIBUTIONS

The other major contribution of this book is the series of research design and methodological choices we devised to better link our analyses with our theoretical implications. While compositional models are not new, in this book, we extended the use of such models to study budgets and add to recent research that has utilized this approach (Breunig and Busemeyer 2012; Philips, Rutherford, and Whitten 2016a). As discussed throughout the book, from a methodological perspective, failing to recognize that budgets are compositional can lead to inferential shortcomings. Namely, researchers may see "impossible" predictions of the proportion of the budget allocated toward a particular category or that over(under)-estimation in one category necessarily occurs together with an under(over)-estimation in at least one other category. Compositional models get us one step closer to the reality of complicated budgetary relationships by taking into consideration these dependent links.

The downside to using compositional methods is that it is difficult to rely on the standard interpretation of tabular results to indicate a model's findings. While compositional models may get researchers closer to reality, that reality is rather complicated to interpret. Here, our innovation was a series of figures designed to better show the context-specific changes to budgets. We favored "effects"-style plots, joining a small, but growing group of researchers who utilize this tool (Lipsmeyer, Philips, and Whitten 2017; Lipsmeyer et al. 2019; Adolph, Breunig, and Koski 2020; Kagalwala, Philips, and Whitten 2021).[3] Such plots can turn a complicated coefficient into a substantively meaningful graph that indicates the change in the proportion of each compositional category. In addition, these plots make compositional models more accessible to both researchers and broader audiences.

The other methodological advance we made in the second half of this book focused on the aggregate budgetary components – total revenues, expenditures, deficits, and budgetary volatility. Recall from our summary of our theory that we noted how these four categories were interdependent. As such, we wanted to avoid placing, at least *a priori*, assumptions about which one of these factors might be causing the others. While previous researchers have made assumptions about the causal relationships of some of these components, we decided to investigate them directly. Our contribution here was to use a panel-version of the popular vector autoregressive model used in the analysis of time series data. This allowed all four budgetary components to be potentially endogenous to

---

[3] See also Jung et al. (2020), who have implemented a series of post-estimation plots – including effects plots – for a wide variety of compositional dynamic models in Stata.

one another, while still allowing for other factors of interest (e.g., globalization, economic growth, and unemployment) to affect these pieces. Such an approach is very rare in both political science and budgeting studies in particular. While there are a few political science articles that use pVAR models (Tang 2008; Windett 2014; Davies 2016), the extension of pVARs proposed by Abrigo and Love (2016) that we incorporate into Chapter 5 has, to the best of our knowledge, only been used once before in political science (Kenny 2020) and, then, only for a robustness check. While we have tried to avoid burdening readers with overly complicated discussions of our research designs and particular methodological choices, interested readers will find the statistical appendices throughout this book useful for their own research.

While not a methodological contribution, we have also amassed a large budgetary dataset for future researchers. By pulling together both historical and contemporary datasets (see Section 2.5), as well as incorporating political, economic, and institutional characteristics, we envision that these data could be useful for anyone interested in budgetary research in the cross-sectional time series setting.

7.3 CHAPTER SUMMARIES AND FINDINGS

After our introductory chapter that outlined the plan of the book, we focused on presenting our theoretical argument in Chapter 2. But first, we needed to evaluate the previous research, so we asked: how has political budgeting been studied to date? We noted that politics and economics have been at the core of many of these theories and studies, a trend that we continue throughout our book. Relying on the framework of the three main approaches to budgetary research, we highlighted two shortcomings in Chapter 2. First, studies that looked at a single expenditure category, such as social spending, failed to take into account the interlinked nature of the budgetary process. Second, when examining work on broader budgetary components, such as expenditures or revenues, we saw a similar shortcoming in failing to acknowledge the dependent nature between these components. To address these concerns, we proposed a more contextual theory of budgets, in which government ideology and preferences of core supporters should translate into governments' budgetary preferences. However, at times domestic and international circumstances, as well as other budgetary components, may clash with these priorities and force governments to adopt alternative allocations.

Next, in Chapter 3, we considered how governments reallocate spending on specific policy areas and argued that left and right governments will distribute funding to different policy areas when given the opportunity. If governments did not have the power to institute their preferred budgets, then their ideological preferences would not drive relative spending allocations. Adding an institutional context to our argument, we contended that only governments with a majority of seats in the lower legislative chamber would be able to reallocate budgetary compositions to fit with their ideological visions. Our findings indicated that majority governments are better able to push through their budgetary priorities, while the conclusions for minority governments point to a mixture of both ideological and, at other times, more strategic decisions about budget allocations.

After testing our expectations about government ideology and institutional power in Chapter 3, in Chapter 4, we turned to other contexts that may affect governments' abilities to alter relative spending in their preferred policy areas. For each electoral, economic, and international circumstance, we created a theoretical "tournament" of expectations. The first expectation relied on an ideological distinction between left and right governments, while the second expectation argued that the context would overtake the ideological preferences of governments. In other words, does ideology or context prevail?

With our models in Chapter 4, we started by evaluating whether left and right governments made different budgetary allocations during elections. Given the mixed results from previous research, we were not surprised by the lack of ideological distinctions on relative spending on the various categories. In the case of domestic economic conditions, we found that governments chose to shift resources to policy areas that fit their ideological priorities during negative circumstances; however, during economic upswings, right and left governments appeared more similar in their budgetary choices. Both government types used the positive economic conditions to cut back relatively on some priorities, such as social protection and defense, while expanding secondary policy areas that at times fit their broader ideals (e.g., education, health, and housing).

When our argument turned to international contexts in Chapter 4, our conclusions pointed to circumstances that appeared to constrain governments. With the opening of borders and markets, right and left governments reallocated to shoring up the bureaucracy to oversee the expansion, while making few, rather small, ideological changes. A similar picture emerged with rising international conflict, where governments traded off

7.3 Chapter Summaries and Findings

butter for guns. Governments from both sides reallocated resources to defense, while making small relative increases to redistributive policies that fit their ideological profiles. In all of these contexts, we found that the reality of budgetary tradeoffs was more complicated than previous research had anticipated.

As we discussed in Chapter 2, researchers analyzing overall budgetary components such as deficits have typically focused on them in isolation. While we have gained an understanding of individual pieces from this work, it is far less clear how these budgetary components might be interconnected. In Chapter 5, we explored the causal relationships between the four budgetary components: expenditures, revenues, deficits, and budgetary volatility. Using a pVAR model, we discovered that some of these budgetary pieces related more to each other than to others. Although there was much discussion about expenditures and revenues driving each other, we found no direct evidence to that effect. Both total expenditures and (weakly) total revenues directly caused budget deficits, but budget deficits in turn only affected revenues, not expenditures. In fact, none of the other budgetary components influenced total expenditures or budgetary volatility. Our examination showed an interesting picture whereby expenditures led to deficits, and revenues reacted to deficits. This causal story suggested that the spending side of the budget (identified as expenditures and volatility) remained largely unaffected by the options governments had to pay for it. Another interesting finding was the lack of a relationship between budgetary volatility – in effect, movements in the very expenditure categories analyzed in Chapters 3 and 4 – and total expenditures. This implied that, as total expenditures grew or shrank, those changes did not significantly cause governments to tradeoff or shift spending at the policy area level; nor did this indicate that tradeoffs at the policy area level translated into movements in total expenditures.

Using the information from these causal relationships, we turned to testing expectations about the relationship between government ideology and institutional context in Chapter 5. Our findings suggested that right majority governments had slightly lower deficits than their left majority counterparts and that right majority governments also had slightly higher budgetary volatility than left majority governments. These effects were quite modest and appeared to occur only over the long-run. It was also interesting that minority governments of differing ideologies did not appear to behave any differently in terms of their budgetary allocations than their majority partners.

Similar to our analysis in Chapter 4 with regard to expenditure allocations, in Chapter 6, we explored how electoral, domestic, and international circumstances affected expenditures, revenues, deficits, and budgetary volatility. We developed a similar argument that, while ideological priorities may take precedent in a vacuum, in reality, context might moderate such shifts in budgetary components. Sure enough, we found very little evidence of partisan differences across elections, domestic circumstances (unemployment and economic growth), and international circumstances (economic openness and hostility). We compared right and left majority governments to a baseline expectation of how all government types behave in response to these sudden changes and found that some of these components – deficits and budgetary volatility – do shift in response to these contextual shocks, although the extent to which they do so often depends on the ideological makeup of government. Once again, these findings point to complicated relationships between governments, budgets, and their situations.

7.4 FUTURE RESEARCH QUESTIONS

While this book has taken a step forward in examining how governments make budgetary decisions when faced with domestic and international factors that can help or hinder their abilities to institute their desired preferences, there remain plenty of unanswered questions about budgets, government behavior, political economy, and methodology. Where do we, as well as other scholars, go from here? In this section, we offer several suggestions on promising areas of future research on the competitive nature of budgets and methods.

7.4.1 Further Budgetary Subcomponents

Many of our questions about budgets raise concerns about redistribution and reallocation for both spending and revenues. Issues about who receives government resources parallel concerns about who pays for them. In both of these situations, the answers lie within the larger umbrella of expenditures, revenues, and deficits. As we have seen throughout this book, many of these research questions require data and methods at a disaggregated level. Our approach for studying and evaluating the composition of expenditures begins to untangle and answer these important questions, and we believe that other scholars will see the utility of looking "under the hood" of policy budgets.

7.4 Future Research Questions

Although, in Chapter 3, we focused on the big ticket policy areas of the spending budget, depending on the research question, scholars can dissect expenditure data into subcomponents that can be further segmented into subcategories. For example, scholars talk about the differences between education levels – i.e., pre-primary, primary, secondary, and tertiary education – where this type of a compositional approach facilitates the analysis of the tradeoffs and competition for resources among the levels. While the "total pie" in our analysis was total spending, the new total would now simply be the entire subcomponent of education.[4] Many scholars have been interested in the reallocation or trading off of resources, especially in the social insurance and welfare literatures (Lynch 2006) and for those working on questions about foreign aid and military tradeoffs (Wenzelburger and Böller 2020), where theories that pit policies (or political supporters by proxy) against each other are common, but the means to rigorously test them empirically have been lacking.[5]

7.4.2 Experiments and Budgets

While our focus in this book has been on various government responses to different international and domestic factors, government spending is, at least in practice, designed for individual citizens or groups of individuals. As our theoretical diagram in Chapter 2 discussed, government preferences on certain expenditure allocations are themselves a function of what their supporters prefer. Moving forward, understanding more about how individuals view budgetary tradeoffs would offer insights into the types of feedback that governments may have from their supporters, voters, or the public at large.

A fruitful area of future research might incorporate our research design on compositions and tradeoffs into survey or experimental research on the preferences of individuals with regard to government expenditures.

---

[4] Another example would be how Busemeyer (2015) is interested in vocational and training opportunities compared with higher education.

[5] Of course, one disadvantage to further dividing budgets is data coverage. The more disaggregated categories become, the less data coverage – at least in terms of datasets such as IMF's COFOG – there tends to be. It becomes more likely that spending categories will be equal to zero. For instance, a landlocked country may not spend funds on a navy, or a resource-poor country may not devote government resources toward mining. We discussed the methodological problems behind analyzing zeros in compositions, especially if they are "essential zeros" (Martín-Fernández, Barceló-Vidal, and Pawlowsky-Glahn 2003), in Section 3.6.

There is already some work on this topic. For instance, Branham and Jessee (2017) examine a large number of policies, such as spending on student loans, arts, mass transit, or roads, to see whether respondents prefer more or less spending in a given area. However, they do not make explicit the nature of budgetary tradeoffs as we discuss throughout this book. The closest work we could find to this approach is where Bonica (2015) prompts respondents to create "a personal federal budget" (p. 1) by explicitly forcing respondents to decrease spending in one (or more) category if they desire to increase spending in another area. Hayo and Neumeier (2019) expand on this idea in the context of Germany. Respondents are asked whether they support increased expenditures for certain policy areas. If they do support an increase, then they are asked how to fund it: either through spending less in other policy areas, through increased taxes, or by increased public borrowing. Other surveys that incorporate these types of designs that make more explicit the competitive nature of budgets will likely reach different conclusions than the many studies that simply ask respondents whether they want to increase or decrease spending on a specific policy in isolation.[6]

7.4.3 Sub-national Budgeting

Another promising area for future research lies at the subnational level. At times, state, provincial, and even local governments face similar budgetary tradeoffs, while withstanding a similar or different set of constraints than national governments. With the variation in both political (e.g., federal versus unitary) and budgetary power (e.g., balanced budgets) among these entities, sub-national governments offer promising avenues to delve further into these complex budgetary relationships.

Some existing work on sub-national budgeting has already started to use the compositional approach we have outlined throughout this book. For example, Adolph, Breunig, and Koski (2020) use the case of US states to show that partisanship matters in setting budgetary allocations; governments take from the policies of their opponents. Such a finding fits with our theoretical argument that governments expand in areas designed to please their political supporters, while retrenching in areas that their

---

[6] Note that many cross-national surveys that include questions about spending on specific policy areas (e.g., education, welfare, or defense) include a caveat that a spending increase may require a tax increase (e.g., Eurobarometer or ISSP). But this type of question does not offer the ability to test a true tradeoff.

ideological rivals tend to prefer Take also the case of Lipsmeyer et al. (2019), who develop a compositional model of budgeting in the US states and create a spatial argument that considers the economic conditions in individual states, as well as "spatially proximate" states on state budgets. They contend that, in addition to geographic proximity – for example, Nevada is closer to California than Arkansas – the economic size of state economies will likely affect how much other state governments pay attention to them. Across five expenditure categories, they find that not only are there partisan differences in budgetary allocations, but also that spillover economic conditions affect states' budgetary allocations.

Sub-national budgeting also takes place at the local level, although few have studied such budgets in a compositional fashion. One exception is Funk and Philips (2019), who find that women mayors in Brazilian municipalities allocate their budgets differently than men. Women mayors spend more (as a proportion of the total budget) on "traditionally feminine" sectors of government, such as education, health, and social assistance, while their male counterparts tend to prioritize areas like transportation and urban development. At this level, we can see how approaching budgetary questions from a compositional angle offers new insights into the relationships between governments, politicians, and budgetary resources.

7.5 CONCLUSION

As the title of this book suggests, budgets are a competitive process. Much like a family fighting over who gets which size slice of pie for dessert, we have shown how governments may not succeed in getting everything they want either. Yet, thinking of policy budgets as simply a zero-sum game with winners and losers remains too simplistic. Understanding the competitive nature of budgets moves our theories and models one step closer to real-world political decision-making. At times, ideological priorities dominate the budget-setting agenda. At other times, the situation at hand – whether it is a minority government, a sagging economy, or a military conflict – may necessitate not achieving those goals in the immediate term and even going against ideological priorities. This could even mean that budgets do not change at all. By maintaining a wider view of the budgetary picture, as we have done throughout this book, we have gained a better understanding of the very real, and very difficult, nature of the budgeting process.

References

Aaskoven, Lasse. 2019. "Partisan-electoral cycles in public employment: Evidence from developed democracies." *Political Studies* 69:190–213.

Abrigo, Michael R. M. and Inessa Love. 2016. "Estimation of panel vector autoregression in Stata." *The Stata Journal* 16(3):778–804.

Adolph, Christopher, Christian Breunig and Chris Koski. 2020. "The political economy of budget trade-offs." *Journal of Public Policy* 40(1):25–50.

Aidt, Toke S. and Graham Mooney. 2014. "Voting suffrage and the political budget cycle: Evidence from the London Metropolitan Boroughs 1902–1937." *Journal of Public Economics* 112:53–71.

Aidt, Toke S., Francisco José Veiga and Linda Gonçalves Veiga. 2011. "Election results and opportunistic policies: A new test of the rational political business cycle model." *Public Choice* 148(1):21–44.

Aitchison, John. 1982. "The statistical analysis of compositional data." *Journal of the Royal Statistical Society. Series B (Methodological)* 44(2):139–177.

1983. "Principal component analysis of compositional data." *Biometrika* 70(1):57–65.

1986. *The Statistical Analysis of Compositional Data*. London: Chapman & Hall, Ltd.

Aitchison, John and Juan José Egozcue. 2005. "Compositional data analysis: Where are we and where should we be heading?" *Mathematical Geology* 37(7):829–850.

Alesina, Alberto. 1988. "Credibility and policy convergence in a two-party system with rational voters." *American Economic Review* 78:796–805.

Alesina, Alberto and Allan Drazen. 1989. Why are stabilizations delayed? Technical report, National Bureau of Economic Research.

Alesina, Alberto and Andrea Passalacqua. 2016. The political economy of government debt. In *Handbook of Macroeconomics*, Vol. 2, ed. John B. Taylor and Harald Uhlig. Oxford: Elsevier, pp. 2599–2651.

Alesina, Alberto and Enrico Spolaore. 2005. "War, peace, and the size of countries." *Journal of Public Economics* 89(7):1333–1354.

2006. "Conflict, defense spending, and the number of nations." *European Economic Review* 50(1):91–120.

Alesina, Alberto and Howard Rosenthal. 1995. *Partisan Politics: Divided Government and the Economy*. Cambridge: Cambridge University Press.

Alesina, Alberto, Gerald D. Cohen and Nouriel Roubini. 1993. "Electoral Business Cycles in Industrial Democracies." *European Journal of Political Economy* 9:1–23.

1999. *Political Cycles and the Macroeconomy*. Cambridge, MA: MIT Press.

Alesina, Alberto and Nouriel Roubini. 1992. "Political Cycles in OECD Economies." *The Review of Economic Studies* 59:663–688.

Alesina, Alberto and Roberto Perotti. 1995. "Fiscal expansions and adjustments in OECD countries." *Economic Policy* 10(21):205–248.

Allan, James P. and Lyle Scruggs. 2004. "Political partisanship and welfare state reform in advanced industrial societies." *American Journal of Political Science* 48:496–512.

Alt, James E. and David Dreyer Lassen. 2006. "Transparency, political polarization, and political budget cycles in OECD countries." *American Journal of Political Science* 50:530–550.

Alt, James E. and Robert C. Lowry. 2000. "A dynamic model of state budget outcomes under divided partisan government." *Journal of Politics* 62(4):1035–1069.

Andrews, Donald W. K. and Biao Lu. 2001. "Consistent model and moment selection procedures for GMM estimation with application to dynamic panel data models." *Journal of Econometrics* 101(1):123–164.

Angelopoulos, Konstantinos, George Economides and Pantelis Kammas. 2012. "Does cabinet ideology matter for the structure of tax policies?" *European Journal of Political Economy* 28(4):620–635.

Ansell, Ben W. 2008. "University challenges: Explaining institutional change in higher education." *World Politics* 60(02):189–230.

2010. *From the Ballot to the Blackboard: The Redistributive Political Economy of Education*. Cambridge: Cambridge University Press.

Ardanaz, Martin and Carlos Scartascini. 2013. "Inequality and personal income taxation: The origins and effects of legislative malapportionment." *Comparative Political Studies* 46(12):1636–1663.

Arellano, Manuel and Olympia Bover. 1995. "Another look at the instrumental variable estimation of error-components models." *Journal of Econometrics* 68(1):29–51.

Arellano, Manuel and Stephen Bond. 1991. "Some tests of specification for panel data: Monte Carlo evidence and an application to employment equations." *The Review of Economic Studies* 58(2):277–297.

Artés, Joaquín and Antonio Bustos. 2008. "Electoral promises and minority governments: An empirical study." *European Journal of Political Research* 47(3):307–333.

Ashworth, John and Bruno Heyndels. 2002. "Tax structure turbulence in OECD countries." *Public Choice* 111(3–4):347–376.

Avelino, George, David S. Brown and Wendy Hunter. 2005. "The effects of capital mobility, trade openness and democracy on social spending in Latin America, 1980–1999." *American Journal of Political Science* 49(3):625–641.

Ayto, John and Ian Crofton. 2011. *Brewer's Dictionary of Modern Phrase and Fable*. Oxford: Oxford University Press.

Bäck, Hanna and Johannes Lindvall. 2015. "Commitment problems in coalitions: A new look at the fiscal policies of multiparty governments." *Political Science Research and Methods* 3(1):53–72.

Bandau, Frank and Leo Ahrens. 2020. "The impact of partisanship in the era of retrenchment: Insights from quantitative welfare state research." *Journal of European Social Policy* 30(1):34–47.

Barberia, Lorena G. and George Avelino. 2011. "Do political budget cycles differ in Latin American democracies?" *Economía* 11(2):101–134.

Basinger, Scott J. and Mark Hallerberg. 2004. "Remodeling the competition for capital: How domestic politics erase the race to the bottom." *American Political Science Review* 98(2):261–276.

Baumgartner, Frank R. and Bryan D. Jones. 1991. "Agenda dynamics and policy subsystems." *The Journal of Politics* 53(4):1044–1074.

Baumgartner, Frank R., Christian Breunig, Christoffer Green-Pedersen, Bryan D. Jones, Peter B. Mortensen, Michiel Nuytemans and Stefaan Walgrave. 2009. "Punctuated equilibrium in comparative perspective." *American Journal of Political Science* 53(3):603–620.

2010. *Agendas and Instability in American Politics*. Chicago: University of Chicago Press.

Bawn, Kathleen and Frances Rosenbluth. 2006. "Short versus long coalitions: Electoral accountability and the size of the public sector." *American Journal of Political Science* 50:251–265.

Bellido, Héctor, Lorena Olmos and Juan Antonio Román-Aso. 2019. "Do political factors influence public health expenditures? Evidence pre- and post-great recession." *The European Journal of Health Economics* 20(3):455–474.

Beramendi, Pablo and David Rueda. 2007. "Social democracy constrained: Indirect taxation in industrialized democracies." *British Journal of Political Science* 37(4):619–641.

Bergh, Andreas. 2021. "The compensation hypothesis revisited and reversed." *Scandinavian Political Studies* 44(2):140–147.

Berry, William D. 1990. "The confusing case of budgetary incrementalism: Too many meanings for a single concept." *The Journal of Politics* 52(1):167–196.

Blais, André, Donald Blake and Stephané Dion. 1993. "Do parties make a difference?" *American Journal of Political Science* 37:40–62.

Blundell, Richard and Stephen Bond. 1998. "Initial conditions and moment restrictions in dynamic panel data models." *Journal of Econometrics* 87(1):115–143.

Blyth, Mark and Richard Katz. 2005. "From catch-all politics to cartelisation: The political economy of the cartel party." *West European Politics* 28(1):33–60.

Boix, Carles. 1998. *Political Parties, Growth and Equality: Conservative and Social Democratic Economic Strategies in the World Economy*. New York: Cambridge University Press.

Boix, Carles. 2000. "Partisan governments, the international economy, and macroeconomic policies in advanced nations, 1960–93." *World Politics* 53(1):38–73.

Bonica, Adam. 2015. "Measuring public spending preferences using an interactive budgeting questionnaire." *Research & Politics* 2(2):2053168015586471.

van den Boogaard, Vanessa, Wilson Prichard, Matthew S. Benson and Nikola Milicic. 2018. "Tax revenue mobilization in conflict-affected developing countries." *Journal of International Development* 30(2):345–364.

Born, Benjamin and Jörg Breitung. 2016. "Testing for serial correlation in fixed-effects panel data models." *Econometric Reviews* 35(7):1290–1316.

Bove, Vincenzo, Georgios Efthyvoulou and Antonio Navas. 2017. "Political cycles in public expenditure: Butter vs guns." *Journal of Comparative Economics* 45(3):582–604.

Branham, J. Alexander and Stephen A. Jessee. 2017. "Modeling spending preferences & public policy." *Electoral Studies* 49:155–172.

Bräuninger, Thomas. 2005. "A partisan model of government expenditure." *Public Choice* 125(3–4):409–429.

Brender, Adi and Allan Drazen. 2005. "Political budget cycles in new versus established democracies." *Journal of Monetary Economics* 52(7):1271–1295.

2008. "How do budget deficits and economic growth affect reelection prospects? Evidence from a large panel of countries." *American Economic Review* 98(5):2203–2220.

2013. "Elections, leaders, and the composition of government spending." *Journal of Public Economics* 97:18–31.

Bretschger, Lucas and Frank Hettich. 2002. "Globalisation, capital mobility and tax competition: Theory and evidence for OECD countries." *European Journal of Political Economy* 18(4):695–716.

Breunig, Christian and Marius R. Busemeyer. 2012. "Fiscal austerity and the trade-off between public investment and social spending." *Journal of European Public Policy* 19(6):921–938.

Breusch, Trevor S. and Adrian R. Pagan. 1980. "The Lagrange multiplier test and its applications to model specification in econometrics." *The Review of Economic Studies* 47(1):239–253.

Brooks, Arthur C. 2001. "Who opposes government arts funding?" *Public Choice* 108(3–4):355–367.

Brown, David S. and Wendy Hunter. 2004. "Democracy and human capital formation: Education spending in Latin America, 1980–1997." *Comparative Political Studies* 37:842–864.

Bunce, Valerie and John M. Echols III. 1978. "Power and policy in communist systems: The problem of 'incrementalism'." *The Journal of Politics* 40(4):911–932.

Burger, Philippe and Ian Hawkesworth. 2013. "Capital budgeting and procurement practices." *OECD Journal on Budgeting* 13(1):57–104.

Burgoon, Brian. 2001. "Globalization and welfare compensation: Distangling the ties and binds." *International Organization* 55(3):509–551.

Busemeyer, Marius R. 2007. "Determinants of public education spending in 21 OECD democracies, 1980-2001." *Journal of European Public Policy* 14(4):582–610.

2015. *Skills and Inequality: Partisan Politics and the Political Economy of Education Reforms in Western Welfare States.* Cambridge: Cambridge University Press.

Busemeyer, Marius R. and Christine Trampusch. 2011. "Review article: Comparative political science and the study of education." *British Journal of Political Science* 41(2):413–443.

Calvo, Ernesto and Maria Victoria Murillo. 2004. "Who delivers? Partisan clients in the Argentine electoral market." *American Journal of Political Science* 48(4):742–757.

Cameron, David R. 1978. "The expansion of the public economy: A comparative analysis." *American Political Science Review* 72(4):1243–1261.

1985. "Does government cause inflation? Taxes, spending and deficits." In *The Politics of Inflation and Economic Stagnation*, ed. Leon N. Lindberg and Charles S. Maier. Washington, DC: Brookings Institution, pp. 224–279.

2012. "European fiscal responses to the great recession." In *Coping with Crisis: Government Reactions to the Great Recession*, ed. Nancy Bermeo and Jonas Pontusson. New York: Russell Sage Foundation, pp. 91–129.

Campbell, James E. 2008. *The American Campaign: US Presidential Campaigns and the National Vote.* College Station: Texas A&M University Press.

Carlsen, Fredrik. 1997. "Counterfiscal policies and partisan politics: Evidence from industrialized countries." *Applied Economics* 29(2):145–151.

Castles, Francis Geoffrey. 1982. *The Impact of Parties: Politics and Policies in Democratic Capitalist States.* Beverly Hills, CA: Sage Publications.

Castro, Vítor and Rodrigo Martins. 2018. "Politically driven cycles in fiscal policy: In depth analysis of the functional components of government expenditures." *European Journal of Political Economy* 55:44–64.

Chang, Eric C. C. 2008. "Electoral incentives and budgetary spending: Rethinking the role of political institutions." *The Journal of Politics* 70(4):1086–1097.

Cheibub, José Antonio. 2006. "Presidentialism, electoral identifiability, and budget balances in democratic systems." *American Political Science Review* 100(3):353–368.

Choi, In. 2001. "Unit root tests for panel data." *Journal of International Money and Finance* 20(2):249–272.

Clark, Tom S. and Drew A. Linzer. 2015. "Should I use fixed or random effects?" *Political Science Research and Methods* 3(2):399–408.

Clarke, Harold, William Mishler and Paul Whiteley. 1990. "Recapturing the Falklands: Models of Conservative popularity, 1979–83." *British Journal of Political Science* 20(1):63–81.

Clayton, Amanda and Pär Zetterberg. 2018. "Quota shocks: Electoral gender quotas and government spending priorities worldwide." *The Journal of Politics* 80(3):916–932.

Compton, Mallory E. and Christine S. Lipsmeyer. 2019. "Everybody hurts sometimes: How personal and collective insecurities shape policy preferences." *The Journal of Politics* 81(2):539–551.

Coutts, Adam, Adel Daoud, Ali Fakih, Walid Marrouch and Bernhard Reinsberg. 2019. "Guns and butter? Military expenditure and health spending on the eve of the Arab Spring." *Defence and Peace Economics* 30(2):227–237.

Cox, Gary W. and Mathew D. McCubbins. 1986. "Electoral politics as a redistributive game." *The Journal of Politics* 48(2):370–389.

Crepaz, Markus M. L. and Ann W. Moser. 2004. "The impact of collective and competitive veto points on public expenditures in the global age." *Comparative Political Studies* 37(3):259–285.

Cruz, Cesi, Philip Keefer and Carlos Scartascini. 2016. *Database of Political Institutions Codebook, 2015 Update (DPI2015)*. Inter-American Development Bank. Updated version of Thorsten Beck, George Clarke, Alberto Groff, Philip Keefer, and Patrick Walsh, 2001. "New tools in comparative political economy: The Database of Political Institutions." *World Bank Economic Review* 15(1):165–176.

Cusack, Thomas R. 1999. "Partisan politics and fiscal policy." *Comparative Political Studies* 32(4):464–486.

Cusack, Thomas R. and Pablo Beramendi. 2006. "Taxing work." *European Journal of Political Research* 45(1):43–73.

Dahl, Robert A. and Charles Lindblom. 1953. *Politics, Economics and Welfare*. New York: Harper and Row.

Dalle Nogare, Chiara and Matteo Maria Galizzi. 2011. "The political economy of cultural spending: Evidence from Italian cities." *Journal of Cultural Economics* 35(3):203.

Danziger, James N. 1976. "Assessing incrementalism in British municipal budgeting." *British Journal of Political Science* 6(3):335–350.

Darby, Julia and Jacques Melitz. 2008. "Social spending and automatic stabilizers in the OECD." *Economic Policy* 23(56):716–756.

Dash, Bharatee Bhusana and Angara V. Raja. 2014. "Do political determinants affect revenue collection? Evidence from the Indian states." *International Review of Economics* 61(3):253–278.

Davies, Graeme A. M. 2016. "Policy selection in the face of political instability: Do states divert, repress, or make concessions?" *Journal of Conflict Resolution* 60(1):118–142.

De Boef, Suzanna and Luke Keele. 2008. "Taking time seriously." *American Journal of Political Science* 52(1):184–200.

De Haan, Jakob and Jeroen Klomp. 2013. "Conditional political budget cycles: A review of recent evidence." *Public Choice* 157(3–4):387–410.

De Haan, Jakob and Jan-Egbert Sturm. 1997. "Political and economic determinants of OECD budget deficits and government expenditures: A reinvestigation." *European Journal of Political Economy* 13(4):739–750.

De Haan, Jakob, Jan-Egbert Sturm and Geert Beekhuis. 1999. "The weak government thesis: Some new evidence." *Public Choice* 101(3–4):163–176.

De Renzio, Paolo and Harika Masud. 2011. "Measuring and promoting budget transparency: The open budget index as a research and advocacy tool." *Governance* 24(3):607–616.

Dellepiane-Avellaneda, Sebastian. 2015. "The political power of economic ideas: The case of 'expansionary fiscal contractions'." *The British Journal of Politics and International Relations* 17(3):391–418.

Devereux, Michael P., Ben Lockwood and Michela Redoano. 2008. "Do countries compete over corporate tax rates?" *Journal of Public Economics* 92(5–6):1210–1235.

Dixit, Avinash and John Londregan. 1996. "The determinants of success of special interests in redistributive politics." *The Journal of Politics* 58(4):1132–1155.

Dolls, Mathias, Clemens Fuest and Andreas Peichl. 2012. "Automatic stabilizers and economic crisis: US vs. Europe." *Journal of Public Economics* 96(3–4):279–294.

Domke, William K., Richard C. Eichenberg and Catherine M. Kelleher. 1983. "The illusion of choice: Defense and welfare in advanced industrial democracies, 1948–1978." *American Political Science Review* 77(1):19–35.

Drazen, Allan and Marcela Eslava. 2010. "Electoral manipulation via voter-friendly spending: Theory and evidence." *Journal of Development Economics* 92(1):39–52.

Dreher, Axel. 2006. "The influence of globalization on taxes and social policy: An empirical analysis for OECD countries." *European Journal of Political Economy* 22(1):179–201.

Dreher, Axel, Jan-Egbert Sturm and Heinrich W. Ursprung. 2008. "The impact of globalization on the composition of government expenditures: Evidence from panel data." *Public Choice* 134(3–4):263–292.

Drukker, David M. 2003. "Testing for serial correlation in linear panel-data models." *The Stata Journal* 3(2):168–177.

Dubois, Eric. 2016. "Political business cycles 40 years after Nordhaus." *Public Choice* 166(1–2):235–259.

Dunne, John Paul. 2012. "Military spending, growth, development and conflict." *Defence and Peace Economics* 23(6):549–557.

Edin, Per-Anders and Henry Ohlsson. 1991. "Political determinants of budget deficits: Coalition effects versus minority effects." *European Economic Review* 35(8):1597–1603.

Enkelmann, Sören and Markus Leibrecht. 2013. "Political expenditure cycles and election outcomes: Evidence from disaggregation of public expenditures by economic functions." *Economics Letters* 121(1):128–132.

Epp, Derek A., John Lovett and Frank R. Baumgartner. 2014. "Partisan priorities and public budgeting." *Political Research Quarterly* 67(4):864–878.

Esping-Anderson, Gosta. 1990. *The Three Worlds of Welfare Capitalsim*. Princeton, NJ: Princeton University Press.

Fagan, Edward J., Bryan D. Jones and Christopher Wlezien. 2017. "Representative systems and policy punctuations." *Journal of European Public Policy* 24(6):809–831.

Falcó-Gimeno, Albert and Ignacio Jurado. 2011. "Minority governments and budget deficits: The role of the opposition." *European Journal of Political Economy* 27(3):554–565.

Franzese, Robert J. 1999. "Partially independent central banks, politically responsive governments and inflation." *American Political Science Review* 43:681–706.
  2002a. "Electoral and partisan cycles in economic policies and outcomes." *Annual Review of Political Science* 5:369–421.
  2002b. *Macroeconomic Policies of Developed Democracies.* Cambridge: Cambridge University Press.
Franzese, Robert J. and Karen Long Jusko. 2005. Political-economic cycles. In *Oxford Handbook of Political Economy,* ed. Donald Wittman and Barry Weingast. Oxford: Oxford University Press, pp. 545–564.
Funk, Kendall D. and Andrew Q. Philips. 2019. "Representative budgeting: Women mayors and the composition of spending in local governments." *Political Research Quarterly* 72(1):19–33.
Galli, Emma and Stefania P. S. Rossi. 2002. "Political budget cycles: The case of the Western German Länder." *Public Choice* 110(3–4):283–303.
Ganghof, Steffen. 2006. "Tax mixes and the size of the welfare state: Causal mechanisms and policy implications." *Journal of European Social Policy* 16(4):360–373.
Garrett, Geoffrey. 1995. "Capital mobility, trade, and the domestic politics of economic policy." *International Organization* 49(4):657–687.
  1998. *Partisan Politics in the Global Economy.* Cambridge: Cambridge University Press.
  2001. "Globalization and government spending around the world." *Studies in Comparative International Development* 35(4):3–29.
Garrett, Geoffrey and Deborah Mitchell. 2001. "Globalization, government spending and taxation in the OECD." *European Journal of Political Research* 39(2):145–177.
Garrett, Geoffrey and Peter Lange. 1991. "Political responses to interdependence: What's 'left' for the left?" *International Organization* 45:539–564.
Garritzmann, Julian L. and Kilian Seng. 2016. "Party politics and education spending: Challenging some common wisdom." *Journal of European Public Policy* 23(4):510–530.
Gemmell, Norman, Richard Kneller and Ismael Sanz. 2008. "Foreign investment, international trade and the size and structure of public expenditures." *European Journal of Political Economy* 24(1):151–171.
Gerber, Elisabeth R. and Daniel J. Hopkins. 2011. "When mayors matter: Estimating the impact of mayoral partisanship on city policy." *American Journal of Political Science* 55(2):326–339.
Getzner, Michael. 2002. "Determinants of public cultural expenditures: An exploratory time series analysis for Austria." *Journal of Cultural Economics* 26(4):287–306.
Giavazzi, Francesco and Marco Pagano. 1990. "Can severe fiscal contractions be expansionary? Tales of two small European countries." *NBER Macroeconomics Annual* 5:75–111.
Gift, Thomas and Erik Wibbels. 2014. "Reading, writing, and the regrettable status of education research in comparative politics." *Annual Review of Political Science* 17:291–312.

Gingrich, Jane R. and Ben W. Ansell. 2012. "Preferences in context: Micro preferences, macro-contexts and the demand for social policy." *Comparative Political Studies* 45(12):1624–1654.

Gist, John R. 1982. "'Stability' and 'competition' in budgetary theory." *American Political Science Review* 76(4):859–872.

Gould, Andrew C. and Peter J. Baker. 2002. "Democracy and taxation." *Annual Review of Political Science* 5(1):87–110.

Granger, Clive W. J. 1969. "Investigating causal relations by econometric models and cross-spectral models." *Econometrica* 37:424–438.

Greene, William H. 2012. *Econometric Analysis*, 7th ed. Old Tappan, NJ: Prentice Hall.

Grilli, Vittorio, Donato Masciandaro and Guido Tabellini. 1991. "Political and monetary institutions and public financial policies in the industrial countries." *Economic Policy* 6(13):341–392.

Gupta, Sanjeev, Benedict Clements, Rina Bhattacharya and Shamit Chakravarti. 2004. "Fiscal consequences of armed conflict and terrorism in low- and middle-income countries." *European Journal of Political Economy* 20(2):403–421.

Ha, Eunyoung. 2008. "Globalization, veto players, and welfare spending." *Comparative Political Studies* 41(6):783–813.

Hahm, Sung Deuk, Mark S. Kamlet and David C. Mowery. 1995. "Influences on deficit spending in industrialized democracies." *Journal of Public Policy* 15:183–197.

Hainmueller, Jens, Jonathan Mummolo and Yiqing Xu. 2019. "How much should we trust estimates from multiplicative interaction models? Simple tools to improve empirical practice." *Political Analysis* 27(2):163–192.

Hall, Peter A. and David Soskice. 2004. *Varieties of Capitalism: The Institutional Foundations of Comparative Advantage*. New York: Oxford University Press.

Hallerberg, Mark and Patrik Marier. 2004. "Executive authority, the personal vote, and budget discipline in Latin America and Caribbean countries." *American Journal of Political Science* 48:571–587.

Hallerberg, Mark, Rolf Strauch and Jürgen Von Hagen. 2007. "The design of fiscal rules and forms of governance in European Union countries." *European Journal of Political Economy* 23(2):338–359.

Hansen, Lars Peter. 1982. "Large sample properties of generalized method of moments estimators." *Econometrica: Journal of the Econometric Society* 50(4):1029–1054.

Harrinvirta, Markku and Mikko Mattila. 2001. "The hard business of balancing budgets: A study of public finances in seventeen OECD countries." *British Journal of Political Science* 31(3):497–521.

Hayakawa, Kazuhiko. 2009. "First difference or forward orthogonal deviation: Which transformation should be used in dynamic panel data models?: A simulation study." *Economics Bulletin* 29(3):2008–2017.

Hayo, Bernd and Florian Neumeier. 2019. "Public preferences for government spending priorities: Survey evidence from Germany." *German Economic Review* 20(4):e1–e37.

Hays, Jude C. 2009. *Globalization and the New Politics of Embedded Liberalism.* New York: Oxford University Press.

Heimberger, Philipp. 2020. "Does economic globalization affect government spending? A meta-analysis." *Public Choice* 187:349–374.

Herwartz, Helmut and Bernd Theilen. 2014. "Health care and ideology: A reconsideration of political determinants of public healthcare funding in the OECD." *Health Economics* 23(2):225–240.

2017. "Ideology and redistribution through public spending." *European Journal of Political Economy* 46:74–90.

2020. "Government ideology and fiscal consolidation: Where and when do government parties adjust public spending?" *Public Choice* 187:375–401.

Hibbs, Douglas A. 1977. "Political parties and macroeconomic policy." *American Political Science Review* 71(4):1467–1487.

Hicks, Alexander and Duane Swank. 1992. "Politics, institutions, and welfare spending in industrialized democracies, 1960–1982." *The American Political Science Review* 86(3):658–674.

Hicks, Alexander, Duane H. Swank and Martin Ambuhl. 1989. "Welfare expansion revisited: Policy routines and their mediation by party, class and crisis, 1957–1982." *European Journal of Political Research* 17(4):401–430.

Hollenbach, Florian M., Christine S. Lipsmeyer and Guy D. Whitten. 2021. "Introduction." *Review of International Organizations* 16(1):183.

Holtz-Eakin, Douglas, Whitney Newey and Harvey S. Rosen. 1988. "Estimating vector autoregressions with panel data." *Econometrica: Journal of the Econometric Society* 56(6):1371–1395.

Honkapohja, Seppo, Erkki Koskela, Stefan Gerlach and Lucrezia Reichlin. 1999. "The economic crisis of the 1990s in Finland." *Economic Policy* 14(29):399–436.

How Government Shutdowns Work. September 10, 2019. Stuff Media LLC. Available at: www.stuffyoushouldknow.com/podcasts/how-government-shutdowns-work.htm5. Last accessed October 12, 2019.

Huber, Evelyne, Charles Ragin and John D. Stephens. 1993. "Social democracy, Christian democracy, constitutional structure, and the welfare state." *The American Journal of Sociology* 99(3):711–749.

Huber, Evelyne and John D. Stephens. 2001. *Development and Crisis of the Welfare State Development and Crisis of the Welfare State: Parties and Policies in Global Markets.* Chicago, IL: University of Chicago Press.

Hwang, Sung-Ha. 2012. "Technology of military conflict, military spending, and war." *Journal of Public Economics* 96(1–2):226–236.

Im, Kyung So, M. Hashem Pesaran and Yongcheol Shin. 2003. "Testing for unit roots in heterogeneous panels." *Journal of Econometrics* 115(1):53–74.

Imbeau, Louis M., François Pétry and Moktar Lamari. 2001. "Left–right party ideology and government policies: A meta-analysis." *European Journal of Political Research* 40(1):1–29.

Iversen, Torben and Thomas R. Cusack. 2000. "The causes of welfare state expansion: Deindustrialization or globalization?" *World Politics* 52(3):313–349.

Iversen, Torben and John D. Stephens. 2008. "Partisan politics, the welfare state, and three worlds of human capital formation." *Comparative Political Studies* 41(4–5):600–637.

Jackson, John E. 2002. "A seemingly unrelated regression model for analyzing multiparty elections." *Political Analysis* 10(1):49–65.

Jacobs, Davina. 2008. "A review of capital budgeting practices." (EPub) *IMF Working Paper No. 08-160*, pp. 1–24.

Jacques, Olivier. 2021. "Austerity and the path of least resistance: How fiscal consolidations crowd out long-term investments." *Journal of European Public Policy* 28(4):551–570.

Jensen, Carsten. 2011a. "Capitalist systems, deindustrialization, and the politics of public education." *Comparative Political Studies* 44(4):412–435.

2011b. "Determinants of welfare service provision after the golden age." *International Journal of Social Welfare* 20(2):125–134.

2011c. "Marketization via compensation: Health care and the politics of the right in advanced industrialized nations." *British Journal of Political Science* 41(4):907–926.

Jochimsen, Beate and Robert Lehmann. 2017. "On the political economy of national tax revenue forecasts: Evidence from OECD countries." *Public Choice* 170(3–4):211–230.

John, Peter and Hugh Ward. 2001. "Political manipulation in a majoritarian democracy: Central government targeting of public funds to English subnational government, in space and across time." *The British Journal of Politics & International Relations* 3(3):308–339.

Jordan, Jason. 2011. "Health care politics in the age of retrenchment." *Journal of Social Policy* 40:113.

Jordan, Soren and Andrew Q. Philips. 2018a. "Cointegration testing and dynamic simulations of autoregressive distributed lag models." *The Stata Journal* 18(4):902–923.

2018b. "Dynamic simulation and testing for single-equation cointegrating and stationary autoregressive distributed lag models." *The R Journal* 10(2):469–488.

2022. "Improving the interpretation of random effects regression results." *Political Studies Review* 1–11.

Jung, Yoo Sun, Flávio D. S. Souza, Andrew Q. Philips, Amanda Rutherford and Guy D. Whitten. 2020. "A command to estimate and interpret models of dynamic compositional dependent variables: New features for dynsimpie." *The Stata Journal* 20(3):584–603.

Kagalwala, Ali, Andrew Q. Philips and Guy D. Whitten. 2021. "What about the rest of the pie? A dynamic compositional approach to modeling inequality." *Social Science Quarterly* 102(4):1534–1552.

Kang, Shin-Goo and G. Bingham Powell. 2010. "Representation and policy responsiveness: The median voter, election rules, and redistributive welfare spending." *The Journal of Politics* 72:1014–1028.

Kanter, Arnold. 1972. "Congress and the defense budget: 1960–1970." *American Political Science Review* 66(1):129–143.

Kato, Junko. 2003. *Regressive Taxation and the Welfare State: Path Dependence and Policy Diffusion.* Cambridge: Cambridge University Press.

Katsimi, Margarita and Vassilis Sarantides. 2012. "Do elections affect the composition of fiscal policy in developed, established democracies?" *Public Choice* 151(1–2):325–362.

Katz, Jonathan N. and Gary King. 1999. "A statistical model for multiparty electoral data." *American Political Science Review* 93(1):15–32.

Kayser, Mark Andreas and Christopher Wlezien. 2011. "Performance pressure: Patterns of partisanship and the economic vote." *European Journal of Political Research* 50(3):365–394.

Kenny, Paul D. 2020. "'The enemy of the people': Populists and press freedom." *Political Research Quarterly* 73(2):261–275.

Kim, So Young. 2007. "Openness, external risk, and volatility: Implications for the compensation hypothesis." *International Organization* 61(1):181–216.

King, Gary, Michael Tomz and Jason Wittenberg. 2000. "Making the most of statistical analyses: Improving interpretation and presentation." *American Journal of Political Science* 44(2):341–355.

Kiser, Edgar and Steven M. Karceski. 2017. "Political economy of taxation." *Annual Review of Political Science* 20:75–92.

Kitschelt, Herbert and Steven I. Wilkinson. 2007. Citizen–politician linkages: An introduction. In *Patrons, Clients and Policies*, ed. Herbert Kitschelt and Steven I. Wilkinson. Cambridge: Cambridge University Press, ch. 1, pp. 1–49.

Kramon, Eric and Daniel N. Posner. 2013. "Who benefits from distributive politics? How the outcome one studies affects the answer one gets." *Perspectives on Politics* 11(2):461–474.

Kwon, Hyeok Yong. 2005. "Targeting public spending in a new democracy: Evidence from South Korea." *British Journal of Political Science* 35(2):321–341.

Laver, Michael and Kenneth A. Shepsle. 1996. *Making and Breaking Governments: Cabinets and Legislatures in Parliamentary Democracy.* New York: Cambridge University Press.

Leibrecht, Markus, Michael Klien and Özlem Onaran. 2011. "Globalization, welfare regimes and social protection expenditures in Western and Eastern European countries." *Public Choice* 148(3–4):569–594.

LeLoup, Lance T. and William B. Moreland. 1978. "Agency strategies and executive review: The hidden politics of budgeting." *Public Administration Review* 38(3):232–239.

Lewis, Gregory B. and Michael Rushton. 2007. "Understanding state spending on the arts, 1976–99." *State and Local Government Review* 39(2):107–114.

Lierse, Hanna and Laura Seelkopf. 2016. "Capital markets and tax policy making: A comparative analysis of European tax reforms since the crisis." *Comparative European Politics* 14(5):686–716.

Lijphart, Arend. 1984. "A note on the meaning of cabinet durability." *Comparative Political Studies* 17:163–166.

1999. *Patterns of Democracy: Government Forms and Performance in 36 Countries.* New Haven, CT: Yale University Press.

Lindbeck, Assar and Jörgen W. Weibull. 1987. "Balanced-budget redistribution as the outcome of political competition." *Public Choice* 52(3):273–297.

Lindblom, Charles E. 1959. "The science of muddling through." *Public Administration Review* 19(2):79–88.

Lipsmeyer, Christine S. 2002. "Parties and policy: Evaluating political party influence on welfare policy spending during the European post-communist transition." *British Journal of Political Science* 32:641–661.

2009. "Post-communist mandates." *Politics & Policy* 37(4):715–734.

2011. "Booms and busts: How parliamentary governments and economic context influence welfare policy." *International Studies Quarterly* 55(4):959–980.

Lipsmeyer, Christine S., Andrew Q. Philips, Amanda Rutherford and Guy D. Whitten. 2019. "Comparing dynamic pies: A strategy for modeling compositional variables in time and space." *Political Science Research and Methods* 7(3):523–540.

Lipsmeyer, Christine S., Andrew Q. Philips and Guy D. Whitten. 2017. "The effects of immigration and integration on European budgetary trade-offs." *Journal of European Public Policy* 24(6):912–930.

Lipsmeyer, Christine S. and Heather Nicole Pierce. 2011. "The eyes that bind: Junior ministers as oversight mechanisms in coalition governments." *The Journal of Politics* 73(4):1152–1164.

Lipsmeyer, Christine S. and Ling Zhu. 2011. "Immigration, globalization, and unemployment benefits in developed EU states." *American Journal of Political Science* 55(3):647–664.

Lütkepohl, Helmut. 2005. *New Introduction to Multiple Time Series Analysis*. Berlin: Springer Science & Business Media.

Lynch, Julia. 2006. *Age in the Welfare State: The Origins of Social Spending on Pensioners, Workers, and Children*. New York: Cambridge University Press.

Martin, Lanny W. and Georg Vanberg. 2004. "Policing the bargain: Coalition government and parliamentary scrutiny." *American Journal of Political Science* 48:13–27.

2011. *Parliaments and Coalitions: The Role of Legislative Institutions in Multiparty Governance*. Oxford: Oxford University Press.

2013. "Multiparty government, fiscal institutions, and public spending." *The Journal of Politics* 75(4):953–967.

2020. "Coalition government, legislative institutions, and public policy in parliamentary democracies." *American Journal of Political Science* 64(2):325–340.

Martin, Lanny W. and Randolph T. Stevenson. 2010. "The conditional impact of incumbency on government formation." *American Political Science Review* 104(3):503–518.

Martín-Fernández, Josep A., Carles Barceló-Vidal and Vera Pawlowsky-Glahn. 2003. "Dealing with zeros and missing values in compositional data sets using nonparametric imputation." *Mathematical Geology* 35(3):253–278.

McGann, Anthony J., Sebastian Dellepiane-Avellaneda and John Bartle. 2022. "Dynamics of public opinion and policy response under proportional and plurality elections." *Economics & Politics* 1–23.

Meinhard, Stephanie and Niklas Potrafke. 2012. "The globalization–welfare state nexus reconsidered." *Review of International Economics* 20(2):271–287.

Mikhailov, Nikolai, Richard G. Niemi and David L. Weimer. 2002. "Application of Theil group logit methods to district-level vote shares: Tests of prospective and retrospective voting in the 1991, 1993, and 1997 Polish elections." *Electoral Studies* 21(4):631–648.

Milesi-Ferretti, Gian Maria, Roberto Perotti and Massimo Rostagno. 2002. "Electoral systems and public spending." *The Quarterly Journal of Economics* 117(2):609–657.

Mintz, Alex. 1989. "Guns versus butter: A disaggregated analysis." *American Political Science Review* 83(4):1285–1293.

Mintz, Alex and Chi Huang. 1991. "Guns versus butter: The indirect link." *American Journal of Political Science* 35(3):738–757.

Müller, Andreas, Kjetil Storesletten and Fabrizio Zilibotti. 2016. "The political color of fiscal responsibility." *Journal of the European Economic Association* 14(1):252–302.

Mummolo, Jonathan and Erik Peterson. 2018. "Improving the interpretation of fixed effects regression results." *Political Science Research and Methods* 6(4):829–835.

Narizny, Kevin. 2003. "Both guns and butter, or neither: Class interests in the political economy of rearmament." *American Political Science Review* 97(2):203–220.

Natchez, Peter B. and Irvin C. Bupp. 1973. "Policy and priority in the budgetary process." *American Political Science Review* 67(3):951–963.

Nerlove, Marc. 1967. *Distributed Lags and Unobserved Components in Economic Time Series*. New Haven, CT: Cowles Foundation for Research in Economics at Yale University.

Newbold, Paul and C. W. J. Granger. 1974. "Spurious regressions in econometrics." *Journal of Econometrics* 2(2):111–120.

Nichter, Simeon. 2008. "Vote buying or turnout buying? Machine politics and the secret ballot." *American Political Science Review* 102(1):19–31.

Nickell, Stephen. 1981. "Biases in dynamic models with fixed effects." *Econometrica: Journal of the Econometric Society* 49(6):1417–1426.

Nordhaus, William D. 1975. "The political business cycle." *The Review of Economic Studies* 42:169–190.

Norpoth, Helmut. 1987. "Guns and butter and government popularity in Britain." *American Political Science Review* 81:949–959.

Oatley, Thomas. 1999. "How constraining is capital mobility? The partisan hypothesis in an open economy." *American Journal of Political Science* 43(4):1003–1027.

O'Mahony, Angela. 2011. "Engineering good times: Fiscal manipulation in a global economy." *British Journal of Political Science* 41(2):315–340.

Ostrom, Charles W. 1978. "A reactive linkage model of the US defense expenditure policymaking process." *American Political Science Review* 72(3):941–957.

Padovano, Fabio. 2012. "The drivers of interregional policy choices: Evidence from Italy." *European Journal of Political Economy* 28(3):324–340.

Palmer, Glenn. 1990. "Alliance politics and issue areas: Determinants of defense spending." *American Journal of Political Science* 34(1):190–211.

References

Perotti, Roberto and Yianos Kontopoulos. 2002. "Fragmented fiscal policy." *Journal of Public Economics* 86(2):191–222.

Persson, Torsten, Gerard Roland and Guido Tabellini. 2007. "Electoral rules and government spending in parliamentary democracies." *Quarterly Journal of Political Science* 2(2):155–188.

Persson, Torsten and Guido Tabellini. 1999. "The size and scope of government: Comparative politics with rational politicians." *European Economic Review* 43(4):699–735.

2000. *Political Economics: Explaining Economic Policy*. Cambridge, MA: MIT Press.

2004. "Constitutional rules and fiscal policy outcomes." *The American Economic Review* 94(1):25–45.

Persson, Torsten and Lars E. O. Svensson. 1989. "Why a stubborn conservative would run a deficit: Policy with time-inconsistent preferences." *The Quarterly Journal of Economics* 104:325–345.

Pesaran, M. Hashem. 2015. *Time Series and Panel Data Econometrics*. Oxford: Oxford University Press.

Philips, Andrew Q. 2016. "Seeing the forest through the trees: A meta-analysis of political budget cycles." *Public Choice* 168(3–4):313–341.

2017. *Manipulating the Masses: New Theories of Political Cycles*. PhD thesis, Texas A&M University.

2021. "How to avoid incorrect inferences (while gaining correct ones) in dynamic models." *Political Science Research and Methods* 1–11.

Philips, Andrew Q., Amanda Rutherford and Guy D. Whitten. 2015. "The dynamic battle for pieces of pie: Modeling party support in multi-party nations." *Electoral Studies* 39:264–274.

2016a. "Dynamic pie: A strategy for modeling trade-offs in compositional variables over time." *American Journal of Political Science* 60(1):268–283.

2016b. "dynsimpie: A command to examine dynamic compositional dependent variables." *Stata Journal* 16(3):662–677.

2020. "Globalization and comparative compositional inequality." *Political Science Research and Methods* 8(3):509–525.

Phillips, Peter C. B. and Hyungsik R. Moon. 1999. "Linear regression limit theory for nonstationary panel data." *Econometrica* 67(5):1057–1111.

Pickup, Mark. 2014. *Introduction to Time Series Analysis*, Vol. 174. Thousand Oaks, CA: Sage Publications.

Pickup, Mark, Paul Gustafson, Davor Cubranic and Geoffrey Evans. 2017. "OrthoPanels: An R package for estimating a dynamic panel model with fixed effects using the orthogonal reparameterization approach." *R Journal* 9(1):60–76.

Pierson, Paul. 2001. *The New Politics of the Welfare State*. New York: Oxford University Press on Demand.

Pitzer, John. 2001. Government Finance Statistics Manual. Technical report. International Monetary Fund.

Plümper, Thomas, Vera E. Troeger and Hannes Winner. 2009. "Why is there no race to the bottom in capital taxation?" *International Studies Quarterly* 53(3):761–786.

Potrafke, Niklas. 2009. "Did globalization restrict partisan politics? An empirical evaluation of social expenditures in a panel of OECD countries." *Public Choice* 140(1–2):105.

2010. "The growth of public health expenditures in OECD countries: Do government ideology and electoral motives matter?" *Journal of Health Economics* 29(6):797–810.

2012. "Political cycles and economic performance in OECD countries: Empirical evidence from 1951–2006." *Public Choice* 150(1–2):155–179.

2017. "Partisan politics: The empirical evidence from OECD panel studies." *Journal of Comparative Economics* 45(4):712–750.

2019. "Fiscal performance of minority governments: New empirical evidence for OECD countries." *Party Politics* 27(3):501–514.

2020. "General or central government? Empirical evidence on political cycles in budget composition using new data for OECD countries." *European Journal of Political Economy* 63:101860.

Quinn, Dennis. 1997. "The correlates of change in international financial regulation." *American Political Science Review* 91(3):531–551.

Raess, Damian and Jonas Pontusson. 2015. "The politics of fiscal policy during economic downturns, 1981–2010." *European Journal of Political Research* 54(1):1–22.

Rauh, Christian, Antje Kirchner and Roland Kappe. 2011. "Political parties and higher education spending: who favours redistribution?" *West European Politics* 34(6):1185–1206.

Remmer, Karen L. 2007. "The political economy of patronage: Expenditure patterns in the Argentine provinces, 1983–2003." *The Journal of Politics* 69(2):363–377.

Rickard, Stephanie J. 2012. "Welfare versus subsidies: Governmental spending decisions in an era of globalization." *The Journal of Politics* 74(4):1171–1183.

Rodrik, Dani. 1998. "Why do more open economies have bigger governments?" *Journal of Political Economy* 106(5):997.

Rogoff, Kenneth. 1990. "Equilibrium political budget cycles." *The American Economic Review* 80(1):21–36.

Rogoff, Kenneth and Anne Sibert. 1988. "Elections and macroeconomic policy cycles." *The Review of Economic Studies* 55:1–16.

Roodman, David. 2009. "A note on the theme of too many instruments." *Oxford Bulletin of Economics and statistics* 71(1):135–158.

Rose, Shanna. 2006. "Do fiscal rules dampen the political business cycle?" *Public Choice* 128(3-4):407–431.

Ross, Catherine E. and Joan Huber. 1985. "Hardship and depression." *Journal of Health and Social Behavior* 26(4):312–327.

Roubini, Nouriel and Jeffrey D. Sachs. 1989a. "Political and economic determinants of budget deficits in the industrial democracies." *European Economic Review* 33(5):903–933.

1989b. "Government spending and budget deficits in the industrial countries." *Economic Policy* 4(8):99–132.

Russett, Bruce. 1982. "Defense expenditures and national well-being." *American Political Science Review* 76:767–777.
Saez, Lawrence and Aseema Sinha. 2010. "Political cycles, political institutions and public expenditure in India, 1980–2000." *British Journal of Political Science* 40(1):91–113.
Sakamoto, Takayuki. 2008. *Economic Policy and Performance in Industrial Democracies: Party Governments, Central Banks and the Fiscal-Monetary Policy Mix*. London: Routledge.
Sanz, Ismael. 2011. "What do OECD countries cut first when faced with fiscal adjustments?" *Southern Economic Journal* 77(3):753–775.
Sausgruber, Rupert and Jean-Robert Tyran. 2005. "Testing the Mill hypothesis of fiscal illusion." *Public Choice* 122(1–2):39–68.
Scheve, Kenneth and David Stasavage. 2010. "The conscription of wealth: Mass warfare and the demand for progressive taxation." *International Organization* 64(4):529–561.
  2012. "Democracy, war, and wealth: Lessons from two centuries of inheritance taxation." *American Political Science Review* 106(1):81–102.
  2016. *Taxing the Rich. A History of Fiscal Fairness in the United States and Europe*. Princeton, NJ: Princeton University Press.
Schmidt, Manfred G. 1996. "When parties matter: A review of the possibilities and limits of partisan influence on public policy." *European Journal of Political Research* 30(2):155–183.
Schuknecht, Ludger. 2000. "Fiscal policy cycles and public expenditure in developing countries." *Public Choice* 102(1–2):113–128.
Schulze, Günther G. and Anselm Rose. 1998. "Public orchestra funding in Germany – An empirical investigation." *Journal of Cultural Economics* 22(4):227–247.
Schulze, Günther G. and Heinrich W. Ursprung. 1999. "Globalisation of the economy and the nation state." *World Economy* 22(3):295–352.
Scruggs, Lyle. 2004. *Welfare State Entitlements Data Set: A Comparative Institutional Analysis of Eighteen Welfare States*. Available at: www.cwep.us. Last accessed October 25, 2022.
Seelkopf, Laura, Moritz Bubek, Edgars Eihmanis, Joseph Ganderson, Julian Limberg, Youssef Mnaili, Paula Zuluaga and Philipp Genschel. 2021. "The rise of modern taxation: A new comprehensive dataset of tax introductions worldwide." *Review of International Organizations* 16:239–263.
Seelkopf, Laura, Hanna Lierse and Carina Schmitt. 2016. "Trade liberalization and the global expansion of modern taxes." *Review of International Political Economy* 23(2):208–231.
Seiferling, Mike. 2013. *Recent Improvements to the Government Finance Statistics Yearbook Database in Response to Analytical Needs*. International Monetary Fund.
  2019. "Fiscal deficits and executive planning horizons." *Political Science Research and Methods* 1–15.
Seki, Katsunori and Laron K. Williams. 2014. "Updating the party government data set." *Electoral Studies* 34:270–279.

Shelton, Cameron A. 2007. "The size and composition of government expenditure." *Journal of Public Economics* 91(11–12):2230–2260.

Shin, Mi Jeong. 2017. "Partisanship, tax policy, and corporate profit-shifting in a globalized world economy." *Comparative Political Studies* 50(14):1998–2026.

Soroka, Stuart N. and Christopher Wlezien. 2010. *Degrees of Democracy: Politics, Public Opinion and Policy*. Cambridge: Cambridge University Press.

Stasavage, David. 2005. "Democracy and education spending in Africa." *American Journal of Political Science* 49:343–358.

StataCorp. 2019. *Stata Statistical Software: Release 16*. College Station, TX: StataCorp LLC.

Streb, Jorge M. and Gustavo Torrens. 2013. "Making rules credible: Divided government and political budget cycles." *Public Choice* 156(3–4):703–722.

Strøm, Kaare. 1990a. "A behavioral theory of competitive political parties." *American Journal of Political Science* 34:565–598.

1990b. *Minority Government and Majority Rule*. Cambridge: Cambridge University Press.

Swank, Duane H. 1988. "The political economy of government domestic expenditure in the affluent democracies, 1960–80." *American Journal of Political Science* 32(4):1120–1150.

2002. *Global Capital, Political Institutions, and Policy Change in Developed Welfare States*. New York: Cambridge University Press.

Swank, Duane H. and Sven Steinmo. 2002. "The new political economy of taxation in advanced capitalist democracies." *American Journal of Political Science* 46:642–655.

Tang, Min. 2008. "Examining the lagged effect of economic development on political democracy: A panel-VAR model." *Democratisation* 15(1):106–122.

Tanzi, Vito. 2002. "Globalization and the future of social protection." *Scottish Journal of Political Economy* 49(1):116–127.

Tavares, José. 2004. "Does right or left matter? Cabinets, credibility and fiscal adjustments." *Journal of Public Economics* 88(12):2447–2468.

Tavits, Margit. 2004. "The size of government in majoritarian and consensus democracies." *Comparative Political Studies* 37(3):340–359.

Thomson, Robert, Terry Royed, Elin Naurin, Joaquín Artés, Rory Costello, Laurenz Ennser-Jedenastik, Mark Ferguson, Petia Kostadinova, Catherine Moury and François Pétry. 2017. "The fulfilment of parties' election pledges: A comparative study on the impact of power sharing." *American Journal of Political Science* 61(3):527–542.

Tilly, Charles. 1990. *Coercion, Capital, and European States, AD 990–1990*. Oxford: Blackwell Publishers.

Tomz, Michael, Jason Wittenberg and Gary King. 2003. "Clarify: Software for interpreting and presenting statistical results." *Journal of Statistics Software* 8(1):1–30.

Tomz, Michael, Joshua A. Tucker and Jason Wittenberg. 2002. "An easy and accurate regression model for multiparty electoral data." *Political Analysis* 10(1):66–83.

Töngür, Ünal, Sara Hsu and Adem Yavuz Elveren. 2015. "Military expenditures and political regimes: Evidence from global data, 1963–2000." *Economic Modelling* 44:68–79.

Tsebelis, George and Eric C. C. Chang. 2004. "Veto players and the structure of budgets in advanced industrialized countries." *European Journal of Political Research* 43(3):449–476.

Tufte, Edward. 1978. *Political Control of the Economy*. Princeton, NJ: Princeton University Press.

Veiga, Linda Gonçalves and Francisco José Veiga. 2007. "Political business cycles at the municipal level." *Public Choice* 131(1):45–64.

Vergne, Clémence. 2009. "Democracy, elections and allocation of public expenditures in developing countries." *European Journal of Political Economy* 25(1):63–77.

Volkerink, Bjørn and Jakob De Haan. 2001. "Fragmented government effects on fiscal policy: New evidence." *Public Choice* 109(3):221–242.

Von Hagen, J. and I. J. Harden. 1995. "Budget processes and commitment to fiscal discipline." *European Economic Review* 39(3):771–779.

Walter, Stefanie. 2010. "Globalization and the welfare state: Testing the microfoundations of the compensation hypothesis." *International Studies Quarterly* 54(2):403–426.

Weisstanner, David. 2017. "The fiscal benefits of repeated cooperation: Coalitions and debt dynamics in 36 democracies." *Journal of Public Policy* 37(2):143–172.

Wenzelburger, Georg. 2015. "Parties, institutions and the politics of law and order: How political institutions and partisan ideologies shape law-and-order spending in twenty western industrialized countries." *British Journal of Political Science* 45(3):663–687.

Wenzelburger, Georg and Florian Böller. 2020. "Bomb or build? How party ideologies affect the balance of foreign aid and defence spending." *The British Journal of Politics and International Relations* 22(1):3–23.

Werck, Kristien, Bruno Heyndels and Benny Geys. 2008. "The impact of 'central places' on spatial spending patterns: evidence from Flemish local government cultural expenditures." *Journal of Cultural Economics* 32(1):35.

Whitten, Guy D. and Laron K. Williams. 2011. "Buttery guns and welfare hawks: The politics of defense spending in advanced industrial democracies." *American Journal of Political Science* 55(1):117–134.

Wickens, Tobias. 2002. *Classification of GFSM 1986 Data to the GFSM 2001 Framework*. Technical report. International Monetary Fund.

Wildavsky, Aaron B. 1964. *Politics of the Budgetary Process*. Boston, MA: Little, Brown.

Williams, Laron K. and Guy D. Whitten. 2012. "But wait, there's more! Maximizing substantive inferences from TSCS models." *The Journal of Politics* 74(3):685–693.

Windett, Jason Harold. 2014. "Gendered campaign strategies in US elections." *American Politics Research* 42(4):628–655.

Wlezien, Christopher. 1995. "The public as thermostat: Dynamics of preferences for spending." *American Journal of Political Science* 39(4):981–1000.

2015. "The myopic voter? The economy and US presidential elections." *Electoral Studies* 39:195–204.

Woldendorp, Jaap, Hans Keman and Ian Budge. 2000. *Party Government in 48 Democracies (1945–1998)*. London: Kluwer Academic Publishers.

Wooldridge, Jeffrey M. 2010. *Econometric Analysis of Cross Section and Panel Data*. Cambridge, MA: MIT Press.

Wursten, Jesse. 2018. "Testing for serial correlation in fixed-effects panel models." *The Stata Journal* 18(1):76–100.

Wyplosz, Charles. 2012. Fiscal rules: Theoretical issues and historical experiences. In *Fiscal Policy after the Financial Crisis*. Chicago: University of Chicago Press, pp. 495–525.

Zellner, Arnold. 1962. "An efficient method of estimating seemingly unrelated regressions and tests for aggregation bias." *Journal of the American Statistical Association* 57(298):348–368.

Zhu, Ling and Christine S. Lipsmeyer. 2015. "Policy feedback and economic risk: The influence of privatization on social policy preferences." *Journal of European Public Policy* 22:1489–1511.

Index

additive logged ratios, 94–96
aggregate budgetary components, literature on, 28–30
  missing elements, 37–40
austere governments, defense expenditures and, 139–140
Australia, budgetary process, 6–7
autocorrelation diagnostics in methodology
  contexts affecting budgets, 242–243
  tradeoffs within expenditures, 102–103
autoregressive distributed lag (ADL) approach in methodology, 104–105

Bolsonaro, Jair, 158
Brazil, sub-national budgetary process, 255
Bryant, Chuck, 5
Budget Hero, 1–2, 244
budgetary incrementalism, 20, 23, 43, 61
budgetary ledger. *See* budgets, components of
budgetary volatility, 164
  economic context, 218–219, 223
  electoral context, 210–211
  expenditure change measure, 52
  globalization and, 228–232
  government ideology and, 180–181, 184–185, 251
  impulse-response functions (IRFs) for shock to, 171
  interconnectedness of budget components, 7
  literature on, 9–10, 25–28
  in methodology, 188–189
  military conflicts and, 235, 237
  as mirror of budgeting process, 35–37
  orthogonalized impulse-response functions (OIRFs) for shock to, 201–202
  results of contexts affecting, 239
budgets
  complexity of, 2–7
  games concerning, 1–2
  sub-national budgetary process, 254–255
budgets, categories within components, 63–65
  data sources explained, 54–58
  left versus right government priorities, 70–75, 81–85
  literature on, 19–22
  methodology for tradeoffs modeling, 77–81
  tradeoffs within, 33–35, 68
  within expenditures, 55–56
budgets, components of, 4, *See also* budgetary volatility; deficits; expenditures; interconnectedness of budget components; revenues
  data sources explained, 54–58
  literature on, 9–10, 28–30
  modeling strategy, 165–168, 205–206
  surveys concerning, 253–254
  tradeoffs among, 158–159

277

budgets, external contexts affecting, 15–16, *See also* economic context affecting budgets; electoral context affecting budgets; international context affecting budgets
  interconnectedness of budget components, 48–51
  significance of research, 10–11
  theoretical contributions of research, 245–247
  theory explained, 14, 40–41, 51–54
  tradeoffs within expenditures, 42–43, 153–156
budgets, literature on, 9–10
  aggregate budgetary components, 28–30
  budgetary changes, 22–28, 62–63
  missing elements, 32, 249
    budgetary volatility, 35–37
    interconnectedness of budget components, 37–40
    tradeoffs within expenditures, 33–35
  political and economic aspects of decision-making, 18–19
  single budgetary categories, 19–22
budgets, political competition in. *See also* contexts affecting budgets; interconnectedness of budget components; tradeoffs within expenditures
  future research questions, 252–255
  institutional context, 44–45
  methodological contributions of research, 247–249
  significance of research, 10–11
  theoretical contributions of research, 245–247
  theory explained, 8, 40–41, 51–54
Bush, George H.W., 208

Casselman, Ben, 245
causal relationships, 159–160, 164–165, 251, *See also* interconnectedness of budget components
Clark, Josh, 5
Classification of Outlays by Function of Government (COFOG), data sources explained, 54–58, 77
coalition governments
  deficits and, 180
  in Denmark and Norway, 61–62

  ideological effect on expenditure tradeoffs, 68–70
  institutional context, 44–45
  in New Zealand, 59
common pool resource problem, 67
compensating argument (international context), 47, 132–138, 149–151
competition. *See* political competition in budgetary process
complexity of budgets, 2–7
compositional theory
  contributions of research, 248
  of expenditures, 41–43
conflict involvement. *See* military conflicts
consensus-oriented goverments
  in budgetary process, 67
  revenues and, 178
contexts affecting budgets, 15–16, *See also* economic context affecting budgets; electoral context affecting budgets; international context affecting budgets
  autocorrelation diagnostics in methodology, 242–243
  interconnectedness of budget components, 48–51, 251–252
  modeling strategy, 142–143, 205–206
  robustness of results, 240–242
  theoretical contributions of research, 245–247
  theory explained, 14, 40–41, 51–54
  tradeoffs within expenditures, 42–43, 115–118, 153–156, 250–251
counterfactual changes in methodology, 98–100

data sources explained, 54–58, 187–189, 249
defense expenditures
  affecting budgets, 48
  in right-leaning governments, 73
  tradeoffs within expenditures, 138–142, 151–153, 155–156
deficits, 162–164, *See also* contexts affecting budgets; interconnectedness of budget components
  data sources explained, 188
  economic context, 217–218, 221–223
  electoral context, 209–211
  expenditures and, 182–183, 187, 251
  globalization and, 227–230

Index

government ideology and, 178–180, 184–185, 251
impulse-response functions (IRFs) for shock to, 171
literature on, 9–10, 28–30
military conflicts and, 234–237
orthogonalized impulse-response functions (OIRFs) for shock to, 200–201
results of contexts affecting, 239
revenues and, 183, 187, 251
Denmark
coalition government in budgetary process, 69
fiscal disagreements in, 203
punctuated equilibrium, 23–25
dependent variables
in methodology, 54–58
in stationarity testing, 101–102
domestic economy. *See* economic context affecting budgets
dovish governments, defense expenditures and, 139–140

economic affairs expenditures in right-leaning governments, 73
economic context affecting budgets, 15, 46–47, 212–214, *See also* globalization
deficits and, 217–218
expenditures and, 214–215
literature on, 18–19, 29
results of methodology, 219–223
revenues and, 215–217
significance of research, 10–11
theory explained, 14
tradeoffs within expenditures, 123–131, 146–149, 154–155, 250
volatility and, 218–219
education expenditures in left- and right-leaning governments, 74
efficiency argument (international context), 47, 132–138, 149–151
electoral context affecting budgets, 15–16, 45–46, 206–207
deficits and, 209–210
expenditures and, 207–208
results of methodology, 210–212
revenues and, 208
significance of research, 10–11
theory explained, 14, 14
tradeoffs within expenditures, 118–123, 143, 154, 156–157, 250

volatility and, 210
environments. *See* contexts affecting budgets
European Union (EU), budgetary process, 5–6
expenditure change measure, 52
expenditures, 160–161
categories of, 55–56, 56
data sources explained, 187–188
deficits and, 182–183, 187, 251
economic context, 214–215, 219–220
electoral context, 207–208, 210–211
globalization and, 223–225, 229
government ideology and, 175–176, 184–185
impulse-response functions (IRFs) for shock to, 168–170
literature on, 9–10, 28–30
military conflicts and, 232–233, 235
orthogonalized impulse-response functions (OIRFs) for shock to, 199–200
results of contexts affecting, 238
as zero-sum game, 4–6
expenditures, tradeoffs within, 14–15, *See also* interconnectedness of budget components,
autoregressive distributed lag (ADL) approach in methodology, 104–105
compositional theory of, 41–43
counterfactual changes in methodology, 98–100
economic context, 123–131, 146–149, 154–155, 250
electoral context, 118–123, 143, 154, 156–157, 250
future research questions, 252–253
independent variables in methodology, 90–91
institutional context, 66–70, 249–250
international context, 131–142, 149–153, 155–156, 250–251
left versus right government priorities, 70–75, 81–85
majority versus minority government priorities, 76–77, 85–88
methodology, 33–35, 77–81
missing elements in literature, 63–65
modeling strategy and simulation approach, 92–98, 142–143
results and robustness of methodology, 114

expenditures, tradeoffs within (*cont.*)
   stationarity diagnostics in methodology, 100–102
   surveys concerning, 253–254
   theoretical contributions of research, 245–247
external contexts. *See* contexts affecting budgets

Finland, aggregate budgetary components, 29–30, 39
Fiscal Ship, 2, 244–245
France, tradeoffs among budget components, 159
future research questions, 252–255

games concerning budgets, 1–2, 244–245
generous governments, defense expenditures and, 139–140
Germany
   budgetary process, 5, 69
   elections and deficits, 209
globalization
   compensation versus efficiency arguments, 132–138, 149–151, 155
   deficits and, 227–228
   expenditures and, 223–225
   government ideology and, 47–48, 149–151, 250
   results of methodology, 229–232
   revenues and, 225–227
   volatility and, 228–229
government administration expenditures in left-leaning governments, 73
government characteristics affecting budgets. *See also* left-leaning governments; majority governments; minority governments; right-leaning governments
   coalition governments, 44–45, 59, 61, 62
   economic context for spending tradeoffs, 123–131, 146–149, 154–155, 214–215
   electoral context for spending tradeoffs, 118–123, 143, 154
   independent variables in methodology, 90–91
   institutional context, 44–45, 66–70, 249–250
   interconnectedness of budget components and, 182–183

left versus right governments, 49–50, 66, 70–75
literature on, 18–19, 29, 62–63
majority versus minority governments, 45, 68–70, 76–77
theoretical contributions of research, 245–247
Granger-causality tests, 171–173, 195–196
growth in economy
   deficits and, 223
   revenues and, 220–221
   total expenditures and, 219–220
   tradeoffs within expenditures affected by, 126, 129–131, 149, 155
   volatility and, 223
"guns versus butter", 138–142, 151–153, 155–156, 234, 250–251

hawkish governments, defense expenditures and, 139–140
healthcare expenditures in left- and right-leaning governments, 74–75
Hollande, François, 159
housing expenditures in left-leaning governments, 73

ideology. *See* government characteristics affecting budgets; left-leaning governments; political competition in budgetary process; right-leaning governments
impulse-response functions (IRFs), 168–171, 196–197
independent variables
   in methodology, 77–81, 90–91, 166
   in stationarity testing, 102
institutional context. *See also* majority governments; minority governments
   in budgetary process, 44–45, 66–70, 249–250
   deficits and, 179–180
   interconnectedness of budget components and, 182–183, 251
   revenues and, 177–178
institutional friction, 23
interconnectedness of budget components, 6–7, 15
   causal relationships, 159–160, 164–165, 251
   government ideology and institutional context, 182–183, 251

Index

Granger-causality tests in methodology, 171–173, 195–196
impulse-response functions (IRFs) in methodology, 168–171, 196–197
lag length selection in methodology, 192–194
methodological contributions of research, 248–249
as missing in literature, 37–40
modeling strategy, 165–168
orthogonalized impulse-response functions (OIRFs) in methodology, 197–202
panel unit root tests in methodology, 189
panel vector autoregressive (pVAR) model in, 189–192
stability in VAR models, 194–195
theoretical contributions of research, 245–247
theory explained, 40–41, 48–54
international context affecting budgets, 15, 47–48, *See also* globalization; military conflicts
deficits and, 227–228, 234–235
expenditures and, 223–225, 232–233
results of methodology, 229–232, 235–237
revenues and, 225–227, 233–234
significance of research, 10–11
theory explained, 14
tradeoffs within expenditures, 131–142, 149–153, 155–156
volatility and, 228–229, 235
Ireland, economic context for spending tradeoffs, 126

kurtosis, 24

lag length selection in methodology, 192–194
left-leaning governments
budgetary priorities, 70–75, 249–250
contexts affecting budgets, 251–252
deficits in, 49–50, 178–180, 184–185, 217–218, 227–228, 234–235
economic context for spending tradeoffs, 126, 214–215, 250
economic growth and, 129–131, 149, 155
electoral context for spending tradeoffs, 119–120, 143, 154, 250

expenditures in, 49–50, 175–176, 184–185, 223–225, 232–233
intervention and redistribution approaches, 66
as majority, 81–85
as minority, 85–88
relationship with economy, 174–175
revenues in, 49–50, 176–178, 184–185, 215–217
unemployment rates and, 128–129, 146–149, 154–155
volatility in, 180–181, 184–185, 228–229, 235
left-leaning governments, globalization and, 47–48, 250
compensation versus efficiency arguments, 132–138, 149–151, 155
deficits, 227–228
expenditures, 223–225
results of methodology, 229–232
volatility, 228–229
left-leaning governments, military conflicts and
deficits, 234–235
expenditures, 232–233
"guns versus butter", 138–142, 151–153, 155–156, 250–251
volatility, 235
literature on budgetary process, 9–10
aggregate budgetary components, 28–30
budgetary changes, 22–28, 62–63
missing elements, 32, 249
budgetary volatility, 35–37
interconnectedness of budget components, 37–40
tradeoffs within expenditures, 33–35
political and economic aspects of decision-making, 18–19
single budgetary categories, 19–22

Macmillan, Harold, 203
Major, John, 213
majority governments
deficits and, 184–185, 251
electoral context for spending tradeoffs, 143
expenditures and, 176, 184–185
ideological effect on expenditure tradeoffs, 45, 68–70, 81–85, 249–250
institutional constraint, 76–77, 175, 249–250

majority governments (*cont.*)
  revenues and, 178, 184–185
  volatility and, 180–181, 184–185, 251
Merkel, Angela, 5, 115
methodology
  for aggregate budgetary categories, 28–29
  autocorrelation diagnostics in, 102–103, 242–243
  autoregressive distributed lag (ADL) approach in, 104–105
  contributions of research, 247–249
  counterfactual changes in, 98–100
  data sources explained, 54–58, 187–189
  economic context, 128–149, 219–223
  electoral context, 121–123, 143, 210–212
  globalization, 136–138, 149–151, 229–232
  Granger-causality tests in, 171–173, 195–196
  impulse-response functions (IRFs) in, 168–171, 196–197
  independent variables in, 77–81, 90–91, 166
  interconnectedness of budget components, 37–40, 165–168
  lag length selection in, 192–194
  military conflicts and spending tradeoffs, 141–142, 151–153
  modeling strategy, 92–98, 142–143, 205–206
  orthogonalized impulse-response functions (OIRFs) in methodology, 197–202
  panel unit root tests in, 189
  panel vector autoregressive (pVAR) model in, 189–192
  for punctuated equilibrium, 23–25
  results and robustness, 114
  significance of, 11–13, 16
  for single budgetary categories, 20–22
  stability in VAR models, 194–195
  stationarity diagnostics in, 100–102
  tradeoffs within expenditures, 33–35, 77–81
  volatility in, 25–28, 188–189
military conflicts. *See also* "guns versus butter"
  deficits and, 184–185, 234–235
  expenditures and, 184–185, 232–233
  government ideology and, 48, 138–142, 151–153
  results of methodology, 235–237
  revenues and, 184–185, 233–234
  volatility and, 184–185, 235
minority governments
  deficits and, 184–185
  expenditures and, 184–185
  ideological effect on expenditure tradeoffs, 45, 68–70, 85–88, 249–250
  institutional constraint, 76–77, 175, 249–250
  revenues and, 178
  volatility and, 180–181
modeling strategy
  for budget component relationships, 165–168
  for contexts affecting budget components, 205–206
  for tradeoffs within expenditures, 92–98, 142–143
multiple-party governments in budgetary process, 67–68

New Zealand, coalition government in budgetary process, 59
Norway, coalition government in budgetary process, 61

Obama, Barack, 17
orthogonalized impulse-response functions (OIRFs), 197–202
Osborne, George, 158

panel unit root tests in methodology
  interconnectedness of budget components, 189
  tradeoffs within expenditures, 100–102
panel vector autoregressive (pVAR) model, 160, 166–168, 189–192, 248–249
parlimentary goverments in budgetary process, 67
policy expenditures. *See* expenditures
political budget cycles, 118–123, 143, 154, 156–157, 207–208
political competition in budgetary process. *See also* contexts affecting budgets; interconnectedness of budget components; tradeoffs within expenditures
  future research questions, 252–255

Index

institutional context, 44–45
methodological contributions of research, 247–249
significance of research, 10–11
theoretical contributions of research, 245–247
theory explained, 8, 14, 40–41, 51–54
presidential governments in budgetary process, 67
priorities. *See* tradeoffs within expenditures
punctuated equilibrium, 23–25

religion and culture expenditures in left- and right-leaning governments, 75
residual autocorrelation tests. *See* autocorrelation diagnostics in methodology
resource allocation. *See* budgets
results of methodology
   economic context, 219–223
   electoral context, 210–212
   globalization, 229–232
   military conflicts, 235–237
   tradeoffs within expenditures, 114
revenues, 161–162, *See also* contexts affecting budgets; interconnectedness of budget components
   data sources explained, 187–188
   deficits and, 183, 187, 251
   economic context, 215–217, 220–221
   electoral context, 208, 211
   globalization and, 225–227, 229
   government ideology and, 176–178, 184–185
   impulse-response functions (IRFs) for shock to, 170–171
   literature on, 9–10, 28–30
   military conflicts and, 233–235
   orthogonalized impulse-response functions (OIRFs) for shock to, 220
   results of contexts affecting, 238–239
right-leaning governments
   budgetary priorities, 70–75, 249–250
   contexts affecting budgets, 251–252
   deficits in, 49–50, 178–180, 184–185, 217–218, 227–228, 234–235
   economic context for spending tradeoffs, 126, 214–215, 250
   economic growth and, 129–131, 149, 155

electoral context for spending tradeoffs, 119–120, 143, 154, 250
   expenditures in, 49–50, 175–176, 184–185, 223–225, 232–233
   intervention and redistribution approaches, 66
   as majority, 81–85
   as minority, 85–88
   relationship with economy, 174–175
   revenues in, 49–50, 176–178, 184–185, 215–217
   unemployment rates and, 128–129, 146–149, 154–155
   volatility in, 180–181, 184–185, 228–229, 235
right-leaning governments, globalization and, 47–48, 250
   compensation versus efficiency arguments, 132–138, 149–151, 155
   deficits, 227–228
   expenditures, 223–225
   results of methodology, 229–232
   volatility, 228–229
right-leaning governments, military conflicts and
   deficits, 234–235
   expenditures, 232–233
   "guns versus butter", 138–142, 151–153, 155–156, 250–251
   volatility, 235
robustness of methodology
   contexts affecting budgets, 240–242
   tradeoffs within expenditures, 114
Romania, decreased revenues, 215

seemingly unrelated regression (SUR), 80, 93
simulation approach for tradeoffs within expenditures, 92–98
Skoler, Michael, 1
social protection expenditures. *See also* "guns versus butter", 115–118,
   defense expenditures versus, 138–142, 151–153, 155–156
   globalization and, 134–135, 149–151
   in left-leaning governments, 73
Spain, punctuated equilibrium, 23–25
spending. *See* expenditures
stability in VAR models, 194–195

stationarity diagnostics in methodology
  interconnectedness of budget
    components, 189
  tradeoffs within expenditures, 100–102
sub-national budgetary process, 254–255
surveys concerning expenditures, 253–254
Sweden, expenditures and government
  ideology, 176

tax turbulence, 25–26
taxes. *See* revenues
Thatcher, Margaret, 59
theoretical contributions of research,
  245–247
tradeoffs among budget components,
  158–159, 245
tradeoffs within expenditures, 14–15, 245,
  See also interconnectedness of budget
  components
  autocorrelation diagnostics in
    methodology, 102–103
  autoregressive distributed lag (ADL)
    approach in methodology, 104–105
  compositional theory of, 41–43
  counterfactual changes in methodology,
    98–100
  economic context, 123–131, 146–149,
    154–155, 250
  electoral context, 118–123, 143, 154,
    156–157, 250
  future research questions, 252–253
  independent variables in methodology,
    90–91
  institutional context, 66–70, 249–250
  international context, 131–142,
    149–153, 155–156, 250–251
  left versus right government priorities,
    70–75, 81–85
  majority versus minority government
    priorities, 76–77, 85–88

methodology, 33–35, 77–81
missing elements in literature, 63–65
modeling strategy and simulation
  approach, 92–98, 142–143
results and robustness of methodology,
  114
stationarity diagnostics in methodology,
  100–102
surveys concerning, 253–254
theoretical contributions of research,
  245–247
Trump, Donald, 158–159

unemployment rates
  deficits and, 221–223
  revenues and, 220–221
  total expenditures and, 219–220
  tradeoffs within expenditures affected
    by, 127–129, 146–149, 154–155
  volatility and, 223
United Kingdom
  budgetary volatility, 26–28
  tradeoffs among budget components,
    158
United States
  budgetary process, 5
  sub-national budgetary process, 254–255
  tradeoffs among budget components,
    158–159

vector autoregressive (VAR) models, 166
  stability in, 194–195
volatility. *See* budgetary volatility

welfare policy. *See* social protection
  expenditures
West Germany, elections and deficits,
  209

zero-sum game, expenditures as, 5–6

Printed in the United States
by Baker & Taylor Publisher Services